10/14

10/18

With Best Wishes
from
Ed Henry
7/25/93

CHANT
THE NAMES OF GOD

Musical Culture In Bhojpuri-speaking India

CHANT THE NAMES OF GOD

Musical Culture In Bhojpuri-speaking India

Edward O. Henry

San Diego State University Press

Permissions
San Diego State University Press
San Diego State University
San Diego, CA 92182

Printed in the United States of America

Library of Congress Cataloging-in-Publication Data

Henry, Edward O., 1941–
Chant the Names of God : Musical Culture in Bhojpuri-speaking India / Edward O. Henry.
p. cm.
Includes index.
ISBN 0–916304–79–5 : $14.00
1. Folk music—India—Bihar—History and criticism. 2. Folk music—India—Uttar Pradesh—History and criticism. 3. Folk songs, Bhojpuri—India—Bihar—history and criticism. 4. Folk-songs, Bhojpuri—India—Uttar Pradesh—History and criticism. 5. Music and society. I. Title.
ML3748.H46 1988
306′.484′09542—dc19 88–15869
CIP
MN

Table of Contents

List of Photographs

Preface

This book reports and interprets research of folk music and related culture in the Bhojpurī-speaking area of northern India (eastern Uttar Pradesh and western Bihar). I first recorded music in this area in 1968 on a music survey of South Asia. After more study in anthropology, ethnomusicology and Hindi, I returned to the area for sixteen months in 1971 and 1972, living for thirteen months in the village whose musical culture dominates this account. The research conducted in that period, supported by grants from the National Institute of Mental Health, was reported in my Ph.D. dissertation, which was supervised by Professor Charles Morrison at Michigan State University. In 1978, with financial support from the Indo-American Subcommission on Culture and Education, and equipment and supplies grants from the College of Arts and Letters at San Diego State University and the San Diego State University Foundation, I returned to the area for six more months of research. This book combines the findings of that research with material from the dissertation as well as other ideas and information accumulated during the interim.

Method

The method used in this research involved tape recording music in the contexts in which it naturally occurred and taking notes on and photographs of the accompanying activities. The songs collected with this method may not be the best available versions. Words, lines or verses may be missing or garbled. But this in itself sheds light on the actual use and condition of folk music. The acoustic results of tape recordings made in such conditions are also inferior to those made in laboratory conditions. Children scream, dogs bark, and crows caw, rendering already slurred or unfamiliar words even more obscure when the tape is played. But the performance of music is observed and recorded as it occurs with other activities in the immediate situation—activities which it may influence or which may influence it. Identification of the situational components of music performance is also important because part of the meaning of music (for the native as well as the analyst) is the association it has with items and actions in the contexts in which it is performed. (See, for example, the *sohar* in Chapter III.) The spontaneous as well as the invited comments people make about music are also important data, and of course general ethnographic information of wide scope is fundamental to this kind of study.

Once music and related data were collected, the songs had to be transcribed from the tapes. Sometimes this was accomplished with the help of local friends, who would dictate as I stopped the recorder after each stanza. Ideally one of the singers should be present at this stage to assist with obscure or obscured words, but this was not always possible. When a capable person who would accept cash compensation could be found, I would play the tapes back with the necessary pauses so he or she could write the lyrics in Devanagari script. Translation of the lyrics also went much faster with, and was sometimes impossible without, the aid of friends or assistants. The dictionaries didn't always contain the words, or they were spelled in ways different from the transcription, or the usage or grammar was opaque.

The next stage of the method required the recognition of connections between different entities in the culture—an understanding of how these entities bear on one another. An obvious example is the relationship between the songs celebrating the birth of sons, patrilineal descent, patrilocal residence, and the dowry. (See Chapter III.)

Limitations

Indian scholars in particular may think it arrogant for someone with relatively little experience in the culture (a total of two years) and with less than perfect command of Hindi or Bhojpurī to attempt a study such as this one. I hope that the curiosity, objectivity, and effort I have brought to the inquiry will compensate to some degree for the many imperfections in my knowledge and understanding, and that this book will stimulate further study.

Before, during and after my thirteen month residence in the village I recorded substantial amounts of folk music in other villages, towns and cities in the Bhojpurī-speaking region and many other areas of India. This experience broadened my conception, but the portrait of musical life presented here is undeniably most valid for a certain village during a certain span of time. Musical institutions had already changed in that village (a new devotional singing group had been formed) when I returned after six years. Nonetheless, I believe that much of what I have described and interpreted accurately represents continuing traditions in this and adjacent regions. I hope that this book will stimulate comparable research in other regions which will ultimately reveal regional similarities and differences. (Distinctive musical regions are probably coincident with language regions, which are also distinct in other aspects of culture. The Maithili-speaking region centered around Madhubani and Darbhanga in northern Bihar, for example, has a distinctive ceremonial life accompanied by types of music substantially different from those found in the Bhojpurī area.)

Acknowledgments

This work could not have been accomplished without the financial support mentioned above, and I am grateful to the people of those institutions for their confidence and assistance. Nor could the work have been completed without the generous aid of many Indian friends, associates, and good Samaritans. I am particularly indebted to scholars and administrators at Banaras Hindu University, including Dr. Prem Lata Sharma, Head of the Department of Musicology, and Sri Maheswar Jha and the late Dr. R. K. Shringy also of that department; Dr. Shukdeo Singh of the Department of Hindi; Dr. Belwant Rai Bhatt and Sri Suk Dev Bhatt of the Department of Music (and to the latter's family, especially his daughter, Usha). Dr. K. D. Upadhyaya of the Folklore Institute in Varanasi, and his friend Sri Datta Treya Pande were most helpful, as was Swami Premananda of Panchbania, Bihar. I also want to express my thanks and affection to four men of the principal research cite: IJP, RKP, KKP, and RSM.

I am grateful to Rounder Records and the editors of *Asian Music, Ethnomusicology, The Journal of Indian Musicology,* and *The Ethnography of Musical Performance* for permission to paraphrase portions of my writing which have appeared in their publications.

Finally, I would like to thank Dr. Charles Morrison of Michigan State University for his supervision of the dissertation; Dr. Linda Hess for inspiration and help with the *nirgun bhajans;* Dr. Robert Holtz, Dr. Merle Hogg, Curtis Bouterse, and Douglas Service for help with the transcriptions; Ms. Beth Ingram, Production Editor, and Mr. Ed Gordon, Managing Editor, San Diego State University Press; Dr. Roger Cunniff, who was Director of the press when the book was accepted for publication in 1983, and who found the means to have some of the music examples copied despite budgetary constraints; Barbara Schloss of the Department of Anthropology, San Diego State University, for her patience and good humor in typing the several drafts of this book; and my wife Connie, for helping with the proofreading and much more.

Dr. Edward O. Henry
San Diego State University
February, 1988

Note on Transliteration

The rules of transliteration used here, except as noted below, are the (more or less) standard rules used to Romanize Sanskrit, Hindi, and other Indian languages.[1] The first time it is used in context the unfamiliar Indian word is italicized and defined, and all necessary diacritics supplied. No italics are used in subsequent occurrences of the word except where needed to prevent confusion. I have tried to include in the index, where all diacritics are supplied, all unfamiliar Indian words used more than once. Familiar anglicized spellings are employed in the case of well known terms such as Krishna and purdah.

The following is a rough guide to pronunciation for the general reader.[2] The vowels ā, ī, ū, e, and o, are long and have approximately the same pronunciation as in Spanish, or as the vowels in the English words father, machine, rule, prey, and go, respectively. A, i, and u (without macrons) are short, and equivalent to the vowels in the English words machine, bit and bull. A common mistake in American pronunciation of Indian words is to pronounce the short a as a long one or as the a in sat. The pronunciation of au varies regionally in North India, but probably the most common pronunciation is like that in caught. Ai has no equivalent in English, but its pronunciation can be approximated by eliding the vowels of the word banning. The r is a flapped one, as in the Spanish word claro. Ṛ is classed as a short vowel, and is pronounced as ri in rich, but with a flapped r.

The aspirated consonant bh is pronounced as in clubhouse; dh as in mudhole, and gh as in the phrase big house. Th and ph are pronounced as in pothole and shepherd. The pronunciation of c is like the ch in church, but less aspirated. Kṣ is also pronounced like the ch in church. Ś and ṣ are both pronounced as the sh in shape. The sub-dotted retroflex consonants ṭ, ṭh, ḍ, ḍh, and ṇ, are pronounced with the tip of the tongue touching the dome of the mouth—further back than it would for the English "dental" consonants t, d, and n.

There are two diphthongs in Bhojpuri which do not occur in Hindi or Sanskrit. These are indicaed by äi and äu. The a is pronounced as the short a of Hindi and Sanskrit; it blends into the second vowel, which varies freely from short to long. The umlaut over the first vowel of these diphthongs is used to denote pronunciations which differ significantly from the ai and au diphthongs of Hindi and Sanskrit.

In most of the song transliterations here preconsonantal vowel nasalization is indicated with a tilda over the vowel, e.g., ãgrezī. In other song transliterations (songs 45 and 47–50, and all nirgun bhajans except 100) where the nasalized vowel precedes a non-sibilant consonant, I have used the more conventional symbol—insertion of an n after the nasalized vowel, e.g., aṅgrezī. Scholars wishing to locate transliterated words in Hindi dictionaries should note that this nasalization will be indicated with the *candrabindu* (ँ) or *anusvāra* (·) above the Devanagari vowel. In those cases where I have used n to indicate pre-consonantal vowel nasalization, I have supplied the conventional diacritical mark with the n, even though it is unnecessary to do so, since the nasal is homorganic with the consonant it precedes and is realized in Hindi dictionaries with the anusvāra or candrabindu.

Notes

1 For the standard rules of transliterating South Asian languages, see A. L. Basham, *The Wonder that Was India* (New York: Grove Press, Inc., 1959), p. 506; and Nazir A. Jairazbhoy, *The Rags of North Indian Music: Their Structure and Evolution* (Middletown, Connecticut: Wesleyan University Press, 1971), pp. 13–15.

2 Adapted from Basham, *The Wonder that Was India*, p. 506.

Chapter I

Introduction

The Place of Music in Indian Culture

Hindu iconography shows clearly the long-standing prominence of music in Indian culture. The deity Krishna is commonly depicted playing a flute, the symbol of his enchanting power over human souls. Hanging from Śiva's trident is a *ḍamarū*, a small, hourglass-shaped drum which ancient texts say sounded the generative vibration of creation. Sarasvatī, the goddess of learning and music, plucks the strings of her *vīnā*, and Viṣṇu carries a conch shell he blows like a bugle to herald his victories over the demons. Temple sculptures and frescoes have featured stringed instruments for perhaps thirteen centuries and drums for over two thousand years.[1]

Music pervades the present as well. Shrilly amplified film songs, the popular music of India, have for decades been a part of the urban ambience, but many other strains compete in the sound space—the devotional chorus of the Hindu temple, the muezzin's call to prayer, the reedy horns of a wedding procession, the droning gourd pipe of the snake charmer, and the intricate melodies of Hindustani and Carnatic classical music issuing from classroom and concert hall, to name but a few. Music is all around, and the mass media cannot yet claim victory.

In the rural Bhojpurī-speaking region of North India (eastern Uttar Pradesh and western Bihar), as in many rural regions of India, live music is abundant. Hardly a day passed in my rural residence there when I did not witness the performance of music, much of it part of one or another ritual ceremony. The diversity of genres and of songs within them shows that music is the focus of much energy and attention. Each of two native collections of folk songs from the region contains roughly three hundred songs of some fifteen genres.[2] Considering no more than the ubiquity of music in urban and rural life and its representation in religious art, it is obvious that music has an important place in the culture of this region.

The village music of the region is interesting as well, in that much of it is folk music in the original sense of the term, orally transmitted and rooted in the rural, illiterate sector of a literate society. Whether for the appeal of their forms or the appropriateness and power of their lyrics, these songs have been found valuable enough by the villagers to learn generation after generation. Here we can observe true folk music thriving in its natural environment, little affected by self-consciousness of tradition or the ravages of mass media.

Previous Studies of Bhojpurī Folk Music and Related Matters

Although this book is based on the first participant-observation study of the full range of village music in the Bhojpurī-speaking area, a number of other books and articles have dealt with various aspects of the subject. George A. Grierson, an outstanding British linguist, published two small collections of Bhojpurī songs with English translations and commentaries in 1884 and 1886.[3] He included meticulous linguistic analyses of the song texts, but provided little information about the situations in which the songs were sung or the musical style.

William G. Archer was a British civil servant in India who wrote many books and articles on Indian art and oral literature. With Sankta Prasad he compiled a substantial collection of village women's song texts, mostly those of Kāyasth caste women in what is now Arrah District in the Bhojpurī-speaking area of western Bihar. Many of these first appeared in a collection in *The Journal of Bihar and Orissa Research Society* in 1942, where they were printed in Devanagari script, without translation or explanation.[4] *Songs for the Bride: Wedding Rites of Rural India*, edited by Mildred Archer, his widow, and Professor Barbara Stoler Miller, is based on a manuscript he was planning to revise when he died in 1979, which incorporated many of the texts from 1942 as well as others obtained subsequently.[5] It interprets the songs in their social and ritual contexts, and provides photographs of women's wall paintings from the nearby Mithila region.

Because *Songs for the Bride* presents material closely related to that in this book, a closer look will be useful. First, although the book contains only women's songs (and thus not the full scope of village music), it is more encompassing than the title suggests. While the majority of the texts are of wedding songs, those of many other genres of women's songs are included—grinding, birth and tonsure rites, mother goddess worship, the rainy season, and love. (The appelation *gajal* for love songs is simply the local pronunciation of the Urdu word *ghazal.*) Most of the texts address the same subjects as the texts included here, although the rituals they accompany differ somewhat. Texts 3, 12 and 13, 30, and 35 are variants of Songs 34, 12, 19, and 33 in this book.

Although *Songs for the Bride* is a worthwhile study, a few idiosyncrasies should be noted. First, Bhojpurī song texts or citations to them are largely absent. Except for three transliterated Bhojpurī texts which serve as examples in a brief discussion of Bhojpurī poetics, no Bhojpurī texts are included. Although the "Complete Bibiography" contains references to works of Archer's which contain some of the original texts, there are no citations which would lead the reader to specific texts. Archer's initial collection of women's songs referred to above is not mentioned. More than thirty of the wedding song texts translated in the book appeared in that collection.

The wedding rituals Archer describes and discusses are specifically those of the Kāyasth caste. Apparently, judging from the acknowledgements, the ritual accounts came largely from Sankta Prasad, who was a Kāyasth. Whether Archer systematically observed any of the rites is not indicated, and one wonders to what extent the rites have been idealized. There is no information about singing, or singers, and their ideas about song.

The interpretation of the rites is quite readable—Archer was a skilled and perceptive writer—but it leaves many details and song texts unexplained, and its many Freudian readings of ritual objects and acts are often unconvincing. His method of presentation was to preface the ritual descriptions with a distilled interpretation (actually a series of themes), thus informing the reading of the ritual acts. Matters not subsumed by his synoptic previews tend to go unexplained.

The editors of *Songs for the Bride* did not adequately relate Archer's work to extant knowledge on the subject. Miller's statement in her preface that ". . . the songs are perceived to enhance the auspiciousness of the rituals, ward off evil influences, and assure the success of the marriage. Like much of the ritual, the songs are also didactic, serving to impress both bride and groom with the reality of their social and sexual union. . . ." follows interpretations made in my earlier study of wedding songs.[6] Although *Songs for the Bride* is somewhat limited, it is nonetheless a valuable contribution to the study of Bhojpurī folklore and North Indian ethnology.

In 1967 Hari S. Upadhyaya submitted a doctoral dissertation to Indiana University which uses 447 songs collected from one informant (included in transliterated form) to support a sociological study of the joint family.[7] Another relevant Ph.D. dissertation is that of Laxmi G. Tewari, "Ceremonial Songs of the Kanyakubja Brahmans."[8] It samples a range of songs from an area around Kanpur in central Uttar Pradesh (west of the Bhojpurī-speaking region) providing musical notations, song texts in Devanagari script, and descriptions of accompanying social events.

The first English-language monograph which approached comprehension of the full range of the Bhojpurī region's music was, oddly, a collection of songs from Surinam. Nearly 35,000 Indians, speaking mainly Bhojpurī and Āvadhī (spoken in the area adjacent to the northwest of the Bhojpurī area), arrived in Surinam between 1873 and 1916. U. Arya's study of their music, *Ritual Songs and Folksongs of the Hindus of Surinam*, reveals many similarities in genres, songs, and social uses with the material presented here.[9] The other English language book which covers a range of Bhojpurī folk music is *Folk Culture and Oral Tradition* by S. L. Srivastava.[10] It compares oral traditions in Rajasthan and eastern Uttar Pradesh, with some anthropological analysis. *Marriage Songs from Bhojpurī Region*, by Chandramani Singh and Ronald Amend, contains texts and translations of seventy-two songs from somewhere in the Bhojpurī region, including some not connected with marriage. It also itemizes many of the wedding customs.[11]

Several Hindi monographs on Bhojpurī folk music have appeared. K. D. Upadhyaya (father of Hari S. Upadhyaya) has published a two-volume collection.[12] The song texts are in Bhojpurī (in Devanagari script) and commentaries and capsule summaries of the songs in Hindi. A similar collection, also in Hindi, is that of Durgaśaṅkarprasād Singh.[13]

Several studies of music and culture outside the Bhojpurī-speaking region are also relevant. Singer and Venkateswaran have provided detailed analyses of the ideology and social framework of *bhajan* (devotional song) singing, a pan-Indian phenomenon.[14] Both Irawati Karve and Oscar Lewis recognized the importance of women's song in the culture and its usefulness in social anthropological study.[15] L. Winifred Bryce's book, although it does not describe actual song performances and contexts, presents culturally sensitive explanations of a good sample of women's songs from Rajasthan.[16] Bonnie Wade's article on women's wedding songs from a village near Delhi includes musical transcriptions, as does her entry on Indian folk song in the latest Grove's Musical Dictionary.[17] Indira Junghare has published articles on the folk music of Maharashtra in *Man in India* and *Ethnomusicology*, including a recent interpretation of the female role as reflected in folk song.[18]

The Scope of this Study: Anthropological Ethnomusicology and Musical Culture

This book is in an area of discourse called ethnomusicology, and within that a narrower one (with blurred boundaries) that can be called anthropological ethnomusicology. Musicological ethnomusicologists tend to be more interested in the particulars of musical style (i.e., the formal aspects of a group's music) than with music as or in culture. The reverse is of course true for the anthropologists. Music attracts their attention first because it is culture. (The term here refers to learned patterns of feeling, thought and action shared by a group of people.) Their interests in music as culture are actually of two different orders.

One line of inquiry is cross-cultural. Music is a universal type of behavior whose uses and features may differ radically in different societies. Three questions loom large:

1. What are the different ways in which people use music in different societies (e.g., for attaining ecstatic states, for divination, and for dancing)?
2. How? and
3. Why does the form of music vary cross-culturally?

Prime examples of the cross-cultural study of music include Alan Merriam's *The Anthropology of Music* and Alan Lomax's *Folk Song Style and Culture.*

The second kind of anthropological study focuses on music in a single society. Here music and the behavior surrounding it are the initial foci. However, in each society music also provides a unique perspective on certain extra-musical culture to which it is related: its study allows us to see something in each way of life that is not seen or is not seen as clearly elsewhere. This approach is thus equally concerned with the larger culture of which music is a part, and with the relationship of music to other parts of the culture. Notable examples of this study include David McAllester's *Enemy Way Music,* Charles Keil's *The Urban Blues,* and Ruth Underhill's *Singing for Power.* Each of these studies could be said to concern a musical culture.

Several scholars have previously used the phrase musical culture. Bruno Nettl urged that "The idea of a musical culture as a system in which parts interrelate, and in which changes in one part inevitably force changes in the others, is one that should be explored further."[19] J. H. K. Nketia defined musical culture as "The aggregate of learned and cultivated cultural traditions associated with music which become evident at the juncture of the social and musical. . . ."[20] My own conceptual system of musical culture is set forth in the following paragraphs.

The idea of musical culture can be useful both as an analytical device, and as a schema for the collection of data in fieldwork. In either case musical culture must be broken down into component categories at one or more intermediate levels of abstraction—categories specific enough to avoid strictly ad hoc analysis but not so narrow that they exclude the unexpected traditional behavior. The model set forth below grew out of my own field work, but draws from the work of two masterful anthropologists—Anthony F. C. Wallace and Bronislaw Malinowski—as well as that of Nettl, Nketia, and Titon.

In Wallace's influential *Religion: An Anthropological View*, he proposes that the study of a society's religion use the cult institution as the basic unit of study, and asserts that a society's religion is likely to be an aggregate of loosely related cult institutions—not necessarily an internally coherent set of beliefs and practices.[21] He defined the cult institution as a set of rituals all having the same general goal, all explicitly rationalized by a set of similar or related beliefs, and all supported by the same social group.

Malinowski similarly proposed that the field study of a society be conducted by examining its institutions. He described basic institutions as consisting of:

> *Groups* attached to a certain part of the *environment* and endowed with *material equipment*, the *knowledge* of how to use this environment and equipment, *linguistic usages* enabling them to cooperate, *rules and laws* governing their behavior and a body of *beliefs and values* shared in common.[22].

The model of musical institution proposed here combines, modifies, and supplements ideas from Wallace's cult institution and Malinowski's basic institution. First, following Nketia's definition of musical culture and roughly paralleling Wallace's cult/religion idea, "musical culture" will refer to the aggregate of a society's musical institutions and related culture. Particularly in complex societies such as India's, there may or may not be sufficient common threads running between these institutions to warrant the assertion of a single unitary musical culture.

Secondly, where Wallace's analysis of religion begins with the performance of a ritual, the musical culture analysis begins with the regular performance of music in a certain social setting: music is of course the primary component in the musical institution paradigm. Also following Wallace, the definition of a musical institution would be a set of musical performances of the same or similar music, having the same general goal, rationalized by the same or similar ideology, and supported by the same group.

Thirdly, music, as well as each of Malinowski's component categories set forth above, is divisible into more specific categories. The music of each musical institution may be divisible into musical genres, with each genre having dimensions of style (which refers to matters such as scale, meter, timbre, and intensity), texts, composition, transmission, and body movement.[23]

The first of Malinowski's components, group, would include the musicians, audience, employer, or agent. These categories would be further subdivisable. We would want to know, for example, about recruitment, training, and remuneration of musicians. Some audiences would be subdivisible into the demonstrative or even participative cogniscenti and those with a more limited interest. Each musical institution is identified with one or more types of social settings analogous to Malinowski's "environment." Each may or may not be attached to a certain type of physical location.

Another basic category, material equipment, would include musical instruments, their makers and construction, and related paraphernalia; printed music or texts; and germaine equipment such as tape recorders.[24] Malinowski's knowledge category would be broadened to include not just knowledge of how to play the instruments, but all knowledge needed to perform the musical role(s) well. Linguistic usages would consist primarily of musical terminology. Rules and laws would include behavioral expectations of musicians within and outside of musical contexts.

Beliefs and values in the musical institutional context would include all concepts, beliefs, sentiments, attitudes and values related to the music apart from those needed for performance. Outstanding among these are ideas about what is and what is not music, where music comes from, talent, musical aesthetics, and the ownership of music. (Many of these categories are explored at some length in Merriam's *The Anthropology of Music*.) This knowledge is likely to be more closely associated with certain roles or categories in the society than with others—especially with the role of musician, of course, but also with the role of ritual specialist.

Finally, to each of the component categories must be added the dimension of change over time. Unfortunately, as discussed below, there is quite often a dearth of information for this slot in the paradigm.

This completes the discussion of the core of musical culture, its musical institutions. We turn now to the periphery of musical culture, the extra-musical culture which influences or is influenced by music. It is convenient to think about these factors in terms of the tripartite techno-economy (material culture)/social structure/ideology (mental culture) model commonly used in cultural anthropology. Although the categories derive from the work of Karl Marx it is not necessary to assume that techno-economy inevitably determines social structure and ideology. The model simply provides a comprehensive set of general categories.

The general technology of a society gives rise to certain kinds of instruments and not others, and thus facilitates in instrumental music certain stylistic traits and inhibits or precludes others. The economy plays a role in the recruitment of musicians, and trade facilitates the movement of music, musical ideas and instruments between societies or sectors of society.

Social structure divides people into groups and categories (a social category consists of people who share one or more traits), each associated in one way or another with a certain type or types of music; and for each social group or category, there is a musical ideology—shared ideas, meanings and feelings conveyed and stimulated by, or resulting in music.

Consonant with the core/periphery idea, the procedure followed in this book is to describe music performances in the contexts of social events, show how their component parts are related, and then point out the relationships between material, social or ideological components of the music and extra-musical material, social and ideological elements that seem to have most influenced them or be most influenced by them. For example, in north India women sing songs to celebrate the birth of sons, but not daughters. Understanding this tradition requires reference to several other social traditions—patrilineal descent, patrilocal residence, and the dowry—as well as to less directly related but nonetheless influential matters such as the physical environment and the mode of adaptation to it.

Equally important to our understanding are the socially-supplied meanings that give rise to, impinge upon, or result from music. For example, the belief that music is auspicious motivates the inclusion of music in all important ritual ceremonies. Or, looking at the reverse process, mother goddess songs convey capabilities of the goddess that promote her worship. Because people sing things they don't say, thorough ethnography demands the study of song lyrics.

The music of most societies is not homogeneous, it is heterogeneous. With its diverse styles go different contexts. The musical institutions of a musical culture and their repertoires often share certain features; however, to assume the existence of a unitary music culture is simply out of keeping with what we know about musical culture in most societies. The headings and subheadings of the chapters that follow identify the main musical institutions of the villages in this region—and the chapters support the assertion of fundamental diversity.

One other theoretical matter that should be discussed here is the relationship between the components of what others might call musical culture and I would call a musical institution. As mentioned above, Nettl believes that these components constitute a true system such that if one part changes, the others must change in response. The research reported here suggests that the relationships between such components are more permissive or engendering than directly causal, and that in many cases the relationship between any two components is rather accidental.

Take, for example, the herders' holler (*khaṛī birahā*). Because it is often sung by herders at a great distance from possible listeners, it must be loud to be heard. So there is a direct relationship between one musical component (loudness, or intensity) and the physical setting. Another distinctive characteristic of the holler is its scale, and there is nothing in any other component in its social or physical setting that can be shown to have any bearing on its scale. It could be sung to any scale in a sufficiently high register and be heard.

In many cases components of the "system" (probably better thought of as an accidental aggregate) will not only conduce another component, but will accept an infinite variety of responses within certain limits. For example, belief in the benefits of hearing the names of God and the religious merit of charitable donations clearly supplies donor motivation which enables *Jogīs* (a Muslim caste of musical mendicants) to support themselves in part through door-to-door begging while singing the names of God. Here, ideology is one of the engendering factors in the performance of a certain type of song, but any type of devotional song sung by any type of mendicant will satisfy the donor's needs. To look at another aspect of the Jogīs' performance, there is nothing about the *sāraṅgī*, the bowed lute the Jogīs use to accompany their songs, that renders it intrinsically suitable except its portability—and other portable instruments are available. The use of the sāraṅgī in this setting is the result of several historical accidents that render it especially available to Muslim musicians, as explained in Chapter VII. In addition to the loose relationship between institutional and musical components, another problem confronts the sociocultural analysis of music.

The systemic mode of explanation is by nature a synchronic one, that is, one that depicts the system at a single moment in time (and thus avoids the problem of dealing with changing patterns of behavior and changing relationships in the constellation of behavioral or ideological patterns to which they belong). This model contributes much to our understanding of music and its relationship with extra-musical culture, but it is not often able to explain satisfactorily the form or stylistic features of music as responses to other parts of the system. The most commonly satisfying explanation of musical form is one which refers to the engendering form, in other words, music history. (The talents and limitations of musical instruments are also of course fundamental to an understanding of the music played on them.) Knowledge of the religious *qawwālī*, for example, contributes much to an understanding of the popular qawwālī that followed it in time. One of the many specific qualities it explains is the fervor of the singing, which stems from its original purpose: to generate ecstasy.

Unfortunately, in many of the musical cultures ethnomusicologists study, historical data are lacking. This is a major problem in the discipline. (It is equally problematic in cultural anthropology in general. As my colleague Victor Goldkind once said off-handedly, the comment that a certain pattern of meaning or behavior is just part of the culture really means that we simply don't know how it originated.)

The lack of music history data has, for the past several decades especially, led ethnomusicologists to attempt to explain stylistic features of music with reference to extra-musical social or ideological structures. In some treatments this is nearly a *cum hoc ergo propter hoc* (with that and therefore because of that) argument: people in a uniquely structured society perform uniquely structured music—it must be the structure of the society that brings about the musical style.[25] Other thinkers have asserted the existence of a deep mental structure which gives rise to both a particular style of music and a somehow homologous structure of society.[26]

Attempts to relate music style to social or ideological (cognitive) structure are implicitly addressed to a profound question for ethnomusicology: Why does music have different styles in different societies? I have suggested above how other, extra-musical aspects of a culture can directly or indirectly influence its music and musical life—how they engender a performance of music within vague stylistic and lyrical limits by certain social types of people for other social types at certain times and places. From there the musicians take over, and in solitary creativity or public performance incrementally or radically alter the music which tradition has given them.

The processes in which people create and re-create music forms can be viewed in micro- and macro-spans. The macro-span changes are the developments in form occurring over years—the kinds of changes treated in music history. The micro-span level includes the private practice *cum* creation session, or the public performance, in which musicians—whether for positive audience response, sheer enjoyment, competition with musical colleagues, ego and prestige enhancement, or relief from boredom—play music and experiment with its form. (One admirably empirical and detailed analysis of a performance showing how audience-musician interaction influences the form the music takes is Regula Qureshi's video-tape-based study of a traditional qawwālī performance.)[27] Changes at the micro-span level (which may or may not be responses to "systemic" components) through generational chains of musicians result in the cumulative deviations that constitute macro-structural changes—and, given isolation, eventually culminate in inter-societal style differences.

One final element of the theory underlying this study should be briefly discussed. A prominent objective of this research was to assess the importance of music in the society. The question is a functionalist one: to answer it requires recognition not only of the intended results of music performance, but of the unintended social and psychological consequences of music performance. For example, wedding songs seem to mobilize sympathy for the bride and thereby ease her adjustment in a new and difficult social situation.

Critics have charged that functionalism is teleological, sometimes tautologous, and that it fails to provide satisfying explanations or to comprehend cultural change. Writing about the functional study of religion, Edward Norbeck asserted that these criticisms at least partially dissolve when the actual results of functional studies are examined. "(Functional studies) have . . . pointed out certain plausible effects of religious beliefs and practices, and they have often traced relationships between religion and other elements of culture in a useful and illuminating way."[28] He goes on to say that, "Recent studies escape the charges of teleology and tautology by explicitly tracing relationship among elements of culture with no dedication to the idea that they are indispensable or to deducing societal or individual needs which they might serve."[27] There is no reason why the same could not be true for functional studies of music.

While Alan Merriam posited a number of general functions for music in all cultures, Bruno Nettl likes the idea "that in each society music has a major function."[30] He cites as an example "upper-caste" Hindu society, in which "[music] may be a way of making the connection between religious values and everyday life. . . ."[31] Again we encounter the assumption of a unitary musical culture with just a single prominent function, which appears untenable. Secondly, it should be recognized that music is an important element of nearly all religions. Thirdly, while Nettl was clearly targeting classical music and the upper echelon of Indian society, this study shows that music is an equally important part of religious life and thought in the village, and that one of its major functions is indeed to express and thus implant, spread, reinforce and perpetuate religious ideology, as well as to provide a vehicle for religious activity and social interaction. Music, however, does have two other common (and sometimes concurrent) functions in the culture: recreation and entertainment.

Language and the Language Region

The language situation in India is complex. There are twenty major literary languages and roughly one hundred and fifty vernacular (unwritten) languages spoken in India. Bhojpurī is one of the latter.

Approximately forty million people in eastern Uttar Pradesh and western Bihar speak Bhojpurī (see the map on the inside front cover).[32] One linguist divides Bhojpurī into Northern, Western, Southern and Nagpuria dialects.[33] The primary site of this research was in the Western Bhojpurī area, which includes the following districts in eastern Uttar Pradesh: western Ghāzipur, southeastern Mirzapur, Banāras, eastern Jaunpur, Āzamgaṛh, and eastern Faizabād.[34] A few of the songs included here came from Balliā District, where Southern Bhojpurī is spoken. The extent of differences between dialects spoken in localities separated by as little as twenty to thirty miles is notable. Villagers say, "The water changes every four miles, the language every eight."

Uneducated people tend to speak more Bhojpurī. Educated people and those with urban experience also speak Standard High Hindi, the medium of education in Uttar Pradesh, or *khaṛī bolī* Hindi, the Delhi-Meerut dialect upon which it is based. Roughly speaking, Bhojpurī is as different from Hindi as Spanish is from French.

Radio broadcasts and newspapers are in a heavily Sanskritized Hindi (i.e., they contain more words drawn or concocted from Sanskrit, the language of the ancient Hindu texts) which is difficult for uneducated villagers to comprehend, or in English, also understood only by the educated. Academicians in this area are also prone to use Sanskritized Hindi. While Bhojpurī predominates in village song, many other languages are also used, as explained in the chapter on fieldwork.

The languages most commonly used in song include khaṛī bolī, Urdu (which has the same grammar as Hindi but uses more Persian and Arabic words), and Bhojpurī. Braj bhāṣā and Āvadhī are found in some of the mendicants' devotional songs. (Braj bhāṣā is the language of the Mathura-Agra area and Āvadhī of the Lucknow area.) Songs also demonstrate the local caste dialects, e.g., the songs of the Camār women are said to use a dialect which differs from that of the main settlement.

Countryside and Village

The Bhojpurī-speaking area is on the wide and fertile alluvial plain which borders the Ganges river from western Uttar Pradesh to the Ganges-Brahmaputra delta in Bangla Desh. Eastern Uttar Pradesh is just inside the western boundary of the area in which rainfall is sufficient to allow rice cultivation. Wheat, barley, and sugar cane are other major crops. Except where flooded rivers have left the land rugged and eroded, it is flat country. The seemingly endless fields are reticulated by elevated footpaths, and cut by irrigation ditches and an occasional road or railroad track. All that protrudes above the horizon are a few groves, and in the distance, clusters of mud-walled, tree-shaded buildings.

The smaller clusters of buildings, the hamlets, generally contain people of only one caste. In the rural areas the untouchable castes always live in such hamlets, but others contain people of Ahir (cowherd),

Nuniā (house-builder) and other castes. Hamlets are scattered randomly around the larger settlements, the multi-caste villages. Each village is separated from the surrounding fields by tanks or man-made ponds which catch the water from monsoon rains and village gutters, and by bare patches which serve as threshing grounds after the two main harvests. Religious shrines—small brick or cement cubicles housing one or more icons—overlook tanks and threshing floors. The most distinctive structure of the village, the school, is also usually located by one of the threshing grounds. It is commonly a long building with a full-length veranda at the edge of a large playground. Conical stacks of cowdung fuel chips stand at the edges of the roads and paths entering the village.

Two major lanes or roads cross-cut Indrapur; these are intersected by the many smaller lanes which wind among the tightly-packed rows and clusters of dwellings. Water buffalo, cows and bullocks are tied by their feeding stations at the edges of lanes and yards, in the shade of the large and sacred *nīm*, *pīpal*, and banyan trees. Nearly a dozen wells, many with wide cement platforms, are scattered throughout the village.

The most obtrusive of the village dwellings are the *pakkā* (first-class) houses—two story plaster-or-brick-walled structures which stand out among the mud-walled, tile-roofed homes of the less affluent. But even the pakkā homes rarely stand alone. They usually share one or more walls with other homes (an economic measure facilitated by the absence of a concept of privacy, or at least a low valuation of it). In these clusters or rows of adjoining dwellings may live families of different castes or even different religions—ten of Indrapur's ninety-nine households are Muslim (which is in keeping with the national proportion of Muslims).

Most homes are divided among several nearby buildings, but in the crowded nucleus of the village one building may contain rooms belonging to two families. The main building, the primary domain of the women, is built around an open courtyard in which they cook and carry out their many other tasks. Most of the main houses have verandas where members of the family and neighbors can sit and chat. The secondary structures are generally thatch-roofed, and open on one side. One of these, the men's sleeping quarters, also at times houses stock, grain, fodder etc.

Neighborhoods, concentrations of much of the daily interaction among villagers, are not demarcated by any particular physical features. One becomes aware of their boundaries after living in the village. In a larger village, residents of widely separated neighborhoods, particularly women, may meet infrequently. Brahman and *Ṭhākur* neighborhoods lie at either end of Indrapur (separated by a distance of approximately three-fourths of a mile). Between them are many neighborhoods of mixed caste composition, e.g., a *Goṇḍ-Kohār* (grain parcher-potter) area, a *Nāī-Kahār* (barber-water carrier) area, and a *Telī-Kānū-Seṭh* area. These last three are now all merchant castes; the front rooms of their dwellings are small shops. In the neighborhood in which Brahman homes predominated there are also *Lohār* (carpenter and blacksmith), *Kalvār* (merchant), *Dhobī* (washerman) and *Ahir* homes. The men in this and other neighborhoods occasionally combine in cooperative work parties such as sugar cane planting and harvesting, and during lulls in the day's activities may be found talking together in a neighborhood sitting-place. The women of the neighborhood convene at each other's homes to sing and gossip.

A Brief Overview of Caste

For the purposes of this book, a *caste* is a ranked, endogamous group, usually associated with a traditional occupation. (Castes of similar occupation may be referred to by people outside the group with a common name. Some anthropologists call these conglomerate units castes and the constituent, endogamous units, sub-castes.)[35]

Castes are regionally concentrated. Certain castes found in the Vārāṇasī region are not found in any number in the Delhi region and vice versa. There are probably several thousand castes; the exact number is not known. The Census of India stopped collecting comprehensive data on caste membership after 1931.[34]

Villagers commonly rank castes by levels. In the south three levels are used (untouchable, non-Brahman and Brahman) and in the north, five. The bottom one of these is the untouchable or scheduled caste level. The upper four levels utilize the names of the four *vārṇas*, divisions of society mentioned in the ancient Hindu collection of hymns called the *Ṛg Veda*. From highest to lowest, the four levels are Brahman (priest), *kṣatriya* (warrior), *vaiśya* (merchant) and *śudra* (artisan, serf). In conveying the approximate rank of a caste a villager would say, for example, "the Kānū caste is of the vaiśya vārṇa." (The Kānū caste is of the merchant or third-ranked level.)

Vārṇa and caste are commonly confused in written accounts, so that one might read in newspapers about "the four great castes," meaning Brahman, kṣatriya, etc. One reason for this confusion of caste and vārṇa is that the priest castes throughout India are called Brahman.[37] Most would be ranked in the Brahman vārṇa, but they do not make up one great group.

One's caste identity is ascribed—it is acquired at birth and immutable. But class ranking, determined largely by affluence, is of increasing importance. Individuals of lower castes who excel economically may be accorded more prestige than people of that caste have traditionally received. Where entire castes are able to raise their economic ranking, they are often able, by emulating higher castes over many years, to raise their caste ranking. (This process has been called Sanskritization.)

Ranking tends to be firmer at the extremes of the hierarchy, looser and more dependent on whom you ask in the middle. Brahmans are the highest everywhere and untouchables the lowest, and usually there is consensus as to which castes are ranked Brahman and which are ranked untouchable. But some middle castes, according to the work they do, don't fit easily into any of the vārṇas. The Ahir caste in Indrapur, for example, was self-ranked in the kṣatriya level, but local Brahmans put it in the śudra level. The ranking of middle and lower castes may vary by region or even village.

It is also at the extremes of the hierarchy that caste identity makes the most difference in social interaction. Members of higher-ranked castes are accorded gestures of deference (including special food when they are feasted), and contact with members of untouchable castes (including touching and interdining) is avoided. Castes in the middle ranks are less concerned with the expressions of caste ranking.

The purity or pollution of a caste's traditional occupation plays an important role in its ranking. Death and bodily emanations, among other things, are polluting; cremators and feces-sweepers, among others, are untouchable castes. Brahmans, more than others, avoid pollution in part because they must be in a pure state in order for the gods to accept their ceremonial offerings (even though a majority of them no longer perform rituals for others).

Traditionally the local extended families of different caste groups were combined in an economic system. Relationships between the *jajmān* landholding family at the hub of the system and the *parjuniā* families who provided services were hereditary. Service castes included priest, blacksmith-carpenter, washerman, barber, and water carrier. They were rewarded with clothing and cooked food on festive occasions, and shares of each harvest. The system survives in diminished form with part of the payments in cash.

Caste intersects with music in various ways. In certain castes, e.g. Nat and Jogī, music is a traditional but optional profession. Certain castes are more musical than others although they are not generally professional entertainers. For example, singing is a part of the Ahir image, and certain genres of song are thought of as Ahir music, but most Ahirs are not professional musicians. Members of lower castes, whose economic prospects are generally dismal, are more often entertainers or processional musicians because employment opportunities in other fields are scarce.

Bazaar and City

Indrapur is several miles from Kamalapur, the nearest bazaar town. (Both community names are pseudonyms to conceal the identity of the locality and thus protect the human rights of the residents.) The road from Kamalapur to Indrapur crosses a river which is impassable by ox cart or motor vehicle from the latter part of June through October due to the heavy monsoon rains. Pedestrians cross the river via a dangerous one-track railway bridge in this season, and by a crude dirt bridge or stepping stones when the monsoon torrents have receded. The village is thus somewhat isolated from the surrounding area for three months a year.

Kamalapur is the site of the Block Development Office, the lowest level of state government and an agricultural extension service and village development agency. Villagers must travel to the bazaar town for a wide range of goods and services not available in the village, including the brass bands and other musical groups which lead processions and entertain in weddings. The men comprising these groups are often artisans and shopkeepers in bazaar towns.

From Kamalapur one can travel by train or bus to the *tehsil* (headquarters of the next higher level of state government) or to the district capital, twelve and sixteen miles distant respectively. Kamalapur is about thirty-five miles from Vārāṇasī, the epicenter and largest city of eastern Uttar Pradesh (1981 population 708,647).[38] Just as villagers must go to the bazaar for the purchase of goods not available in the village, there are other specialized purchases which must be made in Vārāṇasī, particularly in connection with weddings: higher quality, more prestigious entertainment is also hired in Vārāṇasī by more affluent families.

Located on the sacred Ganges (Gaṅgā) river, Vārāṇasī is for Hindus the holiest city, and has been a major pilgrimmage place and an important religious center for several thousand years. A radio station broadcasts from Vārāṇasī, and a daily newspaper is published there, but the penetration of mass media into the hinterlands is restricted by illiteracy, poverty (most families cannot afford radios and many cannot afford to send their children to school because of the labor that would be lost), and limited communication and transportation systems. A postal substation was established in Indrapur in 1971, providing daily mail delivery, but as yet Indrapur has neither telephone nor telegraph service. There were only about ten radios in the village during my residence in 1971–1972.

During that period people spoke of the eastern part of Uttar Pradesh as being technologically "backward" and culturally conservative, but in 1978 substantial increases in motorized transport and the mechanization of larger farms were apparent.

The limited mass media penetration, the nascent industrialization and the poverty contribute to the vitality of folk music and other oral traditions of the area. Even as modernization proceeds, folk traditions are likely to persist in the interior areas.

The Yearly Agricultural Cycle

In a village in which the economy is primarily agricultural, many of the activities of the residents are determined by the annual cycle of cultivation tasks. Ceremonial life and festivals are geared to the agricultural cycle, and these and the seasons themselves, i.e., the cycle of natural changes, determine to a great extent the timings of certain types of music.

The first of the twelve months in the Hindu calendrical year is *Caitr*, which usually begins in March. Caitr is the beginning of the hot season in northern India, when temperatures generally range from the low fifties at night to the mid-eighties in the afternoon. About nine o'clock in the morning the dry west wind (*lū*) becomes noticeable, and picks up force as the day progresses until it begins to diminish about four o'clock in the afternoon. In Balliā District and western Bihar (to the east of Indrapur) a distinctive genre of recreational music, called *caita*, is sung by groups of men throughout the month.

In April the wind and the heat become more intense. People try to stay indoors from about eleven in the morning until four in the afternoon. The agricultural chores of this period, the harvesting, threshing, and winnowing of the *rabī* crop (the group of plants including wheat and barley, planted in October and November) are scheduled for the evening, moonlit nights, or early morning to avoid the severe heat and wind. The singer of the epic Ālhā turned up at harvest time to entertain (for a small share) the harvesters as they worked. Temperatures reach their peak (over 100 degrees in the shade and 115 to 120 in the sun) in the last half of May and early in June.

The period following the winnowing of the rabī crop and planting of sugar cane is one in which the fields require less attention. This agricultural period usually coincides with the month of Vaiśākh (from the last of April to the last of May). This is the most popular time for weddings, and, given the necessity of wedding entertainment, the most musical period of the year.

The first monsoon rains, which usually come in the latter half of June, are necessary for the plowing and planting of the *kharīph* group of plants, whose main crop is rice. Daytime temperatures are slightly lower. Once the season is underway, rain may fall four or five days a week, rendering the narrow lanes of the village slippery and discouraging inter-village travel as well. The evenings are soft, warm and sensuous. The season is generally considered the most erotic of the year, which is reflected in the songs associated with the season, called *kajalīs* (or *kajarīs*).

Another kind of monsoon song is a hymn sung to the smallpox goddess during her worship ceremonies. The worship of the smallpox goddess may occur in the monsoon season because in the recent past epidemics of the diseases with which she is associated were most frequent in this season.

The harvesting of the kharīph crop and the planting of the rabī crop are usually finished by the end of November. From December through February, night time temperatures descend to near freezing, and most of the people are forced to wear their blankets or shawls throughout the day. Warming the hands over fires of dry weeds, twigs, etc. becomes an evening and early morning necessity. One of the campfire pastimes in the evening is the *khisā*, a half-sung, half-recited epic. Harvesting sugar cane and the manufacture of raw cane sugar are the chief agricultural activities of the season.

The *phāgun* season, the period culminating with the *Holī* festival on the first day of Caitr, begins late in January. The weather turns warm and the rabī crops are seen ripening in the fields as Holī approaches. The *phaguā* songs of the Holī season are appropriately high-spirited.

Historical Background

A brief sketch of the area's history from the fifteenth century provides a useful perspective on its diverse music. In the fifteenth century *Rājputs* (ancestors of the castes called Ṭhākur in this region today) began filtering into the area from *Rājputāna*.[39] Rājputāna, literally, land of the Rājputs, is an ancient name for an area comprising western Uttar Pradesh and Rajasthan. Villagers say that already living in the area were some castes still present today, including Ahir, Camār, Goṇḍ, Bārī, Bhar and Musahar groups. The Rājputs gradually supplanted the semi-tribal and Muslim local leaders who controlled the land.

One Rājput family built a moated fortress three miles from Indrapur (still occupied by descendants of the group), and invited Brahmans to come and serve as their ritual specialists. As their clan expanded and the land immediately surrounding their fortress was occupied, factions of the Rājputs moved short distances away to establish new homesteads, one of which was at Indrapur. They again called Brahmans to live nearby.

This account explains the dominance of Ṭhākur and Brahman castes in the region today. It also explains certain linguistic features and thematic elements of local songs, and provides some limited clues to the diversity of their musical forms. Some of the women's wedding songs and the epic Ālhā refer to Rājput institutions of the twelfth century, such as the warring over brides. Several contemporary customs also allude to Rājput origins, such as the seemingly martial *bārāt* (groom's party). Its imperious arrival at the bride's home suggests the legendary military conquests of Rājputāna.

In the latter half of the nineteenth century an increase in emigration from this area resulted in the spread of the local music to such far-flung places as Fiji and Surinam, where they are still performed.[40] The number of men leaving the village to take employment in the major port and industrial cities also began to increase at that time. Today Bhojpurī-speaking neighborhoods exist in Calcutta, Bombay, and other metropolitan areas. In the off-season (after the wedding season), some local musicians travel to these cities to entertain the Bhojpurī-speaking residents.

The most commonly recalled incident of Indrapur's recent past is the 1942 uprising against the British administration. British soldiers reportedly killed a man of the Ahir caste who lived about two miles north of Indrapur. In a violent reprisal, men from the vicinity tore up railroad tracks and telegraph wires and set fire to the district police station. It is said that although most of the women and children had been sent out of the area by their menfolk, the British raped two women. One Indrapur man was killed, and at least seven from Indrapur were among the eighty-five reportedly arrested. Today there are seven men in the village who were imprisoned by the British. They now receive from the government of India "Political Sufferer" pensions of from fifty to sixty rupees monthly. Another man owns land given to him by the government of India as compensation for the death of his father at the hands of the British.

The anti-British sentiment is expressed in songs of that period championing Gandhi and the Congress Party which are still sung in the village (see Chapter II). The Congress Party was highly active in the promotion of anti-British demonstrations and resistance in this region.

Modernization and Social Change

A detailed discussion of the effects of modernization on the village society is not called for by the objectives of this book, but a brief sketch of the more obtrusive changes is helpful in understanding the contexts of contemporary village music. Technological advances are generally reducing village employment, contributing to urban migration and the slow deterioration of rural traditions, including musical ones. Electric tube-wells alleviate the need for traditional oxen and man-powered irrigation arrangements. Hand pumps installed in courtyards have reduced the need for the services of the Kahār caste, whose traditional jobs included carrying water from the wells. Electric threshers are replacing threshing by oxen, mass production has deprived local tailors and jewelers of their markets, and the availability of detergents and razors is reducing the need for washermen and barbers. An electrically powered flour mill now stands at the periphery of the village. Its services are not utilized by all, because of its inconvenient location, but fewer women now use the small stone grinding wheels in their homes, and the songs sung while milling are much less frequently heard.

Communications are also improving. A newspaper published in Vārāṇasī is delivered to the school daily, where it is avidly read by teachers and others. (The literacy rate for Uttar Pradesh is about 34 percent.) The All-India Radio station in Vārāṇasī transmits a considerable amount of music including classical Hindustani, folk and popular music. Popular music, consisting largely of film songs, is enjoyed more by the younger people. Young men sing snatches of it to each other on their evening rambles around the village, and boys and girls alike make up their own verses to film song tunes.

Many men in the village have bicycles, which facilitate working in other communities. Fairly convenient travel to Vārāṇasī from Kamalapur, only a few miles from Indrapur, has been available via the railway for fifty to sixty years. Trips to Vārāṇasī for religious, commercial, or recreational purposes also allow the people to keep appraised of new developments—I was asked many times to explain the hippies then taking advantage of the abundant spiritualism (and marijuana) in Vārāṇasī.

Population pressure on the land is intense. India's population increased by 25 percent from 1961 to 1971, according to the Census Commissioner. The population density is roughly 930 per square mile in the Bhojpurī speaking region.[41] Many village men have no land, either because it has been previously parcelled out to other men in the lineage or because their families did not acquire land at the time of Zamindar Abolition. Those who are unable to farm or find work in or near the village must go to the cities to earn money to support their families and themselves. This is true for members of all castes. I would estimate that over fifty men from Indrapur work most of the year in cities. No doubt this is partly responsible for the many songs depicting the feelings of a woman whose husband or lover is far away.

The urban situation, where the social sanctions supplied by wives and the older people of the village are absent, presses for the adoption of modern ways. The villagers themselves cite the example of the modern urban *hoṭal* (restaurant) in which men of higher (as well as lower) caste ranking take food without inquiring the caste of the cook or waiter. But those who live in cities bow to the conventions of caste discrimination when they return to the village—at least in public life.

Due in part to urban influences, rural life is becoming more secular. Certain sacred ceremonies including the wedding are abbreviated; others are omitted altogether. The divine status of the Brahman is more often disregarded. The Brahmans themselves, with exceptions, are more dependent on their fields and other kinds of employment than on the priestly work which is their legacy. Few of the younger Brahmans are fully trained as ritual specialists because of the declining need for their services. The Brahman's exclusive ritual award of the twice-born string to Brahman boys before puberty (the ritual second birth, the birth of the *divine* human) is observed much less frequently than before. (It occurred once in the thirteen months I spent in the village.)

Polarities in the Order of Reporting

The order of reporting in the chapters below follows two polarities in the nature and function of village music genres: participatory/non-participatory and inner/outer. Participatory music is music in which anyone and ideally everyone present participates. Performers of participatory music are generally not considered by themselves or others as musical specialists—the musical ability required to perform participatory music is not great.

The performers of non-participatory music are specialists who perform for an audience. The following chapters will show how participatory and non-participatory music differ in overt function or use, and consequently in form, the experience of participating individuals, evaluation, and the role of the performer.

Chapters II through V concern women's ceremonial and recreational music, which is participatory music and the innermost music of the village in several senses: it is largely sung in the home, much of it is integral to family-oriented rituals, and, more than any other class of music in the village, it concerns kinship relations. The men's music of Chapter VI is also participatory music performed in the village, but is performed outside the home. Chapter VII proceeds to non-participatory genres, songs performed by specialists for the diversion of their audiences. The first two of these are performed by residents of the village; those that follow reflect another outward movement—the singers are mendicants who do not live in the village. The entertainment and processional genres discussed in Chapter VIII are all performed by outsiders.

Notes

1 B. Chaitanya Deva, *Musical Instruments of India: Their History and Development* (Calcutta: Firma KLM Private Limited, 1978), p. 74, and Curt Sachs, *The History of Musical Instruments* (New York: W. W. Norton, 1940) p. 224.

2 Durgaśankarprasād Singh, *Bhojpurī Lok-git me Karun Ras* (The Pathos in Bhojpurī Folksong) (Allahabad: Hindi Sahitya Sammelan, 1965), and Krishna D. Upadhyaya, *Bhojpurī Lok-git* (Allahabad: Hindi Sahitya Sammelan, 1954 and 1966).

3 G. A. Grierson, "Some Bihari Folksongs," *Journal of the Royal Asian Society* 16 (1884): p. 196, and "Some Bhojpurī Folksongs," *Journal of the Royal Asian Society* 18 (1886): p. 207.

4 W. G. Archer and Sankta Prasad, "Bhojpurī Village Songs," *The Journal of Bihar and Orissa Research Society* (1942): pp. 1-48.

5 William G. Archer, *Songs for the Bride: Wedding Rites of Rural India*, Edited by Barbara Stoler Miller and Mildred Archer (New York: Columbia University Press, 1985).

6 Edward O. Henry, "North Indian Wedding Songs: An Analysis of Functions and Meanings." *The Journal of South Asian Literature* 11 (1975): 62-93, especially pp. 83 and 69.

7 Hari S. Upadhyaya, "The Joint Family Structure and Familial Relationship Patterns in the Bhojpurī Folksongs," Ph.D. diss., Indiana University, (Ann Arbor: University Microfilms, 1967).

8 Laxmi G. Tewari, "Ceremonial Songs of the Kanyakubja Brahmans" Ph.D. diss., Wesleyan Univerity, (Ann Arbor: University Microfilms, 1974).

9 U. Arya, *Ritual Songs and Folksongs of the Hindus of Surinam* (Leiden: E. J. Brill, 1968).

10 S. L. Srivastav, *Folk Culture and Oral Tradition*. New Delhi: Abhinav Publications, 1974).

11 Chandramani Singh and Ronald Amend, *Marriage Songs from Bhojpurī Region* (Jaipur: Champa Lal Ranka & Co., 1979).

12 Krishna Dev Upadhyaya, *Bhojpurī Lok-git*, part 1 (Allahabad: Hindi Sahitya Sammelan, 1954), and part 2 (1966).

13 Singh, *Bhojpurī Lok-git me Karun Ras.*

14 Milton Singer, "The Radha-Krishna Bhajanas of Madras City," in Milton Singer (ed.), *Krishna: Myths, Rites, and Attitudes* (Chicago: University of Chicago Press, 1968), and T. K. Venkateswaran, "Radha-Krishna Bhajanas of South India: A Phenomenological, Theological, and Philosophical Study," in Singer, *Krishna: Myths, Rites, and Attitudes.*

15 Irawati Karve, *Kinship Organization in India* (New York: Asia Publishing House, 1965), and Oscar Lewis, *Village Life in Northern India* (New York: Random House, 1958).

16 L. Winifred Bryce, *Women's Folk Songs of Rājputāna*. Delhi: Ministry of Information and Broadcasting, Government of India, 1961.

17 Bonnie Wade, "Songs of Traditional Wedding Ceremonies in North India," *1972 Yearbook of the International Folk Music Council* (Urbana: University of Illinois Press, 1972), pp. 57-65, and "India: Folk Music," in *The New Grove Dictionary of Music and Musicians.* (Washington, D.C.: Grove's Dictionaries of Music, Inc., 1980).

18 Indira Junghare, "The Position of Women as Reflected in Marathi Folk Song," *Man in India* 61 (1981), pp. 237-253.

19 Bruno Nettl, "Introduction," to Bruno Nettl (ed.), *Eight Urban Musical Cultures: Tradition and Change* (Urbana: University of Illinois Press, 1978), p. 8.

20 J. H. Kwabena Nketia, "The Juncture of the Social and the Musical: The Methodology of Cultural Analysis," *The World of Music* 23 (1981), pp. 22-35.

21 Anthony F. C. Wallace, *Religion: An Anthropological View* (New York: Random House, 1966), p. 78.
22 Audrey Richards, "The Concept of Culture in Malinowski's Work," in Raymond Firth (ed.), *Man and Culture: An Evaluation of the Work of Bronislaw Malinowski.* (New York: Harper and Row, 1957), pp. 24-25.
23 The last four categories come from Jeff Todd Titon, *Worlds of Music: An Introduction to the Music of the World's Peoples* (New York: Schirmer, 1984), pp. 6-7.
24 Ibid. p. 8.
25 For my critique of one such approach, see Edward O. Henry, "The Variety of Music in a North Indian Village: Reassessing Cantometrics," *Ethnomusicology* 20 (1976), pp. 49-66.
26 See, for example, John Blacking, *How Musical is Man?* (Seattle: University of Washington Press, 1973, pp. 89-116), and Marcia Herndon, "The Cherokee Ballgame Cycle: An Ethnomusicologist's View," *Ethnomusicology* 25 (1971): pp. 339-352.
27 Regula Qureshi, "Qawwali: Making the Music Happen in the Sufi Assembly," in Bonnie Wade (ed.), *Performing Arts in India* (Berkeley: Center for South and Southeast Asia Studies, 1983).
28 Edward Norbeck, *Religion in Primitive Society*. (New York: Harper & Row, 1961), p. 136.
29 Ibid.
30 Bruno Nettl, *The Study of Ethnomusicology* (Urbana: University of Illinois Press, 1983), p. 137.
31 Ibid.
32 Shaligram Shukla, *Bhojpurī Grammar* (Washington, D.C.: Georgetown University Press, 1981).
33 Ibid., p. 4.
34 Ibid., p. 4.
35 Pauline Kolenda, *Caste in Contemporary India: Beyond Organic Solidarity* (Menlo Park, California: The Benjamin/Cummings Publishing Company, 1978), pp. 10–11.
36 Ibid., p. 21.
37 Ibid., pp. 20-21.
38 *The Far East and Australia 1984-85*, 16th edition (London: Europa Publications), p. 365. Vārāṇasī is the spelling of the name of the city used in formal contexts. The city is also called Benares, a name used in the British and Mogul periods. (Banāras is the transliteration and reflects the common pronunciation.) Kāśī (Kashi is an alternate spelling) is the name used in the era of the conqueror Harsha (circa 640 A.D.) and before, and is also used in some formal contexts today.
39 Except where otherwise indicated, information in this paragraph comes from Bernard Cohn, "Political Systems in Eighteenth Century India: The Banāras Region," *Journal of the American Oriental Society* 82 (1962), pp. 319-320.
40 For studies of Indian folk music in the Fiji Islands, see Don Brenneis and Ram Padarath, "About Those Scoundrels I'll Let Everyone Know: Challenge Singing in a Fiji Indian Community," *Journal of American Folklore* 88 (1975): pp. 283-291; and Don Brenneis, "The Emerging Soloist: Kavvali in Bhatgaon," *Asian Folklore Studies* 42 (1983), pp. 63-76.
41 Shukla, *Bhojpurī Grammar,* p. 3.

Chapter II

Women's Song: Songs of the Wedding

Introduction

Although women's song has been the focus of surprisingly little anthropological study, it is clearly an important and distinguishing part of the culture. Music is auspicious (*maṅgal*) in connection with any Hindu religious rite, and in many village rites the only music is the singing of the women. All important family rituals, such as birth and wedding rites, require women's song, and women sing for recreational purposes as well. Their songs constitute a vast body of lore. In each of the seven language regions in North India, women sing hundreds of different songs.[1] Very few of these songs are sung by men. In part because fewer women than men are educated, song is an especially important medium for the expression of their mental life. "While the written literature of the modern Indian languages is dominated by men-writers, the oral tradition is rich in women's songs."[2] In its effect on peoples lives, there is no more important music in North India: these songs convey religious knowledge and social sentiments at the heart of everyday life, and the people who sing and hear them number in the hundreds of millions.

Among the most important ceremonial songs women sing are those of the premier social event in the village, the wedding. These songs transmit fundamental religious beliefs, attitudes about certain kinship relations, and even some dated nationalistic ideology. Perhaps more importantly, songs impose unique meanings on the wedding and on marriage, and reinforce others. In so doing, they actually help to achieve the goals of the wedding. To understand the wedding songs fully it is necessary to look first at the system of social relations of which the wedding is part.

Kinship and Marriage among Twice-Born and Śudra Castes in North India

A number of anthropological monographs and articles discuss marriage and kinship in North India, and a thorough description of marriage rites in eastern Uttar Pradesh is available.[3] Accordingly, only those elements needed to provide a context for the presentation and interpretation of wedding songs are mentioned here.

The basic social unit in the village, the extended family, consists of two or more patrilineally-related men (father and son or men related through a common male ancestor), their wives, children, and often other single relatives. Inheritance is patrilineal. Extended families eventually divide, but reside in adjoining or nearby buildings. Authority among males in the household is a matter of generation (sons defer to fathers and uncles) and seniority within generation (younger brothers or cousins to older).

Marriage is endogamous within the caste and exogamous to the clan. A girl's husband should be of a clan of higher ritual ranking or a family which is preferably slightly wealthier than her own. (This does not hold true for some untouchable castes.) A substantial dowry commensurate with the economic status of the families is paid to the husband's family (again excepting most untouchable castes). A man is generally two or three years older than his wife, whose age can vary from pre-pubescent to early twenties, depending upon caste practices and economic status. Despite the Hindu Marriage Act of 1955, which fixes the minimum age for marriage at 15 for girls and 18 for boys, it is common for girls to be married before reaching puberty.[4] Wealthier girls may be sent to high school or college, in which cases marriage or subsequent cohabitation is delayed. Residence after marriage is patrilocal, often with cohabitation delayed three or five years. A distance of ten or more miles usually separates the two families and effectively prevents casual contacts between their members.

Marriage therefore involves the introduction of a young, alien female of a subordinate family into a superordinate household of strangers. Her roles in all but one relationship in the family are deferential. In the company of her husband's father, father's brothers and father's brothers' sons she must speak only when spoken to and keep her sari, which is worn in such a way that the end covers her head, pulled well down over her face. She should speak to her husband, towards whom her attitude should be reverential, only in private. She must defer to the older women of the household, follow their commands, and perform personal service for them. Her husband's sisters may criticize her or try to foist their work on her.[5] Soon after the arrival she will be expected to perform a large share of the household tasks. Only with her husband's younger brother does she have an informal, symmetrical relationship.

Particularly in the first years of her marriage, she will be subject to the restrictions of purdah, whose object is the seclusion of women from public life in order to prevent attack, abduction, or sexual liaison. Hence she is not allowed out of the house and inner courtyard in daylight hours.

There is extreme psychological pressure on a wife to produce a son. His birth extends the patrilineage; his marriage will bring a dowry payment to the family; he will become an economic mainstay in the family by virtue of his work in the fields or elsewhere; and he performs essential rites at the death of his father. It is not surprising that a woman's status in her conjugal home rises noticeably when she gives birth to a son. Failure to do so traditionally resulted in a husband taking a co-wife. The co-wife is mentioned in songs still sung but is actually infrequent today.

Among all save untouchable castes the birth of a daughter is not joyously celebrated as is that of a son. Daughters always leave their natal homes and their dowry is a burden to their families. They are treated with an affection tempered with the ideal that the daughter is an impermanent member of the family.

Enmity is not uncommon between a wife and her husband's mother for several reasons. The mother has nearly unlimited authority to exact service from the new bride. The overbearing mother-in-law is a theme of many women's songs. The relationship between mother and son is very affectionate, as is demonstrated by one of the women's laments below. Not only does the son's wife compete with his mother for his affection and attention, but as she matures she also competes with her for authority in household affairs. These factors can generate much tension and friction in the household. The relations between a woman and her in-laws outlined above are vividly described in women's songs, as seen in this and the following chapters.

A young girl's status in her conjugal family contrasts with her status in her natal family. In her natal home she has freedom of movement in the village and, if there are brothers' wives in the family, fewer chores. After marriage, in addition to assuming a lower status and heavier work load, she is expected to shift her loyalty to her husband's family and to accept the companionship of the women of the house. The distance separating the two households and the bride's young age facilitate her socialization in her new family. Several lengthy visits in her natal home during the first years of marriage serve to ease the adjustment. Despite the obvious difficulties for the young wife, marriages are stable. Divorce is very infrequent among all but untouchable castes.

Marriage also creates an important relationship between two families. This relationship is asymmetrical: Members of the bride's family must play the role of giver and ritual subordinate and the groom's family that of receiver and superordinate. For example, the bride's father symbolically touches the groom's feet in the wedding rite. When a man visits his wife's natal home (usually only to return with her to his home), her father must present him with cash, jewelry or clothing, and the best of hospitality. By tradition, a woman's father avoids her husband's village if possible, but if it is necessary that he go there he must take gifts for her husband, and will not accept hospitality of any sort from his family. Nonetheless, the bond between the two families augments the prestige of both.

Wedding Songs in their Ritual Contexts

The wedding is an event of paramount importance for the Hindu family. It forms new and important relations between two families; it activates nearly all previously established relations by bringing people together or requiring economic exchanges; and it is a prime occasion for the assertion of the prestige of both families by means of the opportunities for display of wealth it provides, including amount of ritual payments, quality of food served, accommodations provided, and band and entertainment hired.

Although there is a fairly stable core of events within a region, variation in the details of ritual acts and their order increases with distance from the village of reference. There is also variation on the vertical axis, with the rites of wealthy families tending to be more elaborate.

While the engagement rite and main ceremony require the services of trained priests, in the homes of both bride and groom the women conduct series of rituals for which they are solely responsible. Wedding songs contribute important meanings to all of the rites. Women of the nuptial families, sometimes accompanied by kin or neighbors, sing at the wedding rites which occur in and around their own homes. It is also common for the women of the bridal priest's family to sing in the weddings he performs, if their home is not too distant for them to walk to the wedding.

Women's wedding songs can be divided into three types according to the specificity of their ritual contexts. One type consists of songs sung only in one designated stage of the wedding, such as the songs accompanying the turmeric application rite (*haldī*) or those sung when the groom's party arrives at the home of the bride (*dvar pūjā*). The second type is called *sagun* (omen or presage). These are sung in the evenings before the wedding as well as in the rites themselves, ideally after such songs as are sung only in that rite. The third type of song is sung when men from outside the family are present—in wedding rites but also on other occasions. These are called *gālīs*, and most of them consist of obscene insults. In addition to the women's songs, weddings involve processional music and musical entertainment, as described in Chapter VIII.

In order to understand the wedding songs as fully as possible, it is important to observe them in their ritual contexts. Song texts are therefore integrated below with brief descriptions of the ritual events they accompany.[6] A discussion of the major themes expressed in the songs follows the presentation of the songs and ritual.

Preliminary Rites and Tilak

It is the sacred duty of a Hindu father to arrange for the marriage of his daughters. With the help of his *purohit* (family priest), friends, associates, and kin, he must locate a young man of suitable family, education, financial prospects and personality. The potential groom's family is approached through an intermediary, and if they find the bride's family satisfactory and the amount of the dowry offered acceptable, the purohits of the two families are consulted. If the prospective couple's astrological charts indicate a positive match, the purohits then determine an auspicious date for the wedding.

A number of rites are then held in the homes of the bride and groom. The first of these, which includes music, is the *tilak*. About one month before the actual wedding the bride's father goes to the home of the groom with a party consisting of selected kinsmen, his barber (a member of the Nāī caste) or a water carrier (Kahā̃r caste). Knowing that his hospitality will be carefully appraised, the groom's father serves sweetmeats (distinctive sweet pastries), tea, betel leaf, cigarettes or even a marijuana preparation called *bhāṅg*, should someone in the party desire it. After the usual *pūjā* (worship ceremony) the groom's purohit performs a ritual in which part or all of the dowry payment is made, and composes the marriage contract document (*laganpatrikā*). This states the names of the bride and groom and their fathers, and when and where the wedding is to take place. The bride's father must give the groom and his brothers small amounts of cash, and the groom's father a *janeū* (a loop of string symbolizing twice-born status). The groom's father gives the bride's father cash to offset the expense of the accompanying servants. The men also negotiate expenditures for band and entertainment, and articles of jewelry which the groom's family will give the bride.

At the end of the meal served to the bride's father and party, the women of the groom's family, concealed behind a curtain, sing the songs called *gālī.* The term gālī generally means either verbal abuse or a song of abuse, but some of the songs called gālī are not abusive—they are given that name because they are sung in the social situation in which gālīs are sung. Such a song was the first one below. It was clearly a bhajan (devotional song) adapted to glorify India's world-famous political leader and nationalist, Mohandas Gandhi, as it originally did the Hindu deity, Śiva. Gandhi's apotheosis is clearly seen as the song identifies his political tenets and symbols in the same way it refers to Śiva's well-known traits—his trident (he resembles the Greek god Neptune in several respects), the sandlewood paste on his forehead (a common element in Hindu ritual), his skull necklace, appetite for bhāṅg, and ḍamarū (a small, hourglass-shaped, double-headed drum with short, loose-hanging, weighted cords that rap the variable tension heads when the drum is oscillated, producing a rapid rat-a-tat-tat).

1.

Arise, citizens of India, arise!
  Touch the feet of Gandhi!
How long will you sleep, how long will you sleep?
  From now on be alert!
The thread of the spinning wheel, the thread of the
  spinning wheel;
  concentrate on the homespun cotton!
Give up the study of English! Give up the study of
  English! Concentrate on Hindi!
Munificent Śiva Śaṅkara, munificent Śiva Saṅkara, the
  trident in his hand.
In his hand the beautifully adorned ḍamarū,
  in his hand the beautifully adorned ḍamarū;
  his forehead adorned with the sandlewood paste.
He eats little balls of bhāṅg, he eats little balls of bhāṅg;
  he sits on the back of the ox.
Around his throat a necklace of skulls,
  around his throat a necklace of skulls;
  the trident in his hand.

The song dates to the 1920s, when Gandhi led the indictment of the British for buying raw cotton cheap in India and selling back British-made mill goods at a considerable profit. Gandhi was promoting the spinning of cotton in village homes as the basis for a cottage industry which has now been realized. Spinning cotton was seen as the way to bolster family and national self-sufficiency. To wear homespun cotton (*khādī*) garments and spin cotton were not only individually and collectively important economic measures, but ways to support and to symbolize support of anti-British, pro-independence sentiments. More abstractly, they were ways of transforming one's identity from that of dependent, exploited peasant to autonomous citizen of an autonomous state. Even today, to symbolize their grass-roots commitment, local politicians in this area wear the rougher homespun cotton garments, rather than the more refined Indian-made goods now available.

The replacement of English with Hindi mentioned in the fourth line of the song was another of Gandhi's goals which has to some degree been realized. After more than 160 years of British rule English was the language of political and intellectual discourse in many quarters as well as the medium of education and government. As Gandhi well knew, language is fundamental to identity, and a sense of autonomy and cultural pride demanded the replacement of English with an Indian language. Although communication between people of different language regions still requires English, Hindi is now the official administrative language and the medium of education in several northern states.

The next two songs are more typical of songs sung in the tilak. They are proper gālīs, which ritually insult the guests. (This custom is interpreted later in the chapter.) The name in line 1 of the first song is that of a member of the groom's father's party. In repetitions of the song the names of other men of the appropriate families are substituted.

2.

Time after time I forbad you, Rām Dharah Singh;
I kept forbidding you to buy the red chiffon.
She wears chiffon, that whore, Murat's sister;
Her pubic hair shows through.

The same sort of substitution occurs in the next gālī, which depicts the visitor's sister as wanton. (The *gaunā* is the departure of the bride to her husband's home for her first period of residence there.)

3.

The green squash planted on the bank of the river are
colorful.

The sister of Sacatā has to go on her gaunā and there is
no one to take her.
A libertine like our Rām Nāth came to take her.
Standing on a fine cot she begs him to kiss her and
ram it in hard.

Reactions of the men to the abuse songs are generally good-natured. A witty member of the groom's party may attempt a humorous retort to the women behind the curtain.

Uradī Chunā

The next rite in the series is observed at both the bride's and the groom's homes on dates fixed by their purohits. At each home five *sadhavā* women (women whose husbands are alive) gather to sing for the first time, in connection with that particular wedding, the songs called sagun. The women must all face in the direction deemed auspicious by the family purhohit. As they sing they winnow some beans. (*Uradī* is a type of bean, and *chunā* means to jiggle or shake. Vertical oscillation of the ingeniously shaped basket creates an air current that blows the chaff and dirt out of the grains or kernels.) The women I asked did not know what winnowing beans symbolized in this situation; perhaps the cleaning, a preparation to cooking beans successfully, suggests (or even *creates*, in the magically-minded) a purifying preparation for a successful marriage.

After they have sung five saguns (five being a ubiquitous and auspicious number in Hindu ritual and lore), the women of the host family rub oil into the hair of the sadhāvā women and apply vermilion to their foreheads. Vermilion so applied symbolizes that the woman is sadhāvā; a woman wears it from the time her groom applies it in her wedding until she dies. Widows are inauspicious; sadhavā women are auspicious and the renewal of their vermilion no doubt enhances this. Clearly, uradī chunā intends to insure the success of the marriage through creating many good omens.

The singing of an auspicious number of auspicious songs by auspicious women is but one of many attempts throughout the wedding to insure its success by magic. Salient others include the astrological reckoning (by a family priest) of dates for all important rites; women's singing in all rites (discussed below in connection with the concept of maṅgal); painting the words *śubh vivāh* (auspicious wedding) and pictures of elephants on the outer front wall of the home; sending wedding invitations with śubh vivāh inscribed on them; wearing new clothing (especially that which has been marked with a spot of the golden-colored turmeric in an inconspicuous place) by all family members during important rites; employing brass or śahnāī bands to lead the wedding procession; and, for wealthier families, the renting of elephants to head the wedding procession. (Elephants are auspicious because of their size, grace and power, and because they are associated with the elephant-headed Gaṇeśa, the god of new endeavor.) Anthropologists have long noted the tendency for magic to be associated with any endeavor where there is fear and uncertainty; this is an excellent example, and shows in its attempt to insure success by every imaginable means the great importance of the wedding.

This session is significant not only as an auspicious beginning. A Brahman pundit and schoolteacher told me that the saguns sung in the weeks preceding a wedding were a way of "advertising" (his words) the impending wedding. When I asked why this was necessary, he said that an impending wedding *must* be known in the community. This was his way of indicating its importance in the lives of villagers. So this gathering of neighborhood women not only confers their blessings upon and insures the success of the wedding, it serves to call to the attention of the neighborhood the approaching rite of passage. Ideally women sing saguns every night after this until the culminating rite. In reality, they may miss a night or two due to illness or other exigency.

In both the bride's and groom's villages, the women of the neighborhood gather at the home of the bride or groom after the evening meal to sing saguns. This is an inter-caste affair, since neighbors may happen to belong to different castes as they did in the center of the village. Several typical sagun sessions I attended were held at the home of a Lohār groom. Other women and girls present were members of the Dhobī (śudra level), Ṭhākur (kṣatriya level), Kalvār and Kānū (vaiśya level), and Brahman castes. This series of rites was the first to shatter my image of castes as socially isolated groups. In this part of the village women from castes of śudra to Brahman levels regularly took part in each other's rituals as well as exchanging other neighborly favors and gossip. (See Chapter VI for further examples of inter-caste interactions.)

The proceedings were informal and relaxed in these and other of the women's song sessions I observed, with no visible efforts made to produce a precise musical product. Women converse and joke between songs and sometimes during responsorial songs when their half of the group is not singing. One or two of the women might nurse infants or toddlers, and older children run in and out at will. Pauses between songs are frequent as the women gossip, take betel leaf provided by the host family, or try to recall other songs to sing. Literacy is an advantage in that respect: some educated women keep notebooks for preserving and recalling the texts of songs they like.

These were rather large gatherings with fifteen or twenty girls and women in attendance. Women's song groups generally ran from three to twelve people.

The women did not participate equally in the singing, which is commonly the case. A middle-aged woman with a strong voice and a relatively large repertoire led many of the songs. Such domination by a strong singer is not unusual. Not all of the women knew all of the songs, and songs were terminated if no one joined in. Some songs were sung by only the girls. I was told that these were largely songs learned from the newsprint booklets sold at fairs and railway stations, and set to common folk tunes or film music.

Saguns are also sung in other of the wedding rituals, ideally after such songs as are sung only in connection with that rite. It is the context in which it is sung and not the text or tune which defines a sagun. Those songs women called saguns were all sung in wedding-related rites, to different tunes, and about different topics. Some do concern marriage and the wedding, but here we begin to see the impress of *Vaiṣṇava* devotional religion, (which in this region revolves largely around the deities Rām, Krishna, and Hanumān), and again the nationalistic theme, as in the first of the seven songs below. These were recorded at different wedding rites in the village.

The first sagun dates from the early 1940s, when to be a member of the Congress Party was to be a revolutionary. At this time the Congress Party was leading an occasionally violent anti-British independence movement, the *svaraj* or self-rule movement. The actions depicted in the song remind one of how Gandhi and others used fasting as a political strategy.

4.

My husband having become a member of the Congress
party, I will not stay alive.
I will not live; he will not eat the carefully prepared food.
Without self-rule he will not come to the door.
I will not live, he will not drink from the water pot.
Without self-rule, he will not come into the courtyard.
Without self-rule, he will not take *pān*.
Without self-rule, he will not sleep on the bed.[7]

Pān is a very popular chewed stimulant in South and Southeast Asia consisting of lime, catechu, pieces of areca nut and optional tobacco wrapped in a leaf from certain Indian varieties of pepper plant.

The structure of this song is typical of the women's songs: each line is a repetition of a basic theme with one or two words changed.

It is this repetitious, formulaic quality which makes it possible for women to learn these songs without formal training. The single theme and structure of songs like this one also make additional verses easy to compose.

The next song also concerns husband and wife. An informant said that songs such as this one actually have a didactic function in warning the bride of marital situations she might face.

5.

What mistake have I made, husband, that you are giving
  me so much trouble?
Have I spoiled the food, husband, did I put in
  too little salt?
Have I spoiled the food, husband, did I put in
  too little bay leaf?
Did I use too little perfume, husband, that you are giving
  me so much trouble?
Have I spoiled the pān, husband?
Have I spoiled the catechu, husband?
Have I spoiled the bed, husband?
Didn't you get enough sleep?

The husband-wife relationship is not solely a matter of wife pleasing husband, as the next song shows. Songs based on this theme are fairly common.[8] (Informants said that lime-colored saris were in vogue several decades ago.)

6.

Order me a lime-colored sari, dear;
  without wearing one my heart can't be satisfied.
Have a room built, have a loft built,
  have them cut a little window in it, dear.
Without peeping out my heart can't be satisfied.
Without seeing my heart can't be satisfied.
Order me a lime-colored sari, dear;
  without wearing one my heart can't be satisfied.
Have a grove planted, have a garden planted.
Have a little lemon tree planted.
  without plucking them my heart can't be satisfied.

More closely related to the matter at hand, the wedding, were the following two songs. The first typifies those songs which describe the splendor of the ideal wedding, showing a great concern with the quality (and price) of dress and ornaments. The hyperbole is reminiscent of that used to describe the wedding of Sītā and Rām in the *Rāmcaritmānas*, one of the primary texts of Vaiṣṇava devotional religion. (See Chapter VI.) A version of this song survived, at least until recently, among Bhojpurī-speaking immigrants to Surinam.[9]

7.

Such a wondrous boy has come, of a rich family.
Your crown is worth millions, the fringe alone
  worth thousands.
Your wedding trousers worth millions, your robe
  worth thousands.
Your shoes worth millions, your socks worth thousands.
The bride worth millions, the veil worth thousands.

Everyone in this society is extremely concerned that everything in a wedding must be of the highest quality possible, or at least be maximally impressive, so it is funny to think of a wedding in which all the items are rotten vegetables, as in the parody which follows.[10] (The *śahnāī* is a double reed horn. See Chapter VIII.)

8.

Krishna came to the wedding, girls, everyone came to
  dance.
The wedding pole a wretched cucumber,
The wedding canopy betel leaves, girls, everyone came to
  dance.
The groom a wretched banana,
The bride an orange, girls, everyone came to dance.
The drum a pumpkin,
The śahnāī a wretched squash, girls, everyone came to
  dance.
The groom's party goes, a lot of wretched potatoes,
Fanned with wretched radishes, girls, everyone came to
  dance.
The bed covered with wretched greens,
The pillow, a long squash, lay on it, girls, everyone came
  to dance.

The deity Krishna, whose name occurs only in passing in the previous song, is the subject of a great many songs and other lore.

People of this area know more about Krishna and Rām, another principal deity in Vaiṣṇava religion, than about any other deities. This is in part because of their popularity as song subjects.

The events depicted in the song below, along with multitudinous other stories, are found in the *Bhāgavata Purāṇa* (an enormous compendium of Hindu mythology fundamental to Vaiṣṇava religion, written in the ninth century A.D.), and in the poetry of Surdās, a popular medieval Hindi devotional poet. Surdās' poetry and the *Bhāgavata Purāṇa* are both important literature in the Vaiṣṇava devotional movements, religious movements that have had great influence on the folk song of this area and most of north India. (See Chapter VI for more on the Vaiṣṇava movement.)

Lāl, in the first line of the song, is a term of endearment which a woman uses to address her son. It is also an epithet (name) of Krishna. Braj (also spelled Vṛj and Vraj) is the area around Mathura in western Uttar Pradesh, the legendary childhood home of Krishna.

9.

In the middle of the bank of the Jamunā, my Lāl snatched
 the ornaments
The women of Braj go toward the bank of the Jamunā
 to fill water vessels.
In the middle of the group Krishna appeared and
 roughly snatched the ornaments from me.
He ate my yogurt, broke the vessel that was on my head,
 and floated the carrying ring in the Jamunā.
He took our clothes and climbed the almond tree.
We were naked in the water, my Lāl snatched the
 ornaments.
In exchange for the clothes we gave a yellow silk cloth
 when we came out of the water.
You, then, are Lāl, Nanda Bābā's,
I am the daughter of Bṛṣbhan.
Whenever you meet Krishna in the lane, he pinches your
 cheeks.
Wearing a lotus leaf, Rādhā came out.
Krishna clapped, my Lāl snatched the ornaments.
Restrain your child, Mother Jāsodā!
He roughs me up, my Lāl snatched the ornaments.
Just now Lāl plays in the lane.
When did he abuse you? You don't admonish him.
He shouts from the direction of the brush, my Lāl
 snatched the ornaments.

The pranks and erotic exploits of the youthful Krishna have an obvious appeal to younger singers, and are common song topics, as subsequent texts demonstrate. The story of Krishna's theft of the *gopīs'* (young women who tend cows) clothes while they were bathing is especially popular and is depicted in some of the polychrome calendars villagers hang in their devotional rooms. This song is a rather incoherent telling with admixtures of unrelated motifs such as Krishna's meeting with Rādhā and his pinching of the gopīs' cheeks. In some prose versions of the story Krishna refuses to give the gopīs their garments until they clap, fully revealing themselves.[11]

The next song also transmits Vaiṣṇava lore. It outlines a myth that explains some of the features of a major Hindu festival called Holī. (See Chapter VI.) The mortal son of a demi-divine king named Hirankascyp, Prahalād was a devotee of the god Rām, and refused to worship his father. His father directed Holikā, his own super-human and non-flammable sister, to hold Prahalād in a burning pyre after other plots had failed. Rām intervened, Holikā was consumed in the flames, and the devoted Prahalād survived. The lyrics of this song are in Hindi, which suggests that it originated outside the Bhojpurī region.*

10.

It has become a habit, father, it has become a habit.
  [This is the refrain.]
He chants the name of Rām, father. [refrain]
The fine food in the golden tray; Prahalād will not eat
  the fine food, father. [refrain]
Burn him in the fire, press him down in water, tie him to
  a post. [refrain]
I have put water from the Himālya mountains in the
  vessel; he will not drink the water, father. [refrain]
I fasten his betel leaf with cloves; he won't eat it. [refrain]
I decorate his bed with flowers;
  Prahalād will not sleep on the bed. [refrain]

Haldī

The next ceremony in the sequence, called haldī or *hardī* (turmeric), is performed in the bride's and groom's homes on a date fixed by the purohits. Women from the neighborhood are again involved. In addition to rubbing the body of the bride or groom with a turmeric-mustard seed oil mixture thought to render the skin smooth and lustrous, they perform *cumāvan,* in which each takes a stem of *dūb* grass

*This song may be heard on the LP disc, *Chant the Names of God*. See Henry, 1981.

in each hand and touches the bride's or groom's feet, knees, chest and shoulders, and then makes a circle around his or her head. Turmeric, and the bright yellow color it imparts, are thought to be auspicious. Cumāvan is considered a personal blessing of the nuptial person, as shown in Song 11 below.

The bride and groom in their respective homes are not allowed to bathe, work, or approach well or cooking fire. They enter what Turner, following Van Gennep's analyses of rites of passage, calls a liminal condition, in which the individual is symbolically detached from the previous status and plays a role that has few or none of the attributes of the past or future status.[12] The first song below, recorded during a turmeric rubbing, refers to this liminality. (The blanks in lines 4 and 6 indicate incomprehensible phrases I inadvertantly failed to check with the singers.)

11.

The girl I saw playing, Mother, I see seated on the flour
design.
I see a beautiful flour design, Mother. [2X]
Oh Mother, I don't know when the barber's wife
plastered,
I don't know ———.
I see a pretty pot, I see a pretty pot.
Oh Mother, I don't know when the potter made it, I don't
know ———.
I see a pretty plow shaft, I see a pretty plow shaft.
Oh Mother, I don't know when the Lohār made it or
when he cut it.
I see a pretty bride, I see a pretty bride.
Oh Mother, I don't know when the god made her or
when she was born.

This song acknowledges the liminal condition of the bride-to-be by contrasting the image of her as a playful girl with the figure seated on the flour design, who seems to have lost her identity—"I don't know when the god made her or when she was born." ("Plastering" in the third line refers to the preparation of an area of ground or floor for use in a ceremony by sweeping it with cow dung plaster, which ritually purifies the area, and picks up the dust.)

In their specification of ritual acts and objects, this song and the following one perform the mnemonic function of insuring that the rites, their successive steps and necessary objects, will be remembered. It is the women of the household who conduct these "folk" rites—the rituals are not officiated by purohits, and thus neither preserved nor regulated by authoritative texts.

The following song connects the important ritual objects with their traditional providers. The *Koirin* is the wife of a *Koirī*, a man of the vegetable growing caste; The *Telin* is the wife of a *Telī*, a man of the caste whose traditional job was the extraction of vegetable oils from seeds. Sympathy for the bride (expressed in referring to her tenderness) is found in several other songs of the wedding (nos. 27–29 and 31). Rādhikā Devī is the name of the bride.

12.

Koirin Koirin, you are a great queen;
  from where have you brought the turmeric today?
My Rādhikā Devī so tender cannot bear the harsh
  turmeric.
Telin Telin, you are a great queen;
  from where have you brought the mustard seed oil
  today?
My Rādhikā Devī so tender cannot bear the harsh
  mustard seed oil.[13]

The women also sang a sagun at one turmeric-rubbing session I observed, another of those songs warning the bride of possible disappointments or problems in marriage.

13.

I didn't get a husband as vibrant as I.
His hair is not as pretty as mine.
I didn't get an ornament as pretty as my forehead.
His complexion is not as good as mine.

Rituals, as well as their usual chores, keep the women busy on this day. After the turmeric rubbing women at the groom's home erect a ceremonial pole to be used in subsequent wedding rites. At the bride's home women decorate and consecrate the *maṇḍap* (the canopy under which major wedding rites are held) and the *kohabar* (the ritually designated room in which wedding paraphernalia is stored and some wedding rites are conducted). Then they proceed to a local pond to secure a mother goddess's blessing, singing saguns en route.

Pitra Nevatinā

On the day of the *vivāh* (wedding) at the bride's home, and on the evening before the departure of the bārāt at the groom's home, there is a rite called *pitra nevatinā* (invitation of ancestors). The women of the household invoke the ancestors with a song in which the names of three generations of ancestors are enumerated.

In the rite called *koharā kī patī* (leaves of the sweet pumpkin) which follows, the groom and other unmarried boys and the bride and other unmarried girls eat from leaves of the *koharā* in their respective homes. Rites are performed which again symbolize the changing statuses of the bride and groom.[14] After the groom eats, the rest of the family is served rice. Wealthier families or those wishing to give the impression of wealth may invite all those men who will comprise the bārāt—friends, associates, and all members of the patrilineage living nearby.

Bārāt

On the morning of the departure of the bārāt, the band hired by the groom's father comes to the home of the groom. Led by the blaring band, the women of the family and their neighbors sing saguns as they proceed through the village to the grain-parching ovens of the family's Goṇḍ. The women often sing different songs than the band plays, but at the same time. Here one or several of the women dance to the music of the band, and the Goṇḍ gives them the *lāvā* (parched rice) made from grain which had been brought to her on the day of the turmeric rubbing. The group returns to the home of the groom, where the lāvā and the board seat upon which the groom sits during the wedding rites are consecrated in a brief pūjā (worship ceremony). The bārāt will take these items, along with a pot containing water from the groom's bath of that morning, to the wedding ceremony. Cumāvan is again performed, with the appropriate songs, and the groom is fed yogurt (a pure and auspicious food).

Wearing a special costume for the wedding, the groom rides with a younger brother in a four-man, enclosed palanquin usually carried by Kahārs. (See Photo 4.) Several men explained this with reference to the *Rāmcaritmānas*, in which Rām is accompanied on his journey and in his wedding by Lakṣman, his younger brother. The groom carries a white onion in his pocket to protect him from the seasonal hot west wind. Led by the band and followed by the women, they carry the groom to the edge of the village, where the mother of the groom performs a *parachan* by revolving a pestle around or over his head. This act is believed to drive away evil spirits.

Here again one or two of the women dance to the music of the band, spurred on by the ribald shouts of the others. As with the gathering at the Goṇḍ's ovens, and in accordance with purdah restrictions, no men are present except those in the band. There are many idiosyncracies, but generally the dancer moves in a circle, her torso upright and relaxed, and hips oscillating gracefully as her feet perform tight, almost mincing steps. The more sophisticated dancers, such as the one in Photo 17 learn to use their hands, eyes, and head expressively, as in the classical Indian dance styles, often seeming to mime a woman coyly teasing her lover. Sometimes dancers move in ways which allude to the sex act, encouraged by the bawdy remarks of their friends.

After the dancing, the groom's mother showers the collected women and children with coins, and there is a mad scramble. The women return to their homes and the Kahārs carry the palanquin off toward the bride's village.

Transportation of the groom and bārāt offers another arena for prestigious display. Wealthier families charter a bus if the distance warrants. Others send the groom and close male kin in a taxi and let the *bārātī*s travel at their own expense. Many bārāts take bus or train; public conveyances are jammed beyond belief and sanity during the wedding months.

Dvar Pūjā

The bārāt, band, groom and members of the bride's family convene on the edge of the bride's village. If the families are wealthy, there may occur what appears to be a mock charge after the groom has arrived. In one such event, I observed the groom's party form a line facing the line of the bride's party which was about thirty yards away. Esteemed members of the groom's party rode rented elephants, (the auspicious symbols of Gaṇeśa, the elephant-headed son of Śiva and the deity who ensures the success of new endeavor, but here also symbolic of the role of conqueror, which surfaces at several points in the wedding rites). The bārātīs fired their shotguns, and the elephants charged at full tilt towards the bridal line, the band and bārāt in their wake. Once they reached the bridal line, the bārātīs retarded the pace and the entire group proceeded to the bride's home.[15] In most cases, upon the arrival of the groom the band merely leads the procession to the bridal home. As they approach, the women sing from the veranda of the house, where everyone has been eagerly anticipating the bārāt's arrival. The singing again coincides with the playing of the band and is thus heard only intermittently by anyone but the women themselves. The scene is one of great chaos and excitement, with hordes of screaming children converging to see the spectacle and hear the band.

The following songs (14-18) were recorded at the arrivals of bārāts. The occasion is referred to as *dvar pūjā* (worship at the door). Their fragmentary nature is due in part to the noisy conditions and in part to the fact that the women occasionally forget words and run songs together.

The royal status given to the groom in the first song is expressed in song and ritual throughout the wedding rites. It shows that the women are expected to revere the groom. (They may also resent him, as expressed in later songs.) Rājā Bali was a virtuous king whose story is told in the *Vāmana* and *Bhāgavata Purāṇas* (ancient Hindu texts). His domain once included heaven and hell as well as the earth. (See explanation of Song 100 for details.) Unique in its theme among the wedding songs I collected, the song expresses gratitude to the lineage and its head for searching out a groom and thus for arranging the marriage.

14.

What group gets down under the mango and tamarind
trees, the shade as cool as that of the almond?
Because of your sacrifice, grandfather, we searched out a
groom like Rājā Bali.
A crown installed upon the head of the groom,
He comes to the door like Rājā Bali.

The following song simply recognizes the long-awaited moment, the arrival of the groom. Song 16 is the first of many that insult the groom and his party. *Bhagara* is a plant only vaguely known by informants. "Thieves" is ambiguous: it may be merely an insult, or it may be another of the several references to conquest and bride seizure which occur in the wedding. Dudhaura is the groom's village.

15.

Lo le lo le he comes to the home of the bride's father.
The handsome groom comes to the home of the bride's
father.

16.

Hey groom, grow a proper mustache.
Apply the color of the bhagara.
Oh people of Mardapur, shine the lights, the thieves of
Dudhaura come.
Thieves of mothers, thieves of sisters, the thieves of
Dudhaura come.

Song 17 continues the attack on the bārāt, insulting the groom's family by calling them deceitful and miserly. The presence of elephants or horses and a brightly-outfitted band are signs of the economic status of the groom's family and thereby the bride's family. Their absence is an affront to the bride's family and robs it of prestige.

17.

You shouted that you would bring elephants; you didn't
bring elephants!
Fuck your sister; you didn't bring elephants!
You come to steal the bride!
You shouted that you would bring a band; you didn't
bring a band!

Song 18 seems to be another reference to conquest and fighting between the two families.

18.

When the bārāt forms a crowd at the door;
Hit! Hit the target!

After the bride's mother and sisters protect the groom by performing a parachan, the dvar pūjā begins. On a small area which has been ritually purified by sweeping with cow dung and water, a design (*cauk*) has been drawn with flour. This sanctifies the ground, converting it into a sacred place for the duration of the ceremony. Here the purohit leads the bride's father and groom through a pūjā. The men of the bārāt are then led to the area in which lines of cots have been placed for lounging and sleeping, where they are served the best refreshments the bride's family can manage and are entertained by a musical group. Later in the evening the hosts provide a full-scale dinner, and at about midnight, the vivāh finally begins.

Vivāh: *The Culminating Rite*

Before the vivāh, the barber's wife, who is the bride's chief attendant, washes the bride using some of the water from the groom's bath (brought by the bārāt). This "symbolizes the first intimate contact between the couple."[16] The bride's *māmā* (classificatory mother's brother) presents gifts to the bride's mother and her parjuniās and the women provide levity with a few gālīs aimed at him.

The women of the bride's family and neighborhood always sing in the vivāh. Their songs, like all music in ritual contexts, are deemed maṅgal (auspicious). Its importance as a ritual ingredient is clear; I observed no weddings lacking it and a wedding without it was inconceivable to villagers. If the bridal purohit lives nearby, women from his family may also attend and sing. The presence of the Brahman women is considered auspicious, and the bride's family rewards them with token payments called *dakṣinā* (the same term given to the payments made to a Brahman priest). The groom's father must also make a token payment to the women of the bride's party who sing. The groups do not sing together, and sometimes even sing different songs simultaneously.

After attending members of the bārāt are seated in the maṇḍap with the bride's close kinsmen and the chorus(es), a purohit performs the pūjā of the presiding deities. Then, her drooping form supported by the barber's wife, the bride makes her way slowly into the maṇḍap. Throughout her presence there she is hunched over with her sari completely covering her head and face, and seems to verge on collapse. Her limp and passive bearing symbolizes her modesty and abject humility, the latter also being expressed in some of the songs below. While the groom's side presents the bridal ornaments and clothing to the bridal purohit, the women sing:

19.

The ornaments you're flashing in my wedding canopy are borrowed.
Elder brother of the groom, you fuck your sister.

As well as obscenely insulting the groom's elder brother, this song in effect accuses the groom's party of having taken the ornaments from their own female kin (to be confiscated from the bride when she comes to live with her husband, and returned to their owners). The suspicion and obscene hostility of the gālī contrast profoundly with the sober awe of the next song, whose bare description of the groom's entrance indicate that it is a momentous occasion for the women.

20.

The groom took the box of ornaments and came into the wedding canopy.
He came, the groom came, the groom took the box of vermilion and came into the wedding canopy.

He came, the groom came, the groom took the gold and
silver and came into the wedding canopy.
He came, the groom came, the groom came into the
wedding canopy with great pomp and show.

After the ornaments are consecrated by the purohit, everyone scrutinizes them and the purohit enumerates each item aloud. Attention again shifts to the groom's older brother. The women sing:

21.

The groom's elder brother has a nose like a marijuana
pipe.
He stares at my daughter under the wedding canopy.
The groom's elder brother has long, long legs.
These legs stride into my wedding canopy.
The teeth of the groom's elder brother could split big
chunks of wood.

The groom's elder brother then worships the bride with many ritual offerings. Informants always said that this is the only time he touches the bride. (Their relationship is normatively one of avoidance.) The women then serenade the groom, who sits nearby with his father.

22.

Mother asks Supher, the groom: "Why are you smeared
looking?"
"Your mother slept under a palm tree; you are that very
color."
"Your mother slept with a dog; you are black like that."
Mother asks Supher, the groom: "Why do you bark like
that?'
"Your mother slept with a wolf; you bark just like that."

But the insults are again contradicted with an expression of concern. This sagun also depicts the finishing touches put on the groom's finery before his departure, including adjustment of his splendidly ornamented crown. (See Photo 5.) It suggests the fears and worries that abound on this important occasion, and the response to such fears—worship of a deity who can provide protection.

23.

In the upper room the groom adjusts the crown.
There the groom's mother supplicates Suraj [the sun, who is a deity]:
"Don't let anyone put the evil eye on my groom today."
In the upper room the groom adjusts the golden ornaments.
There the groom's father's sister supplicates Suraj:
"Don't let anyone put the evil eye on my groom today."
In the upper room the groom adjusts his pajama.
There the groom's sister supplicates Suraj:
"Don't let anyone put the evil eye on my groom today."
In the upper room the groom adjusts his *dhotī*.
There the groom's father's brother's wife supplicates Suraj:
"Don't let anyone put the evil eye on my groom today."

(The dhotī is a man's skirt-like garment, generally of white cotton, the front part being passed between the thighs and tucked in behind.) The reverential mood is quickly shattered with another obscene accusation of deceit.

24.

Look at the crown! Don't forget, mister, that the crown is borrowed.
The groom is of a whore; the bride is of a faithful woman.
Look at the bracelet! Don't forget, mister, that the bracelet is borrowed.

After the groom declares to the gods his intentions of marrying, the bride's father seats him and worships him with ritual offerings. Informants pointed out that this treatment, worthy of a *rājā* (king), symbolizes the ascendency of the groom's family to the bride's in all relations. The groom dons the new yellow dhotī given to him by the bride's father and the women sing:

25.

Put on the lower and upper garments sewn by your Muslim father.
Put on the dhotī spun by a concubine, son of a whore.
Put on the dhotī spun by a concubine, son of a Muslim.

Here a sung expression contradicts a simultaneous ritual expression in another medium. The contradicting expressions of ritualized groom-worship and sung groom-abuse clearly reflect the ambiguity and ambivalence of affinal relationship—as do the contrasting messages of the women's raucous insult songs with the solemn songs of ritual description.

The purohits start the sacrificial fire and release the ancestral spirits from the captivity of the clay dishes, while the bride re-enters and with her groom again worships the gods. With the climactic moment of the bride's transfer approaching, the women empathize with her in song. The first song depicts the bride's feelings at being given away by her father.

26.

Rām has brought them together.
The barber found the groom, the Brahman reckoned the day.
Burn the barber's beard! Burn the Brahman's books!
"Oh, Father has taken great advantage of me, Mother."
"Oh, how can I curse him enough, Mother?"

This second song empathizing with the bride uses the metaphor of celestial eclipse to symbolize the taking of the bride by the groom's family. In Hindu mythology (e.g., the *Viṣṇu Purāṇa*), eclipse is presented as the seizure and swallowing of the sun or moon by the demon-god Rahu.[17] Thus the song likens the taking of the bride to her being seized and devoured by the groom's family—which is no doubt how it seems to some brides.

27.

What kind of eclipse occurs from evening to morning?
What kind of eclipse occurs when half the night is passed?
What kind of eclipse occurs under the wedding canopy?
When will the sun come?
What kind of eclipse occurs at four in the morning?
Oh, the eclipse of the sun occurs from evening to morning.
The eclipse of the daughter occurs under the wedding canopy when half the night is passed.
In the morning the sun will come.

The song ends on a positive note, suggesting the daughter's eventual re-emergence and recovery. A woman's position in her husband's family does improve with time. Giving birth to a son elevates her status dramatically, and by the time most women are middle-aged they are in positions of considerable power and respect in the homes which have become theirs.

The next stage is called *kanyadān* (the gift of the virgin daughter). After the father announces to the gods that he is giving his daughter, the purohit places the bride's hands together palms up on the similarly held hands of her father, and the groom's hands likewise upon hers. Then the purohit places various ritual items in the groom's hands, and the bride's brother pours water over the layers of hands and ritual objects.

The first lines of the song sung during these symbolic acts refer to the acts themselves. Pouring water over their combined hands purifies their participation in the formation of this new union. The bulk of the song again suggests family conquest and bridal seizure. Fighting with the groom for her possession is in keeping with the close relationship the North Indian man has with his sister, and the protection he is expected to provide. The final lines of the song remind the bride's brother of a central fact of the patrilineal descent groups: its daughters and sisters are but temporary members in the local group—in most cases they will marry and live with their husband's families.

28.

Oh brother Dasarath Rām, don't stop the flow of water.
If the flow is broken your sister will become angry.
Brother Dasarath Rām, don the bow and arrow.
Oh brother, your sister's husband will surely come, he
  will fight with you on the battlefield.
My brother fought all day but he lost in the evening.
Oh he loses Tīlā Devī, his sister; Supher the groom has
  won.
Ho, brother Dasarath Rām, what have you forgotten?
Brother, you have not lost cows or oxen, you have lost
  your sister.
Oh it is good to forget about sister Tīlā Devī.
Cows and oxen are our wealth, brother; sisters that of
  another.[18]

After the purohits declare to the gods and spirits of the ancestors that the bride's family is donating the bride, the bride's father is made to say by the purohit that he is giving the groom his daughter for him to protect, support, and master. He places his daughter's hands palms down in those of the groom to signify that she is given.

The rite called *kriśnarpan* (presentation of gifts) follows. The bride's father gives dakṣinā to the pandits, the vow of *godān* (the gift of cows to a Brahman), and token payments to the purohits and clients of the family (parjuniās). The bride stands by the groom and her father blesses them: "May you live as long as there is water in the Ganges and Jamunā rivers." With his arms crossed, he tosses rice on them. The groom gives the purohits token payments and his own purohit the godān vow. As the purohits perform yet another fire sacrifice the women are singing the following gālīs, which show that even the Brahman purohit, whose divinity demands that (ideally) in everyday life he be treated "as a god on earth," is the object of ritual insult. The first song accuses the groom's purohit and party of incest with their sisters. The second song again shows sympathy for the bride, while insulting the purohit. (The shopkeeper's balance always hangs unevenly; the spindly bamboo cane tends to lean and catch the clothes of passers-by.)

29.

The bārāt's pandit, pretending to need water, calls for his sister.
"Slam the door! I will die of shame before my father." [she says]
"My brother is honorable." [says the narrator of the song]
All the members of the bārāt call for their sisters!

30.

The Brahman's mother is like the midden covered with weeds.
Listen, Brahman, quickly perform my daughter's fire sacrifice.
The smoke has spread to the young and tender girl.
The Brahman is a half-mind, like a clod from the tank.
Listen, Brahman, quickly perform my daughter's fire sacrifice.
The Brahman's scrotum is like the shopkeeper's balance.
The Brahman's sister is like the bamboo cane.

In the following stage the groom stands behind the bride, his arms around her and a basket in his hands. Her brother pours the parched rice (lāvā) from both the bride's and the groom's sides into the basket. The song the women sing expresses in a rather surprising metaphor the new social union which has been established, not only of bride and groom, but of all members of their families.

31.

Mix your lāvā and our lāvā together.
Have our father and your mother sleep together.
Have our father's brother and your father's brother's wife
sleep together.[19]

The groom then pours the lāvā onto the maṇḍap floor, a purohit divides it into seven small piles, and the groom walks on them. One purohit said that this symbolizes the seven circumambulations of the marriage pole and sacrificial fire by the bride and groom. The presiding purohit then proclaims the rules of marriage incumbent upon husband and wife. The bride and groom circumambulate the fire and ritual items three times and sit, the bride to the left of the groom.

Sindur dān (the gift of vermilion) is the title of the apical stage of the vivāh. People commonly say that this is the point at which the bride becomes the groom's. The groom applies the consecrated vermilion (a red powder) in the parting of the bride's hair. She will wear vermilion there as long as her husband is living. The women are singing songs such as these, which depict the stereotypical emotions of the bride. The first one expresses her embarrassment and humility under the wedding canopy, where she is the focus of public attention.

32.

I am embarrassed before my grandfather, my long-haired
grandfather.
I am embarrassed before my father's brother, my long-
haired father's brother.
I am embarrassed before my brother, my long-haired
brother.

This second sindur song suggests that the bride feels betrayed at her abandonment by the males of her family.

33.

Oh, I call Grandfather himself; he does not speak.
Oh, Grandfather forces the groom to apply vermilion.

Oh, Father's brother forces the groom to apply vermilion.
Oh, my brother forces the groom to apply vermilion.

The bride's sisters come forward and touch up the vermilion; the groom's father gives them saris and money. Then the groom gets up and sits down on the left of the bride, which also symbolizes that she is his.

After finalizing rites conducted by the purohits, who again receive cash payments, everyone leaves the wedding canopy but the bride and her friends. They perform cumāvan, singing among others the following song, whose final simile was a common one in classical Sanskrit poetry.[20]

34.

With rice and green grass, let us go to the cumāvan of
Chotū Rām's daughter.
Touch her head, give the blessing.
Live, bride and groom, 100,000 years.
Live as long as the earth and sky.
Enjoy as the night enjoys the moon.

The women of the bride's family (but not the bride) proceed to the kohabar, where there are informal rites involving the groom. The women sing gālīs such as the following: The first one expresses what may be a common feeling—that the other family is inferior to one's own. The second castigates the mean mother-in-law and shows how she can make her daughter-in-law's life miserable. The stereotypical mother-in-law is jealous of her son's wife and resents their intimacy.

35.

This new kohabar of gold and brass.
With great commotion goes the groom, born of a
plowman.
Slowly, slowly goes my daughter, born of an emperor.

36.

Whose mother comes in to awaken, Tīlā Devī?
"Get up, son, it's dawn."Give that kind of a mother into
the hands of the Turks, into the hands
of the Moghuls, into the hands of the Pathans.

Who says, when only half the night has passed, that it's
morning.

I did not have the opportunity to attend the activities at the home of a groom during the evening of the vivāh, but according to Planalp:

> While the marriage rites are taking place at the bride's house, the women of the groom's family, and their friends, sing and dance throughout the evening. This occasion is referred to as *nakata*. At the time when they estimate the ancestral spirits are being invoked in the bride's village, they too release the *pitrīs* (ancestral spirits) confined in the clay cup on the miniature stove near the marriage pole. It is believed that the ancestral spirits are instantly transported to the place of the wedding.[21]

Khicarī

Khicarī is the name given to *dāl* (lentil soup) mixed with rice. It is customarily eaten by the bride and groom on the second day of the wedding. One more-educated informant told me that khicarī symbolizes the new couple, the rice being conceived as masculine and the dāl feminine.

Khicarī is held in the forenoon or afternoon of the second day. All of the dowry items are displayed on a table in the home of the bride. (These often include wristwatches, stainless steel dishes, transistor radios, etc.) The groom is expected to object to the quality of the items given or to demand more, and may refuse to eat until he extracts a commitment for something else. After the haggling he and the younger boys from his party are seated for the eating of khicarī. As they dine, the bride's female kin sing gālīs from behind a curtain or from some semi-concealed location. For this "service" they must be compensated with a small payment from the groom's father.

The gālīs presented below were recorded in a different ritual context but are the same as would be sung at khicarī and tilak rites. The first one is typical in addressing obscene insults at both the targeted men (here including the author) and their female kin.

37.

Brother, Patna is a pleasant city, brother, Patna is a
pleasant city.
Corrupted in childhood, Henarī Rām and Rām Sāgar
Miśra are the sons of whores.
Their sister was corrupted by Rām Candra.
They eat from their sister's earnings; tears come into her
eyes.

Henarī and Rām Sāgar eat from the earnings of their
sisters.
They submit themselves to sodomy, brother, Patna is a
pleasant city.

Informants could not explain the refrain "Patna is a pleasant city"; perhaps the song is an adaptation of another with that refrain. The next one is one of that type in which men of the bride's family are depicted taking sexual advantage of the women of the visitor's family. The foreign words are local terms for the different parts of the sari.

38.

At the low bathing place of the high pond there is a
pleasant bungalow.
There Henarī's sister takes a bath.
Daya Śaṅkar's sister takes a bath.
Our Kesau Rām went there to ogle.
Our Laukāī Rām went there to ogle.
Open the *gughat*, they will look at her cheeks.
Her cheeks are like a red wave.
Open the *colī*, look at the goods.
The goods are like limes and pomegranates.
Open the *pūpatī*, they will look at the pubic hair.
Open the petticoat, they will look at the moon.
It is like lightning.

The gughat is the part of the sari a woman pulls over her face. The colī is the brief blouse worn beneath the sari. The pūpatī is the lower part of the sari. Moon symbolizes vagina.[22] Perhaps the last line means "it gives great light [like a large moon]."

The next song insults both the visiting males and their female kin; however, this one charges the men with failure to control the young women of their families, rather than with immoral sexual conduct. Apparently Indra Rām is the man with whom their sister or daughter is consorting. On the holy Ganges river, Kāśī Viśāsar Ganj is a place where one would bathe to be absolved of the sin of irresponsibliity for one's female kin. Feasting Brahmans is another means of absolution. "Mister Henarī" refers to the author, who was visiting when this song was sung.

39.

The rain starts, the clouds are dense and black, every
lane is inundated.

She starts to come out, wearing golden clogs; she slips in the middle of the courtyard.
I ask you, Mister Henarī, is your sister running away?
I ask you, Mister Rām Candra, is your sister being lured away?
Will judgement be given nowhere but at the door of Indra Rām?
You must feed five or ten Brahmans, Henarī.
You must feed five or ten Brahmans, Candra.
The sin will be expiated.
You must bathe at Kāśī Viśāsar Ganj, Henarī.
Myself, I keep my father's daughter's and grandfather's granddaughters under my control.
Who will pass judgement?

This final gālī combines the different types of insults and ends by demanding payment for the "service" of gālī-singing from those who have been enjoying it.

40.

Flee, son of a whore, flee on to Delhi!
Henarī's sister copulates in a field on the plains of Delhi.
Hindu, Muslim, that cumin seed, that coriander seed, one climbs on before, one behind.
There is saliva in your father's mouth, in your father's mouth there is water.
Give the price of my gālī, Henarī Rām, give, relatives!
My Indra fucks your sisters. Give, relatives!

In most cases the *vidāī* (formal farewell) follows khicarī on the second day of the wedding. After the purohits receive their payments of cash and clothing, the fathers of the newlyweds ritually embrace and shake hands, and the groom's party departs.

Arrangements for the bride's departure vary according to the circumstances. In some cases she accompanies the groom to his home after the vidāī to stay a few days before returning to her father's home. In many cases she remains in her home until the gaunā.

Other ethnographers have reported songs sung on the occasion of the bride's departure, songs indicating the distress and the fright which she feels at the imminent changes in her life.[23] I did not observe the singing of such songs but their primary theme is one of the prominent themes of wedding (vivāh) songs.

Prominent Themes of Wedding Songs

Three themes turned up most frequently in the wedding songs: the plight of the bride, conquest, and insult. The songs' treatment of these themes contributes to the effectiveness of the wedding as a right of passage. It also provides an interesting ethnohistorical perspective.

The Plight of the Bride

A wedding is a rite of passage, a ritual or series of rites that makes and marks a change of role for one or more individuals. Many roles change with a wedding: two single people become spouses and two families become in-laws. But in the North Indian wedding, one person undergoes changes more radical than any of the others—the bride. She leaves her family to assume a role of low status in an alien family, and the role of wife to a stranger.

Throughout the vivāh, the bride assumes a flexed, stooped posture, which symbolizes her feelings about the proceedings and her future. When she moves to and from the wedding canopy, she is so limp she must be supported by an attendant. Her sari is pulled down to completely hide her face. When I asked people why the bride assumed this bearing, they said *śarm kī vajah se* (because of embarrassment). Song 32, sung as the bride is being given away by her father, enunciates these feelings: "I am embarrassed before my grandfather, my long-haired grandfather. / I am embarrassed before my father's brother, my long-haired father's brother. . . ."

The bride's bearing and the above song not only symbolize her embarrassment and humility under the maṇḍap, they also allude to the new roles which the bride is assuming, roles in some of which she is nearly a non-entity. The daughter who becomes a wife stereotypically exchanges independence and affection for strictly-delimited freedom, deference, and rivalry. The stereotypical response is expressed in songs 26 and 33, which indicate that the bride feels angry and betrayed at her disposal by the males of her family: " 'Oh, Father has taken great advantage of me, Mother.' / 'Oh, how can I curse him enough, Mother?' " and "Oh, Grandfather forces the groom to apply vermilion."

The eloquent simile of song 27 reveals the awfulness and helplessness women feel at the moment of their transfer to the groom's family: it is like an eclipse of the sun, the swallowing of the heavenly light by an evil monster. It implies that the bride's identity is swallowed up by her husband's family.

Song 28 vividly illuminates the structural principle responsible for the grief: the daughters of the lineage are only temporary members who will, after they marry, be more closely affiliated with their husband's lineages than with the lineage of their birth. "Cows and oxen are our wealth, brother; sisters that of another." This song also shows that the men of the family, too, undergo emotional strain at the loss of the bride to another family.

> You have not lost cows and oxen, you have lost your sister.
> Oh it is good to forget about sister Tīlā Devī.

A woman's relationship with her brothers tends to be affectionate. Except for occasional visits in the first years of marriage, these relations are severed by her marriage. This song recognizes the sadness of the brother at the loss of his sister, and then reminds him and the others present that, in accordance with the rules of the society, sisters belong not to the family into which they are born, but to that into which they marry. The open acknowledgment of the emotions of the bride by the singing of these songs mobilizes sympathy for her and thereby facilitates her adjustment.

Conquest

Song 28 also states that the brother must surrender his sister because of his loss on the battlefield. This may well refer to the time Rājput kings feuded over the marriage of their daughters.

> In the twelfth century . . . the country [Rājputāna, the area from which masses of people migrated into Bhojpurī-speaking area] was ruled by hundreds of small independent Rajput kings or lords, who fought among themselves constantly and over the most trifling matters. Whenever a beautiful daughter of one of these kings or chieftains became nubile, his rivals would often attack him in order to force him to marry his daughter to one of their number. If the girl's side was defeated, the marriage preparations were made. However, her supporters usually sought to surprise the victorious groom's side with an attack while they were busy with the marriage rites. Thus, there grew up a tradition of fighting under the mandap.[24]

A number of other elements in the wedding allude to conquest. One is the descent of the groom and his "forces" upon the bride's village and home. The band playing its brassy tunes; the formidable elephants or aristocratic horses (sometimes used in mock attacks on the bride's home); and the use of firearms are highly appreciated ostentation. But they also allude to the era when a rājā's army marched into the village to forcefully take a bride, and embody the martial ethos of that situation. The reference to wars between the feudal rājās is found in other of the women's songs: Song 16, in which the bārāt is depicted as thieves of mothers and daughters, and Song 18, containing the call to shoot at the bārāt as it crowds beneath the wedding canopy.[25]

The identification of the groom's party as the conquerors in these songs, and the singing of the songs before the groom and his party under the wedding canopy, emphasize the dominance of the groom's family in the wedding and its ascendance in the marriage alliance. The songs also express hostility between the two families, a theme fully developed in the gālīs.

The Meaning of Gālī

Informants defined gālī as an obscene insult, and twelve of the sixteen included here are obscene. The use of raw, rude sexual imagery is common in verbal abuse (or at least, it is familiar to Americans). What is distinctive is the strategy of the insult. In over half of these gālīs the insult is made by attributing sexually immoral behavior to the men's close female kin—usually sisters, but also mothers. (Songs 2, 3, 17, 22, 30, 37-40, and, indirectly, 19 and 24-26.) This is typical of verbal abuse in this region, where one of the most common spoken (actually shouted) epithets is *tohār bahan chondo* (fuck your sister). These insults show that a woman's virtue is the vessel of her family's honor, and that fathers and brothers are held responsible for the sexual conduct of daughters and sisters. Song 39 makes this explicit. "You (and the addressees are always male) must feed five or ten Brahmans . . . the sin (of having one's sister defiled) will be expiated."

In three of the songs the women are defiled by male relatives of the singers (Songs 3, 37, and 38). These express another principal meaning of five of the insults, assertion of the inferiority of the target's families to that of the singers. The assertion may be phrased in terms of dominance of the singers' family over that of the targets, subtly symbolized by the image "Our men screw your women" in songs 3, 37, and 38; it may refer to the relative social position of the families (Song 35, the groom born of a plowman and the bride an emperor); or it may refer to some other relative quality (Song 24, the groom of a whore, the bride of a faithful woman).

One other strategy, which refers to the immediate situation, is the accusation of deceit or untrustworthiness. Songs 19 and 24 accuse the groom's family of not buying the groom's crown and the jewelry for the bride, but of only borrowing them. Song 17 accuses them of reneging on their promise to bring elephants, a serious default. The prestige gained by the bride's family from an impressive bārāt (with brightly uniformed band and elephants or horses etc.) is one of the expected benefits of the marriage—it is as important as many of the tangible items involved.

In discussing the relationship between gālī and the social contexts in which it is sung, it must be remembered that the targets of gālī have two things in common: each is outside the patrilineage of the women singing, and each is owed something by the joint family of the bride. It is not only the groom's family that is abused, as one would expect given its acquisition of bride, dowry, and superordinate status at the expense of the bride's family. Rather, males in both families receive the abuse sung by their female affines. In the wedding rites, the attending purohits also receive some choice epithets.

A consideration of the nature of the affinal and purohit-jajmān relationships, particularly with respect to the wedding, helps to understand the custom. In each of the meetings of members of the two families, particularized financial transactions or commitments are negotiated. For example, the tilak involves payment of the dowry, gifts of cash to the groom and his brothers, payment of the bride's father's parjuniās by the groom's father, settling the quality of entertainment which will be hired, and the jewelry which the bride will receive from the groom's family. Although there are ranges of expectations governing each amount, there are no "fixed prices," and bitterness is not an uncommon result. Disappointments also arise for both parties when hospitality, accommodations, and "pomp and show" do not meet with expectations. Conflict and competition are inherent in the relationship, with both parties attempting to maximize gain and prestige, and minimize expenditure.

The conflict is intensified by the concept of *ādar* (honor) which is in turn compounded by the public knowledge of all wedding arrangements and events—everyone in the village has expectations regarding the scale and quality of hospitality, entertainment, etc. Any misunderstanding, deception, or scrimping resulting in the disappointment of the other family is liable to be interpreted by it as well as the rest of the village as an intentional affront to the family.

Conflict is inherent not only in the wedding, but in the enduring affinal relationship as well. Jacobson has observed that:

> Both groups of kinsmen feel they have rights in the woman, rights to her company and to her labor. . . . In-laws who refuse to allow a woman appropriate visits to her natal home arouse much antagonism, as do parents who keep a daughter from her husband's family too long. . . .[26]

Jacobson goes on to point out that potential tension between affines is recognized and dealt with ritually as well as objectively, through distance mechanisms of avoidance, respect, and joking behavior.

There is also a basic conflict between the bridal purohit, who presides in the vivāh, and his jajmān, the bride's father. The purohit's role is such that he can threaten to withhold consecration of the rites, which would jeopardize the marriage by offending the gods, if he is not remunerated as he sees fit. In the course of the wedding there are many points at which he can demand payment. Some of these situations are legitimized by tradition, but some are not clear-cut. The term *lālcī* (greedy) is often heard at these times. His demands are tempered, however, by the necessity of maintaining his long-term relationship with his jajmān, and by fear of general censure. (The groom's purohit was insulted in the vivāh [Song 30] as a member of the groom's party rather than as a purohit.)

Villagers themselves explained gālī by saying that it is a kind of "joke" (one of those I asked actually used the English word) which relaxes the guests and promotes harmony. Given the conflict-endowed nature of the affinal and purohit-jajmān relationships, this is a persuasive explanation, and one supported by the cross-cultural research of anthropologists.

A. R. Radcliffe-Browne has pointed out that joking relationships tend to arise in relations in which there are strong conjunctive and disjunctive forces, i.e., in relationships in which it is in the interests of both parties to maintain the relationship in spite of the many conflicts inherent in it. He argues that:

> Any serious hostility is prevented by the playful antagonism of teasing, and this in its regular repetition is a constant expression or reminder of that social disjunction which is one of the essential components of the relation, while the social conjunction is maintained by the friendliness that takes no offense at insult.[27]

The desirability of establishing and maintaining affinal relations, i.e., the conjunctive forces in the relationship, include the necessity of marrying offspring, the prestige gained by the wedding, and alliance with a family of comparable or greater prestige, as well as economic strengthening. The conflicts inherent in the affinal relationship and the conjunctive and disjunctive components of the purohit-jajmān relationship have been brought out above. The theory also accounts for the tolerant reactions of those being insulted, who, as mentioned above, rarely express any hostility.

The obscene nature of the songs is also an important factor. Evans-Pritchard noted that the withdrawal by society of its normal prohibitions on the use of obscenity gives special emphasis to the social value of the activity. In such situations obscenity also provides a socially acceptable means of catharsis.[28]

The situations in which gālī is sung suggest that gālī is primarily a response to inherent difficulties between the bride's family, affines and purohits. But since gālī-singing in effect opposes (active) female singers to (passive) male listeners, there is a feeling that the situation is basically one of women taunting men. Any discomfiture experienced is certainly confined to the males present, and the mirthful vehemence with which some of the older women sing suggests that gālī constitutes an acceptable means of asserting and expressing themselves despite the generally subordinate role women play in any public event.

Summary

Song injects into the wedding rites a wide range of meanings that are not symbolized by the other ritual acts it accompanies. Saguns transmit religious lore and in particular the Vaiṣṇava lore of Rām and Krishna, whose predominance in the folk song of this region will become clear in subsequent chapters. We also see in this category a song of the new ideology, nationalism, which finds expression in other genres of folk songs explored in later chapters. A few of the saguns (e.g., 5 and 13) clearly have didactic functions, while others (e.g., 11 and 12) serve as ritual mnemonics. In the tilak, dvar pūjā, vivāh and khicarī rites the gālī songs express the bridal family's antagonism toward outsiders (primarily affines) to whom they are obligated, at the same time easing the tension of the immediate situation with their bawdy humor. In the vivāh itself, it is only the songs that convey the blessings of their singers, express sympathy for the bride, acknowledge her feelings of humility and anger, and her brother's feelings of loss. In so doing they assist in effecting the role changes at which the wedding is aimed.

Wedding songs are only one of many divisions of women's songs. A second type is that sung in connection with another social event of great importance to the family, the birth of a son.

Notes

1 Clarence Maloney, in *Peoples of South Asia* (New York: Holt, Rinehart and Winston, 1974) includes the following major north Indian language regions in his main linguistic map of India: Panjabi, Sindhi, Gujarati, Marathi, Hindi, Uriya, and Bangali. In their revision of G. A. Grierson's seminal *Language Survey of India*, Drs. S. K. Catterji and S. M. Katre classify north Indian languages into seven somewhat differently constituted regions. See their book, *India: Languages* (New Delhi: Publications Division, Ministry of Information and Broadcasting, 1970).

2 Irawati Karve, *Kinship Organization in India* (New York: Asia Publishing House, 1965), p. 131.

3 Ibid, and Oscar Lewis, *Village Life in Northern India* (New York: Random House, 1958). For marriage in eastern North India see Jack M. Planalp, "Religious Life and Values in a North Indian Village," Ph.D. diss., Cornell University. (Ann Arbor: University Microfilms, 1956).

4 Giri Raj Gupta, *Marriage, Religion and Society: Patterns of Change in an Indian Village* (New York: John Wiley & Sons, 1974), p. 65.

5 Karve, Kinship Organization, p. 137.

6 The culminating rite of the wedding (*vivāh*) I recorded in the home of a fairly well-to-do Ahir caste family in Indrapur. I transcribed the tape and pieced together the ritual events and song texts with the help of two Brahman school teachers, one of whom was also a purohit and thus a specialist in weddings and other ritual matters. I recorded and observed the other songs and rites in numerous weddings held by Nau, Lohār, Ahir, Ṭhakūr, and Brahman families in and around Indrapur. I have included the most complete, vivid, and representative songs and excluded most of the obviously fragmentary and incoherent ones.

7 For variants see Hari S. Upadhyaya, "The Joint Family Structure and Familial Relationship Patterns in the Bhojpurī Folksongs," Ph.D. diss., Indiana University. (Ann Arbor: University Microfilms, 1967), p. 339.

8 For variants see D. N. Majumdar, *Caste & Communication in an Indian Village* (New Delhi: Asia Publishing House, 1958), pp. 310-12; and Upadhyaya, "The Joint Family Structure," p. 320.

9 U. Arya, *Ritual Songs and Folk Songs of the Hindus of Surinam* (Leiden: E. J. Brill, 1968), p. 80.

10 For a song based on a similar theme, see Ruth S. Freed and Stanley A. Freed, *Rites of Passage in Shanti Nagar* (New York: The American Museum of Natural History, 1980), p. 472.

11 For three variants, see Laxmi G. Tewari, "Folk Music of India: Uttar Pradesh," Ph.D. diss., Wesleyan University. (Ann Arbor: University Microfilms, 1974), pp. 189-91.

12 Victor Turner, *The Ritual Process: Structure and Anti-Structure* (Chicago: Aldine Press, 1969), p. 94.

13 For variant see Planalp, *Religious Life*, p. 479.

14 Planalp, *Religious Life*, p. 488.

15 For another observation of this mock charge see Planalp, *Religious Life*, p. 500.

16 Ibid., p. 504.

17 John Dowson, *A Classical Dictionary of Hindu Mythology and Religion, Geography, History and Literature* (London: Routledge & Kegan Paul Ltd., 1972), pp. 114 and 252-53.

18 For another version, see Chandramani Singh and Ronald Amend, *Marriage Songs in Bhojpurī Region* (Jaipur: Champa Lal Ranka & Co., 1979), p. 66.

19 For a variant see Arya, *Ritual Songs*, p. 78.

20 Daniel Ingalls, *Sanskrit Poetry* (Cambridge: Harvard University Press, 1968), pp. 130, 142, and 148.

21 Planalp, *Religious Life*, p. 513.

22 Cf. Deben Battacharya, *Love Songs of Vidyapathi* (London: George Allen & Unwin, 1963), p. 106.

23 Planalp, *Religious Life*, p. 531 and Lewis, *Village Life*, p. 183.

24 Planalp, *Religious Life*, p. 522.

25 For another song indicating bridal conquest, see Chandramani Singh and Ronald Amend, *Marriage Songs*, pp. 61-62.

26 Doranne Jacobson, "Songs of Social Distance," *Journal of South Asian Literature* 9 (1975): 45-60.

27 A. R. Radcliffe-Brown, *Structure and Function in Primitive Society* (New York: The Free Press, 1965), pp. 90-95.

28 Edward E. Evans-Pritchard, *The Position of Women in Primitive Society* (London: Faber & Faber, 1965), p. 101.

III

Women's Songs of Sons

Introduction

When a woman gives birth to a son the other women in her joint family gather to sing auspicious songs called *sohar*s. Songs the women sing in worshipping the mother goddess, a goddess they believe can provide sons if she is pleased or smallpox if she is not, also indicate the extra importance of sons.

Morris Opler has interpreted such ritually expressed concern with males as part of a culture theme he calls "the ascendancy of the male principle."[1] The eighteen sohars and mother goddess songs below and the social occasions in which such songs are sung clearly indicate the preference for sons and concern for male longevity which Professor Opler has subsumed under the ascendant male theme. In discussing the preference for sons I argue that it is essentially practical, deriving from economic and social factors.

The sohars and mother goddess songs presented below also demonstrate that songs are much more important in the transmission of religious ideology than previous ethnography has shown. They objectify a part of women's religious ideology not elsewhere accessible and show that women understand their deities, whether high (Sanskritic) or low (non-Sanskritic) in terms of one paradigm, and not two as has been asserted elsewhere.

The Contexts of Sohar

The women of the joint family, and later, women in the neighborhood, sing sohars upon the birth of a son. Like other music in special situations, the singing of sohars is commonly deemed mańgal—it provides a favorable omen. It is thus a kind of mild magic, a manipulation of unseen forces to insure a good life. Some women also think of sohar as an expression of gratitude to supernatural forces. The singing of sohars undoubtedly provides a way for the women to express their gladness, and perhaps unintentionally serves to signal the neighborhood of the blessed event.

Soon after the birth of a child, be it boy or girl, the family calls a midwife of the untouchable Camār caste, who will stay with the mother for at least six days after birth. She cuts and ties the umbilical cord and performs other tasks too polluting to be undertaken by anyone of a higher caste. (All bodily emanations are considered polluting, and childbirth is especially so, rendering not only the mother, but members of the extended family and the house itself polluted.)

Sometime within the first day after birth the women of the neighborhood come to rub the mother and child with mustard seed oil, which is considered a kind of personal blessing, like cumāvan. If the newborn is a male they join with the women of the extended family to sing sohar then and for the next five successive nights (eleven nights if the family is particularly traditional). The singing of sohars continues the celebration of this most appreciated event.

Two types of professional musicians also perform the sohar in this region. One type is the notorious *hinjaṛās*, who wear women's clothing and are said to be hermaphroditic (or otherwise genitally abnormal), and who support themselves primarily through musical performances. The other well-known type is called *pauriyā*. Those pauriyās I recorded in Vārāṇasī were Muslims. In this area, I was told, the hinjaṛās perform for those families in the city proper in which a son has been born, while the pauriyās perform at such homes in outlying areas. Both types of groups come to the homes of newborn sons without being called, and are paid for their services in part because the groups will broadcast the family's stinginess in song to all neighbors and passers-by if they are not compensated as they see fit.

Although villagers define the sohar as a song sung at the birth of a son, it is also sung in other rites. In those contexts in which it does not refer directly to the birth of a son, I would argue that the reference is implicit. Thus, rites are made auspicious by singing songs associated with an event of maximum auspiciousness—the birth of a son.[2] Like the birth of a son, each rite in which sohar is sung marks the beginning of a new period in the lives of family members:

1. In the *muṇḍan sanskār* (the tonsure ceremony of a boy), the family's barber shaves the infant's head, and the women offer the hair to the mother goddess Śītalā. This is a culturally recognized rite of passage, in which the child moves from polluted to unpolluted condition, and, generally, into the toddler stage of life.

2. *Mul śāntī.* (Mul is the name of the 19th lunar mansion, considered the most inauspicious; śāntī means peace.) This rite is performed to prevent misfortune from coming to the parents of a child born during an inauspicious lunar mansion. It marks the end of the inauspicious period and the beginning of an auspicious period.

3. The *kathā*, the recitation of a moral parable and performance of a fire sacrifice (*havan*) by a Brahman priest, is an occasional rite of transition. It is usually performed when a member of the family is beginning or has completed some endeavor, a bachelor's degree, for example. It thus recognizes a change in the family's circumstances.

In these three rituals sohars are included to maximize the benefits of the ceremonies by suggesting the birth of a son. Women also sing sohars in the holiday *Janamāśthamī* which commemorates the birth of the deity Krishna. Here the reference to the birth of a son is explicit.

There are two recognized types of sohar texts: those regarding matters of devotion and those concerning childbirth. The devotional sohars articulate certain beliefs and practices in the highly complex village religion, an overview of which is necessary to make sense of the songs.

Village Hinduism

The beliefs and practices of village Hinduism can be roughly divided into complexes called Sanskritic and non-Sanskritic. These terms are somewhat misleading, as is the dichotomy in religious beliefs and practices which they imply. Nevertheless, they serve to introduce some order into a complex subject.[3]

The Sanskritic complex consists of the beliefs and practices regarding deities who are the subject of Sanskrit (and a few other Indian language) texts. Although not all of the deities mentioned in Sanskrit texts are worshipped in India by any means, we can say that a majority of the deities whose worship has a pan-Indian distribution are the subjects of Sanskrit texts.

The non-Sanskritic complex is found more in rural areas but in cities as well. Some non-Sanskritic beliefs and practices are common only to a community (some only to a family, lineage, or caste); others have a regional distribution, and a few, like the worship of a mother goddess who is not the subject of a Sanskrit text, are found across the sub-continent. Most are orally transmitted; some are transmitted by means of cheap books or booklets.

Sanskritic deities have the sanction of the state-supported village schools, in which the children read stories about them in their Hindi primers. In rural eastern Uttar Pradesh the most important deities of this group are: Rām (spelled Rāma in formal contexts) and his auxilliary, Hanumān, a god in the form of a monkey; Śiva and Gaṇeśa, his elephant-headed son; Krishna; and several of the mother goddesses, especially Kālī and Durgā.

Non-Sanskritic deities are by definition those not elaborated in Sanskrit texts. Many of them have apparently been adopted from non-Aryan groups. The non-Sanskritic deities worshipped by residents of Indrapur include Mātā Māī and other aspects of the mother goddess; Ḍih Bābā, the auxilliary (*sahāiyak*) of Mātā Māī and guardian of the village; and Sāyad Bābā, a Muslim saint worshipped by both Muslims and Hindus.

While Brahman priests perform life-cycle rites and Sanskritic ceremonies, other kinds of priests perform non-Sanskritic rites. With few exceptions these are of the śudra and untouchable levels of caste. Most important are: the *pūjārī*, who maintains a shrine and performs in it a daily pūjā of the deity or deities represented; the *darśaniā*, who attains through devotions direct communication with a deity, but doesn't maintain a shrine; and the *ojhā*—a kind of shaman. The ojhā's performances usually involve possession by a mother goddess. He functions most often as a diviner and exorcist, and occasionally as a sorcerer. The rites performed by these practitioners share some elements with Brahmanic ritual, such as the consecration of the ritual area by means of a rice flour design (cauk) on ground which has been purified by plastering it with cow dung. Other elements, such as the use of cloves as seats for the deities involved, and the use of liquor as a consecrating fluid, are found only in shamanic rituals.

Sanskritic deities play a larger part in the devotions of members of the Brahman caste and generally in the twice-born castes than they do in the devotions of the lower castes.[4] However, there is an important exception to this generalization: in the higher castes women and a few men worship the non-Sanskritic mother goddesses.[5] (See Photo 7.) Relatively more women worship, in part because they believe that the mother goddess, if pleased, will bestow a son or sons to the devotee, or that she may afflict smallpox or cholera upon those families in which she is not worshipped.

Education, with its rational and Sanskritic biases, is also a factor in both sex and caste correlations with Sanskritic and non-Sanskritic complexes. Although the proportion of lower caste boys receiving at least a primary education (and thereby a Sanskritic bias) is much greater than in the past, in 1971 and 1972 few girls of any caste were formally educated.

A third fact is urban experience. Many men whose families remain in the village work in cities, where they are subject to Sanskritizing and Westernizing influences. Women rarely leave the village except to make religious pilgrimages and attend local fairs. Education and urban experience of males have the effect of discouraging their adherence to non-Sanskritic religion. Most of the educated men in Indrapur were disdainful of non-Sanskritic cults including that of the mother goddess.

The division of Sanskritic and non-Sanskritic religious complexes is thus apparent in texts, in deities, in functionaries, and in the religious tendencies of certain categories of people. But in a number of important ways the two complexes merge or overlap. For example, both Sanskritic and non-Sanskritic deities can be worshipped on a personal basis, i.e., without mediation.[6] Such personal devotions are performed at shrines in or near the village or in the devotional rooms of devotees' homes.

The manifest functions of the two complexes also tend to overlap. Professor David Mandlebaum stated that the Sanskritic complex "is used to ensure the long-term welfare of society, to explain and help maintain village institutions, to guarantee the proper transition of individuals from state to state within the institutions," and the non-Sanskritic complex ". . . is used for local exigencies, for personal benefit, for individual welfare."[7] The data presented here suggests that the division is not as clear-cut as this statement suggests. Anyone may privately worship a favorite Sanskritic deity from whom they seek personal aid in time of sickness or other trouble. Some Brahman priests do provide protective charms for individuals, and treat illness by magical means. And at least one of the non-Sanskritic calendrical rites, the mother goddess rite, has as a goal the long-term welfare of the society. Furthermore, sohars the women sing suggest that women do not distinguish the deities on the basis of Sanskritic and non-Sanskritic factors. This is clearly visible in the first song below.

The first four sohars refer generally to village Hinduism; the last seven to childbirth and the family. Songs such as the first one which pay respect to various deities are usually sung first in sohar sessions, among all castes. (This and the following three songs were recorded at rituals of a Brahman family in Indrapur; I have also recorded songs like the first one at the homes of Camār women near Vārāṇasī.) This song indicates that Sanskritic deities (Śiva, Kālī and Satya Nārāyaṇa, an aspect of Viṣṇu) and non-Sanskritic deities (Bhavanī Māī, a mother goddess) are not treated as belonging to different categories of deities.

41.

From where does Kālī Māī come, from where
  Bhavanī Māī?
From where does Śiv Śaṅkar come, from where Satya
  Nārāyan?
Kālī Māī comes from the east and Bhavanī Māī comes
  from the west.

Oh Satya Narāyan comes from the south and Śiv from the north.
Where do you seat Kālī Māī, where Bhavanī Māī?
Where do you seat Śiv Śaṅkar, where Satya Nārāyan?
We seat Kālī Māī and Bhavanī Māī in the grove.
We seat Śiv Śaṅkar in the *yonī*, Satya Nārāyan on the cauk.
What do you offer Kālī Māī, what Bhavanī Māī?
Now what do you offer Śiv Śaṅkar, what Satya Nārāyan?
We offer Kālī Māī *dhar*, Bhavanī Māī flowers.
We offer Śiv Śaṅkar rice, Satya Nārāyan *mevā*.
What does Kālī Māī give me, what Bhavanī Māī?
What does Śiv Śaṅkar give, what Satya Nārāyan?
Kālī Māī and Bhavanī Māī give offspring.
Śiv Śaṅkar gives wealth; Satya Nārāyan *mokṣa*.
The person who sings and spreads this song
Will go to heaven and eat *sādā*.

This song constitutes a paradigm of religious cognition with four dimensions:

1. Directional proveniences. (Their implicatons are unclear.)
2. Location for worship. (The *yonī* is the basin-shaped symbol of the vagina in which the phallic *liṅga*, the symbol of Śiva, is placed.)
3. Favored offerings. (*Dhar* is a mixture of cane sugar, flower petals, other "sweet" things and water. *Mevā* is a mixture of raisins, coconut and other dried fruit.)
4. Domains of human welfare. With respect to the last category, mother goddesses are attributed the power of awarding offspring; Satya Nārāyaṇa spiritual emancipation (salvation) and Śiva, wealth.

This song shows no clear-cut division between the functions of Sanskritic and non-Sanskritic deities.

In line 18 *sādā* is the fruit of the *kal* (or *kalpa*) tree that is thought to grow in heaven. The sense of the line is that the persons who sing the song will attain immortality. Lines 17 and 18 thus express a common belief underlying the singing of devotional songs—that singing and other devotions are a path to salvation.[8] Both this song and the next one may well act as devices for remembering ritual recipes.

The goal of the next song is quite tangible—a husband like the ideal Rām. The kinds of austerities depicted as means to that end are also used by women to insure the longevity of their husbands and other male relatives, and to obtain male offspring.*

*This song may be heard on the LP disc, *Chant the Names of God*. See Henry, 1981.

42.

Rām sits on the sandalwood platform as he bathes.
All her girlfriends ask Sītā, What austerities did you do
to get a groom such as Rām?
I bathed in the month of *Māgh* (January-February)
and did not warm myself by the fire.
Every day I arose and worshipped Śiv; I got the groom
Rām.
In *Jet* (April-May) I fasted on the eleventh and twelfth
days of the lunar fortnight.
I ate the prescribed foods every Sunday; I got the groom
Rām.
I feasted the Brahmans; I picked up the food they left.
I gave them the crust of the curds, girls, and thus got the
groom Rām.

Feasting brahmans (in the penultimate line) to gain boons and religious merit is commonly practiced. Food left on another's plate has been polluted by the possibility of its contact with saliva; to eat such food is a gesture of extreme deference, symbolically attributing divine status to the person. The crust of homemade yogurt (in the last line) is considered a delicacy.

The next song provides a ritual formula for obtaining not only an ideal husband, but ideal in-laws as well. As Rām and Sītā (Rām's wife in the Rāmāyaṇa) are the model couple, the other members of their families are upheld as the ideals for the corresponding roles in the marital alliance.

43.

Make and decorate the pedestal in the courtyard.
Sister, install Satya Nārāyan upon it and cover it with the
cloth of yellow silk.
Knowing that Satya Nārāyan is on it, I would cover it
with the cloth of yellow silk.
Sister, I would squat, touch and wash his feet, and drink
the water.
I would request a father-in-law like Dasarath and a
mother-in-law like Kausilyā.
Sister, a husband's older brother who reads books.
I would ask for only one husband's brother's wife, and a
man like Rām.

Sister, a husband's younger brother like Lakṣman,
a daughter like a clove, a son like a lotus.
I got a father-in-law like Rājā Dasarath, a mother-in-law like Kausilyā.
I got only one husband's brother's wife, a man like Rām,
a husband's younger brother like Lakṣman.
Sister, a daughter like a clove, a son like a lotus.
My request was fulfilled; I obtained residence in Ayodhyā.

In Song 41 Śiva is said to be worshipped to gain wealth. In Song 42 he is said to have been worshipped to get the ideal husband. In Song 43 Satya Nārāyaṇa (an aspect of Viṣṇu) is said to be worshipped to get the ideal husband and affines. (More than one husband's brother's wife, in line 7, would render life in the joint family less peaceful and more competitive. One sister-in-law would be desireable, however, to help with the many chores.) According to these songs, then, Sanskritic deities as well as non-Sanskritic deities are attributed specific relevance and domains immediate to human needs and desires; the songs indicate that people appeal directly to these gods for concrete assistance.

Songs 42 and 43 are combined in a popular sohar collected among the descendants of Indian immigrants in Surinam.[9] There the deity supplicated is Brahmā, another Sanskritic deity ("the supreme spirit manifested as the active creator of the universe").[10] As in the following song, Brahmā is identified throughout India as the writer of personal destiny—fate made an entity and somewhat personalized. He is thus often blamed for one of the most dreadful tragedies that can befall an Indian woman: barrenness.

44.

As all were seated the queen said to the king:
"All of your offspring have died; I will become an ascetic."
"If the queen will be an ascetic, I too will be an ascetic."
The king will rub ashes on himself and the queen and they will beg for alms in the forest.
Twelve years have passed and Brahmā has not come into the forest.
Brahmā has given boys to everyone without exception.
"Go to your dwelling, barren woman, your turn has not yet come."

"Brahmā has not had enough ink to write that you should
bear children."

This song refers to the epic of Rājā Bharatharī, a king without progeny who elected to become a yogi. (See Chapter VII.) His wife wanted to accompany him on his ascetic odyssey but he forbad it. In this song the wife wants to become an ascetic because she has failed to bear her husband children. (In the fourth line, some ascetics consecrate themselves by smearing their bodies with the ashes of sacrificial fires.) Her husband first offers (perhaps playfully) to join her but then tries to console her, saying that it just has not yet been her fate—Brahmā has not written it. Holding Brahmā responsible again reflects the immediate relevance of Sanskritic deities.

The next song and the six following it are less concerned with deities; their concern is childbirth and its many implications for relationships in the joint family.

45.

My girl friends and kindred gather together.
The girls fill the big clay pots and bring the pure Ganges
water.
One girl may get water; one may get sand.
One sister stands in a sad mood, she doesn't fill the pot.
"Hey, sister, fill the pot and take it home."
"What is your problem; you won't fill the pot?"
"Has your mother-in-law bitten you or your sister-in-law
abused you?"
"Sister, has your husband gone to Madhubanī?"
"You stand there so sadly, you don't fill the pot."
"No, my mother-in-law has not bitten me, nor has my
sister-in-law abused me."
"Girls, my husband has not gone to Madhubanī."
"You stand there so sadly, you don't fill the pot."
"Sisters, he taunts me about conceiving a son, I cannot
tolerate it."
"Fill the pot, sister, and take it home."
"Sister, I have two sons, take one."
"Keep it as your own."
"We can borrow such things as salt and oil."
"Sister, who can borrow conception?"
"It isn't purchased, it isn't bought."

The theme of this song, the plight of the barren woman, is a common one among sohars.[11] The third line draws a parallel between fertile and sterile women and the girls who get water in their pots and those who get sand. This song was sung by the Camār women of Karauṇḍī (on the outskirts of Vārāṇasī).

The following three songs reveal some of the many tensions in the family having to do with conception and childbirth. The first song, from Indrapur, shows the attention due a child-bearing wife from family members and a problem she may have with her husband.

46.

"Rājā (husband), bring your mother, the pain is becoming intense.
If you humble yourself I will esteem you."
"The women will take the narrow path and, walking gracefully, come to the house."
The old woman will take the narrow path and, walking gracefully, come to the house.
Then the old woman will climb and sit on the doorstep.
"You, old woman, will eat the left-over food and fix my hair."
"Rājā, call your brother's wife, the pain is becoming intense.
If you humble yourself I will esteem you."
The old woman will take the narrow path and, walking gracefully, come to the house.
When the women come they will sit on the bed.
"Hey women, call my thin husband, then comb my hair."
"Rājā, bring your sister, the pain is becoming intense.
If you are too proud I will think you small."
The husband will take the narrow path and, walking gracefully, come to the house.
Now the husband's sister will come and sit on the bed.
"Hey, husband's sister, clear out the refuse, then comb my hair."

The next song, from the pauriyās of Vārāṇasī, enumerates social rituals attendant upon the birth of a child, and illuminates tensions between the woman giving birth and her husband's mother and sister. The last six lines of the song comprise a retort to the child-bearing wife from whose point of view the first part of the song is sung.

47.

Now the band starts to play; the women sing sohar.
Now the band starts to play; the women sing sohar.
The baby wiggles about in his mother's lap.
He squirms in his father's lap.
I will not call your sister, oh my husband.
I will not call your sister, oh my husband.
If I call your sister, she will demand her gift.
Where can I get a *neg* [gift] for her, my husband?
If I call your mother, she will demand her gift.
Where can I get the yellow sari to give her, my husband?
I will request the stone bowl and pound the dry ginger.
I will myself sift the dry ginger, my husband.
I will order the mortar and grind the ginger; you will cook and I will eat, my husband.
Instead of your sister I will call my own and I will give her the gift.
I will not call your sister, my husband.
I will take everything and spend it on myself.
When your mother comes to demand her gift, I will hide the money and show only a cowry.
When your sister comes to plaster the labor room I will steal the money bag and show her the empty mud pot.
When the women come to sing sohar, I will steal the betel leaf and show the chewing tobacco.
When the neighbors come to see my dear baby I will cover its face and show the feet.
When the midwife comes to cook my food I will hide the bread board and show the rolling pin.
"Hey *bhaujī* [brother's wife], since I have heard your song, hey bhaujī, I think I will take your jewelled bracelet."
The venerable old man sits on the royal stool.
"Hey Bābā, I will take the nose ring."
The venerable brother sits on the royal stool. "Hey brother, I will take the *bindī*".
The venerable mother sits on the royal stool. "Hey mother, I will take the yellow cotton sari."
"Hey bhaujī, since I have heard your song, hey bhaujī, I think I will take your jewelled bracelet."

When a woman gives birth she must present a gift to her husband's sister, which compensates her for rituals she performs and assistance she gives. She physically cares for her, as mentioned in the last line of Song 46, and traditionally makes a specially recuperative postal-natal food consisting of dried fruit, molasses, dry ginger and other spices. With a gift called *devtā* the woman must also reward her husband's mother for worship rites she performs which are thought to insure the life of the new-born infant. The defiant woman of this song not only resents having to make these presentations, but resents ritual obligations to the neighbor women as well, and doesn't even want anything to do with the midwife.

The last six lines of this song were not separated in performance, from the previous lines, but a reliable informant said that they are a different song. The husband's sister taunts his wife, saying that for the neg she will take various prized possessions, including the *bindī*, a small disk placed between a woman's eyebrows in place of the circular mark usually worn there for beautification and good luck.[12] This is a common motif in the sohars which touch on the relationship between a man's sister and his wife.

On the other hand, a number of women's songs indicate close friendship between the two. S. L. Srivastava states that the relationship has two phases.[13] After an initial period of adjustment when she begins living at her husband's home a woman is often on friendly terms with her husband's sister. But when her husband's sister marries and begins living at her own husband's home, the husband's sister sees her brother's wife become the mistress of the house "in which she was free to do anything." In her new, restricted position this is doubly aggravating. She begins to find fault with her brother's wife, and the relationship declines.

The following song also concerns the birth of a son, again revealing the psychological pressure it places on a woman, and showing how it affects feelings between husband and wife. Angered by her husband, a woman conceals good news from him.

48.

Thin as the betel leaf, beautiful as the golden flowers,
My wife slept on her husband's bed.
She slept in sweet slumber, she slept in sweet slumber.
It is dawn, it is dawn.
"Husband, let go of my sari".
It is dawn, it is dawn.
"Wife, your mother-in-law is calling you. Your sister-in-law is calling you."
"Oh, my wife, have you a son in your lap?"
She was crying, she was crying; "Get up."

"No, my mother-in-law is not calling me, nor is my sister-in-law.
Nor is there a son in my lap.
Don't taunt me, don't taunt me."
It is dawn, it is dawn.
"Husband, let go of my sari."
It is dawn, it is dawn.
The lady but heard these words,
The lady takes off her good sari, she puts on old clothes.
The lady takes off her good sari, she puts on old clothes.
The lady puts on old torn clothes.
Angry, she leaves for her parent's house. Angry she leaves for her parent's house.
She went to the first, the second, and the third forest.
Her father's house was in the third forest.
She goes into the house, she goes into the house.
She placed one foot in the doorway and the second foot in the middle of the doorway,
With the third step she was in the corridor.
Her third step was into the labor room.
There a baby was born, there a baby boy was born.
Oh washerman, oh barber of the village, come quickly.
Oh, my barber, take this announcement,
But don't tell my husband.
The first announcement to my mother-in-law, the second to my father-in-law,
Oh barber, the third invitation to my husband's younger brother.
He went to the first forest, the second, and the third.
In the third forest was her father-in-law's pond.
There her husband was brushing his teeth.
"My barber, what auspicious news do you bring?"
You are beaming, you are beaming.
"The first announcement to my mother-in-law, the second to my father-in-law.
Oh barber, the third invitation to my husband's younger brother."
He but heard these words.
He threw down five rupies and a finger ring.
My barber, you have brought the announcement,
So don't tell my wife.
The barber went from there to the mother-in-law in the morning.
He brought the first announcement to her mother-in-law,

The second announcement to the father-in-law, the
second to the father-in-law,
My barber, the third to her husband's younger brother.
"Don't tell my husband, don't tell my husband."
The mother-in-law arose and sang, the sisters-in-law
played instruments.
The husband's younger brother tossed coins, the women
played instruments.

This ballad, from the Camār women of Karauṇḍī, tells a story of spiteful satisfaction. At dawn a woman sleeping with her husband tells him to let go of her sari so she can arise. He chides her, asking sarcastically if her mother- or sister-in-law is calling, and then taunts her about not having produced a son. Piqued, she dons old clothes and starts for her parent's home. She must walk through three forests—a convention for indicating great distance and the passage of time. No sooner does she arrive than the child is born. She calls her father's barber to deliver the birth announcements, but spitefully tells him not to inform her husband.[14] Nonetheless, when her husband sees the beaming barber, he senses what has happened and throws the ritual payment at his feet. While the women of the family play musical instruments, the man's younger brother throws coins to the children who have gathered.[15]

The final two sohars concern matters related to childbirth in local versions of the great Hindu epic, the Rāmāyaṇa. In the transmission of the Rāmāyaṇa story and related lore, song is undoubtedly as important if not more important than any other medium. The first song is from the pauriyās of Vārāṇasī. After the introductory lines honoring the father of the new-born child who was present during the singing of the song, it tells how King Dasarath's three queens become pregnant by eating a forest herb which they had received from a *Mālī* (a man of the Mālī caste, whose traditional occupation is gardening).[16] After they each bear a son, they send for a Brahman pandit, who astrologically divines the future: Bhārat will become King of Ayodhyā, Rām and Laksman will be banished from the kingdom with Rām's wife, Sītā. The demon king Rāvaṇa will kidnap her but Rām and Lakṣman will overcome his forces and with Sītā return to Ayodhyā.* The final sixteen lines, while sung as a part of this song, comprise another version of the second sohar in this collection.

49.

Now the band starts to play and sound the name of Sotī.
The band starts to play and the women sing sohar.

"Now, my husband, the handsome Mālī is in back, come now without delay."
"Mālī, what is your hoe made of? What is your basket made of?
Mālī, why is it red? Why is it red?"
"Queen, my hoe is made of gold my basket of silver."
"Mālī, go to the plantain forest and bring the sweet root."
He took the hoe on his shoulder to the forest, the basket on his head.
The mālī goes to the first forest, the second forest, and to the third.
The mālī arrived in the plantain forest where the sweet roots are.
He started to dig, he prayed to the goddess of the forest.
He dug again, he prayed to his parents.
He dug a third time he pulled out the sweet root.
He dug and dug and filled the basket with the queen's medicine.
Then he took the hoe on his shoulder and the basket on his head.
The mālī came to the first forest, the second forest, and the third.
The mālī came to the village boundary, he approached Ayodhyā.
Then Queen Kausilyā got the message that the mālī was coming.
Queen, where is the mortar, where in the world is the pestle?
Queen, where will you find your husband's sister so she can grind?
The queen says, we will get the mortar somewhere, the pestle from Ayodhyā.
We will call my husband's sister from far away to grind.
Then Kausilyā drank a full cup and Sumitra drank the second cup.
Queen Kaikeyī washed the mortar and drank; they were born sterile.
Queen, from drinking that very medicine the three queens became pregnant.
Queen Kausilyā began to show, and Sumitra,
And Queen Kaikeyī; who were born sterile.
Rām was born of Kausilyā, Lakṣman of Sumitra,
Bhārat Satrughan of Kaikeyī, three houses full of joy.
Queen, make a design of pure pearls and call the pandit.

Then the pandit of Kāśī (Vārāṇasī) came and sat in my courtyard.
Pandit, open the old book and read.
The queen asks, in which auspicious time was my son born?
Rām was born at a good time, and Lakṣman was also born at a good time,
At the third time Bhārat Satrughan, who will become the king of Ayodhyā.
Then Rām born of Kausilyā and Lakṣman born of Sumitra,
When they became twelve years old, they will have to leave Ayodhyā.
Then they will go to Lanka to attack; Rāvan deceived Rām.
King Rām will kill Rāvan and they will take Sītā,
They bring Sītā back in the palanquin and again dwell in Ayodhyā.
[No break in singing here, but what follows is another song.]
Sītā will light a four-directional oil lamp.
She goes to worship Girijā [wife of Śaṅkar].
She worshipped, oh sister, Girijā, and she requests five boons.
Now my first wish, Sītā asks, somehow, fulfill my wishes.
She begged to become the queen of Ayodhyā, to see the Sarjū river always.
My second wish, Sītā asks, somehow, fulfill my wish.
Sītā wishes a mother-in-law like Kausilyā, a father-in-law like Dasarath.
The third wish, Sītā, asks, somehow, fulfill my wishes.
A husband's younger brother like Lakṣman, a husband like Rām.
Now my fourth wish, Sītā asks, somehow, fulfill my wish.
Sītā wishes for a bed made of flowers and a boy in her lap.
The fifth wish Sītā asks, somehow, fulfill my wishes.
Now Sītā wishes for a bed made of flowers and a baby in her lap.
Now the band begins to play and the women sing sohar.
Now the band begins to play and sound the name of Sukkhū.
Now the band begins to play and the women sing sohar.

[Sukkhū, in the penultimate line, is probably a
misremembering of Sotī, the father named in line 1.]

The final sohar, from the Camār women of Karauṇḍī, tells how Rām's mother Kausilyā forbids sending to her co-wife Kaikeyī an invitation to Rām's wedding. When at the time of the wedding Dasarath feels it is incomplete without Kaikeyī's attendance, he goes to her. She refuses to come and demands that Dasarath decree her son Bhārat to rule and Rām to be banished to the forest.

50.

Queen Kausilyā sits on the stool; King Dasarath sits on
the throne.
"King, arrange the distribution of Rām's wedding
announcements."
He has to take announcements here and there and to the
mother's brother's house.
"King, there is one forbidden invitation: Kaikeyī. Kaikekyī
is my enemy."
The people come from here and there and from the
mother's brother's house.
"King, one didn't come—Kaikeyī. So the courtyard seems
lifeless."
Having heard this much the king could listen no longer.
The king put on golden sandals to please Kaikeyī.
He awoke the sleeping queen and sat cross-legged.
Queen, give up that sad mood, go to my courtyard.
I won't give it up, I won't go to your courtyard.
King, decree that Rām go to the forest, and that Bhārat be
King.
Then I will come to your courtyard.
If you talk like that, you don't know how to talk.
Queen, tear out this heart of mine, which you have made
so sad.

The two vignettes related in these two songs both depart from the lines of the story as related in Tulsī Dās' *Rāmcaritmānas*, the authoritative popular version of the Rāmāyaṇa story. In that telling the queens become pregnant after consuming the oblation from a fire sacrifice which the king had a saint perform.[17] The *Rāmcaritmānas* does not mention Kausilyā forbidding Kaikeyī an invitation to Rām's wedding.

These songs are thus variations on a pan-Indian theme. More research is needed to show whether the variations are common in this region.

The texts of birth-related sohars, as well as the singing of all sohars when a male is born, reveal an obsession with the birth of sons. This theme finds further expression in the songs of the mother goddess.

Worship Songs of the Mother Goddess

"A goddess who is thought to control smallpox, and often a variety of other contagious diseases, is found in almost every part of India."[18] Although it is not clear when disease first became associated with a mother goddess, her worship probably predates the arrival of the Aryans in South Asia. For reasons made clear in the following pages, the cult of the mother goddess in rural eastern Uttar Pradesh is still vital despite the abatement of diseases thought to be in her control. In Indrapur the more elaborate of two calendrical rites devoted to her worship is the only institution which convenes representatives of all families. She is instrumental in shamanic exoricism and important in personal devotions as well. Women learn the basic concepts and beliefs of the mother goddess cult from the songs they sing as expressions of their devotion.

"Mother goddess" is used here to refer collectively to different female deities or "aspects". At the Sanskritic level the important female deities can be divided into two groups. One group includes Pārvatī and Lakṣmī, consorts of the male deities Śiva and Viṣṇu. They are characterized by a mildness consistent with their subordination to and dominance by their male consorts.[19] The goddesses of the other group, including Durgā, Kālī, and Śītalā, have a dual nature. They can be either benevolent or destructive. The non-Sanskritic mother goddesses have the same dangerous character—they are benevolent if worshipped, and may even favor the earnest devotee with a son. But they may be vindictive if they feel they have not received adequate worship, and punish the negligent by inflicting smallpox, cholera, or chicken pox. These diseases are traditionally considered visitations or manifestations of one of the mother goddesses. Although smallpox has been eliminated, epidemics of smallpox and cholera were common just a few decades ago.

For convenience and clarity in the section, the term "mother goddess" will not denote the mild Sanskritic aspects of the goddess, Lakṣmī and Pārvatī, but will refer only to the aspects which are potentially destructive.

The fierce character of the deities is obstrusive. Durgā is depicted in the songs and religious calendar portraits found in the village as a fierce goddess attacking her enemies from the lion on which she is mounted. Kālī is shown in most calendar pictures standing on the corpse of Bhairav, an aspect of Śiva, her tongue lolling out, a necklace of skulls around her neck, and a machette dripping with blood in one hand. Oddly, Śītalā is not visually depicted, nor is her physical image verbalized in song.

At the Sanskritic level in Indrapur, devotees worship the mother goddess by commissioning a Brahman priest to read from the Śrī Durgā Saptāsatī kā Paṭh (a sacred text of 700 Sanskrit mantras [see Chapter V] devoted to the goddess in a number of manifestations) and perform a pūjā. At the non-Sanskritic level, devotees worship the mother goddess in several calendrical rites (described below) involving women's songs. Mediation by priests is not an integral part of these rites. In these contexts the mother goddess is called Mātā Mäī, Mäiyā Morī, Śītalā, Bhagavatī Mäī, Bhavanī Mäī, the Seven Sisters, and other names. But as the songs below demonstrate, devotees equate Sanskritic and non-Sanskritic goddesses. Most villagers do not have precise ideas about the relationships of these deities one to another nor about their distinctive traits. The term "mother goddess" refers to any of a number of female deities who probably emerged in different times and places and whose attributes have become merged or blurred through movement of peoples, diffusion, and confusion.

Calendrical Mother Goddess Rituals

In Indrapur, communal worship of Mātā Mäī occurs on nine days in the bright lunar fortnight of the monsoon month of Sāvan (mid or latter July to mid or latter August). Informants said that Sāvan is a month in which Śītalā is widely worshipped, and that during Sāvan each non-Brahman caste in the village would sacrifice a goat to her at her temple some distance from the village. In fact, the barber caste was the only one which did so during my stay in the village; perhaps such worship was more popular previously.

The first site of communal mother goddess worship is the shrine of Ḍih Bābā, the guardian spirit of the village, who is considered by some to be an auxiliary of the mother goddess. The shrine itself is of the genre called caurā (altar). It is a brick platform mounted by twin hemispheres of stone about seven inches in diameter. Standing by the hemispheres were one or two clay horse figurines. No one was able to explain the significance of the hemispheres or the horses. The horses may be symbolic mounts for the Ḍih Bābā or the mother goddess.

The worshippers included a few men and about thirty women. (See Photo 7.) None of the women was under about thirty-five years of age. One informant explained that it was the duty of the female heads of the household (almost always older women) to perform the worship to insure that it was done correctly, but a younger informant said that younger people do not attend because they do not consider Mātā Māī as important as their parents do.

As they reached the site each woman drew a small pot of water from a well, dropped into it a mixture of sweets, spices, and flowers, and offered it to Mātā Māī by pouring it at the base of the Ḍih shrine and another shrine ten feet away. Planalp states that they propitiate the village guardian because he allows Mātā Māī to enter the village only if he is angered by their neglect.[20] The other shrine is thought by some to represent Sāyad Bābā, a Muslim deity; others think it is a *celā* (servant-apprentice) of Ḍih. Such differences in basic conception are by no means unusual in the village.

After enough women had collected they sang songs of the mother goddess (*mātā māī kī gīt*, sometimes also called *pacaṛās*). The people believe that the goddess is greatly pleased by the singing of these songs.

Proceeding to the Kālī shrine, each woman again made the same offering. In a stage of the rite which seemed an appendage, a Brahman of a lower caste than the rest of the Brahmans in the village performed a fire sacrifice while the women again sang pacaṛās. He was assisted by a man of the Ahir caste, said to be an aspiring ojhā. All of the offerings went to a Camār drummer who with his *daphalā* (a shallow drum of large diameter—see Photo 00) had provided plenty of auspicious noise for the occasion.

On the eighth evening men, women, and children gathered at the center of the village. Again, there is supposed to be one adult representative from each household in attendance. Among them was a group of Goṇḍ musicians who sang songs generally unrelated to the mother goddess, accompanying themselves with cymbals and an hourglass-shaped drum with variable tension heads (*huṛuk*), which produces a distinctive gulping sound. The same Brahman as before performed a fire sacrifice. The group then paraded around the village in a clockwise direction, stopping at the Kālī shrine, at the Ḍih shrine, at a point southwest of the village, and then at the Śiva shrine in the center of the village. The men erected at each stop a bamboo pole on which was tied a red flag and a miniature cot. These are thought to divert the goddess, who, as the songs show, likes to sleep, and to prevent her entrance into the village. The procession around the village thus erects a magical perimeter defense against the pestilential mother goddess.

During the procession there was singing by the Goṇḍs and the women—not of the same songs, but at times simultaneously. For the villagers the intermittent cacophony is incidental to the double measure of auspiciousness resulting from the two musical offerings.

The other most important period of mother goddess worship in the village is called *Nau Rātrī* (nine nights). It begins on the first day of the month of Caitr (approximately March 12-April 10). There is another Nau Rātrī in the month of *Kuār* (approximately September 15-October 14), but it is one of less goddess-related activity. During Caitr Nau Rātrī those with problems they believe amenable to the methods of ojhās attended their special nightly seances. In the two which I attended, the ojhā (of the Lohār caste), contacted his tutelary deity (a goddess) by singing a song in which he addressed the deity as *Māi* ('mother') and requested her to possess him. Following the goddess' appropriation of his body—marked by a convincing combination of arm-flapping, whistling, sucking noises and convulsive tremors—he began to speak in a peculiar voice created by vocalizing words as he inhaled. He spoke to his clients as the godling herself, asking them to relate their problems and, usually, attributing them to some supernatural cause such as *bhūt* (the malevolent soul of a person who died violently or in unhappy circumstances). During the session I observed he addressed two problems: an expiring ox which various treatments had not revived, and a lost document. In some cases the divination is followed by exorcism of the harrassing spirit.

More affluent people may express their deference toward the mother goddess in higher style during Caitr Nau Rātrī by contracting a Brahman to recite from the *Durgā Saptāsatī kā Paṭh*. Here the goal seems to be the maintenance of favorable relations with the deity rather than obtaining assistance with specific problems.

The eighth day of this period is a holiday locally called *Basiaurā*. The name derives from *bāsī* (leftover food). In the Sanskritic tradition this holiday is called *Durgaśtamī*—'Durgā eighth.' The women of each family spend the day cleaning and plastering the house. After the evening meal, while they are preparing food for the next day, they sing the songs of the mother goddess discussed below. The next morning they perform a special ritual in which food is offered to the mother goddess, and paint circles around the outside drain openings and doors of the house and courtyard to prevent her entrance. During the day women are prohibited from cooking or house-cleaning of any kind. (All food consumed is the bāsī prepared the previous night.) The prohibition of cooking fires on Basiaurā is, like the fanning of a person afflicted with smallpox, explained with reference to the belief that the goddess does not like heat. (The name Śītalā means "the cool one.")

There is another discrete cluster of occasions in which a mother goddess is important—exorcism, divination, and sorcery performed by the ojhā. (For convenience' sake I will refer to this as the shamanic context.) Whether the goddess invoked in these rites can be equated with the one outlined above is uncertain. In most shamanic contexts she is addressed as Māī, like the aforementioned goddess. But the functions she performs (aiding with divination, exorcism, and sorcery) differ, and they usually benefit an individual or family rather than the village as a whole. Moreover, the manner in which the ojhā approaches his tutelary goddess differs from the manner in which she is addressed in group worship. Devotees are cautious and appeasing; the ojhā is bold and demanding, as seen in these first lines of an exorcism which I recorded.

> Listen to me Mother!
> Speak to me of what is in that dark room, Mother!
> Answer this question, *joginiyā*! [a female yogi]
> Mother, today my eyes cannot see, but by my ears I hear you. . . .

Rather than relating the attributes or promoting the powers of the goddess, as most of the women's songs do, the ojhā's songs directly invoke, address, and command the goddess by which he divines and exorcises. The musical style of the ojhās' songs, which are also called pacarās, was quite distinct from that of the women's songs, and most closely resembled the kharī birahā. (See Chapter VIII.)

Mother Goddess Songs

The pushy attitude of the ojhā contrasts sharply with the reverential, laudatory tone of the women's songs, such as the first two below (from the Camār women of Karauṇḍī). In these songs the mother goddess is swinging in a swing. Swinging is a frequent pastime of young villagers in the monsoon season, which in this region is also the season of the primary communal mother goddess worship. In the second song the swing is suspended from the branch of a nīm (Latin *azidiricta indica*) tree. The association of the nīm tree with the goddess is a fundamental belief in her cult. The nīm is a large shade tree which villagers associate with coolness. The goddess swings beneath the nīm to enjoy its cooling effects. Consonant with this is the traditional treatment for smallpox: to fan the afflicted with a nīm branch, which cools the goddess who is manifest in the pox.

Both of these songs also connect the goddess with the Mālī caste, another widely held connection.[21] The Mālī and *Mālin* (wife of a Mālī) are commonly the pūjāriś of the mother goddess, that is, they keep her shrines and temples clean and make regular offerings to her. Mālī denotes a member of the Mālī caste, the śudra caste of gardeners who traditionally raise and sell flowers and betel leaf. People in Indrapur said that the Mālī is associated with the goddess because she likes sweet things, including scented flowers. Five of the eight mother goddess songs included here refer to the close association of the Mālī caste and the mother goddess.

51.

Oh, Mālī, Mother is spinning around in the swing in
  your garden.
All seven sisters at once are spinning around in the swing
  in your garden.
The Mālī arranges a sitting place for the seven sisters
  on the jeweled sandlewood in your garden.
The seven sisters are spinning in the swing in your
  garden.
With the Ganges water in the vessel,
  the Mālī washes her feet,
Oh Mālī, in your garden.
The Mālī makes an offering of dried fruit on the
  embossed plate,
Oh Mālī, in your garden.
You perform *āratī* with the camphor candle and clarified
  butter,
Oh Mālī, in your garden.

This song simply lists acts which comprise worship of the goddess, and probably serves as a mnemonic for remembering the ritual. The Mālī arranges a sitting place for her/them, washes her feet (the feet of the icon), makes a dried offering, and moves an oil lamp in a vertical circle before the image (i.e., performs āratī).

In the following song the identity of the two men who push her is unclear. The third to push her is her auxiliary, Ḍih Bābā. The promised rewards in this song are deliberately vague: perhaps she will only ease the suffering of the devotee's husband and community, or perhaps she will refrain from afflicting them. In addressing the mother goddess the woman of this song refers to her baby as "your (i.e., the mother goddess') servant" as a way of pledging her child to the service of the goddess and thereby expressing her deep devotion.

52.

Māiyā is swinging on the swing she has hung from the branch of the nīm tree.
Māiyā sings songs as she swings.
Sitting on the swing, the seven sisters are pumping.
Dear Lālcand Rām is pushing.
Dear Agivān Singh is pushing.
Ḍih Bābā is pushing.
The bough undulates as dear Lālcand gently pushes.
The fragile nīm bough undulates.
That clove bough undulates.
After swinging a long time, Māiyā left feeling thirsty.
She left on the path to the Mālin's house.
Are you in or out, Mālin, so that I can get a drop of water?
Give me a drop of water.
How can I give you water, Śītalā Māī, when your servant is in my lap?
Baby Ganpat, Māiyā, is in my lap.
Baby Ganpat is in my lap.
Put Ganpat to sleep on the golden bed, Mālin, and give me a drop.
Give me water, Mālin, just a drop.
How can I give the seven sisters water, when there is a baby on my lap?
When your servant is in my lap?
Put the servant to sleep on the golden bed, Mālin.
Give me water, Mālin, just a drop.
The cot will break, Māiyā, he will fall to the ground.
Mother, your servant will fall to the ground.
When my servant, Mālin, falls to the ground, I will lift him up.
I will lift him up in my golden sari.
In her right hand she takes the water pot, in her left the silken rope.
The Mālin goes to let the rope down at the little well, to let that silken rope down.
The well was so deep the water was in the nether world.
How can I give Māiyā water?
If you have the skill, Mālin, tie the rope to your sari.
Give me water with the tied sari.
Pulling out one pot she washes her hands and pulls out a second pot.

She gives Māiyā water with the second pot.
She gives all the goddesses water with the second pot.
She gives all the unremembered goddesses water with
the second pot.
Just as you have soothed me, Mālin, in the same way,
all of your people will be soothed.
Your husband will be soothed.
Your village will be honored.[22]

The next song makes clear other rewards of mother goddess worship: the devotee bargains her devotions for a baby as well as for her husband's longevity ("the vermilion will stay on my forehead"). The precious nature of the goddess' appointments (temple of gold, earrings of pearl etc.) indicate her awesome glory. This song was sung by Smti. Usha Bhatt, a professional folk singer of Vārāṇasī, who learned it from her mother.*

53.

Of what is the goddess' temple made? What is on the
door?
I will wipe clean your temple with my sari, the vermilion
will stay on my forehead, Mother.
The temple of the goddess is made of gold, the door of
silver,
Sandalwood is on the door.
I will wipe clean your temple with my sari, the vermilion
will stay on my forehead, Mother.
Of what, Mother, are your earrings made, of what your
necklace, of what your necklace?
My eyes keep sweeping the path.
Of gold, and pearls Mother, the earrings, the necklace of
rosemary.
Mother, I will wash your feet with tears; the vermilion
will stay on my forehead.
I will keep fanning you if you will put a baby in my lap.

The following song, from a village-wide mother goddess ritual in Indrapur, also indicates belief in the mother goddess' power to grant longevity to men—longevity, but not immortality. The near identity of the goddesses is suggested by the way their names are interchanged. This is another of the many songs telling of the goddess' power to grant wealth and sons. Half of the mother goddess songs in this collection and six of the sixteen songs in Upadhyaya's 1954 chapter on mother goddess songs emphasize the mother goddess' ability to award sons.

54.

I picked and picked the flowers and fashioned them into
  a garland
I took them to the court of Śītalā, Mother.
I took them to the court of Kālī, Mother.
Are you asleep or awake, Kālī Mother?
The Mālin stands at the door, Mother.
Ask, ask, Mālin, I will give what you ask, whatever is in
  your heart.
Are the seven sisters inside or outside?
How long does the Mālin stand at the door?
Ask, ask, Mālin, I will give what you ask, whatever is in
  your heart.
You give me riches and sons, Mother.
Will you give immortality to the Mālī, Mother?
Even if the moon of the east goes to the west,
  the Mālī will not be immortal, Mālin.

There is a striking similarity between the character of the mother goddess and the social significance of in-marrying women to the family. The primary mother goddess attributes—the source of wealth and sons if pleased, and destruction if displeased, correspond to the primary traits of women as seen by the patrilineal, patrilocal North Indian family. Among all but the lowest castes women bring wealth in the form of a dowry and subsequent gifts, and they can provide the sons needed to continue the lineage and permit a man proper funerary rites. The indulgence of pregnant women so that they might provide sons is well known, and corresponds to the worship of the goddess for the same purpose. The destructive aspect of woman, which corresponds to the pestilential aspect of the goddess, is expressed in the conventional belief that the arrival of a bride brings continued disruption as well as the stereotype of women's "pettiness and penchant for quarreling."[23] Conflict between a man's mother and his wife, as we have seen, is also a problem. Catastrophes occurring to the family after her arrival are sometimes blamed on the young bride, who is said to have brought malevolent ghosts with her.

Corollary to the goddess' favorable disposition toward her devotees is her antagonism toward those who do not worship her, seen in the following two songs. In these and subsequent songs the names Kālī, Śītalā, and Mātā are again used interchangeably.

55.

Riding a lion Śītalā comes roaring, villagers.
You don't know Mother, villagers.
The son of the Mālī does know her, he takes a garland.
He takes a garland to the goddess, standing in the doorway.
Riding a lion Kālī comes roaring, villagers.
You don't know Mother, villagers.
The son of the devotee does know her, he takes an offering.
He takes an offering to the goddess, standing in the door.
Riding a lion Durgā comes roaring, villagers.
You don't know Mother, villagers.
The son of the shepherd does know her, he takes a young male goat.
He takes a young male goat to the goddess, standing in the doorway.
Riding a lion Amaliyā comes roaring, villagers.
You don't know Mother, villagers.
The son of the potter does know her, he takes a pot.
He takes a pot to the goddess, standing in the doorway.

56.

Mother so thin,
Omnipresence of Bengal,
To whom do you give, Śītalā?
To whom do you give, Kālī?
Five or ten sons?
Whom do you make childless?
I give to the pious, the devotees,
Five or ten sons.
I make the proud childless.
To whom do you give, Mother?
Mother so thin,
Omnipresence of Bengal,
Five or ten pox?

On whose back do you rub hot coals?
To the religious devotees, five or ten pox;
I rub hot coals on the backs of the proud.
Mother so thin,
Omnipresence of Bengal.

These two songs, both from rites in Indrapur, express a fundamental theme of this and other North Indian mother goddess cults: the opposition of the mother goddess to those who do not worship her. In Song 55 this is expressed by opposing the villagers who don't "know" the goddess to the sons of the Mālī, the devotee, the shepherd, and the potter, who "know" and worship the goddess through their offerings. It is interesting that all of the castes named as devotees are of the śudra varṇa (the lowest varṇa). This suggests that the "proud" who refuse to worship the goddess are of the higher castes. One of the two mother goddess songs in Chandramani Singh's collection also suggests opposition of the goddess to the higher strata of society:

Shitala goes to pick flowers in the guise of a gardening woman
On this side Mother Shitala is picking flowers [and] on that side
The king's son was staring on that side
[Shitala says]—O son of the king, how dare you stare at me, I will smite you [with smallpox]
O son of the king, I will smite your body
[King's son says]—O Shitala, please excuse this error [because you were] in the guise of a gardening woman
O Mother, I stared at you [because] you were in the guise of a gardening woman.[24]

In Song 56 the opposition is more dramatic. The goddess rewards the faithful with songs, and lets them off with only a few pox. But she makes the proud childless, and severely afflicts them with smallpox (indicated by the phrase "I rub hot coals on the backs of the proud").[25]

The following song is rather obscure, but also seems to identify the mother goddess with the lower, generally poorer castes.

57.

Your father's household is very poor, oh Mother.
The barley bread inedible, oh Mother.
Mother, with it weed spinach.
Śītalā Māī, your father's household is very poor, oh
Mother.

Seven Sisters, your father's household is very poor, oh
Mother,
The barley bread inedible, oh Mother.
Mother, with it weed spinach.
Marukā Māī, your father's household is very poor, oh
Mother.
Durgā Māī, your father's household is very poor.
The barley bread inedible, oh Mother.
Mother, with it weed spinach.
Sakathā Māī, your father's household is very poor, oh
Mother.
Durgā Māī, your father's household is very poor, oh
Mother.
Gaṅgā Māī, your father's household is very poor, oh
Mother.
The barley bread inedible, oh Mother.
Mother, with it weed spinach.
Ḍih Bābā, your father's household is very poor, oh
Mother.
Caurā Māī, your father's household is very poor, oh
Mother.
The barley bread inedible, oh Mother.
Mother, with it weed spinach.
Vindhyācal Māī, your father's household is very poor, oh
Mother.
Sāyr Māī, your father's household is very poor, oh
Mother.
The barley bread inedible, oh Mother.
Mother, with it weed spinach.
All goddesses and gods, your father's household is very
poor, oh Mother.
Whoever has been forgotten, your father's household is
very poor, oh Mother.
The barley bread inedible, oh Mother.
Mother, with it weed spinach.

A group of Camār women on the outskirts of Vārāṇasī sang this song in a mother goddess worship rite. The deities named, most but not all of whom are goddesses, have shrines in the neighborhood. With the final stanza of the song the women carefully avoid offending any deity they may have neglected. By revealing seemingly innocent young ladies to be goddesses, the following song also alludes to the ominous aspects of the goddess' character.

58.

The little girls pick flowers and bamboo branches
The Mālī's garden is his temple
The Mālī calls, "Whose daughters, people?"
He treads in the garden. "Whose daughters, people?"
"We are neither daughters nor son's wives."
"We are the seven sisters of Śītalā."
"We are Vindhyācal, Bhagavatī, Kālī, Bhavanī."

In this song from Indrapur there are two implications of the line "We are neither daughters nor son's wives." This is a way of stating the alien and therefore somewhat frightening nature of goddesses, because ordinarily all young women in the village are either daughters or son's wives. It also draws attention to one of the mother goddess' distinguishing traits—her status as a mature female without a consort.

Summary and Interpretation

The singing of sohars and mother goddess songs is an important part of their respective rituals. By specifying ritual acts some of the songs work to preserve the very rituals in which they are sung.

Both kinds of songs are much more important in the transmission of religious ideology than has been recognized. The texts of devotional sohars transmit the attributes of both Sanskritic and non-Sanskritic deities; a variety of beliefs supporting religious activities such as the benefits of austerities and singing devotional songs; Vaishnavite devotional lore, especially of the Rāmāyaṇa; and ideas regarding the pantheon which are basic to ritual practices. The beliefs expressed in the songs reveal the absence of a Sanskritic/non-Sanskritic dichotomy in the women's religious thinking, and show that Sanskritic dieties as well as non-Sanskritic deities are thought to govern matters of personal benefit.

The sohar texts related specifically to childbirth transmit to women and reveal to us the terrible importance bearing a son has for a woman, and some of the tensions between a woman and her husband, his sisters and mother.

The songs of the mother goddess also transmit concepts, beliefs and attitudes fundamental to her cult. One of these is her dualistic nature. Like the girls of the village, she likes to cool herself by swinging in the shade of the nīm tree, and like these girls she can bring sons to the family. Also like these girls she can create havoc. If not respected the mother goddess can afflict those too proud to worship her with smallpox.

Several songs suggest that the mother goddess is affiliated primarily with lower castes. Certainly her association with the Mālīs, a śudra caste of gardeners, is clear. The Mālī and his wife are described as the chief caretakers of her shrines and her steadfast devotees. Other of the songs suggest that the goddess is poor, like most of the lower castes in the village, and that her devotees are of lower castes. In another place I have elaborated upon the notions that the mother goddess is affiliated especially with lower castes, that higher caste women are attracted to the essentially low cult by the compelling beliefs regarding fertility and disease, and that the lower castes gain influence over high castes through special rapport they are believed to have with the goddess.[26]

Male Ascendancy and the Desire for Sons

The texts of mother goddess songs and sohars, as well as the singing of sohars at the birth of a son, demonstrate women's preference for male offspring. Professor Morris Opler interpreted both songs for sons and ritually expressed concern with male longevity as part of a culture theme he called "the ascendancy of the male principle." What I wish to show here is that preference for sons and concern with male longevity are essentially pragmatic, deriving ultimately from economic and social structures.

In the introductory sketch of social organization in the previous chapter two factors were identified which are fundamental to the desire for sons: Descent is patrilineal (i.e., inheritance of land and the tracing of descent are through the male line), and residence after marriage is patrilocal (the bride leaving her own family to reside with her husband and in many cases, other members of his family). These two factors are in turn the result of other forces.

The most widely held explanation of patrilineal descent is that it is a social structure which keeps men in the family so that they may more effectively get or produce food.[27] In plow agriculture societies such as this one, males are better suited to plowing and other heavy tasks, because of their greater stature and strength; women are also handicapped by the consistent imposition of childbearing and nurturance chores during their most able years. (Because of high mortality a woman must bear many children to insure the survival of even one male.) Males are thus fundamentally necessary for food production; females are also necessary, but males can do the crop-related work usually assigned to females more easily than the females can do the work usually assigned to males. Patrilocal residence not only retains men for food production, it minimizes changes in the membership of the work force, which minimizes the number of times tasks have to be allocated, and the number of times new personnel must be trained and taught the lay of the land.

Land is a scarce resource in agricultural societies, and retaining control over the land is crucial. Maintaining the male work group intact through patrilocal residence, in which sons stay with the family and daughters move away, also facilitates the transfer of control over the land from father to son. This is another factor that leads to concern with male line of descent—patrilineality—and the consequent wish for males to serve as heirs.

Plow agriculture and patrilocal residence have other important consequences with respect to differential valuation of male and female offspring. Until she is married men of the family must keep careful watch over the sexually mature daughter, because talk of her sexual misconduct would jeopardize her marriageability and bring great shame to the family. (Villagers give this as one reason a girl should be married as soon as she is mature.) In order that a daughter can be married, her father (with the help of kinsmen) must find her a suitable groom, which can be time-consuming, expensive, and frustrating. He must then host a wedding whose elaborateness and expense are commensurate with his prestige. He and other members of his family will, by custom, play a deferential role in all relations with his daughter's husband's family. Added to this is the burden of the dowry, a substantial amount relative to income among all but the lowest castes. This influences gender preference not only because marrying off a daugher requires expenditure of savings or assumption of loans, but because a son represents potential dowry income. His daughter will then leave the family; her visits become increasingly short and seldom. Only sons will be there in the parents' later years, first to assist them in limited ways but ultimately to provide for their complete support.

One other social factor in son preference is the need for physical protection. Feuding and warfare are common in the histories of most, if not all, localities. Men are better suited to fighting and other military activities by stature and strength, and by freedom from childbearing and nurturance. More men in the family means more protection from marauding troops or neighbors.

A son is of ritual importance as well. Ideally it is a son who administers the blow to the skull of his deceased father which releases the soul so that it can begin its journey to the land of the dead. Also, especially among Brahmans, it is believed that a man is born with three debts: to ancestors, teachers, and deities.[28] The debt to ancestors can only be paid by fathering a son.

The other side of the preference-for-sons coin is discrimination against daughters. Girls are usually treated with care and affection by their parents, but they are sometimes the victims of neglect or outright infanticide, particularly in families where there are already several daughters, or where there are sons and scarce means to sustain all of the children. Barbara D. Miller has shown that hospital admissions favor boys over girls at a ratio of about two to one in North India (implying greater concern for welfare of boys), and that girls die at much higher rates in the north than do boys.[29] Miller hypothesized that daughters are discriminated against not only because of the marriage expense they impose, but because among propertied families they are excluded from agricultural work and thus are economically less valuable. In testing this proposition she found that where female labor participation (f.l.p.—women working outside the home) is high there is high preservation of female life, but where f.l.p. is low, female children may or may not be preserved.[30] She explains the discrepancy with reference to ideological factors. Although f.l.p. is high among low castes in the North, female life is not preserved, she believes, because those castes accept the dominant ideology, which favors males.[31]

The idea that lower castes accept *in toto* the dominant ideology favoring males is controverted by a musical practice alluded to above (Song 45). In 1978 I observed that women of the Camār caste (an untouchable caste) in two villages on the periphery of Vārāṇasī (Citurpur and Karauṇḍī) celebrate and sing sohars at the births of daughters as well as sons. Unfortunately, whether this is generally true of Camār and other untouchables, or of other lower castes in this region, has yet to be determined.

A thorough evaluaton of Miller's study is beyond the scope of this book, but should her hypothesis be valid it is clear that f.l.p. would still be only one of many factors contributing to a value orientation favoring sons that is manifest, among other places, in the musical culture. A son will be there in later years to produce food, protect the family, bring in a dowry, assist his parents, and continue the family's endeavors. For these and related reasons women make pilgrimmages, visit men thought to have supernatural powers (*siddh phakirs*), wear special amulets, and perform a variety of devotions and austerities in order to conceive sons. Moreover, a woman is often little respected in her husband's home unless she gives birth to a son.[32] Little wonder that women sing paeans to a mother goddess who can assure sons, and celebrate their birth with auspicious songs.

The concern with male longevity, a goal of private and group rituals, is similarly practical. Females are dependent for support first on their fathers, then their husbands, and finally their sons.[33] They depend on their fathers also to find them grooms, and subsequently, their brothers to maintain a connection with the natal family. It is thus not surprising that women perform several rituals whose explicit goal is the longevity of the males in their lives.[34] What appears in mother goddess and birth songs as the pervasive cultural elevation of males is in large part a recognition of their economic importance to women.

The songs women sing in wedding rites, mother goddess worship, and the celebration of male births are those whose contexts and lyrics tell us much about the lives of these women. But women's singing is not confined to ritual ceremonies: other kinds of songs and a type of near-song they perform provide further insight into their culture.

Notes

1 Morris Opler, "Introduction: North Indian Themes—Caste and Untouchability." In *The Untouchables of Contemporary India*, edited by J. Michael Mahar. (Tucson: The University of Arizona Press, 1972).

2 This was pointed out to me by Professor Charles Morrison.

3 For a lucid discussion of these and other problems with the Sanskritic/non-Sanskritic dichotomy, see Lawrence Babb, *The Divine Hierarchy: Popular Hinduism in Central India* (New York: Columbia University Press, 1975), pp. 23-29.

4 McKim Marriott, "Little Communities in an Indigenous Civilization." In *Village India: Studies in the Little Community*, edited by McKim Marriott (Chicago: University of Chicago Press), p. 209, and Jack M. Planalp, "Religious Life and Values in a North Indian Village," Ph.D. diss., Cornell University. (Ann Arbor: University Microfilms, 1956), pp. 720-21.

5 Planalp, *Religious Life*, pp. 720-21.

6 Ibid., p. 778.

7 David G. Mandlebaum, "Transcendential and Pragmatic Aspect of Religion," *American Anthropologist* 68 (1966): 1174-91.

8 For related songs, see U. Arya, *Ritual Songs and Folksongs of the Hindus of Surinam* (Leiden: E. J. Brill, 1968), pp. 39 and 67.

9 Ibid., pp. 38-40.

10 John Dowson, *A Classical Dictionary of Hindu Mythology and Religion, Geography, History and Literature* (London: Routledge and Kegan Paul, Ltd., 1972), p. 56.

11 Krishna Dev Upadhyaya, *Bhojpurī Lok Gīt* (*Bhāg* 1). (Allahabad, India: Hindi Sahitya Sammelan, 1954), pp. 101-142, especially pp. 115, 126, 129, 135, and 137.

12 For a related song see Laxmi G. Tewari, "Ceremonial Songs of the Kanyakubja Brahmins." In *Essays in Arts and Sciences* 6 (1977) p. 33.

13 S. L. Srivastava, *Folk Culture and Oral Tradition* (New Delhi: Abinav Publications, 1974), pp. 33-39.

14 For a related song see Hari S. Upadhyaya, "The Joint Family Structure and Familial Relationship Patterns in the Bhojpurī Folksongs," Ph.D. diss. Indiana University, (Ann Arbor: University Microfilms, 1967), pp. 253-54.

15 For a song with many of the same motifs, see Upadahyaya, *Bhojpurī Lok Gīt*, p. 131.

16 For variants see Upadhyaya, *Bhojpurī Lok Gīt*, p. 147, and Upadhyaya, The Joint Family Structure, pp. 246-47.

17 F. S. Growse, *The Rāmāyaṇa of Tulsī Dās* (Allahabad, India: Ram Narain Lal Beni Prasad), p. 89.

18 Ralph Nicholas, "Sitala and the Art of Printing: The Transmission and Propagation of the Myth of the Goddess of Smallpox in Rural West Bengal." In Mahadev Apte, ed. *Mass Culture, Language and Arts in India* (Bombay: Popular Prakashan, 1978), p. 155.

19 Lawrence A. Babb, "Marriage and Malevolence: the Uses of Sexual Opposition in a Hindu Pantheon," *Ethnology* 9 (1970): 141-42.

20 Planalp, *Religious Life*, pp. 760-761.

21 Upadhyaya, *Bhojpurī Lok Git*, p. 343.

22 For another version of this song, see Chandramani Singh and Ronald Amend, *Marriage Songs from Bhojpurī Region* (Jaipur: Champa Lal Ranka & Co., 1979), pp. 42-43.

23 Opler, "North Indian Themes," p. 6.

24 Chandramani Singh and Ronald Amend, *Marriage Songs*, pp. 44-45.

25 Textual evidence shows that smallpox has been associated with a mother goddess in India since the twelfth century A.D. There is, however, some likehood that those songs about her referring to smallpox date to a more recent period of epidemics. See Ralph Nicholas, "The Goddess Sitala and Epidemic Smallpox in Bengal," *Journal of Asian Studies* 41 (1981): 26, 32-34.

26 Edward O. Henry, "The Mother Goddess Cult and Interaction between Little and Great Traditions," in Giri Raj Gupta, ed. *Religion in Modern India. Main Currents in Indian Sociology, Volume V* (New Delhi: Vikas Publishing House PvtLtd, 1983), pp. 174-197. A serious error was made in the typesetting of the second paragraph of that essay. It should read: "This paper analyzes the mother goddess cult in eastern Uttar Pradesh as a product of the interaction between the religion of the upper social groups, represented by the Brahmans, and the cults of the masses."

27 For example, see Roger M. Keesing, *Kin Groups and Social Structure* (New York: Holt, Rinehart, and Winston, 1975), p. 135.

28 Tewari, "Ceremonial Songs . . . ," p. 50.

29 Barbara D. Miller, *The Endangered Sex: Neglect of Female Children in Rural North India*. (Ithaca, New York: Cornell University Press, 1981), pp. 89, 100.

30 Ibid., p. 117.

31 Ibid., pp. 158-159.

32 Premchand's short story, "A Desparate Case," portrays this situation at its worst. See David Rubin, *The World of Premchand* (Bloomington: Indiana University Press, 1969).

33 Doranne Jacobson, "The Women of North and Central India." In *Women in India: Two Perspectives* (Columbia, Missouri: South Asia Books, 1977), p. 66.

34 Opler, "North Indian Themes," p. 6.

* This song may be heard on the LP disc, *Chant the Names of God*. See Henry, 1981.

IV

Other Women's Songs and Dirges

Introduction

The foregoing pages have been concerned with the women's ceremonial songs that seem most important—the wedding songs, songs sung at the birth of a son, and songs about the mother goddess. Women also occasionally sing for recreation or to help pass the time and ease the tedium of monotonous tasks. These occasions include recreation in the monsoon season, rice-transplanting, and flour-milling. Women also perform a kind of dirge after the death of a family member and in other highly emotional situations. Each of these different types of song provides more insight into the world of the women who sing them.

Recreation in the Monsoon Season

On monsoon evenings, when it isn't raining, girls of a neighborhood often get together to swing and sing kajalīs. The swings are bamboo harrows, which allow up to five people to swing together (see Photo 10). The girls also sing their kajalīs when they dance a group dance which they call *dhunmuniā*. The girls stand in two lines about eight feet apart, facing each other. One line begins to sing and advances toward the other line. When they stop, approximately at the end of the stanza, the girls in the two lines are face to face. The girls of the second line begin to sing and advance, the girls in the first line having to walk backwards to their position. On the next stanza the cycle begins anew. The girls' postures are those of normal standing or walking.

I observed the women's dance and tape recorded the kajalīs on the afternoon of a holiday called *tīj* (on August 24 in 1971), when married women fast for their husband's longevity. Younger women who have been living at their husband's homes for only several years receive gifts of saris and food from their fathers and brothers. The younger women of the southern part of the village (Brahman, Lohār, Kalvār, and Dhobī castes) had gone together to the river to perform the ritual ablutions of the day, and to don their new apparel. They performed the dance upon returning to a flat, open place on the path to the river.

Due to the low quality of the recordings, I did not fully transcribe the women's songs, however, I did determine the general topics of the songs. They depicted scenes and concerns mostly familiar in other village songs: episodes of the youthful Krishna, vignettes from the Rāmāyaṇa, amorous relations between husband and wife, and the importance of devotion.

Rice-transplanting Songs

While transplanting rice in September, women, generally of the Camār caste, sing *ropanī kī gīt* (songs of rice-transplanting) to make the time pass more quickly. To perform the back-breaking task, the women stand in six to eight inches of water and bend at the waist to insert the bundles of rice plants in the mud.

I was able to record only one of their songs, but it is a ribald gem. A girl named Myna (after the speech-mimicking bird of the same name) is married but has yet to cohabit with her husband. She makes flimsy excuses to her brother's wife for telltale changes in her anatomy. Arrangements for her gaunā are made with alacrity, but not quite soon enough.

59.

"I ask you Myna, my husband's sister,
How is it that your cheeks are yellow, my husband's
sister?"
"I went to Father's grove to grind turmeric and it
splashed on my face and made it yellow."
"How is it that your stomach has become swollen,
husband's sister?"
"I went to Father's grove to grind chickpea flour;
I ate it and my stomach swelled up."
"How did your breast get blackened, sweetheart?"
"I went to Father's grove, brother's wife, to scrub pots;
the pots stained my breasts black."

The honorable mother-in-law sat on the stool;
"Set the date for Myna's gaunā, sweetheart!"
But now Myna's husband is just a brat—he must still play with toys.
"Have your husband's younger brother take a letter, daughter-in-law; set a date for Myna's gaunā."
When the groom's party took position near the village, Myna got a headache.
When the groom's party came into the courtyard, to Myna was born Nanda Lāl.
Hearing the sound of the crying, Myna's brother beat his head;
"Shall we celebrate *biyahal* or *sudevas*?"
"Heed me, oh brother who beats his head, play both kinds of music!"

At the end of the song Myna says to her brother, who is pounding his head in humiliation—"Don't worry, we'll just celebrate both occasions at once" (the rite of departure of the bride and the rite of the mother and new-born son).[1]

Milling Songs

Women formerly spent much time converting grain into flour by means of a *cakkī* (small hand-turned millstone—see Photo 8). Today this work is increasingly done at motorized mills owned by village entrepreneurs. I recorded the milling song below at a session convened for me in Narhī, Balliā District, by Śrī Datta Treya Pāṇḍe, a most hospitable secondary-school principal. The singers were Brahman women. The song tells of a stereotypically difficult family relationship and one of its worst possible consequences.

60.

With a golden broom, oh Rāma, she sweeps out the courtyard.
She goes out of the courtyard, oh Rāma, her sari falls open.
Sitting on a stool, oh Rāma, the honorable mother-in-law says,
"I will kill your brother, the wife of your elder brother, and your brother's daughter."

The mother-in-law gives, oh Rāma, the golden pitcher.
The daughter-in-law takes in her hand, oh Rāma,
the silken draw-rope,
To fill the pitcher, to fill the pitcher at the bank.
She drowns herself, oh Rāma, she sinks in the Jamunā
river.[2]

Difficulties between a man's wife and his mother are sufficiently common that the relation is stereotypically one of conflict (somewhat more so than are mother-in-law relations in our own society). Not only is there competition between the two for the loyalty and affection of the man, and later, power in the household, but initially the mother is the taskmaster to a man's wife. This sets the stage for conflict because, as Doranne Jacobson has noted, few north Indian women, even young brides, are willing to be subservient to anyone, and some find it impossible to even pretend to be so.[3]

The Chanted Lament

When a family member dies, one or more of the (usually) older women in the family may spend a half hour or more each day in a half-cried, half-chanted lament. Educated villagers called this a *vilāp;* others simply called it "crying." If the grief is deeply felt she may continue to do this intermittently for weeks or even months. The woman's death lament exists in a more developed form in south India and in Greece, and is found in varying forms throughout the Middle East.[4]

The departure of the bride from her natal home, whether with the marriage party or later, is an occasion for scenes of acute emotion also involving the vilāp.[5] Some women also chant in this manner when they leave their natal for their conjugal homes after an extended visit. Other laments are heard in a happier situation—when a woman meets a relative or old friend after a long separation. The women squat down, embracing, each with her head on the other's shoulder, sometimes each holding the other's ankles, and chant for a while.

The three tones of the lament span only a minor third. They are sung in free rhythm, their few lines repeated over and over. Villagers did not consider them to be song (*gīt*). There is, of course, no clear dividing line between singing, speaking, chanting and crying; examples of these performances are included here because they are on the periphery of song.

People told me that the texts of the laments are spontaneous. They are probably improvised on the traditional themes. Because I would be invading someone's privacy and exploiting her grief, I did not tape-record the lamenting I observed. The texts below were provided by a reliable informant, one of the village school-teachers, who said they were typical. Their brevity here provides a certain intensity; in performance there is much repetition.

Mother's Lament

Hey child, oh child!
Having left me where have you gone, oh child?
How can I go on without you, oh child?
I can't forget your face, oh child.
Who will call me mother?

Wife's Lament

Hey love, oh love!
To whom can I go for support, oh love?
How will my life pass, oh love?
My life's succour, where have you gone, oh love?

Sister's Lament

Hey brother, oh brother!
Whom, whom shall I call, oh brother?
Who will look after my welfare, oh brother?

Daughter's Lament

Oh father, where are you going?
Who will bring clothes for me?
Whom shall I call father?
I have become an orphan.

As the titles indicate, the content of the lament varies according to the kinship relation between the singer and the deceased. Each of the laments begins by calling out to the deceased as though he or she could hear. Three of the laments then ask in bewilderment: "Who can satisfy those needs you satisfied?" The specific needs vary with the kinship relationship. A wife grieves, "To whom can I go for support, oh love?" A sister grieves, "Whom, whom shall I call, oh brother?/ Who will look after my welfare, oh brother?" A daughter grieves, "Who will bring clothes for me?/Whom shall I call father?" These laments thus call attention to the fundamentally relational nature of the loss, i.e., the loss of a dyad. The exception is the mother's lament for her child, in which the loss is clearly personal: "How can I go on without you, oh child?/I can't forget your face."

The laments serve to define the intense emotions of the bereaved or otherwise upset, and provide an acceptable means for the cathartic expression of their feelings. They also signal those nearby of the family's emotional condition. In form and performance, they contrast markedly with other women's song.

Notes

1 Arya recorded a version of this song in Surinam. See U. Arya, *Ritual Songs and Folksongs of the Hindus of Surinam* (Leiden: E. J. Brill, 1968), pp. 133-34.

2 *Ibid.*, p. 134.

3 Doranne Jacobson, "Songs of Social Distance," *Journal of South Asian Literature* 9 (1975):49.

4 Brenda Beck, *The Three Twins: The Telling of a South Indian Folk Epic* (Bloomington, Indiana: Indiana University Press, 1982), p. 45. Margaret Alexiou, *The Ritual Lament in Greek Tradition* (New York: Cambridge University Press, 1974). Fredrik Barth, *Nomads of South Persia* (Boston: Little, Brown and Company, 1961), pp. 143-144.

5 Jack M. Planalp, "Religious Life and Values in a North Indian Village," Ph.D. diss., Cornell University (Ann Arbor: University Microfilms, 1956), pp. 530-531.

V

Women's Song: Song Structure and Social Structure, Valuation and Change

Form and Classification

Most uneducated village women are inarticulate about the musical characteristics of their songs—the text is the important thing to them. Some of the songs are nonetheless musically interesting. There is a variety of scales and rhythms, and the occasional pretty or intricate melody. In comparison with the musical style of men's songs, certain features of the women's song style assume particular significance.

Women classify their songs according to use, as opposed to classifying them by text, melody, or rhythm (men do the same). This is most clearly seen in the gālī category, which includes songs that are not abusive but are called gālīs because they are sung along with the abusive ones (e.g., Song 1). In like manner, sohars concern various subjects and have various tunes, but are all sung at male births or on other momentous occasions. Saguns, likewise, have different texts and tunes, but are all sung in the same wedding contexts.

Like most music in India, the music of women's songs is monophonic or monodic—a single tonal line prevails. (This is as opposed to the polyphony and harmony common in Western music, where two or more tonal lines are performed simultaneously.) A majority of women's songs are divided into two melodic phrases or sections, which can be designated A and B. The range of the B part almost always differs from that of the A part, and is usually higher (e.g., Song 1 in Appendix B [B.1.]). This is the folk counterpart and perhaps the precursor of the *sthāyī* and *antarā* of Hindustani classical music.[1] In some cases, such as B.1., the scales of the A and B parts differ slightly. The A and B parts may be combined in various rondo forms (e.g., AABBCC or ABACAB). There is often involuntary variation in this matter. There are also some songs consisting only of repetitions of one melody (e.g., B.3.), and a few with three. A majority of song performances involve a responsorial section, with roughly half of the group echoing the final part or all of the line the other half of the group has just sung (e.g., B.5.). Quite often the responsorial line is not as elaborately ornamented as its precedent. Singers differ in the degree to which they embellish the melody: those who take a deep interest in music tend to incorporate more, and more diverse ornaments (example B.5.).

Most of the melodies encompass a fairly narrow range—a seventh or less. Conjunct movement (from one tone to an adjacent tone in the scale) predominates, giving the melodies a smooth quality, but jumps of a third or fourth are not unusual.

Melodic contour varies, but the most common shape is a gentle arc. This is seen in four of the five songs included here (B.2-5). In these examples the melody ascends by first a second and then a minor third to arrive at a fourth above the starting pitch, where it hovers before descending to the starting pitch.

Most songs have scales whose intervals are close to those of the Western diatonic scale, although they are, of course, not equal-tempered. Others are chromatic variations of the diatonic scales, such as B.1., which includes both natural and flatted seconds.

The songs are strophic, that is, two or more verses or lines are sung to the same melody or melodic phrase. Often the songs are quite repetitious. One song of ten brief lines of text may last as many minutes as a result of repetitions of individual lines and responsorial singing. The amount of repetition varies from session to session, and there is no doubt less repetition among accomplished singers. When I asked one educated singer about the repetitiousness, she said, "Music has its own effect." By this she meant that the singing itself, as a social and physical activity, and without consideration of the verbal content, is gratifying. Extreme repetitiousness undoubtedly has significant psychological effects, and invites comparison with *japa-yoga*, the repeated chanting of a word or phrase in order to approach union with the divine, and with the chant-like *harikīrtan* the men sing, which some men say is soothing and relaxing.

Song Structure and Social Structure

Older women tend to sing in a lower range; girls in a higher one—sometimes so high that they can't quite reach the high tones.

Wade found these same tendencies among women she recorded in a village near Delhi.[2] This is probably due both to older women's diminished range and to their additional experience in pitching the songs when beginning them, but it may also be due to a different timbral preference among the younger generation—one closer to the timbres of film song music. The songs older women sing, especially the ritual songs, tend also to be slower, and they are no doubt older than the recreational songs the younger women sing.

Women's songs move easily between castes. As mentioned above, women sing in neighborhood groups which may include members of different castes. Female laborers and women of client (parjuniā) families, such as the Kahā̃r women, sing for and hear songs sung by the women in their employer's or jajmān families.

The songs also travel easily between villages. A woman moves to her husband's village (usually at least ten miles away) when she marries, taking with her songs sung in her natal home, as well as, in some cases, songs she learned on visits to her mother's natal village.

The melodies of women's songs are, with some exceptions, distinct from those of men's songs. Some of the Dhobī women's melodies resembled those Dhobī men sang, and the same was true in the Kahā̃r caste.[3] But generally the melodies of women's songs differ from those of the men's. They are also distinctive rhythmically.

My recordings from Rajasthan, Uttar Pradesh and Bihar show in all three states the coexistence of regular and irregular meters among women's songs, but with irregular meter, sometimes called mixed meter or stretched meter, predominating. Other ethnomusicologists' transcriptions' of women's songs from diverse locales in the north show this same irregularity.[4] Occasionally one hears a group of women singing in which one woman provides percussive accompaniment with a drum called *ḍholak* (a double-headed, wood-bodied drum played with both hands). But even then the song meter is usually irregular, and does not correspond with that of the drumming.[5] The irregular rhythm of the women's songs contrasts with the largely regular rhythm of the men's participatory songs.

In some cases the irregular meter of a song appears to result from intentional change for expressive purposes or to accommodate an ill-fitting word or phrase. Or singers may unwittingly change the rhythm here and there, especially in the "odd" meters, such as 5/8 and 7/8, so that the meter is no longer maintained. (An example is B.1., where in the sixth measure one tone is elaborated at the expense of the meter.) But the meters of some songs, such as B.4-7, are too irregular to suggest that they evolved from regular meters. The rhythmic irregularity of the women's songs may also be the result of social factors. This is taken up in the following chapter.

The frequent melisma (where several tones are sung to one syllable of text), such as in B.5., suggests that the rhythm is influenced by melody as well as by words. That is, words are broken and extended in ways they wouldn't be in speech for the sake of providing a vocable for melodic development. In summary, the metric irregularity of women's songs apparently has no single cause.

The language of women's songs differs in several ways from the language of ordinary village speech. One of the most notable characterisitics is the addition of meaningless vowels and syllables which fit the words to the melody, e.g., the additon of *a* betwen *sab* and *nācan* in line 1 of B.1., the addition of *re* after *sukuvar* in B.3., and the addition of *ho* at the ends of all lines of Song 17. The addition of the potentially confusing *nā* as a meaningless syllable, e.g., in Song 28, line 4, is not uncommon (*Nā* in the spoken language is a negative marker). Vowels are also both lengthened and shortened.

A final troublesome phenomenon of the women's song language is the confusion of inflectional markers. In Song 47, for example, *āvelī* in line 1 is *āve* in line 2. This is a change made to meet metric and melodic requirements. In B.1. half of the women sang *koi* and half sang *ko* (after *sab a nācan*) through the entire song. This difference cannot be given the same explanation. (The transliterations reflect a standardization that does not occur; I relied on my helpers in the determination of the appropriate or consensual marker in each instance.)

The confusion of inflectional markers results in part from the mixture of dialects encompassed by the body of women's songs. A majority of the songs are in sub-dialects of Bhojpurī, but dialects from western areas are also represented. For example, the words of Song 10 are in khaṛī bolī Hindi (the Delhi-Meerut dialect).

The Valuation of Women's Song

Singing ability is recognized and brings prestige to a woman and her family.[6] When men return from a wedding women in their family will ask about the singing ability of the bridal family women. A woman's adjustment in her new home will be eased if she can sing and has some songs to share. Even men may comment that a woman has a good "throat" (*galā*). But if prestige attaches to good singing, it is surprising at first that so much of it is so dismally lacking in unison. The reasons for this provide some insight into the musical culture.

Better group singing may result from the presence of a woman who has had the advantage of musical training in private school education (this would generally mean women of upper castes), or it may result from the presence of one or more strongly musical individuals who transmit their songs, interests, and technique and who enforce, one way or another, their musical standards and preferences on the group. One middle-aged woman's musical dominance in one of the groups in Indrapur was quite apparent, and other observers have commented on especially musical women.[7] Finally, group singing is more strongly established as a tradition in some families than in others, perhaps in part as a result of the presence or former presence of strongly musical women.

If none of these conditions happens to have been realized, the absence of good singers does not prevent songs from being sung: the *doing* of song is in some cases imperative, and the ultimate quality of the music is of lower priority.

Participatory music, of which women's song is an example, generally has a more functional or instrumental significance than it does an esthetic significance. That is to say that people generally consider participatory music more as an imperative part and a means to the desired end of the occasion in which it is performed than they consider it as art. The singing of Happy Birthday in America is a good example. ("Art" is here used to mean "master craftsmanship extended to convey emotion.")[8] People do recognize and appreciate good singers. But performance and participation take precedence over concern with formal refinement and demonstration of skill in ritual and recreational situations.

The women's singing in wedding rites and other contexts provides considerable evidence to support the idea that the functional significance of their music has primacy over its esthetic significance. No group I observed excluded those who sang out of tune or rhythm, including fifth-singers (people who unknowingly sing a melody at an interval of a fifth from the normative melody). Women's wedding songs consistently compete with other noise and music, including the loud chanting and talking of the purohits and sometimes other groups of women singers. In a few weddings, where no women present could sing well, unison was lacking to such a degree that normative melody could not be discerned in the cacophonous screeching. In their prewedding song rituals women frequently ran songs together, that is, they began a new song without pausing at the end of the previous one. They also paused for awkward intervals to recall verses, and gossiped or joked when their moiety wasn't singing in antiphonal songs. Clearly the performance and the process of which it was part were more important than the musical product in all these cases. A comment made by Dr. Belwānt Rāī Bhaṭṭ, an outstanding classical singer and professor of music at Banaras Hindu University, further testifies as to the functional primacy of women's song. When I mentioned the offhand way in which village women's singing seems to be treated, he said, "Yes, they don't expect that anyone will listen to them—singing is enough."

Informants' statements also corroborate the functional primacy of participatory music. In interviews with villagers I noted two complementary ideas about the value of women's ritual song. One is that the songs, like all music in ritual situations, are maṅgal (Sanskrit *maṅgala*). The word has two primary senses. One is "happiness, welfare, bliss. . . ." The other is "anything auspicious or tending to a lucky issue (e.g., a good omen, a prayer, benediction. . . .)"[9] Women's songs are thought to augment the happiness and glory of the wedding and to insure its success and the success of the marriage. This concept was explained by a Brahman priest, and seemed to be held mostly by Brahman males.

The second idea, which emerged through conversations with women, is that music is required in a particular context or ritual, and has its value as a part of that activity. Enjoyment of the "beauty" of the songs was not an expressed reason for their performance. When I asked if they had any favorite type of music, many said only that they were all good. Two women did mention their preference for bhajans, which for them are songs mentioning Hindu deities. But one young woman who was more educated and articulate than the others said, when I asked if there were any songs which she found especially pretty:

> In its own place, every song is pretty. On its occasion, each is pretty. If a wedding song was sung now, it wouldn't be liked. When will it be considered beautiful? When there will be a wedding, then. So at every time, the [appropriate] song is felt to be beautiful. When it is its time, then it is felt to be good. And if the time is passed it doesn't have a good effect.

The Efficacy of Music

Arya argues in his study of Hindu folksong in Surinam that women's ritual music is auspicious because it contains the names of deities, and thereby utilizes the efficacy of the name.[10] "The efficacy of the name" refers to the idea in Hinduism that the name (of a deity) has the power to produce a desired effect, either because the uttered name invokes the assistance of the deity or because the utterance itself has magical power.[11] Arya further asserts that this auspiciousness, which is essentially a belief in the power of the music to influence the outcome of mundane affairs, effectively equates women's ritual songs with mantras, the magical words and formulas intoned by Hindu priests in their sacred ceremonies. But priests and other people in Indrapur explained the ritual importance of *all* music with the term maṅgal—

whether or not the music included the singing of a deity's name—so for them music's auspiciousness does not depend on the efficacy of the name.

My impression is that music in general is thought to be auspicious because it is believed to enhance the prospects of attaining the goals of the ritual by glorifying and pleasing the gods. In this way music is like other ritual acts that affect the senses—the burning of incense and ghī, the garlanding with flowers, etc.[12] Part of the underlying strategy of the sacrifice which is basic to every rite is to extend symbolically to the gods the kind of hospitality one would bestow upon a royal guest (*atithī*): each deity invoked in the pūjā is thus symbolically bathed, perfumed, garlanded, clothed and fed the purest and finest of foods and pān. In the same anthropomorphic mode, the gods are provided with the diversion of music. Music that lauds the gods is of course doubly effective in inducing their benevolence.

Women's song does parallel the priests' mantras in a few provocative ways. The strongest support for the idea that women's ritual song is a kind of mantra is the context of its use. Just as the priest accompanies each stage of his ritual with a mantra, the women accompany each of their rituals with a song. The dirge-like sound of some of the women's songs, especially the older, lower-pitched and slower ones, also vaguely resembles the chanting of the priests' mantras. But villagers did not express the idea that the women's songs were like mantras or even that they had power. (They only said they were auspicious.) Furthermore, while priests say that their mantras express the desired goal of the ritual act—that the god enter the designated vessel, sanction on action, receive an offering or whatever—only a few of the women's ritual songs specify desired goals (Songs 23, 31, 34, 52, 54, and the pitra nevatinā songs). And whereas the priests emphasize the importance of correct performance of mantras, women do not express such a dictum for their ritual songs, nor do the performances reflect it. The inclusion of women's song in important rituals suggests that it is felt to assist in the attainment of the ritual's goals, but support is lacking for the statement that all or even most women's ritual song functions like mantra.

Change in Women's Singing Traditions

Women's songs and the institutions of ceremonial singing are changing, especially in cities and more accessible villages. One area in which this is apparent is song transmission. For many years song booklets with the texts of commercially composed songs have been sold at fairs and in bazaars and railway stations. Increasingly these texts are set not to traditional tunes or modes, but to the melodies of film songs. The melodies of these songs are largely of tempered scale, and the rhythms more regular. The distinctive flavor of local music traditions with their irregular meters and scales are thus lost, as the mass media homogenize another culture. Song texts available in booklet form include sohars and wedding songs as well as a variety of other types. My impression is that the printed wedding songs are usually those of general relevance, like the saguns, but I did record one song associated specifically with the sindur dān rite which was set to a tune from the film *Nagin*. Young women themselves compose songs to the film songs they hear in theaters, on the radio, and broadcast at weddings over electronic amplification systems.

Electric amplification itself threatens the persistence of women's folk song and other orally transmitted music traditions. In Vārāṇasī and nearby villages (as in most North Indian cities and their hinterlands) it is fashionable and prestigious to hire disc jockeys for weddings and other festivities, who broadcast songs at ear-splitting volume with their auto-battery-powered turntables and amplifiers. This practice, in addition to aggravating neighbors, discourages or precludes the singing of wedding songs by the women of the family and neighborhood.

Tewari reports that in the cities of Uttar Pradesh, young people generally turn away from the traditional toward the modern. Girls have other distractions and outlets than ritual ceremonies and consequently do not learn the songs of their older female kin. Professional singers are hired, in some cases, to lead women's ceremonial singing.[13]

Countering the threat of mass media homogenization and eradication is a small but growing consciousness of the beauty and value of traditional folksong. Several annotated collections of Bhojpurī folk songs have certainly generated some awareness of the meaningfulness of folk song. Some women preserve and teach folk songs in girls' schools. There is now in Vārāṇasī a folklore institute (the Indian Folk-Culture Research Institute, headed by an eminent scholar of Bhojpurī folk culture, Dr. K. D. Upadhyaya) dedicated to the research and preservation of folk music in the region, and there are no doubt others like it in the state.

In Shahpura, a small city not far from Bhilvara in central Rajasthan, I recorded a group of educated men and women and their children who comprised a voluntary folksinging association, and there are no doubt some like it in Uttar Pradesh. Even though such groups perform traditional songs divorced from their traditional contexts, the songs are preserved and perform an important, if different function. They symbolize a past way of life, a common heritage or common roots, and by organizing their interaction and expressing their common cultural background, reinforce bonds between the singers.

The foregoing has been concerned with the music at the heart of the society, the music of the household. The perspective will now begin its outward progress and move into the realm of males.

Notes

1 "The composed piece in both instrumental and vocal music generally has two sections, *sthāyī* (*astāī*) and *antrā*. The former is the main part of the composition and is said to be usually limited to the lower and middle registers, while the antrā extends from the middle to the upper registers." Nazir A. Jairazbhoy, *The Rags of North Indian Music: Their Structure and Evolution* (Middletown, Connecticut: Wesleyan University Press, 1971), p. 30.

2 Bonnie Wade, "Songs of Traditional Wedding Ceremonies in North India," *1972 Yearbook of the International Folk Music Council* (Urbana: University of Illinois Press, 1972), pp. 57-65.

3 Indira Junghare informed me that men and women of the *Kolī* fisher caste in Maharashtra also sing the same melodies.

4 Bonnie Wade, "Songs of Wedding Ceremonies"; Laxmi G. Tewari, "Ceremonial Songs of the Kanyakubja Brahmans," Ph.D. diss., Wesleyan University (Ann Arbor: Xerox Microfilms, 1974), and Naomi Owens, "Mahapatra Wedding songs: A Preliminary Look at Context and Melodic Structure," mimeographed and undated.

5 Cf. Rosina Schlenker, *Lower Caste Religious Music from India* (an LP disc) (New York: Lyrichord Discs, n.d.), Side B, no. 2.

6 Cf. Susan S. Wadley, "Folk Literature in Karimpur," *Journal of South Asian Literature* 9 (1975): pp. 7-18.

7 Hari S. Upadhyaya, "The Joint Family Structure and Familial Relationship Patterns in the Bhojpurī Folksongs," Ph.D. diss., Indiana University (Ann Arbor: University Microfilms, 1967), p. 3, and Laxmi G. Tewari, Ceremonial Songs, p. 27.

8 John Greenway, *Ethnomusicology* (Minneapolis: Burgess Publishing Company, 1976), p. 28.

9 Monier Monier-Williams, *Sanskrit-English Dictionary* (London: Oxford Univesity Press, 1964), p. 772.

10 U. Arya, *Ritual Songs and Folksongs of the Hindus of Surinam* (Leiden: E. J. Brill, 1968), p. 13.

11 T. K. Venkateswaran, "Rādhā-Krishna Bhajanas of South India: A Phenomenological, Theological, and Philosophical Study," in Milton Singer, *Krishna: Myths, Rites and Attitudes* (Chicago: University of Chicago Press, 1968), pp. 168-69.

12 This was pointed out to me by Professor Charles Morrison.

13 Laxmi G. Tewari, "Ceremonial Songs of the Kanyakubja Brahmans," *Essays in Arts and Sciences* 6 (1977): p. 47.

VI

Men's Group Song

Introduction

Outsiders tend to think of Indian castes as somewhat isolated, rigidly stratified social groups. The anthropological literature has contributed much to this view. It has consistently emphasized the rigidly controlled and hierarchical interaction between members of differing castes, while commonly ignoring intercaste activities that feature equal interaction. This passage from a popular introductory anthropology text is typical.

> Castes are always higher and lower in a hierarchical order. Castes are rigid; a person is born into his caste and can rarely escape from it; he must (usually) marry within his (or her) caste, and the offspring will remain in it. Castes usually have traditionally prescribed occupations within the productive and service system of the society. Caste behavior toward members of other castes is rigidly prescribed . . . Although social intercourse between members of different castes may be highly circumscribed and severely limited, the intercaste relations form a functional social and economic network of interdependence in which even the lowliest and most economically deprived caste has its own autonomy and degree of interdependence.[1]

It is true that castes are ranked, largely endogamous groups, and that members of higher castes expect deference from lower castes and will not publicly accept certain kinds of food from them. It is also true that rural untouchable castes are segregated—their hamlets are separated from those of other castes—and contact with them is avoided.[2]

It was quite surprising to learn, however, that above the untouchable level, people of different castes mix freely in this area of

North India, and that much, if not most, interaction between members of quite differently ranked castes is no more marked by subordination and superordination than most day-to-day public interaction in the West. We have already seen this to be true in the case of women's song sessions, in which women of the neighborhood participate without regard to caste identity. Another important finding of my research was the existence throughout the Bhojpurī-speaking region of voluntary men's singing associations that include men from castes ranked all the way from śudra to Brahman. Such singing groups no doubt exist in the other regions of North India as well.

Equal ranking is not confined to group music making, but is found in many other cooperative activities in the village, such as sugar cane cultivation, seasonal rituals, roof-raising, canal building, private interdining, and day-to-day interaction and leisure conversation. The Gandhian democratic ideal, the tenets of devotional religion, and the establishment of contractual law all legitimate such institutions. These patterns of rank-free interaction contravene the principle of hierarchy (the tendency to rank) that Dumont and others believe to pervade Indian society and culture.[3] As useful as the notion of hierarchy may be in understanding Indian life, it must be qualified.

In Indrapur voluntary groups of men and boys sing two types of seasonal songs and a genre of ecstatic devotional music.[4] Like the women's songs, men's songs transmit much more ideology than has previously been recognized. Before discussing the men's songs and their particular contribution to the culture, however, attention will be given to the social significance of group singing in general. A comparison of men's and women's songs and their positions in the society concludes the chapter.

Music: Linking the Individual and Society

Group singing such as that discussed in this and the previous chapters has a social significance that transcends the particular meanings (ritual requirement, recreation, devotion or whatever) it has for Indian participants. Group singing and dancing are unique in the repertoire of human behavior in the way they join individuals in social relation through individual, psycho-physiological gratification. This is an individually and socially beneficial mode of behavior that, unfortunately, has lost ground to the forces of individualism and specialization in the recent evolution of civilizations. True, church congregations still sing together, and people do perform group music without special training in the West, but these are much less frequent activities and involve a smaller proportion of society in the West than they do in India.

Radcliffe-Brown, the British social anthropologist, had considerable insight into the individual music experience and the process by which group music performance links the individual with society. Except where otherwise indicated the following discussion of group music-making draws from his exposition in *The Andaman Islanders*, and incorporates a few of my own observations. Radcliffe-Brown uses the word 'dance' to denote dancing, singing, clapping, and stomping, "all parts of the one common action in which all join,"[5] but his insights are also applicable, with slight modification, to group singing without dance.

Singing gives pleasure to the individual in several ways: first, it is a form of play. Secondly, muscular activity of the variety required to sing, propelled by the pulse of rhythm, is transformed into a pleasureful exertion. It gives the performer a feeling of heightened energy, which is reinforced by the excitement produced by the movements and sounds of group, "and intensified, as all collective states of emotion are intensified, by reason of being collective. . . ."[6]

Now focusing on the relationship of individual to group, we first see that the group provides a platform for the individual to demonstrate his skill at singing, dancing, or whatever, invoking the admiration of others and a feeling of self-worth which stimulates in return a sense of good will toward his fellows.[7] Secondly, the phenomena of rhythm and the mutual coordination of voices are keys to the process of the individual-group relationship.

> . . . through the effect of rhythm the (song or) dance affords an experience of a constraint or force of a peculiar kind acting upon the individual and inducing in him when he yields himself to it a pleasure of self-surrender. The peculiarity of the force in question is that it seems to act upon the individual both from without (since it is the sight of his friends dancing and the sound of the singing and marking time that occasions it), and also from within (since the impulse to yield himself to the constraining rhythm comes from his own organism).[8]

This same rhythm allows all the members of the group to join in the same actions and perform them as one body.[9] The participant must direct his senses to the sounds and movements of the others to enable him to keep time to the music and to coordinate his voice with the others—he is in a condition "in which all bodily and mental activities are harmoniously directed to one end."[10] I would add that the experience of joining one's voice with others provides a unique and exciting sense of union, which is further increased by the enunciation of commonly felt sentiments in song. Radcliffe-Brown concludes that "Dancing (or music-making) is a means of uniting individuals into a harmonious whole and at the same time making them actually and intensely experience their relation to that unity of which they are members."[11]

Keeping in mind the social cohesion created through individual gratification in any group music performance, we can turn now to the special qualities of men's group song.

Men's Group Song and Vaiṣṇava Devotionalism

The three genres of men's groups song most commonly performed in Indrapur are all related through their connection with Vaiṣṇava devotional religion. The songs of harikīrtan, whose texts are quite brief and repetitious, enunciate the names of Krishna; Rām; Hanumān, the model devotee of Rām; and Viṣṇu (called Hari in the songs). The two other genres of men's songs are seasonal; they also include many about Rām and Krishna.

The popularity of songs about Rām and Krishna is a result of the *Vaiṣṇava bhakti* (devotional) religious movements that spread across northern India in the fourteenth to seventeenth centuries. Collectively, the cults centering on Rām and Krishna are called Vaiṣṇava because the two figures are both seen (at least by authors of authoritative religious texts, and by educated Hindus) as *avatārs* (descents of god into human or animal form) of the deity Viṣṇu. Most of the characters, images and events of the men's seasonal songs about Rām and Krishna can be found in the literature of the Vaiṣṇava movement.

The Krishna Literature

According to the chronology of the texts in which they appear, there are three distinguishable Krishnas, although a few of their attributes overlap.

> There is Krishna the chief of the Yadavas, who served as Arjuna's charioteer in the Bharata epic. There is Krishna the god incarnate, the instructor of Arjuna and through him all mankind, who appears, not in the old epic, but in that larger religious work, the Mahabharata, into which it was expanded. Then there is Krishna of Gokula, the god brought up among cowherds, the mischievous child, the endearing lover. . . .[12]

It is the third Krishna who is the subject of so many of the folksongs of this region—Krishna the mischievous child and endearing lover. The stories about this Krishna fill many different volumes, but one compendium stands out—the *Bhāgavata Purāṇa*. It was probably composed by a group of ascetic devotees in Tamil-speaking South India in the ninth century A.D.[13] Bhakti cults emerged later in Bengal and North India. It is not clear to what extent they diffused from the movements of the South, but the *Bhāgavata Purāṇa* is fundamental to all, and all share the spirit of impassioned personal devotion which characterizes the *Bhāgavata Purāṇa*.

In Bengal and North India, bhakti poets, drawing freely from the *Bhāgavata Purāṇa* but admixing other materials as well, produced devotional literature in both Sanskrit and the vernacular languages. There were many such poets, but in seeking correspondences with the songs sung in this part of India, two stand out.

The first is Jayadeva, a Bengali who wrote the Sanskrit love poem, *Gīta Govinda* (Song of the Cowherd), around 1150 A.D.[14] This poem "quickly achieved renown in northern and western India and from the early thirteenth century became a leading model for all poets who were enthralled by Krishna as God and lover."[15] Relative to the themes of rural songs, this poem is significant in a number of respects. The poem is the lyrical narration of the love of Krishna and one of gopīs, Rādhā (who was married to another, unnamed man). Introductory verses refer to their first tryst (which is very briefly depicted in the *Bhāgavata Purāṇa*, although the gopī is unnamed). The poem then dwells on their painful longing for each other in the subsequent period of separation, and concludes with their passionate reunion. Rādhā's longing for Krishna became the conceptual model for ecstatic devotion to Krishna; it is thought to symbolize the soul's intense longing for union with God. Rādhā's willingness to commit adultery was thought to express the ultimate priority which must be accorded to love for God.[16]

In emphasizing their separation with its attendant longing, the poem employs the *virahādukh* (pain of separation in love) motif which is found in earlier Sanskrit court poetry. The older Sanskrit poems also contain two other conventions used in the *Gīta Govinda*—the sexually arousing effects of the breeze, flower scents and other natural phenomena; and the darting glances of the woman which pierce the heart of her lover like arrows.

Natural beauty's enhancement of desire and the pain of separation are popular themes in village songs, some of which depict season by season their effects on a woman separated from her lover or husband. The combined theme is called *barahmāsa* (twelve months). (All these themes, both with and without references to Krishna, are found in Songs 64, 71, and 73, and Songs 1 and 4 from Sir, a village near Vārāṇasi.

The next phase in the development of Krishna motifs is the emergence of vernacular (as opposed to Sanskrit) bhakti poetry. Surdās, (c. 1478-1581) one of the most popular vernacular bhakti poets in northern India, was the most famous member of a school of literature called the *Astchaps* (eight seals).[17] The founder of this school, Vāllabhacārya, introduced Surdās to the tenth chapter of the *Bhāgavata Purāṇa*. Vāllabhacārya and his son each had four disciples (hence the name of the school). All resided near Mathurā, the mythical home of Krishna, and wrote in the language of that area, Braj bhāṣā. Although the work of Surdās was based on the *Bhāgavata Purāṇa*, he adapted, omitted and added material freely. According to Pandey and Zide, many of the themes of songs presented below are those Surdās admixed with the *Bhāgavata Purāṇa* material.[18]

To summarize, the depictions of Krishna in the songs below are those of Krishna the pranksterish child and Krishna the entrancing flautist and lover. Some of the themes are identical with those of Surdās' poetry. Others are shared with and may have derived from the *Gīta Govinda* and earlier Sanskrit court poetry. The Krishna motifs of rural song are never the philosophical abstractions used to rationalize his unique and somewhat randy traits by the scholars, nor is Krishna really glorified by song as is, for example, the mother goddess. He is instead merely the mischievous and sensual protagonist of narrative fragments. Krishna's character, and his place in the village pantheon contrast with those aspects of Rām, the other major Vaiṣṇava deity.

The Rām Motifs

The motifs regarding Rām also derive from Vaiṣṇava bhakti literature, but in this case there is one source to which most of the rural song motifs can be traced. This is the Rāmcaritmānas (Lake of the Deeds of Rām), composed by Tulsī Dās *circa* 1575-1600 A.D.[19] Although most people in this region identify it with the much earlier Sanskrit Rāmāyaṇa attributed to Vālmīki, it is not a translation of it and is similar to it only in the broad outline of the story. Many episodes not found in the Rāmāyaṇa have been added. Composed largely in Āvadhī, a dialect of eastern Hindi, or Kosali, it uses words from other dialects as well.

The story of Rām is an odyssey told by Tulsī Dās with much hyperbole. Here is a very brief summary of the story, including episodes depicted in the songs in this study:

> Rām (called Rāma in formal Hindi and Sanskrit contexts) was the elder son of Dasarath, a king of Oudh. (The modern Ayodhyā in East-central Uttar Pradesh is said to have been the site of the royal court.) In the court of Janak, a Bihari king, Rām competed in a bow-breaking contest for the hand of Sītā, the king's daughter. He won, they were married in the most glorious of ceremonies, and returned to Ayodhyā. In accordance with unwitting vows made by his father, Rām was passed over in the succession to the monarchy in favor of the son of a younger wife, and banished for fourteen years. Rām went into exile with Sītā and Lakṣman, his

> half brother, refusing to return at the death of his bereaved father. While dwelling in their forest abode Sītā was kidnapped by Rāvan, an evil god of Lanka (identified with the insular nation now called Sri Lanka). In searching for her, Rām and Lakṣman became allied with an army of monkeys and bears including Angad and Hanumān. When Lakṣman was struck by the poisoned arrow of one of Rāvan's henchmen, he was saved by Hanumān's bringing from the Himalayas an entire mountain containing the required antidotal herb. After Angad had failed to negotiate Sītā's release with Rāvan, Rām and his allies attacked and defeated them and rescued Sītā. Rām, Sītā, Lakṣman, and all the valiant monkey-chiefs then flew to Ayodhyā in an aerial car, where they received a glorious welcome and lived happily ever after.

The story emphasizes the ideal moral qualities of its characters: the power and courage of Rām; the faithfulness of Sītā; the honor of their fathers; the devotion and loyalty of Hanumān and Lakṣman. Lakṣman and especially Hanumān are upheld as the model devotees of Rām.

The Rām of the *Rāmcaritmānas* is merged in the minds of many villagers with *Bhagvān*, the omnipotent overseer of the mundane world—God. Men greet each other with *Jāya Rām*—(Hail to Rām), or *Rām Rām, bhāiyā*—(Rām Rām, brother).

In their anthropomorphic depictions Rām and Krishna constitute opposing ideal types. The character of Rām is moral and serious as opposed to the lusty, spirited and captivating Krishna. Most of the songs about Krishna describe his pranksterish activities as a child or his amorous activities as a youth. His amorous pastimes are quite contrary to Brahmanical morality, and his *līlā* (sport) the opposite of the martial Rājput ethos. Krishna is more worldly, and less an ethereal ideal than Rām.

The following paragraphs on the music of Holī and the monsoon season show how elements of Vaiṣṇava bhakti ideology discussed above have become entrenched in village culture and song—not only the in context of ecstatic devotion *per se*, but in recreation and widely-celebrated festivals as well.

Holī and its Music

In the cold season the temperature descends to near freezing at night, and there are occasional rain showers. The houses are unheated save by the sun.

> People generally go to bed earlier in the winter, often by nine o'clock. For Camars and other poor families, it is the only way to keep warm, since they cannot afford fuel for fire. Often a whole

> family sleeps together on two charpoys [cots] placed side by side, with a single quilt or blanket stretched over them. And many poor families go to bed hungry, for January is a month of food scarcity. . . .[20]

The festive period of Holī, about five weeks long, begins in late January or early February, just as the weather begins to warm. According to the Indian lunar calendar, the Holī season extends from a holiday called *Vasant Pancmī* (spring fifth) through the day called Holī. The climactic day of the season is also the first day of the lunar year. The now-verdant fields and warm weather inspire the exuberant celebration of this holiday, a true rite of spring. For many it is the most eagerly anticipated and enjoyed of the Hindu festivals.

Two of my informants' statements about Holī illuminate the local perception of it. One man said that Holī was originally a śudra (vārṇa) rite. The śudra vārṇa is the lowest level of castes in the classical (Vedic) hierarchy, and today the lowest level of "clean" castes. The association of Holī with śudra castes reflects a vārṇa stereotype: Holī has the spontaneity, absence of inhibition, and earthiness associated by many with the śudra level as opposed to, for example, the formality, asceticism, and piety that characterize the uppermost of the classical vārṇas.

The second idea, expressed by several young men with a word that has no English analog, was that Holī was a very *mast* time. The dictionary definitions of mast are: "intoxicated, drunk, proud, wanton, lustful, happy . . ." and "sexually excited."[21] I also heard mast used to refer to a class of rowdy, high-spirited children, and to men who tended to laugh and crack jokes. In the context of Holī, it seems to refer to a heady and sensual excitement resulting from social and sensory stimulation.

A third idea held by Hindus about the meaning of Holī is that it is a time of social cleansing and renewal. "It is believed that one should throw enmity, jealousy, and ill feelings into the fire of Holī and start afresh for the new year."[22]

These three clusters of meanings are easily seen in the descriptions of Holī rituals and music that follow.

Holikā Gārnā: The First Rite of Holī

In Indrapur people explain the first two rites connected with Holī, *Holikā gārnā* (the establishment of the Holikā pyre) and *Holikā dahan* (the burning of the Holī pyre), with reference to the widely known story of an evil king. One informant said he was a *rākṣas* (demon, monster). Prahalād spent all of his time worshipping Rām. Prahalād's father considered himself divine, and was angered that he was not receiving proper obeisance. He forbade Prahalād to worship Rām. When Prahalād persisted in his devotions, his father tried in various ways to have him killed. Finally he had his sister Holikā, whom fire could not harm, hold Prahalād in her lap while a pyre was built around her and ignited. But Rām intervened, Holikā was burned to death and Prahalād emerged unscathed.

I observed the rite of Holikā gārnā (gārnā means to pitch, to erect a pole or stick by planting it in a hole in the ground) in Indrapur on the evening of January 23, 1972. The rite was led by several of the younger men who regularly took an interest in music and recreation. It was an inter-caste association including Brahmans, Kalvārs, Lohārs, Dhobīs and Nāī.

The rite began at the veranda of one of the Brahman members, the location of many of the social activities connected with Holī. One of the men there had a ḍholak (the most common type of drum in this area), and several others had pairs of cymbals from three to five inches in diameter called *jhāl.*

After ten or fifteen men and boys had arrived the group proceeded towards the edge of the village, playing their instruments, singing and cheering as they went. Others heard the noise and rushed to join the group. The cheers, such as *jāya candra kī jai*! (Hail to Lord Rām), are regular features of the larger public religious celebrations. They sang the phaguās which are sung only at this time of the year.

When they arrived at the traditional site, the older men erected a tall branch and buried auspicious symbols at its base. This was to be the pyre of Holikā. Others packed cow dung fuel chips around the branch, and the entire crowd then circled the branch five times, singing phaguās and clapping in time. In returning to the starting point, the group stopped at the homes of two men with whom most members of the group were on friendly terms. There they shouted a special Holī cheer—*sā rā rā rā kabīr*. Informants were unable to explain this apparently obscene epithet. One man said it means "you are like Holikā," but this meaning seems too mild to provoke the laughter and cheering it evoked. The crowd then returned to sing phaguās at the veranda whence it started.

I observed the final stage of another Holikā gārnā rite of somewhat greater scale at a nearby bazaar town. There were garlands of flowers on the ceremonial branch, a fire sacrifice had been performed, a four-piece brass band played, and a female impersonator was dancing with typically sexual pelvic and hand gestures (see Chapter VIII). This indicates how such rites are amplified given the interest and economic means of the celebrants.

Phaguā Sessions

The phaguā sessions, occurring once or twice a week in Indrapur for the next five weeks, took place at the home of a Brahman man who loves music and owns a harmonium (a small hand-pumped organ) and several sets of cymbals.

The phaguā sessions were unscheduled and informal. A few of the regular participants would meet by chance during the day and decide whether they would like to sing that evening. After the singing began, more people would inevitably drop in to join the singing or listen and comment. There were usually ten to twenty people there after the session had begun.

Leadership of the singing rotated among the capable singers—a Kahār, Lohārs, Dhobīs, and Brahmans. All sat on the floor while some clanged a rhythmic accompaniment with their cymbals and others clapped in time.

The singing of *cahakā*, the most popular genre of phaguā, is antiphonal—first one half of the groups sings a line, then the other half repeats that line. The line is sometimes repeated two or more times by each side. A strong singer may introduce melodic variations which the repeaters attempt to duplicate. The songs begin slowly and singers sing and play their cymbals with moderation. Through the course of the song the tempo and volume of voice and percussion increase, and singers begin to cheer at the ends of the stanzas. Before the song ends the tempo is fast, the clashing of cymbals and loudly pounding ḍholak are deafening, and many singers rise to their knees to sing with maximum force. As they finish, singers give a great cheer and throw their arms into the air. In each song this pattern—from a restrained beginning to a frenzied climax—is repeated. The style of cahakā is much like that of the harikīrtan in its rhythm, some of its melodies, and particularly its use of the repeated climax. The exuberance of Indrapur phaguā sessions was matched by those I saw in villages around Vārāṇasī and in the adjacent Balliā district.

Rarely spanning more than an octave, the melodies of phaguās are commonly in an untempered diatonic scale. (See Photo 11.)

The Burning of the Holī Pyre

The burning of the Holī pyre took place on February 29, 1972, at the site mentioned above. After supper men and boys congregated near the ceremonial branch, which had become the center of a great pile of tinder. More fuel chips were thrown on, a Brahman performed a brief fire sacrifice, and Holikā's pyre was ignited. The ḍholak player then set the rhythm with his drum and everyone sang and circled the burning pyre, shouting, "Sā rā rā rā kabīr" and other epithets between songs. When the blazing fire began to recede, young boys ignited torches from it and ran towards the river south of the village. (See

Photo 9.) Many then assembled at the Brahman's veranda to sing phaguā.

Holī: The Culminating Day

On the morning of Holī people dress in their oldest, most ragged clothes to "play colors" (*raṅg khelnā*). It is a time when everyone is permitted to be aggressive in conventional modes. Using squeeze bottles and spray guns, children and younger men squirt each other with colored water (whose traces are visible on skin, hair, and clothing for several weeks). Some nefarious players would act in a disarming way until they were close to a friend, then grab him with a headlock and rub colored powder all over his face. There is a lot of hollering and chasing around. About noon everyone bathes and throws their dye-stained clothes away or sets them aside for later donation to wandering mendicants.

In the afternoon men began gathering at the Brahman's veranda. Each arriving guest approached each man present and with his thumb applied red powder (*abīr*) in a vertical line in the center of his forehead (and always with an upward motion). The other man would return the gesture, considered a blessing, and they would embrace, symbolizing the renewal of social bonds. Most of the men took bhāṅg, which had been prepared by the hosts. Some of this had been rolled into little balls for eating and some had mixed with water, milk, and crude cane sugar to make a drink called *ṭhanḍāī*. In the quantities consumed by most men the preparations are mildly intoxicating.

The Brahman host recited funny chants called *kabīr* and *jogīrā*. These are collations of crudely poetic lines, full of word play, often incoherent and sometimes obscene. Their names and their humorous whimsy suggest that they are in some way related to the *ultabāśī* songs of the Jogīs. (See the following chapter.) Perhaps they are satires of those songs, but informants could shed no light on this apparent connection or on the apparent inclusion of Kabīr's name in the sā rā rā rā kabīr epithet. (Kabīr was a reknowned medieval Hindi poet to whom many of the Jogīs' songs are attributed.)

For half an hour chants were interspersed with phaguās. I was again encouraged to shout insults at my older friends. Young men transformed an old man into a *launḍā* (a female-impersonating dancer, usually a young man) by painting his lips and wrapping a shawl around him to serve as a sari. With their launḍā in tow (looking somewhat like a dancing bear) the party began its clamorous rounds of the village, stopping at the verandas of more affluent families to perform chants and phaguās and enjoy ṭhanḍāī and other refreshments.

Below are some phaguās, a kabīr and a jogīra recorded in various Holī festivities. The first song relates an episode from the *Rāmcarit-*

mānas. Rājā Janak held a bow-breaking contest for the hand of his daughter, Sītā. It was won by the god Rām, one of "two boys" mentioned in line 8.*

61.

Listen, listen to the story of Janak, friends, listen to
  the story of Janak.
Rājā Janak made this promise.
He placed a bow at his door.
The sovereigns of many countries came.
The bow was neither moved nor removed, friend,
  listen to the story of Janak.
Bara Sur and Rāvan came.
They fled when half the night was gone, friend,
  listen to the story of Janak.
Two boys came with a holy man.
One grasped and broke the bow, friend,
  listen to the story of Janak.

The next two songs concern Krishna, the most popular phaguā topic. The first one is a dialogue from Krishna's first meeting with Rādhā, his favorite gopī (milkmaid). Nanda Lāl here means dear son of Nanda, who was Krishna's social father. *Gvāl* is the caste name of the cowherds.

62.

"Buy yogurt, Nanda Lāl, dear boy buy my yogurt."
"Where are you from, gopī?
What is your name?"
"I am a Gvāl gopī of Mathurā,
Rādhā is my name.
My mother-in-law made this yogurt
I came to sell today."
"When was the milk taken from the cow?
When did it thicken?
When did you add it to the lentils?"
"Dear boy, buy my yogurt.
The morning's milking, it was thickened that very
  evening.
Dear boy, buy my yogurt.

*This song may be heard on the LP disc, *Chant the Name of God*. See Henry, 1981.

It was added to the lentils in the evening.
Dear boy, buy my yogurt."
Rām Nāth Pānde sang this cahakā
Today Henarī sits with us. Dear boy, buy my yogurt.
Today he is a guest.
Today is the Holī festival. Dear boy, buy my yogurt.

Henarī, in the antepenultimate line, is the local pronunciation of my name. The song's acknowledgment of my presence shows the latitude for lyrical improvisation in these songs.

The next song, one of the less coherent ones, shows the close association of Krishna with the Holī festival, and introduces several other bits of Krishna lore: two of his common names (Hari and Mohan); his flute and captivating flute playing; and his home in Braj.

63.

Hari celebrates Holī in Braj.
Rādhā soothes her friends.
Group by group all the little ones come. Harī celebrates Holī in Braj.
Mohan, who took your flute and beads?
We will wear nose ornaments. Harī celebrates Holī in Braj.
Where did Mother Dasomat go? Harī celebrates Holī in Braj.
Turning his head this way and that, Krishna asks:
Where did they go, clever one?

"Clever one" refers to Rādhā. Her friends took pleasure in hearing about her affair with Krishna (line 2). The following song concerns a later stage in Krishna's affairs with the gopīs. After all of the gopīs had fallen in love with Krishna, he left them. This separation is combined here, as it is in much vernacular and Sanskrit poetry, with the virahādukh and barahmāsa themes. Banvārī, Āvadh Bihārī, and Man Mohan are all epithets of Krishna.

64.

Friend, what have we done to cause Banvārī to abandon us?
In the month of May the body becomes hot,
the sari is uncomfortable.

In the month of June the sorrow of separation increases,
and the sixth lunar mansion antagonizes,
The month of July is pleasant.
Ādvadh Bihārī went to swing under the branch of the
mango tree.
In August, the sky is heavy and the pain of separation is
great in the heart.
Krishna promised to come in September
but he became involved with my co-wife.
In October, Man Mohan plays joyfully.
The cuckoo begins to call from the mango branch.

Phaguās are not confined to mythological topics. "The piercing glances of his lover," an image in the next song, dates back to the *Gīta Govinda* and older Sanskrit poetry. Authors' or singers' names are commonly inserted near the end of songs, especially entertainment songs. Śiv Prasād is here the name of the ostensible composer.

65.

My sweetheart's eyes are a dagger.
Since then there has been no rest in my heart.
Darkness came and there arose a flame.
My sweetheart's eyes are a dagger.
Food and such means nothing to me.
Inside there has arisen a flame.
My sweetheart's eyes are a dagger.
Śiv Prasād is struck speechless.
As though he had been struck dead.
My sweetheart's eyes are a dagger.

The next two phaguās are topical songs. The first of these obviously dates to the British occupation, and shows that their treatment of the natives was not always noted for its fairness. Some older villagers still react with fear and suspicion to white-skinned people, who are automatically assumed to be some kind of "inspectors."

66.

For what offense has the police inspector arrested my
husband?
My husband is neither a very short nor a very thin man.
Intoxicated by bhāṅg, my husband went to sleep on the
street.

I will have to give five rupees to the officer, ten to the
inspector.
I will have to surrender my charms to the white man, ten
to the inspector.
I will have to kidnap my husband.

The last phaguā concerns cultural change. It was composed by Nangau, the patriarch of a musical clan of the Ahir caste in Sir. It describes changes which took place some years ago, when the young men began to abandon sandals for shoes, and dhotīs for *lungīs* (sarongs). Now instead of *biṛīs* (crude cigarettes made from a rolled leaf) they prefer cheap cigarettes, and in lieu of lungīs, western trousers. *Dhur māṭī* refers to the dirt which wrestlers rub on their bodies before a match. Wrestling is perhaps less popular in the cities than before, but still very popular in villages.

67.

All are captivated by the new fashions, brother, everyone
abandons the old ways.
Oh, they want boots on their feet.
They wear multicolored sarongs.
Heavy dhotīs are not considered attractive.
Bengali style hair cuts, everyone abandons the old ways.
The boys happily smoke biṛīs,
They apply fragrant oil and soap.
They chew great wads of betel leaf at work.
They have abandoned the dhur māṭī, everyone abandons
the old ways.
High prices have come.
Homemade ghī has become but a dream.
The stomach is filled with chutney and potato salad.
Hearts are ensnared in romantic love, brother, everyone
abandons the old ways.
Before, the young men advanced the name of Sir
Bacau felled the tiger.
Madhu earned a name in wrestling.
Nangau says: "Please explain it, brother, everyone
abandons the old ways."

It is at first surprising that a tiger was killed in or near Sir within Nangau's time, for there is very little forest remaining in the area, but a great deal of forest in India has fallen to the cultivator's axe in this century.

The final two items are rhythmically recited rather than sung. Clearly, rhyming word play and obscenity take precedence over coherence in the first type of verse, the jogirā. The second type of rhyme recited on these occasions, the kabīr, is an obscene insult, and the strategy of the one chosen for inclusion here is the same as that of many of the women's gālīs—degrading one's female kin.

68.

The instruments play in the grove. Who are the players?
Mother Earth has gone to sleep. Who will wake her?
Here people will mix and dance.
Let's go to the grove. I will serve you fruit.
When the fruit branch breaks, I will spread the spread.
If the corner of the spread tears, I will call the tailor.
If the tailor's needle breaks, I will make the horse run.
If the horse's leg breaks, I will apply turmeric.
If the turmeric leaves a yellow stain, the yellow color doesn't come out.
If the old man doesn't let go of the old woman, bugger the old man!

69.

Listen to my kabīr, Henarī, I say.
Henarī's sister's vagina expands until it is as big as the tank at Ujainī.
In one half Henarī kneads dough, in the other his father bathes.
Teeth grind the penis.
Ouch! The clitoris will cut, the vagina is lined with thorns.
The vagina pounds like the collar of the hoe blade.
Hai hai Holī! Your vagina climbs up the penis.

The Meaning of Holī

It should first be mentioned that all calendrical rites are institutionalized departures from monotonous daily routines—culturally authorized escapes from the ordinary. Holī is an especially vibrant one.

An overview of the five stages of the rites and their primary activities readily reveals the overlapping themes of Holī: uninhibited, even licentious spontaneity; sensual excitement; and social renewal:

1. Establishing the Holikā pyre: singing, cheering, abusive epithets.

2. Phaguā sessions: singing, cheering.
3. The burning of Holikā: singing, abusive epithets, fire and torches.
4. Playing colors: squirting and throwing dye, rubbing colored powders.
5. Finale: singing, obscene songs, abusive epithets, application of red powder, embracing, dancing, mild intoxication.

The music of Holī contributes to all three of the themes. First, the men's group singing of phaguā is intoxicating in and of itself. The pulse-quickening synchrony of voices, clashing cymbals, and crackling, booming drum, plus the repeated crescendo and accelerando of the songs, play an important part in establishing the noisy, fervid gaiety villagers call *mastī*.

Secondly, adding to the heavy spirit of the music are the frequently erotic or sexual lyrics. Listed below are the themes of nineteen other phaguās I recorded. Of these and the seven songs presented above, fifteen are concerned with some aspect of the heterosexual relationship, with eleven of these at least somewhat erotic (Song 64 above, and Songs 4, 6 and 7 from Indrapur, 1 and 4 from Sir, and 1-5 from Surinam).

Other phaguās from Indrapur:

1. Sītā and Rām provide for all.
2. (the name of any friendly visitor is put in the slot) is selling the services of his sister.
3. Krishna and the gopīs celebrate Holī.
4. My husband, who lives far away, is coming to see me.
5. My husband's younger brother will take the thorns from my fingers; my husband will drive away the pain.
6. I long for my husband.
7. Krishna is pushing Rādhā in the swing.
8. The wondrous features of Rādhā.
9. A woman says to her husband that she wants to sew.
10. The attributes of famous river-banks (e.g., that of the Ganges in Vārāṇasī is justice-dispensing).

From Sir:

1. The intoxicating season of Phāgun has come, my youth is waning, my husband lives far away.
2. Bacau killed the tiger that came into the village.
3. The wants of the modern rural wife—specific types of clothing, ornaments, and to be taken to the cinema.
4. The intoxicating season of Holī has come; Krishna plays with the alluring gopīs.

From Surinam:
1. Krishna teases a gopī and commits lawless behavior with her.
2. Beloved Krishna, do not leave me in this lovely spring season, my body aches for you (a gopī's request).
3. Why do you manhandle me, Krishna? You will not get what you want.
4. Where has my lover taken me? We passed the whole day in a strange hills and forests; we mixed with the rustics.
5. Where has my king (lover) gone? The signs of youth (breasts) are swollen. Remember me, master, only you can console me.[23]

Many of the sexual songs are those pertaining to Krishna. Six of the 21 songs collected in Indrapur and Sir are concerned with Krishna, as are three of the five phaguās from Surinam. The references to Krishna in these songs are to his cowherd aspect, in which he consorts with Rādhā and the gopīs. In a devotional context such as the Vaiṣṇava cults of Bengal and Madras the involvement of Krishna and Rādhā or Krishna and the other gopīs focus on the gopīs' adoration of Krishna, which is taken as a model the devotee's submissive worship of the deity.[24] Embedded in the context of Holī, however, the sentiments expressed in the songs are more secular than sacred, more sensual than devotional.

The sexual excitement is manifest in three other ways: The first is the intentionally enticing lauṇḍā, the female-impersonating dancer. His demeanor in the dance is that of a coquettish, provocative woman, sometimes describing a phallus with hand gestures, and coition with "bump and grind" pelvic movements. The second is the uninhibited chanting or shouting of normally prohibited expressions, many of them sexual. Everyone becomes more excited by enunciating or hearing these normally unutterable expressions.

The third pattern visible in the rites of Holī which must contribute to the exciting experience of the participants is the occurrence of vivid sensory symbols.[25] Bright objects, bright colors and sexual symbols obtrude in three of the five stages. In the burning of Holikā all of the activity is centered around a huge bonfire, with people partaking of its brightness and heat with their torches. In the playing of the colors, everyone ultimately wears rainbow combinations of bright colors—a vivid departure from the standard off-white garments. The squirting of dye from plastic squeeze bottles (some in the form of Krishna) and giant, phallic syringes is blatantly sexual. On the afternoon of the day of Holī, the wearing of the blood-red abīr powder on the forehead (which is thought to make the brain hot) is another occurrence of a bright-hot symbol.

This stage combines all of the intoxicating and sensually exciting elements—the use of normally prohibited language, sensory symbolism, group singing and female-impersonating dancing—under the amplifying effect of bhāṅg. Village men say that when one takes bhāṅg, "Everything one does, one does *khūb*" (very much). If my experience of this climactic rite is typical, one becomes merely a particle in a colorful, phantasmagoric swirl of music, cheering, and camaraderie.

The social renewal theme is most apparent in the mutual application of red powder on the forehead and the subsequent embrace. We can speculate that the playing of colors, with its licensed aggression, renews bonds by venting hostile feelings and providing shared experiences. Social renewal also results from men stepping out of their ordinary roles, some of which are ranked relative to one another, to interact on an equal basis in all of the Holī proceedings.

In conclusion, the culminating Holī rites constitute a break in routine social interaction and boring work regimens, a joyous time-out period exempt from certain norms and taboos. In the spirit of good fun people engage in harmless combat, sing obscene and erotic group songs, and reaffirm their mutual regard and good will. Phaguā, the music of Holī, is an important agent in the intoxicating mood which permeates the spring season and its ritual celebrations. Another genre of men's group song expresses the mood of a later season.

The Music of the Monsoon Season

Kajalī or kajarī is the name given to a song about the monsoon season or a song sung in the monsoon season about some related topic. The monsoon season begins in June and ends in October (the period of Āṣāṛh, Sāvan, and Bhādõ of the Indian lunar calendar). Temperatures decline somewhat from the hellish heights of the previous season. At first the rains are occasional, but later they increase in frequency and duration, and at the peak of the season (August-September), they may last for two or three days without much interruption. Travel is curtailed. Winds are moderate and humid, and the evenings, when it is not raining, are soft and sensuous. The often erotic and romantic kajalīs fit very well the mood of the thick monsoon nights.

Young people, in sexually segregated groups, like to swing and sing in the evenings. Suspending a bamboo harrow by rope at each end from a strong tree branch, several people sit or stand on it to swing. It moves in an arc parallel to itself, rather than perpendicular to it as it would in America. (See Photo 10.)

The same group of men who most often sang phaguā, sometimes with one or two older men, would gather at a well once every four or five days to sing kajalī. The well was a large, recently built circular concrete structure. Around its opening was an elevated surface about three feet high which provided seating space free of crawling insects. On Nāg Pancmī (snake fifth; July 27 in 1971) and on several other occasions when they were in the mood and the weather permitted, they gathered at the school playground or at some other open, flat space to sing kajalī as they peformed a simple dance called dhunmuniā.[26]

The dance was said to have evolved in Mirzapur District, seventy or eighty miles south of Indrapur, and spread throughout eastern Uttar Pradesh. (Mirzapur is also famous for its kajalīs, and many people say the genre originated there.) Informants gave several etymological explanations of the dance name. A musician from western Bihar said that the word derives from *dhunmun* (the uneven gait of a child). Two of the teachers in Indrapur said that the root *dhun* in *dhunmuniā* means "to search, to wander." This was not the case in available Hindi dictionaries, but there is a Hindi verb *dhurḥnā* which means "to search, investigate." They said that the dance was originally performed by young women, and symbolized their search for husbands.

Seen from above, the dance resembles the revolving of a spoked wheel. Each "spoke" is composed of two or three men. Side by side, each has one arm about the other's waist. The units of two or three trace the paths of spokes as they step and snap their fingers in time with music. Their postures somewhat stylized and knees bent, they glide around smoothly and gracefully. The music is antiphonal. When one or more couples are singing they stand in one place as the other couples move around to come up behind them. At the completion of the stanza the now-silent unit begins to move around the arc, and the couple(s) that had come up behind them initiate a new stanza. There was no instrumental accompaniment of the dances I observed.

The men's kajalīs all employ a duple metre and the same melodic mode. Each consists of from two to five melodic phrases of eight or sixteen beats (see Appendix B). With a flatted seventh and flatted third, and spanning only a fifth, the songs have a sinuous, minor feeling. The beginning tempo is moderate but, as in the other men's genres, tends to speed up over the course of the song.

The girls of the village also sing kajalī and dance dhumuniā, but their dance differs from the men's, as do the tunes of their songs. Their kajalīs treat the same topics, however.

The following five songs were all sung at the time of the dhunmuniā dancing by the men on Nāg Pancmī. The mood was gay, but less riotous than that of holī. The first song was the subject of several kajalīs I recorded and is a variant of Song 6. It relates an erotic incident from Krishna's wild adolescence (a story told in the *Bhāgavata Pur-*

āṇa).[27] The scene is also one of those depicted on the religious calendars used in devotions.

70.

The women of Braj stand and make a request.
Give me my sari, Krishna.
He took their clothes and climbed the almond tree.
We are naked in the water.
My companions are naked in the water.
I will give you your clothes,
When you leave the water.
All the girls beg together.
Keep our honor.
Companions, keep our honor.
Rādhā covered herself with a lotus leaf and came out.
Krishna clapped his hands.
Krishna clapped his hands.

The following song is a barahmāsa which portrays the anguish of a woman separated from her lover. Mention of every month of the year conveys the sense of prolonged waiting. The final lines resume the eroticism of the previous song.

71.

Woman, be patient for twelve months.
In June give up your lover, my lady.
In July mix with the girls of the village and sing with them.
Stay in the house all August; don't go to your father's house.
It won't be easy for you in September—don't cry.
In October send one letter c.o.d.
In November go to your father's with all your girlfriends.
In December I will send you a parrot to play with.
In January go to Allāhābād and bathe on *Makar Saṅkrāntī.*
In February you won't be able to play Holī and get colors on your sari.
In March I will worry and send a messenger.
In April I will come home and fulfill your desire.
In May we will meet, we will surely meet.

The months of the Indian lunar calendar named in this song do not correspond to the months of our calendar as precisely as the translation indicates.[28] *Makar Saṅkrāntī* is the Hindu celebration of the winter solstice. Bathing on that chilly day is a must and bathing at Allāhābād on the Ganges is particularly meritorious.

Separation is also basic to the following song, but here it results in pragmatic warnings rather than pained longings. Assam and Bengal do have occult reputations, so the final lines are not just deceits intended to keep her husband true.*

72.

Mind what I say: be careful on the way, dear,
  Bengal is a bad country.
You will go there and your face will turn black.
The water will get to your heart and it will become
  riddled, it will become riddled, dear.
Whoever eats too many coconuts and bananas becomes
  ill.
He eats them and becomes more ill.
They are always sold cheaply; there are bazaars in every
  direction.
They are always sold cheaply; there are cities in every
  direction.
The Bengali woman is a clever one.
Each casts spells.
They have long hair and thin waists, dear.
You won't be able to understand their zig-zag language.
She will cast her spell and turn you into a ram.
She will bring you under her control and keep you on her
  bed, dear.

In 1972 about twenty-five men from the village worked in Bengal and Assam. Although the number had no doubt increased in recent years, men from the village have worked in far-away places for as long as anyone could remember.

The next song again combines the barahmāsa and virah themes. It also expresses some of the popular concepts about the erotic effects of the monsoon season. People believe that sexual desire, particularly that of a woman, reaches its peak in the monsoon month of Sāvan (roughly, July), hence the "blossoming" of the gaunā and the desired consumation of the marriage. Savaliyā, Hari, and Śyām are all epithets of Krishna used here as metaphors for husband.

73.

Take this letter and go, Brahman.
July passes.
Take my letter, the clouds in the sky are thundering.
In July the gaunā blossomed, Savaliyā, the gaunā
  blossomed.
The way can't be seen in August.
The rain drops pitter-patter in the courtyard.
In September the heavenly moonlight shines daily.
In October the lamps burn, Savaliyā, the lamps burn.
November is not a bit pleasant.
All my friends go to their gaunās.
In December the cold hurts.
In January I am waiting in the courtyard.
In February with whom will I play colors?
Harī has gone to the Madhu forest.
In March the scent of the *palāś* tree in the forest blows,
Savaliyā, the scent of the palas blows.
In May beautiful Śyām does not come.
Twelve months have passed.

The burning of lamps in October alludes to the Dipāvalī festival, which celebrates Rām's victory over Rāvaṇa—the victory of good over evil. The Madhu forest is that in which Krishna slew the monster Madhu. The scent of the *palāś* tree (Latin *butea frondosa*) is thought to be an aphrodisiac.

The final song of this group, self-identified as a kajalī, shows the latitude of kajalī topics. It describes the charms of a woman of the Kahā̃r caste, whose traditional occupation includes filling the water jugs of the patron's homes. There were still Kahā̃r women so occupied in Indrapur in 1978, although wealthier families had installed hand-pumps in their courtyards so that water did not have to be brought from the well.

74.

The young bride fills the water jugs of the well-to-do.
The eye makeup of the fair lady is excruciatingly lovely.
Her eyes radiant as flower blossoms.

Wearing a blue petticoat; her waist thin.
The fair lady's colī like that of a Multānī woman.
Light green bangles on her waist.
A *dhakavā* print shawl covers the pretty woman.
A chain of gold on the fair woman's waist.
Anklets on her feet,
The woman walks on the path, casting her glance from
  side to side.
Chaube Master sings.
A brand new kajalī is prepared.
His home in Indrapur in District Ghāzipur,
The bride fills the water jugs of the well-to-do.

Multānī is a city in Afghanistan noted for its well-built women. The colī is the abbreviated, tight-fitting blouse worn under the sari. *Dhakavā* print saris were in vogue when the song was composed.

A Time for Lovers

"The rainy season is the time for lovers, the time when the earth is lush and green again, when the wind is filled with the scent of sandalwood. It is poignant, when lovers are apart . . ."[29] Just as suggested by this quotation, the villagers associate the mood of the rainy season with its natural phenomena, such as the aphrodisiac scent of the palāś tree, the thundering clouds, the pitter-patter of rain drops in the courtyard, and the heavenly moonlight of September.

The composer of the final kajalī above told me that the monsoon season was a very mast time, and therefore his favorite kind of song was the kajalī. When asked to explain, he referred to natural characteristics of the season, particularly to the call of the *koel* (cuckoo) and the movement of the dark clouds in the sky, both images found widely in Hindi and Sanskrit poetry and song, and both of which are thought to enhance desire. He liked kajalīs, in other words, because their texts were so appropriate to the season. (His aesthetic is like that of the woman mentioned above who said that song is good when it was sung at the right time.)

The texts of kajalīs reflect and reinforce the romantic and sensual mood of the season. There are a number of obviously erotic images in the songs above—Rādhā and the other gopīs standing naked before Krishna; the long-haired, thin-waisted Bengali women who entrance men and keep them on their beds, and the reunion of husband and wife after a year's separation. For the villagers, the natural phenomena described in the songs—the thundering clouds, patter of rain and so forth—are equally evocative.

Kajalīs share several themes with phaguās: Krishna in Braj is the general setting of Kajalī 70 and Phaguās 62 and 63, Indrapur 3 and 7, Sir 4, and Surinam 1, 2, and 3. The barahmāsa theme found in Kajalīs 71 and 73 is found in Phaguā 64 and Indrapur 6. Phaguā 64 combines the theme of the barahmāsa with the theme of the separation of the gopīs from Krishna.

Songs about the desire of a woman separated from her lover in which the lover is identified as Krishna are an important part of his devotional worship. The devotee of Krishna is often depicted as the wife separated from her husband or lover. But songs incorporating this theme are not confined to worship and doctrine; they are common in many genres of North Indian folk song.

The poetic theme of separation is for most men and women a vivid and emotive situation, and for many villagers, a familiar one. Many village men are employed elsewhere for the greater part of the year. They rarely take their wives with them, and thus spend only three weeks or a month with them in the course of a year. Husband and wife are also separated by the duolocal residence common in the first years of marriage. It is not uncommon for newly-wedded women to spend only about half of their time with their husbands during the first two or three years after their gaunās. Often the month of Sāvan in particular is spent at their father's homes. Several young men of the village whose wives were living in their natal homes confided a longing for their return.

Even though many phaguās and kajalīs concern major deities, the mood of their singing is hardly one of reverence. Like informally sung Christmas carols in the United States, they are somewhat sacred in text but secular in context. The remaining type of men's group music to be discussed is explicitly devotional in both.

The Music of Ecstatic Devotion

Harikīrtan is a popular kind of devotional music in this region, a part of many religious rites as well as an independent institution. Chant-like and extremely repetitious, it transforms the consciousness of its singers as well as satisfying social needs. From the perspective of the singers, it provides a means to approach union with the divine.

Harī most commonly refers to Viṣṇu or to either of two of his incarnations, Rām and Krishna. Kīrtan refers to devotional music sung in groups. Devotional singing was a part of the Vaiṣṇava bhakti movement which, under Caitanya, spread from Bengal throughout eastern North India. While kīrtan refers to any group devotional song, or to recitation accompanied by music, harikīrtan refers to antiphonal Vaiṣṇavite songs with short, simple stanzas continuously repeated, e.g., *Hari Krishna Hari Krishna, Krishna Krishna Hari Hari,* one of the most common, and *Jai Sīa Rām Jai Jai Sīa Rām*—(Hail Sītā-Rām, hail hail Sītā-Rām!) Harikīrtans are of indefinite length, and one may last anywhere from five to twenty minutes. Ḍholak, cymbals, hand-clapping, and often a harmonium accompany the singing. (See Photo 11.)

Men sing harikīrtan in several contexts. One is the regular, institutionalized performances of informal voluntary singing associations in villages, towns and cities. In the village the harikīrtan group consisted of men from different neighborhoods and castes ranging from śudra through Brahman level, plus visiting friends and relatives. The location of harikīrtan singing is often a temple, but can also be a shop, veranda or roof of someone's home, or any convenient and sufficiently large place. Harikīrtans are commonly sung on the *ghāt*s (bathing places along the river) in Vārāṇasī as well as in many shops and temples there. In Asī and other neighborhoods in Vārāṇasī harikīrtan and other devotional music is often electrically amplified for the entire neighborhood to enjoy.

Singer's study of the *bhajana* of Madras offers several insights into the significance of this kind of religious institution in the urban context. (The bhajana has several forms. Among them, the weekly form corresponds most closely with harikīrtan session.) Singer noted that the bhajana links domestic and temple cults, providing an easier path to salvation in an age when the paths of strict ritual observances, religious knowledge, and ascetic withdrawal have become difficult or inaccessible. They have the latent function of reducing the consciousness of caste, sect, and regional differences and the tensions generated by this consciousness. Singer also feels that bhajanas satisfy needs for sociability, intimacy, and affiliation in the impersonal urban context.[30]

In the contexts mentioned above, the harikīrtan is an autonomous institution. In other situations, such as the pūjās described below, harikīrtan is optional and ancillary to the ritual activities which it accompanies. In Indrapur devout families of some means had religious ceremonies performed by their Brahman priests to recognize and signal to the rest of the village some event important to the family. Harikīrtans accompanied some of these. The most common ceremony of this type is the kathā, which refers to the moral parables recited by a Brahman pundit as well as pūjā in which the story telling is contained. I was told by a Brahman pundit that the type of kathā performed in this area, the *Satyanārāyaṇavratakathā* (*Satya*—truth, *nārāyaṇa*—an epithet of Viṣṇu, *vrata*—vow, *kathā*—story) derives from the *Reva Khaṇḍ* portion of the *Skanda Purāṇa*. According to the pundit, the name Satyanārāyaṇa means "the Lord, who is truth," and the stories emphasize the importance of honesty.[31] The kathā is sometimes a *manavtī* (a vow to offer something to a deity or to worship it after the fulfillment of one's wishes), but informants said that the kathā can also be performed when a householder wants to express gratitude or devotion, or wishes to obtain a blessing. For example, one man of the Kānū caste had a kathā performed before he left the village to return to Bombay to run his shop there for another year; several Brahman families and one Lohār family had kathās performed when one of their members obtained bachelor's degrees. The kathā is thus seen to be a family rite of transition. Usually all members of the joint family, to whom the rites are of primary importance, are in attendance. Neighbors and biradari may also attend.

If the family performing this kathā wishes to stress the significance of the occasion, it may sponsor harikīrtan singing beginning the day before the kathā and running continuously, with changes in personnel, until the kathā is completed. Otherwise, the harikīrtan singing can begin any time on the day the kathā is performed, the sooner the better. The householder invites the singers in advance. They come with their instrument and sit in the *baiṭhak* (the men's lounging and sleeping quarters) or wherever the daily household ritual offerings are performed. They are remunerated with *prasād* (the food offered to deities in the course of a ritual and subsequently distributed to participants, family and friends) and other meals, to which family and friends are optionally invited.

Another context for harikīrtan is the *yagya* (Sanskrit *yajna*). The yagya is "a religious offering, an oblation."[32] As with kathā, in actual use the term is extended to include a cluster of ritual ceremonies and other activities of which the offering is the most important. At its core the yagya is a series of pūjās thought to benefit all the residents of a locality as well as the sponsor(s). Sponsors provide a feast or feasts and often arrange for harikīrtan singing.

Repeated Climax

Like the cahakā (the most popular kind of phaguā), the texts of harikīrtans are simple and repetitious, and the music is antiphonal and strophic, usually with only a few basic melodic lines of narrow range (a sixth or less). The primary meter is duple. A drummer provides the basic propulsion with a ḍholak, and singers keep time with small cymbals or handclapping. The songs proceed in cycles. Beginning at moderate tempo and intensity, the men sing the brief lines over and over, faster and louder, until a fever pitch is attained. The force with which singers hammer their cymbals together increases through the course of each cycle until at the climactic point the clangor may overshadow the singing, which is at shouting intensity. After each climax the cycle begins anew with its initial moderation.

Leadership of the group shifts among those who know the songs. Each leader seems to have one or more favorite melodic modes which serve as bases for variation. A creative leader can elaborate the singing to keep it interesting without detracting from the building climax. He can introduce variations in melody and phrasing, which the "choir" attempts to reproduce exactly, or he might sing the last half of the first stanza and the first half of the last stanza; the "choir" must then sing the last half of the last stanza and the first half of the first stanza. Thus there is scope for artistry in the harikīrtan, as there is in the kajalī and cahakā. But, as with the women's music, an aesthetically pleasing musical product is not the primary goal.

Control of the tempo and intensity of the singing is also shared by the ḍholak player, the master timekeeper. He and the lead singer and other singers signal each other by nods or shouts when they want to increase the tempo, or the ḍholak player may do so independently. The ḍholak player beats out not only the basic synchronizing pulses, but a complex, varying set of complementary accents—the skills of some ḍholak players are dazzling. Those who do not play instruments clap, and many wag their heads laterally in time with the beat.

Gāñja (marijuana) smoking is a regular element in the sessions of many harikīrtan groups. The *cilam* (stemless clay pipe) is passed from person to person, each smoker invoking Kālī or Śiva and touching the cilam to his forehead in reverant salute before inhaling. Like the ingestion of bhāṅg, the smoking of gāñja no doubt augments the intensity of the singing experience. Knit brows, bulging neck muscles, closed eyes, and heads and bodies weaving to and fro testify to the intensity of the experience. An informant in Indrapur told me that when one sings harikīrtan one forgets everything else.

Such ecstasy in the more secular context of Holī was called mastī—"intoxication." But in the context of devotional singing men explained the desired state of mind with reference to devotions to Bhagvān (God) and the peace of mind it provides. One man said, when I asked him how he felt when he sang harikīrtan:

> I put my faith in Bhagvān. I keep love. For this reason I have great liking for this, and from it I get great happiness. In it I pray to Bhagvān. I do his prayer, supplication, like, "Bhagvān, keep me in happiness." For this he will give a reward, I do his praise, his worship, I call him by his name so that he will protect me. He will drive my sorrows away. For this reason I like it very much.

When I asked what went on in his mind when he heard harikīrtan he said,

> In the mind a love is born. For Bhagvān, in the mind. And the love grows. From hearing harikīrtan a new light is born for Bhagvān

> in the heart. Just as I have lost my way and some man tells me, the way is not that way, it goes this way . . . So in my mind it is understood that I was wrong. So in this way, that which I am doing day long, week long, year long, some bad deed is being done by me, so I don't remember, but hearing harikīrtan, I remember my bad deeds, from praying to Bhagvān, I find the way. . . .

He added that after singing harikīrtan,

> A kind of peace is found in the soul that I have sung a harikīrtan, from this Bhagvān will certainly drive my pains away. For this reason there is fulfillment in the heart. Worries have gone away. The mind becomes light. . . .

In response to the same questions another man also mentioned the peaceful, worriless state of mind he attained. Another mentioned that the mind is totally occupied with Rām (God).

Babb has stated that the singing of devotional songs such as harikīrtan is thought of as a form of worship (pūjā), and an expression of devotion that imparts *punya* (merit) to the participants, which may lead to good fortune in this life or better fortune in the next.[33]

Another way in which harikīrtan has meaning to the villager is as maṅgal (auspiciousness). It will be recalled that all music is thought to lend auspiciousness to the events it accompanies. The auspiciousness of music is enhanced when the text includes the names of deities: according to Venkateswaran, even hearing the Name is considered beneficial.[34] This would account for the tolerance with which endless electrically amplified harikīrtans are received by non-participants.

There is also an apparent connection between the repetitious singing of harikīrtan and the continuous repetition of spoken phrases to attain salvation (japa-yoga). While both practices are considered means of attaining salvation, concepts vary (even among one group of devotees) as to how this is accomplished. Some think that it is through the glorification of God and invocation of his grace, others think that it is through the assimilation of the god or state of sanctity.[35] Whatever the ideology, chanting or singing results in a changed state of consciousness which practitioners value.

Conclusion and Comparison of Men's and Women's Song

Like the women's groups songs, the men's provide participants with the simultaneous experiences of play, personal power, and union with a group whose membership cross-cuts caste lines. Both also transmit much ideology—people learn much of their culture through these participatory songs as well as through the songs of specialists such as those presented in the following chapters. They learn such disparate things as patriotism, role expectations, procedures for religious rituals, and a great deal of Hindu mythology.

Although men's and women's songs and group singing have much in common, sex role differences are quite visible in music and music-making. They can be seen in five areas. First, women sing more frequently than men do; singing is a more obtrusive part of women's role. Secondly, women sing about Rām, Krishna, and other figures, but they also sing about an array of topics that men don't: birth, kin roles and relations, the scurrilous traits of their in-laws (in jest), the benefits of austerities, and the mother goddess. These are clearly topics of greater immediate importance to women. They must bear sons, they endure more relational difficulties, and they are charged with gaining the goddess' and other deities' aid in maintaining the domestic welfare.

The third difference is in musical style. Men's singing is most always strongly rhythmic. In sharp contrast, the irregular meters of a majority of women's songs are not conducive to foot-tapping or hand-clapping—even with drum accompaniment. This surprising difference in the style of men's and women's participatory song is suggested in a presumably ancient Sanskrit couplet: *śruti mārtā layah pitā*—roughly: melody is the mother, rhythm the father.[36] None of the women's sessions ever reached the frenzied heights of the men's harikīrtan and cahakā.

Why does women's song style differ from men's? Perhaps women's songs simply descend from different times and places than do men's. But the general absence of strong rhythmic drive from women's music is in keeping with the restraint which pervades women's role in married life—at least in the upper castes. As her life proceeds a woman is economically dependent of her father, her husband, and her sons. She cannot risk behavior that would upset or alienate them. Furthermore, until she is older, a woman is expected to quietly subjugate her individual wishes to those of her in-laws. Music as noisy and boisterous as the men's would attract attention unseemly for a woman; it would be inappropriate to the woman's role.

I did witness some driving and rowdy singing by Camār women. This is consonant with a general difference between the public presence and conduct of untouchable caste women and those of higher castes: they are more often present publically because they are more often employed outside the home and less restricted by purdah, and they are sometimes more jolly in their public groups than other women.

Differences in the contexts of men's and women's singing also reflect sexual segregation. Men sing in open, public places. Women also sing in public, but they sing more often in the protective confines of the courtyard, where they spend most of their married lives. That women sing more often in the courtyard, and men and women never sing together reflects purdah and the segregation of the sexes. Whenever women do appear in groups in public, they sing. Song thus seems to license their appearance, as well as to constitute a medium for their public statements.

Finally, men's singing is generally an end in itself: it is the focus of their musical gatherings. A substantial part of women's singing, on the other hand, is perceived as an important ingredient of a larger ritual, usually one whose object is the health and prosperity of the family. In summary, music expresses the contrast in sex roles in the village in five ways: frequency of singing, song topics, song style, social context of performance, and overt function.

Phaguās, kajalīs and harikīrtans, like the women's group songs, are fairly simple songs. In that the songs belong to and are sung by everyone with a modicum of musical ability, they are truly folk songs, and distinct from the songs of the following chapters. Moving outward once more, the next chapter will view genres not found in every home or lane, those which for one reason or another are not easy to learn, and belong only to a relatively few specialists who live in or circulate through the village.

Notes

1 E. Adamson Hoebel, *Anthropology: The Study of Man* (New York: McGraw-Hill Book Company, 1972), p. 491.

2 R. A. Schermerhorn, *Ethnic Plurality in India* (Tucson: University of Arizona Press, 1978), p. 33.

3 Louis Dumont, *Homo Hierarchicus* (Chicago: University of Chicago Press, 1970).

4 On my trip to Indrapur in 1978 I attended a session in which men were singing songs they called only *bhajans* (devotional songs). The songs were varied in tune and text, more developed than the harikīrtan in both respects, and different from both of the seasonal genres. Most concerned Rām or Krishna.

5 Alfred R. Radcliffe-Brown, *The Andaman Islanders* (New York: The Macmillan Company, 1964), pp. 246-52, 326.

6 Ibid., p. 250.

7 Ibid., p. 251.

8 Ibid., p. 249.

9 Ibid., p. 247.

10 Ibid., p. 248.

11 Ibid., p. 253.

12 Daniel H. H. Ingalls, "Foreward," in Milton Singer (ed.), *Krishna, Myths, Rites, and Attitudes* (Chicago: University of Chicago Press, 1968), pp. v-vi.

13 Thomas J. Hopkins, "The Social Teaching of the Bhāgavata Purāṇa," in Milton Singer (ed.), *Krishna: Myths, Rites, and Attitudes* (Chicago: University of Chicago Press, 1968), pp. 5-6.

14 George Keyt, *Jayadeva's Gīta Govinda: The Loves of Krishna and Rādhā* (Bombay: Kutub-Popular Pvt. Ltd.), p. 9.

15 William G. Archer, *The Loves of Krishna in Indian Painting and Poetry* (New York: Grove Press, 1958), p. 84.
16 Ibid., p. 75.
17 S. M. Pandey and Norman Zide, "Surdas and his Krishna-bhakti," in Milton Singer (ed.), *Krishna: Myths, Rites, and Attitudes* (Chicago: University of Chicago Press, 1968), p. 174.
18 These include his poems on the child Krishna (Songs 6, 62, 63, and 70); descriptions of Rādhā (one of the themes of other phaguās mentioned on p. 00); the hypnotic effect of his flute on Rādhā and other gopīs (Song 79); and the bee songs (*bhramargīts*), which concerns Uddhava's futile mission to Gokula to console the gopīs with a monotheistic philosophy after Krishna had departed. (This was a theme of a few fragmentary songs which I recorded but have not included here.)
19 Frank Keay, *A History of Hindi Literature* (Calcutta: Y.M.C.A. Publishing House, 1960), p. 50.
20 Jack Planalp, "Religious Life and Values in a North Indian Village," Ph.D. diss., Cornell University (Ann Arbor: University Microfilms, 1956), p. 358.
21 R. C. Pathak, *Bhargava's Standard Illustrated Dictionary of the Hindi Language* (Hindi-English Edition) (Vārāṇasī: Bhargava Book Depot, 1969), p. 859, and Mahendra Chaturvedi and Dr. Bhola Nath Tiwari, *A Practical Hindi-English Dictionary* (Delhi: National Publishing House, 1975), p. 584.
22 Laxmi G. Tewari, "Folk Music of India: Uttar Pradesh," Ph.D. diss., Wesleyan University. (Ann Arbor: University Microfilms, 1974), p. 96.
23 U. Arya, *Ritual Songs and Folksongs of the Hindus of Surinam* (Leiden: E. J. Brill, 1968).
24 Edward C. Dimock, "Doctrine and Practice among the Vaiṣṇavas of Bengal," in Milton Singer, (ed.), *Krishna: Myths, Rites, and Attitudes* (Chicago: University of Chicago Press, 1969).
25 Victor Turner holds that a symbol has both ideological and sensory meanings. The former is an arrangement of norms and values that guide and control persons as members of social groups and categories. The sensory meanings are "closely related to the outward form of the symbol" and are usually "natural and physiological phenomena and processes." See Victor Turner, *A Forest of Symbols* (Ithaca: Cornell University Press,1967) pp. 27-30.
26 Nāg Pancmī is a day on which women make offerings to a snake deity to placate the snakes, which are driven to higher ground by the heavy rains and thus become a problem.
27 Archer, *The Loves of Krishna*, p. 37.
28 See Ruth and Stanley Freed, "Calendars, Ceremonies and Festivals in a North Indian Village," *Southwestern Journal of Anthropology* 20: (1964): 67-90 for a thorough discussion of Indian calendars.
29 Edward C. Dimock and Denise Levertov, *In Praise of Krishna: Songs from the Bengali* (Garden City, New York: Doubleday & Company, Inc.), p. 18.
30 Milton Singer, "The Rādhā-Krishna Bhajanas of Madras City," in Milton Singer (ed.), *Krishna: Myths, Rites, and Attitudes* (Chicago: University of Chicago Press, 1968), pp. 121-23.
31 D. N. Majumdar, *Caste and Communication in an Indian Village* (New Delhi: Asia Publishing House, 1958), pp. 291-92.
32 R. C. Pathak,*Bhargava's Standard Dictionary*, p. 909.
33 Lawrence A. Babb, *The Divine Hierarchy: Popular Hinduism in Central India* (New York: Columbia University Press, 1975), p. 39.
34 T. K. Venkateswaran, "Rādhā-Krishna Bhajanas of South India: A Phenomenological, Theological, and Philosophical Study," in Milton Singer (ed.), *Krishna: Myths, Rites, and Attitudes* (Chicago: University of Chicago Press, 1968), p. 168.

35 Ibid., p. 169, and Mircea Eliade, *Yoga: Immortality and Freedom* (Princeton: Princeton University Press, 1969), p. 216.

36 David Reck, "India/South India," in *Worlds of Music*, ed. Jeff Todd Titon. (New York: Schirmer Books, 1984), p. 252.

*This song may be heard on the LP disc, *Chant the Names of God*. See Henry, 1981.

PHOTO 1: A launḍā and colleague sing and dance at a Camār celebration marking a new-born girl's ninth day.

PHOTO 2: A typical women's song session. The ḍholak is optional.

PHOTO 3: A village woman dances to brass band music.

PHOTO 4: A groom departs for the bride's village in a palanquin.

PHOTO 5: The bridal attendant, bride and groom in the vivāh.

PHOTO 6: Pāvariās singing a sohar.

PHOTO 7: Women singing a mother goddess song at her worship ceremony in the grove.

PHOTO 8: Women singing a milling song as they grind flour on a cakkī (quern).

PHOTO 9: Young men with their torches at Holikā Dahan, the burning of Holikā.

PHOTO 10: Young men singing kajalī as they swing in the monsoon season.

PHOTO 11: Men singing harikīrtan on a temple veranda at a yagya. Visible are the cymbals (jhāl) and drum (ḍholak).

PHOTO 12: Kharī birahā singer Rām Candra Yādav. The Ahirs often cover one or both ears when singing. They say it improves their hearing of the vocal line.

PHOTO 13: Ālhā singer Hanīph Nat with ḍholak.

PHOTO 14: Jogī Jān Mohāmmad at an impromptu recording session in Khalīsā.

PHOTO 15: A jogī calling himself Kabīr Dās, in typical working garb playing a sāraṅgī.

PHOTO 16: Kāśī Nāth Gosā̃ī, a mendicant singer of nirgun bhajans, playing a one-stringed drone instrument called *ektāra,* and wooden castanets.

PHOTO 17: A female entertainer teasingly sings to a man in her audience on the second day of a wedding.

PHOTO 18: A birahā group. The man standing is playing kartāl. One of the seated musicians is playing ḍholak.

PHOTO 19: The qawwālī band at the Nizāmuddin Auliā shrine in Delhi (1978). The leader, playing the harmonium on the left, is Gulām Hussein Khān.

PHOTO 20: The Cānd Putalī qawwālī band of Vārāṇasī.

PHOTO 21: Murat Lāl Bhāratī, the lead singer of this qawwālī group, sits behind the harmonium (to our right). This is a typical bārāt entertainment setting in Indrapur.

PHOTO 22: A Camār daphalī group with daphalā (large frame drum), nagāṛā (kettle drum), and kasāvar (gong) plays dance music for the lauṇḍā (foreground), while women in the procession the musicians have led sing an unrelated song. Males with trays are bringing food for the "ninth day" celebration.

PHOTO 23: Mhmd. Iśahaq and party of Sādāt, Ghāzipur District.

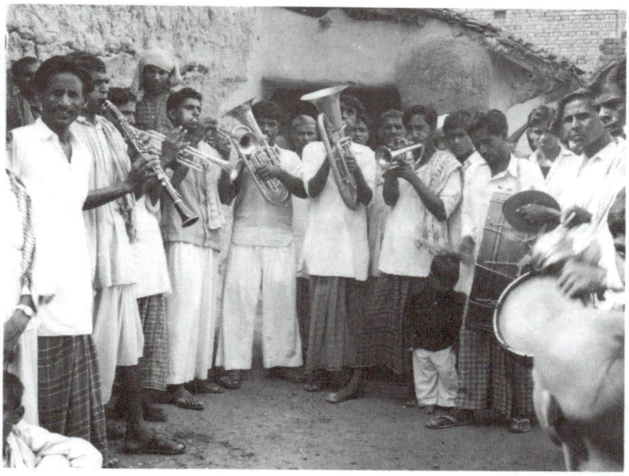

PHOTO 24: English (brass) band, in uniform, with lauṇḍā. Notice the Scottish bass drum, the center drum in this picture.

PHOTO 25: Ustād Rosan Āhmad.

PHOTO 26:
A śahnāī band provides dance music for Camār women on the outskirts of Vārāṇasī. They are celebrating the twentieth day of a new-born girl.

PHOTO 27: The śahnāī band. Note ḍuggī and khurḍak drums, thoughtful listeners.

VII

Unpaid Specialists and Mendicants

Introduction

The non-participatory songs and music presented in this and following chapters differ from the participatory songs of the previous chapters in several important ways. Participatory songs join untrained individuals in mutual monitoring and self-adjustment aimed at sonic unity; their forms tend to be simple. In non-participatory music the social situation is not one of unity, but of the dichotomy of performer and audience. In order to entertain, the non-participatory songs must also be more interesting—textually, musically, or extra-musically—more developed and complex, than the participatory songs everyone knows and can sing.

Another difference between the two broad divisions is that the performers of participatory music are of no special type. Non-participatory songs tend to be performed only by persons of certain social categories. For example, only men of Ahir (cowherding) and *Gaṛer* (sheep herding) castes perform the field holler called khaṛī birahā.

Except for the relatively infrequent performances of the *Natin,* a female tatooist, and the singing of the female entertainer, all non-participatory music is performed by males. This reflects the dominant role males play in public life in the village.

The categories of music in the taxonomy below are listed in order of the cost involved in a performance. The first two categories are non-remunerative; the mendicants receive small donations of grain, old clothing, etc.; and the entertainers are paid in cash. These categories are discussed in the following order below.

A. Unpaid specialists
   1. Khaṛī birahā: the herders' field call
   2. Khisā: the story-song
B. Music of mendicants
   1. Ālhā: a martial epic
   2. Blind mendicants
   3. Songs of the jogīs
C. Entertainment and Processional Music
   1. The informal performance
   2. *Birahā*
   3. *Purvī*
   4. *Qawwālī*
   5. Processional Music

Khaṛī Birahā: The Herder's Field Call

The khaṛī birahā is a brief, highly ornamented and very forceful field call cow and sheep herders perform while tending their herds or relaxing with their caste brothers and friends. When, from a distance of a quarter mile, I first heard an Ahir sing a khaṛī birahā I thought, "That man has an incredible voice; it's unfortunate he has no sense of pitch." Some weeks later his guru (who was also his uncle) came to visit. (See Photo 12.) Lo and behold, his song was out of tune in precisely the same way as his nephew's. This was not two singers who lacked pitch sense, but a genre whose scale and other traits differed radically from others in the region. The performances of two other men, one of the Gaṛer caste and the other an Ahir from Vārāṇasī, confirmed that the khaṛī birahā was a widespread and unique genre.

Although residents of Indrapur consider it singing, the khaṛī birahā is more precisely designated a field call or holler. This has been defined as ". . . a vocal performance intended to project information or emotions over long distances."[1] It is reminiscent of the call of the *muezzin* (the crier who, from a minaret or other part of the mosque, calls Muslims to prayer). However, it is even more strenuous—in the quiet evening hours it can be heard for several miles across the open countryside. In this part of rural India a man still hollers to signal someone far away; the khaṛī birahā is apparently an embellished descendant of the signal holler. In the words of one of the great ethnomusicolgists, A. H. Fox-Strangways, "A man sings because it is a splendid thing to do, and because he cannot help it."[2] But in addition to the diversion and gratification it offers singer and listeners, the khaṛī birahā no doubt maintains a feeling of community between separated herders or the herder and people in the homestead or village. It is thus peculiarly suitable for herders to perform. Most of the men who do so, belong to two herding castes, the cowherding Ahirs (also called *Yādavs* and *Gvāls*) and the goat and sheepherding Gaṛers. Perhaps because Ahirs far outnumber Gaṛers, khaṛī birahā is more often thought of as Ahir music.

The resident khaṛī birahā singer of Indrapur said that just after sundown and just before sunrise were the best times to sing khaṛī birahā. Every once in a while, apparently when the mood struck him, he would send a few of his birahās floating out over the village just after dusk. He also performed at night if caste brothers were visiting, and occasionally when he returned with the herds in the evening. In most cases his hollers were heard by all residents of the southern part of the village. As brought out below, it may be significant that this is a neighborhood in which the Brahmans predominate.

The variety of embellishment packed into the khaṛī birahā's brief verses is remarkable. The uncle/guru starts the first several lines with an upward swoop to the tonic, singing each line in near monotony, and ending with a downward swoop. But in the climactic ending lines, his voice slides up to the seventh (or in some cases, the sixth) and after one or two instantaneous upward flares, makes its way down in (roughly) semitonic intervals, flattens out, constricts slightly and then makes glottal vibrations for several seconds, glides down another interval, levels off again, but this time with a markedly raspier tone quality, and ends with a final descending portamento. (A good performance can be heard on the lp disc *Chant the Names of God*, Henry 1981.) When he sings in the company of a kinsmen, they often chime in on the portamento (glide), which, coming at the end of a line, is usually a predictable verb. Subsequent lines are built of structural elements contained in the climactic line, repeating the descending motion. The scale is not a tempered one and is distinct from the diatonic scale.[3] The vocal ornamentations used, the heavy vibrato, the change of vocal tone quality, and the passion of the singing are arresting even to one who does not understand the words. The texts are distinguished chiefly by their condensation and imagery; most of the themes are shared with other song genres. The songs presented below were all recorded in Indrapur from the uncle and nephew mentioned above.

In *nirgun bhajans* (discussed later) the parrot and other birds are metaphors for the soul. But in the first song below, parrot stands for a person who accepted the composer's love and then spurned him.

75.

I say, brother, I came to know that parrot, I fed it milk;
  the parrot turns on me.

Oh, brother, had I known the parrot would turn on me I
  would have hurt the wee bird's wing.
Oh, I would have torn the little bird's wing.

The next one is an imaginative expansion of an early episode in the Rāmāyaṇa. When Rām was exiled from Ayodhyā, his father's kingdom, he and his wife Sītā and his half-brother Lakṣman went to live the life of a *sādhū* (religious ascetic) in the forest. The composer imagines them wearing the sādhū's costume, which includes a necklace made of basil (*tulsī*), thought to have magical protective powers. Elaborating further on the ascetic image, he depicts them begging in the cities as sādhūs do today. These images are not in F. S. Growse's translation of the *Rāmcaritmānas*.

76.

Oh I say Rām, brother, Rām has become a yogi;
  Lakṣman, an ascetic.
Both brothers have become fakirs.
Oh, in this very lane they wear their necklaces of basil
  beads.
They wander in the cities begging alms.

While dwelling in their forest abode Sītā is abducted by Rāvaṇa, the evil god-king of Lanka (Śrī Lanka). In the war to regain her, Rāvaṇa's aide shoots Lakṣman with a poison arrow.

77.

Oh, Brother Lakṣman has been hit by the poison arrow.
Rām takes him in his lap and cries.
"In the dawn Lakṣman will die.
Then who will return with me to Ayodhyā
Who will return with me to Ayodhyā?"

The following two songs deal with Krishna, who is probably mentioned in more songs in this region than any other deity. The first one tells how Rādhā was so entranced by Krishna's flute playing she could not even pick the ripe plums.

78.

In the forest of Brindāban there were ripe plums.
Rādhā bowed the branch, but she couldn't pluck one:
Krishna was playing his flute.

Several songs collected in Indrapur refer to the marriage of Krishna with Kubarī after he had left Gokulā, the home of Rādhā and the other gopīs. In the *Bhāgavata Purāṇa*, Kubarī is called Kubjā. She was a misshapened girl whom Krishna miraculously restored to beauty. Although Krishna initially accepted her insistently-offered love, he left her, according to the scriptures, because of her low and worldly attitude toward him.[4]

79.

The women of Gokulā lament: Kubariyā, your fate is rich.
All have gotten cripples and paralytics.
And Kubarī got Krishna.

This last pair of songs links a dramatic episode of the Rāmāyaṇa, the kidnapping of Sītā by the demon Rāvaṇa, with Hindu cosmogony set forth in the Viṣṇu Purāṇa. That story of the development of the universe posits four epochs (*yugas*). The first was a time of perfect comfort, peace, and virtue; the condition and morality of man deteriorate further with each successive yuga. A Brahman informant said that Sītā was not kidnapped in the Treta Yuga. According to him and my references, there is no Sat Yuga; the singer was apparently mistaken.

80.

I say, at which time was the earth quaking?
At which time was the sky shifting?
At which time was Sītā kidnapped?
Where had Rām gone?

This is a riddle answered by the next song.

81.

The earth was quaking at the time of the Kali Yuga.
The sky was shifting at the time of the Sat Yuga.
Sītā was kidnapped in the Treta Yuga.
Where to kill the deer, my people.
Oh, Rām had gone to kill the deer.

These few texts are typical of the kharī birahā texts sung in Indrapur in that they are largely vignettes from the Rām and Krishna stories. In 1884 George Grierson, the eminent British linguist and folklorist, published a collection of Bhojpurī khaṛī birahās he had recorded in western Bihar. The songs have the same brief poetic form as those included here, but they encompass a wider range of topics, including the mother goddess and secular subjects, such as the pain of separated lovers and the erotic charms of young women.[5] Additional research is needed to explain the narrow scope of the songs sung in Indrapur. It could be due merely to the limited tastes of the singers I happened to record. Since the vitality of the genre appears to be waning, many songs could simply have been forgotten. It might also be a result of contextual factors, such as singing for a predominantly Brahman audience—the pious facet of the Brahman caste image might constrain the song choice of a singer who knew Brahmans to predominate in his audience.

Khaṛī birahā singing contributes to the unique caste image of the Ahirs. Although the caste ranking ascribed to them by villagers is in the lower-middle range, their generally robust physiques and virility evoke respect even from members of higher castes. Many of the men exercise daily; their prowess at wrestling and gymnastics is part of their stereotyped image. The Ahirs encourage their young men to sing virahas and *Lorikī*, a lengthy epic about the life of an Ahir hero.[6] Their music is a hallmark of their caste, and an expression of pride in caste identity. Although the texts of the khaṛī birahā are largely conventional, its form and intensity render it unique and uniquely suitable to the context in which it is most often performed—the wide open spaces.

Khisā: The Lustful Stepmother

Another type of unpaid specialist music performed in the village is a cante fable consisting of spoken narration interspersed with sung verses of four or six lines. Villagers refer to it merely as *khisā* (story). Although the story it tells is of diminished relevance today, the social process of its telling is still valued.

During the long and chilly winter evenings, the young men in one neighborhood of Indrapur—Dhobīs, Lohārs, Kalvārs, Ahirs, and Brahmans, gathered on the large veranda of one of the Brahman's houses to talk and take part in reciting a khisā.

A Dhobī man narrated, and a Lohār friend joined him in singing the verses. Although the Dhobī narrator predominated, audience members took part by interjecting humorous remarks, exclamations, or questions. Often the narrator would pause before the verb at the end of a sentence, and an "assistant" he had selected would supply the appropriate word. (Tandon states that such an "assistant" [my term] plays a named and regular role in story telling sessions, ". . . by making suitable interjections like, 'yes; and then what happened' and 'so the prince said.' ")[7] Thus there was cooperative interaction between the performers and members of the audience, with the narrator leading and providing the basis for the contributions of the others. (The form thus lies between participatory and non-participatory.) Many members of the group were the same young men who constituted the communal seasonal song groups and were thus accustomed to interacting on an equal basis.

The melodic line of the song begins a fourth above the tonic, slowly descends to it, then twice rises to the vicinity of the flatted third, and again descends to the tonic. The scalar intervals are somewhat like that of the khaṛī birahā—not at all diatonic. Also like the khaṛī birahā, the singing is rubato. The sung portions of the epic occur every three to five minutes in the telling of the story.

A favorite khisā in Indrapur is *Puran Mal*. It is an epic odyssey of classical structure and proportion, requiring three or four evenings to perform. One of its important motifs, the lustful stepmother, is found in a number of North Indian narratives.[8] When Puran Mal rejects his stepmother's advances, she tells his father that he has attempted to seduce her. Enraged, he evicts Puran, who becomes an ascetic. Wandering far and wide he meets a lovely woman, but circumstances prevent their marriage. In the end, by virtue of his noble character, he is happily united with both his parents and his beloved, and he forgives his stepmother. The moral value of the story was no doubt greater in times when polygyny was more common; songs of several genres mention the "co-wife" and problems arising from her presence in the family.

The Dhobī who performed *Puran Mal* learned it from his father, who was renowned for his repertoire of stories. The role of traditional story teller seems to be disappearing as the world depicted in the old stories becomes further and further removed from present-day reality, and the value attached to folklore and the folk music declines in favor of more modern and chic entertainment, such as film music.

Puran Mal is also performed in Rajasthan, sometimes as a staged drama. The story in song-form is available there in a cheap newsprint booklet, and is probably known throughout northern India. Another epic set to music is also said to be available in booklet form. This is the *Ālhā*. Because it is sung by an intinerant mendicant, our focus once more shifts outward, from the songs villagers sing to songs sung in the village by outsiders.

Ālhā, A Martial Epic

Unlike the khisā, performance of the epic ballad called *Ālhā* allows no participation by audience members. The settings of its performance and the roles played by participants differ accordingly, as pointed out below. The importance of the *Ālhā* for its listeners derives from the stories it relates, more than from the interaction which accompanies its performance. These stories express a pervasive element in North Indian culture: the martial theme. The form of the song and accompaniment are also important because they engage and maintain the attention of the audience, and underscore dramatic points in the song.

The singer of the *Ālhā* occupies a role of a different order than that of the khaṛī birahā and khisā singer—he receives compensation for his livelihood. One obvious difference this makes is in the settings of his performances, which must be convenient for his listeners—he can hardly afford to sing from afar or join them at his leisure. Also, inasmuch as he is performing a service or justifying a donation, it is even more important than for the voluntary singers that his songs be valued by listeners.

Singers of the *Ālhā* in this region belong to the Muslim *Nat* caste, a caste with an unusual history and *modus operandi*. Majumdar shows a wide distribution of the caste, over an area stretching from Punjab and Rajasthan to Bengal on his map of "Ex-Criminal Tribes of India."[9] Hutton states that this is "A caste of singers, dancers, acrobats, and professional criminals . . . who generally move about without a permanent territorial location."[10] In northern Bihar, in 1978, I did observe an obviously mobile group of Nat familes camped on the edge of a large town. Several men of this group journied daily to a bazaar in town to perform the *Ālhā*. Not all of the Nat groups are itinerant, however. The two Nat singers who performed in Indrapur indicated that selling cattle was their primary occupation; singing *Ālhā*s was limited to certain seasons. They returned whenever possible from their work-related travel to their permanently located families (one near Indrapur and one in Āzamgaṛh District). Each of these singers had exclusive singing rights over a certain territory.

The Nat caste in this area is Muslim, but it is not made obtrusive. The singers preferred pajama or dhotī to the lungī, the patterned sarong often worn by Muslims in this area.

One Nat, who travelled alone, said he would not take food or water from the sub-caste of the Nat who lived near Indrapur. He said that the sub-caste to which he belonged was higher than that of the other Nat partly because they could keep their women at home. The wife of the Nat who sang around the village was a tattooist. As she worked she sometimes sang songs similar to the saguns in Chapter II (especially Songs 5 and 6).

Previous reports indicated that *Ālhā* singers perform for weddings and for other occasional gatherings of men, often in the monsoon season when people are kept indoors by the rain.[11] But the *Ālhā* singer who sang the canto below moved from field to field in the morning and late afternoon during the harvest, performing for donations of grain. At night, after everyone had eaten and the marijuana pipe had gone around in the untouchables' hamlet where he slept, he would sing for several hours to an entranced audience. This sometimes included higher caste boys from the main settlement, who were sufficiently interested in the *Ālhā* performance to risk parental punishment for frequenting the polluting hamlet.

The *Ālhā* is sung throughout northern India. It relates the exploits of Ālhā and his younger brother, Rudal (in some versions called Udal). They were legendary Rājput generals of the army of a twelfth-century Rājput ruler, and belonged to an inferior clan of Rājputs. Because of the hypergamous marriage system, no other Rājput clan would give them their daughters in marriage. They were thus forced to fight continuously in order to secure wives for their sons and other male relatives.

The canto (division) of the *Ālhā* condensed here is of great interest to villagers, because it dramatizes an event of utmost concern and importance—the conduct of a wedding. The singer said he learned the epic from a booklet purchased in the bazaar.

Accompanied by a heavily armed and highly decorated bārāt, Rudal Singh, the chief of the clan, Debha Tivārī, his advisor, and Malkhā, the prospective groom, arrived at a grove outside the village of the Rājā of Junāgaṛh. (Junagaṛh is in what is today the state of Gujarat.) There they set up camp and imported dancing girls to entertain them while they awaited amicable gestures from the Rājā of Junāgaṛh which would indicate he was willing to marry his daughter to Malkhā. But the Rājā did not welcome them with the customary ceremonies, nor did he send provisions. After several days Rudal had his men fire continuous vollies to communicate his displeasure.

The Rājā's advisor, Curā (apparently after arguing with the Rājā), took the dowry goods to Rudal's camp. Rudal refused them, and sent Curā away as he pretended to go hunting with several other men. Instead they ambushed Curā without harming him and snatched the dowry, which they gave to Malkhā. Rudal's party then moved their camp to a pond near the Rājā's fortress and began to prepare for the wedding.

The Rājā argued with Curā that if he married his daughter to Malkhā the family honor would be stained and "the water pipe would be finished," i.e., they would be excommunicated from the caste because of the low ranking of Rudal's clan. They finally agreed that if Curā could deliver Malkhā to the Rājā, the Rājā would give Curā half his kingdom. Curā went to Rudal's camp where they angrily asked why the preliminary rites had not been performed. Curā told them that all preparations had been made and requested that Malkhā come along with him. Rudal, fooled by Curā, told Malkhā to go with him. As Malkhā departed there were unfavorable omens—someone sneezed, a one-eyed Telī ("oil presser") appeared, and a dead man's skull spoke, saying that he too had gone to Junāgaṛh to marry. Malkhā returned to camp crying but Rudal and the rest of the family were unsympathetic and ordered him to Junāgaṛh.

Like other cantos I heard, this one ends at a point of suspense—presumably to insure listeners for the next performance. Also like other cantos it is packed with romance, splendor, scheming, and above all, battle and bravery. The hyperbole serves to attract and hold the attention and imagination of the audience. This is no small task, given that the performance of one canto may require several hours. (The entire text is quite lengthy—one singer said he knew eleven or twelve cantos.)

Several other traits of the *Ālhā* serve to enhance listeners' attention during the lengthy performances, notably the variation of melody and percussion. In one *Ālhā* the singer employed five different melodies, all in a diatonic scale, for the verses of his text. The two Nat singers who sang in Indrapur delivered these melodies with a rich, throaty timbre that seems to be particular to their caste (at least in the Vārāṇasī-Ghāzipur area). It was immediately apparent in the singing of Kāśī Nāth Gosāĩ, a mendicant bhajan singer of the Nat caste living in Vārāṇasī (discussed below).

The tune of the *Ālhā* recorded by Nazir Jairazbhoy in a village north of Allāhābād (eighty miles west of Vārāṇasī) is essentially different from the melodies used by *Ālhā* singers around Indrapur. Whether tunes vary regionally, semi-regionally, by clan or family obviously needs further investigation.

The drum used is the ubiquitous ḍholak. It is a barrel-shaped, double-headed, wood bodied drum, over two feet long and a foot in diameter. Like many other Indian drums and drum sets, it provides two complementary percussive textures. On the higher pitched right head, the drummer taps out sharply defined, busier patterns; on the left head he beats out the less frequent thumping and gulping sounds. Some drummers tie small splints of bamboo on the first and second fingers of their right hands to get an even crisper sound.) The drumming not only provides a highly propulsive rhythmic accompaniment, but also punctuates and dramatizes the narrative.* As the story becomes more exciting, the drumming becomes more fervent, sometimes symbolizing the bombast of battle. When the singer wants to cover some less interesting but necessary material in the text he stops drumming altogether and half-talks-half-sings the narrative very rapidly. He also sometimes interjects a *he bābājī* (like "hey, mister," but more deferential) to regain the attention of the audience.

The traditional *Ālhā* is said to derive from epic poems written by Jagnīk (or Jagnāyak), a royal bard. These epic poems are the earliest modern vernacular literature of Hindustan.[12] The epic has survived only in oral versions which were later printed (and still are in cheap newsprint booklets). The period in which they were written is designated, in the history of Hindi literature, as that of *vir* (or *bir*) *ras*—"the heroic emotion."

The heroic emotion is intimately related with a strand of North Indian culture which anthropologist John Hitchcock has called "the martial idea of the Rājput," and I will refer to as "the martial theme."[13] It is notable in part because it is so contrary to the non-violent, ascetic, and metaphysical image of India and Indians which is common in the West. The martial theme is expressed in the depiction of battles in folk and historical tales; in the classical martial epics, the Mahabharata and the Rāmāyaṇa, as well as in the folk epics such as the *Ālhā*, and in other folk songs such as those of the following chapter. It is also seen in varying degrees in such personal traits and propensities as courage, personal pride, pride in physical strength and political power, a stern and unsmiling demeanor, swagger, quickness to perceive personal slight, and the love of swords, guns, horses, elephants, and military-style bands. The names of the genres birahā (sometimes spelled *virahā*) and khaṛī birahā may allude to this theme, as does the intensity with which they and the *qawwālī* (below) are sung. Although it is an intrinsic aspect of *kṣatriya vārṇa* (warrior division) caste identities, the martial ethos is by no means confined to members of those castes. Many Indian men, including Brahmans, are strongly attracted to things martial, and the *Ālhā* singer capitalizes on this value.

In summary, the mendicant Nat caters to his listeners by performing at a location convenient to them, be it field or veranda. With virtuoso drumming, melodic variety, hyperbolic lyrics, and dramatic story lines he holds their attention to the performance. The epic reflects and reinforces the martial theme, a salient facet of North Indian culture.

Blind Mendicants

Unlike the *Ālhā* singers, most musical mendicants sing bhajans. In India as in many other parts of the world, one of the few occupations open to the blind is that of musician; the most commonly seen blind performers comprise one class of musical mendicants. Most of those I saw accompanied their bhajans with small frame drums (*daph*) or tambourines. (See Photo 16.) Around Vārāṇasī these musicians frequent the busy lanes, especially near temples, but many of those I saw were on trains. Typically, a mendicant would ride singly, without a ticket, boarding with the help of a sighted passenger, who helpd him find a place where he could sing a bhajan or two and hold his own in the mad traffic of a third-class railway compartment. Later he would get down to catch another train back to his starting point. A few people donate and are rewarded with the mendicant's blessing, plus the thought that they are nearer salvation for the charity. Most turn the other way, and in so doing sometimes miss a moment's beauty—there is artistry to be found in this genre as there is in others more profitable.

A blind mendicant singer is usually addressed as Surdās, after the blind sixteenth-century poet-saint who composed and sang Vaiṣṇava poetry. Song texts of the one such singer I was able to record defied adequate comprehension and have not been included.* Another category of bhajan-singing mendicants consists of those who call themselves *Jogīs*.

The Mendicants called Jogīs, and their Songs

Introduction

A Jogī would usually arrive in Indrapur in the morning, well before the blistering noonday sun. As though to assure residents of his identity, he would sing loudly and play his *sāraṅgī* (See Photo 15.) as he moved from house to house. At each door he would sing until someone in the home gave him some grain or other produce, or it became apparent that he was being ignored. Villagers said that a Jogī works several villages in this fashion before returning to his temporary quarters, which may be several days' journey from his home.

The word jogī is the vernacular of the word yogi, which refers to a person who practices some physical or mental discipline in order to unify with a supreme being or force—a religious ascetic. However, in different regions of North India there are different castes, each of which is called Jogī by people in the vicinity. This leads to some confusion. Like many, if not most, of the residents of Indrapur, I assumed that the local Jogīs were religious ascetics. They often wear white turbans, pajamas and *kurtās* (loose, long-sleeved tunics), so their appearance lives up to their name, and they call themselves by names like Gorakh Bābā or Kabīr Das (see below) which also suggest their ascetic role.

Subsequent research revealed that the Jogīs of this region are not ascetics, but householders, and many if not all of them are Muslims. It is thus ironic that the songs of the Jogīs play an important role in the religious life of the village Hindus, and odd that they are sung by Muslims. The songs themselves are unusual in their obsession with death and the luxuriance of their metaphorical language.

The Songs of the Jogīs

Songs in the Jogīs' repertoires can be classified in three categories: songs about Rājā Bharthari, songs most villagers simply call bhajans, and a special kind of bhajan called the *nirgun bhajan*, for which the Jogīs are especially noted.

Although many Jogīs no longer sing songs about Rājā Bharatharī, they were an essential part of a Jogī's repertoire at one time. Several men in Indrapur said to be sure to ask the Jogīs for such songs, and Dasgupta indicates that the Jogīs of Uttar Pradesh (which would encompass those discussed here) used to be called Bharatharīs, and sing the teachings of Bharatharī.[14]

Bharatharī was a prominent figure in an eary medieval mystical cult called the Nāth cult. One of the fragments of the epic I collected tells how Bharatharī, a king without progeny, became a disciple of Gorakhnāth, a saint of miraculous powers whose name is associated with an extant sect of Jogīs.[15] Initiates of the order, claiming Gorakhnāth as its founder, wear huge wooden earrings which pass not through the lobe, but through the cartilege or hollow of the ear, and are thus called *kānphaṭa*—"split-ear" Jogīs. A legend tells how Gorakhnāth split Bharatharī's ears, thus originating the practice.[16]

The second category of Jogīs' songs, which educated men call *sagun bhajans*, concerns miscellaneous deities and philosophical matters. The third category consists of *nirgun bhajans*. Nirgun is the vernacular of the Sanskrit *nirguṇa*, which means "without form," and refers to a supernatural entity without personal traits, an attributeless divine. Nirgun bhajans dwell on the transitory nature of life, the inevitability of death, non-attachment to the mundane, and salvation through devotion to an impersonal divine.

They represent a religion that differs in important respects from *sagun bhakti*, the style of the Vaiṣṇava movement outlined in the previous chapter and the style of Hinduism most popular in India today. Sagun means "endowed with qualities, possessed of attributes."[17] Sagun bhakti refers to the devotional worship of the deities with personal attributes, especially Krishna, Rām, and Rām's auxiliary, Hanumān. Sagun bhakti is an emotional approach to a personal god represented in pictures and icons. The approach to the divine is modeled after Rādhā's passionate longing for Krishna, or Hanumān's steadfast loyalty to Rām—it is envisioned in terms of familiar social relations. The fervent harikīrtan singing described above is a characteristic expression of sagun bhakti.

The nirgun bhakti shares with the sagun an emphasis on bhajan—rememberance of god's name. But the true nirgun devotee worships no image. In the words of one informant, the divine is *binā rūp, binā śarīr*—"without form, without body." Nirgun bhakti advocates participation in the divine through detachment from the mundane world, and through internal as opposed to external expressions of devotion.

Villagers said that nirgun bhakti is a Vedic religion. It is true that the idea of a divine absolute without characteristics is found in the Atharva Veda, and is prominent in the early Upanishads. There have been however, other, more recent influences. One less commonly recognized is that of early Buddhist mysticism (c. 1000-1200 A.D.), whose chief exponents were the Bengali Siddhs such as Sarahpada. Their teachings were in large part absorbed by the Nāth cults which subsequently spread throughout India but were most influential in the north. Bharatharī, Gorakhnāth, and Gopicand are held to have been the chief exponents.[18]

Many of the nirgun bhajans attribute themselves to Kabīr, who is commonly cited as the greatest of the nirgun poets. At least two authorities on South Asian religions have noted in Kabīr's poetry the combination of Islamic notions with the primarily Hindu devotional ideology. Hopkins points to the strict monotheism of Islam and DeBary to Islamic rejection of caste and idolatry.[19] He also holds that, "The mystical conceptions and the phraseology itself of Kabīr's verses reflect strong Sufi influences. . . ."[20]

The Music of the Jogīs' Songs

It is the accompaniment that renders the Jogīs' songs distinctive in local village music. The instrument is the sāraṅgī. The sāraṅgī has a long history in northern India (but not in the south), where it has been used to accompany the singing and dancing of courtesans as well as the classical Hindustani vocalists of the royal courts; more recently, the concert halls and soirees of the upper classes.

The main or bowed strings of the sārangī are tuned to the tonic of the song and to the fifth degree of the scale below it. The melody is played mostly on the tonic string, while the fifth often acts as a drone. (Some players do not use the second string.) The singer usually plays a brief prelude before singing an *alāp* (a wordless, rubato prelude) of less than thirty seconds, playing more or less in unison with the alāp and with most of the text. Between vocal lines he plays little fillups, and between stanzas he might play a short interlude, often based on the *sthāyī* (the first melod strain). The more skilled players, such as Jān Mohāmmad, even punctuate lyrical phrases with sāraṅgī interjections. The sāraṅgī playing of some of the singers (e.g., Meghū Sāi) was too intricate and generally skilled for a casual mendicant—some of the Jogīs have clearly worked as professional accompanists. This was corroborated when one of the older Jogīs of Khalisa sang a nirgun bhajan to a sixteen-beat rhythmic cycle like the *tīn tāl* of Hindustani classical music, and called it a *ṭhumrī*, which is a type of light classical vocal music.

While generally reducible to but ten or fifteen lines of poetry at most, the Jogīs' nirgun bhajans run from three and a half to over five minutes in length, including the brief prelude and alāp. They are lengthened not only by the occasional sāraṅgī interlude, but by repetition of sung lines (the first line especially, which is repeated immediately, at the end of the song, and often in the middle) and by paraphrasing or repeating the line prior to the one sung. The repetition of the first line is one of a number of practices in this genre which are shared with *g͟hazal* and *qawwālī*. (G͟hazal is a type of song whose texts are couplets of the premier classical Urdu poems also called g͟hazals. Qawwālī is another Muslim-originated genre.)

No two of the nirgun bhajans recorded have similar melodies, and as shown in the musical examples, some melodies are much more complex than others. This supports the idea that the melodies derive from those of other genres. The songs do share a few general features of tonal structure. A few of the songs have a narrow range (a fifth or sixth), but most span an octave. In a majority of the songs collected the scale employs both alternatives of certain degrees of the scale. For example, the scale of song 82 uses both the minor and major third. Almost all of the songs feature the sthāyī-antarā form of delivery in which there is an initial and basic melodic strain (sthāyī) which alternates with one or more strains (antarās) in a higher range (tessitura). As in the g͟hazal and qawwālī, the antarā is often delivered in rubato tempo (free rhythm). About half of the songs shared another feature, a monotonic, chant-like delivery of certain lines (e.g., song 82).

The outstanding rhythmic features of the songs are two: first is the mixture of steady-pulsed and rubato rhythms in almost all of the songs. Some were sung almost completely in free rhythm, some almost completely with a regular pulse, and many were sung with more equal amounts of the two. The mixture of rubato and pulsed rhythms is typical of both g͟hazal and qawwālī singing. Secondly, the pulsed passages in many of the songs were propelled by a strong backbeat (emphasis on the up-beat) from the sāraṅgī. This was particularly noticeable when there were jingle bells mounted on the bow, as Jān Mohāmmad had done.

The Texts of the Nirgun Bhajans and Other Jogīs' Songs

The first song concerns a dominant theme in the nirgun bhajans, the transience of bodily existence. The body will be only a corpse, a feast for the vultures. The soul, the bird of life, shall transcend it.

82.

Oh Rām, on which day will the bird of life go to the
forest?
The body will burn, everything will burn.
Like branches and leaves, everything will fall off.
Don't be proud of the body.
It will be but a feast for the crows and vultures.
That woman who has put betel leaf in your mouth,
even she will be repulsèd by the sight of you.
"Oh, quickly take it out of the home, before it becomes a
demon and consumes the household."
The ruling king will go, the queen, gazing on her beauty,
will go.
Oh, all the Veda-readers will go.
All the proud persons will go.
The moon will be left behind, the sun whose light is
bright will be left behind.
But, says Kabīr, good deeds will leave their mark.
Oh, reputation will remain.
On which day will the bird of life go to the forest,
oh Rām, on which day?

This and the following song were performed by Jān Mohāmmad, one of the most talented of the Jogī singers from Khalīsā, Āzamgaṛh District. He sang in a kind of teeth-clenched way, sometimes out of one side of his mouth, with a hard and arresting tone. The ferocity of his vocal and instrumental attacks was quite in keeping with his personality. His brusque arrogance and wit were unusual among the closed-mouthed and deferential Jogīs. His sāraṅgī reflected the care with which he approached his music. It was one of the few I saw which had all the strings attached and the skin head intact. The bow was adorned with red ribbons at both ends, the jangles tied to the hand end added percussion and drive to the music.

There is much in the above song of Jān Mohāmmad that typifies the nirgun bhajan. The use of a bird to symbolize the personal soul is a poetic convention extending back to the Upanishads, the basis of Hindu philosophical speculation.[21] In the songs below swan, myna, and parrot all symbolize the personal soul.

"Oh Rām" in the first line may be merely a conventional exclamation, like "Oh, Lord," or it may be intended to address the divine. At any rate, in the nirgun context the word Rām refers not to the incarnation of Viṣṇu and hero of the Rāmāyaṇa, but to Nirgun *Iśvar* or Brahman, the attributeless God.[22] Although nirgun is by definition a concept of an impersonal supernatural entity, many of these songs inadvertantly attribute personality to the supernatural power. According to Hopkins, this paradox dates back to the late Upanishads.[23] It reflects the recurring domination of sagun over nirgun beliefs. This song is very similar to one attributed to Surdās but it seems a very unlikely product of his.[24]

The name Kabīr appears in the closing lines of this song as it does in many of the nirgun bhajans. Kabīr was a mystic poet and saint who probably lived in the last half of the fifteenth century A.D. An outstanding scholar of Hindu literature has written of Kabīr, "His best utterances are probably the loftiest work in the Hindi language; and hundreds of his couplets have laid hold of the common heart of Hindustan."[25] There are three collections of Kabīr's poetry, from three regions: the Bījak from Bihar, the Granthāwalī (or Pāncvanī) from Rajasthan, and the Guru Granth from Punjab. The three collections differ somewhat in the main trends of the philosophy/theology they set forth, the western collections favoring the more common sagun bhakti.

Kabīr's poetry sets forth a theistic, devotional philosophy which eschews ritualism, asceticism, idolatry, and temple-worship, as well as caste and religious discrimination. The songs of the Jogīs and the poetry attributed to Kabīr have much in common.

As with Sanskrit and other Hindi poetry, the name appearing at the end of a song often only identifies the famous poet in whose style the song is composed. It is not a reliable indication of authorship. This song is, however, very much in the spirit of poetry attributed to Kabīr. Its acute, sometimes brutal images, its contempt for Brahmans (the "Veda-readers") and royalty, and its stern tone are all elements common in the poetry of Kabīr. So too is its depiction of a woman's reaction to the death of her husband. Images of a man's kin reacting to his death occur frequently in these songs.

83.

One day there will be a theft in the body
Oh mind, stay alert.
Oh, there are ten doors in the body.
When people are gathered around you on all sides.
When life begins to leave,
Oh, where does the soul go?
Oh, mother weeps, "Oh, my son has died."
Oh, sister weeps, "My brother."

And when a newly-wed bride weeps,
Oh, she feels life is without hope.
Oh, says Kabir, listen, brother Sādhū.
The hemp is cut and the shroud is woven.
Who knows, oh Rām, what will become of the body?

This song about death, like many of the nirgun bhajans, depicts family reactions to drive home its point. The third line refers to a yogic concept that there are ten orifices in the body through which the soul can escape. (For those who might attempt to tally them, the tenth is said to be the mind.) The last two lines again refer to the impermanence of corporal life.

This song is addressed to fellow sādhūs (holy men), a convention so common in the nirgun bhajan as to be stereotypical. Sādhūs still sing these songs to each other in their periodic assemblies as they probably did more frequently in the past. Today "sādhū" in these songs is also understood to apply to any individual who is striving for truth and liberation.[26]

The following song also focuses on the meaninglessness of bodily existence, but with a unique strategy and without many of the conventional lyrics.*

84.

Oh wood, you wood of the forest, now see the spectacle of wood.
When you came from the womb, the swinging cradle was of wood.
When you were five, the toy in your hand was of wood.
Oh wood, you wood of the forest, now see the spectacle of wood.
When you were twenty, you began to worry about marriage.
Then the decorated palanquin was of basil wood.
When you were forty, you began to worry about old age.
When you were sixty, the cane in your hand was of wood.
When you were eighty, you began to worry about passing on.
When four persons collected to lift the cot, the death litter was made of wood.
They took you to the bank of the Jamunā and gave you a Ganges bath.

Wood below and wood above, the pyre was made of
  wood.
It was lit like the Holi bonfire in the month of Phalgun,
  the blow was struck with wood.
Says Kabīr, listen, brother sādhū, all is a game and
  spectacle of wood.
Oh wood, you wood of the forest, now see the spectacle
  of wood.

This outstanding song belittles the importance of bodily existence by depicting life as a drama in each stage of which wood has the starring role; bodies merely pass through this world of wood. The idea is similar to Shakespeare's "All the world's a stage . . ."[27] The song also deflates major preoccupations—marriage, old age and death—by rendering them as nothing more than common features of certain stages of life.

Departures from parallel structure in lines 7-9 suggest incorrect or incomplete transmission. The line "They took you to the bank of the Jamunā and gave you a Ganges bath" is also problematic. (The Jamunā and Ganges are both rivers in North India.) Kabīr was known to have used the terms Jamunā and Ganges to refer to the left and right nostrils, in yoga terminology often called the *īda* and the *pīṅgala*, but that meaning does not seem to fit here.

The refrain of the song, that life is but a play or spectacle of wood, is reminiscent of a saying common among sādhūs of this area—"All of this world is but a plaything of *māyā*," (*yeh sab māyā kā khelwār hai*). Māyā is usually translated "illusion," but it refers to all phenomenal experience and particularly to the web of invisible constraints imposed on an individual by social relations, desires, and emotions—constraints which militate against salvation. From the perspective of these songs, the phenomenal world, the world of human experience, is insignificant and illusory. The following six songs all deal with the problem of māyā, a fundamental concept in the nirgun ideology. The first of these adds to a rather random collation of nirgun bhajan conventions two ideas unique in this collection.

85.

A field of little trees; the air does not move, oh Rām.
Yes, in this world no one is yours; so with whom can one
  speak, oh Rām?
The swan says, "Listen, pond, it is *I* that shall fly."
This is our last meeting; I will not return.

Oh, where did the soul come from? Where does it go?
Where did you fix your resting place, and where did you get stuck?
Oh, the soul came from that-without-form, it went into that-with-form.
You fixed the resting place in the fortress of the body, and you were stuck in māyā.
Where did you fall asleep? A thief has robbed everybody, oh Rām.
But Kabīr Sāheb recognized the robber; he achieved the steadfast, immortal home.

The singer of this song was not a Jogī, but a man of the Musahar caste named Jagat, who lives in Kesat, near Dumrāo in western Bihar. He said that he had learned the songs through participation in the Kabīr Panth Satsaṅg, a society he said was founded on the idea that knowledge and understanding are gained through group discussion of the works of Kabīr and other nirgun poet-saints. The poetry of this group generally employs the honorific *sāheb* after Kabīr's name. Unique in this collection is the final line of this song. It shows that Kabīr, like most all of the Indian saints, is thought to have transcended death through spiritual perfection.

None of my informants could explain the first line of the song. The second refers to the illusory quality of social bonds and the ultimate isolation of the individual. We see again the bird/soul simile, and again death as the thief of the soul. This is the only song in this collection in which the relation of the personal soul to the attributeless divine ("that-without-form"—the nirgun) is expressed.

The following five songs further elucidate the concept of māyā and indicate what is to be done to escape its nasty effects. The precious diamond and the fly stuck in the molasses are two of the most common conventions of the genre.

86.

Now someone squanders the precious diamond and leaves the world, brother.
Keep the precious diamond with care; lock it up!
Today some saint-buyer will come; the diamond will be sold at a high price.
You have to leave the world, brother.
The fly sits down on the wet molasses; his leg gets stuck.
Then he hasn't the power to escape; in confusion he will die.

You have to leave the world, brother.
The parrot remains in the forest of cottonwool trees;
Look, brother!
Then he hasn't the power to escape; in confusion he will die.
You have to leave the world, brother.
Says Kabīr, listen brother sādhū:
Concentrate on your devotions; salvation is not achieved without devotions.
Life will be spent in vain.
You have to leave the world, brother.

This song was sung by Abul Hassan of Khalīsā. Since corporal existence is ephemeral, life is misspent if it is not used to realize the true existence, or to get in tune with the supreme being. Some people in the region hold the belief that human existence is awarded only once in 84 lacs of births (a lac is 100,000), and offers the only opportunity to escape from the cycle of rebirth. The precious diamond can thus be taken as the soul, as life itself, or as the opportunity to reunite with the godhead. Whichever, its inestimable value is squandered when the individual succumbs to the insidious, illusory promises of the phenomenal world. Then he becomes like the fly who gets stuck in molasses, or the parrot that lingers in a forest of cottonwool trees whose attractive pods ultimately yield only an inedible down. Without remembering god's name in devotions, there can be no escape from māyā's hollow promises and no salvation. The same point is made in the following song, which was performed not by a Jogī, but by a cowherd tending his cattle outside the village of Indrapur in 1971. It is a kharī birahā.

87.

I say that I was going to Badrinarain when Brahmā delayed me.
I used to count my basil beads; in māyā I forgot.
Oh, in my māyā I forgot.

The singer laments that it was not in his fate (written by Brahmā) to arrive at Badrinarain (a prominent Hindu pilgrimage place in the Himalayas), i.e., it was not in his fate to devote himself to God. Again, māyā distracted him from his devotions—here, the repetition of God's name as the basil rosary beads are fingered. Apparently either māyā is defined as a part of fate or the two explanations for failure to practice devotion are simply not recognized as contradictory.

The next three songs further elaborate the importance of devotions in combatting māyā. The first of these combines a stoic comment attributed to Kabīr with conventions seen in previous songs—the scourge of māyā, the futility of material wealth, and the reactions of kin at death.*

88.

Brother, now in the mind there is māyā, māyā,
  now there is māyā in the mind.
Brother, the mind collects māyā. Pray! The mind collects
  māyā.
I accumulated the hundreds and thousands of elephants,
  horses, and oxen.
I jumped at every chance to get money; even then I said
  it wasn't enough.
Pray, mind. Brother, now the mind collects māyā.
Five and twenty-five convened in the marriage party;
  they raised the wooden horse.
Now it goes; the mouth utters not the name of God, the
  shroud covers from head to toe.
Pray, mind. Brother, the mind collects māyā, pray, the
  mind collects māyā.
I thought some person would go with me, or cow, water
  buffalo, money or horse.
The anus goes uncovered; God attaches his rope.
Now in the mind there is māyā, māyā, now the mind
  collects māyā.
Mother grasps the hand and cries; sister grasps the arm
  and says, "My brother."
Remember mind, she grasps the arm and says, "My
  brother."
Says Kabīr, "Why do you weep? He who puts it together
  breaks it apart."
Hey mind, māyā, now the mind collects māyā.

The singer of this song was a mendicant who called himself Kāśī Nāth Gosāī̃, a name that no doubt enhances his credibility. Kāśī is an ancient sacred name for Vārāṇasī, the premier Hindu pilgrimmage place. Nāth literally means Lord, and was an appelation used by mem-

*This may be heard on *Chant the Names of God*, Henry, 1981.

bers of the of the medieval Nāth cults. Gosāī̃ is a name used by the disciples of the Bengali Vaiṣṇava saint, Caitanya, and a caste which may have derived from a sect of Caitanya devotees. It turned out, as explained in the chapter on field work, that the singer was actually a member of the Nat caste. Many men of this caste sing for alms, but they do not generally perform bhajans. Perhaps the number of garbled phrases in his songs is the result of unfamiliarity with the tradition.

The song was recorded as the singer performed in the streets of Asī on the Hindu festival called *Maunī Amavās*. Asī is a neighborhood on the banks of the Ganges river in Vārāṇasī; the hundreds of pious people who flock there on Maunī Amavās, when they accrue special ritual merit for bathing in the Ganges, constitute a fruitful crowd for mendicants.

"Five and twenty-five convened in the groom's party" refers to gaunā, the bride removal custom. The use of gaunā as a metaphor for death is another convention in this genre. "Wooden horse" is obscure but may be an ironic reference to the death litter. Mention of the uncovered orifice in line 19 is unusual and seems out of place. It may refer to the naked condition of the body on the funeral pyre, or it may merely be a garbled phrase. The singer himself could not explain it.

The following song, in large part conventional, also exhorts listeners to practice their devotions (but with an interesting metaphor), and sheds a bit more light on the problems of māyā.

89.

Oh myna, speak the speech of Rām.
Speak myna, speak the speech of Rām.
Why are you sleeping in illusion? The day is dawning.
You are a pilgrim of four days.
You have to leave the world, myna, speak the speech of Rām.
Speak the speech of Rām a good while.
In which cage do you live, myna?
The bird of breath will leave; you won't be able to move.
Oh speak, myna, speak the speech of Rām a good while.
Half the day has passed in confusion; why do you sit with head hung down?
Says Kabīr, listen brother sādhū, remember God's name always.
Myna, speak the speech of Rām, speak the speech of Rām a good while.

This was sung by an older Jogī, Meghū Sāī, who lives in Khalīsā (Āzamgaṛh District). Here myna refers to both the person and the personal soul. "Speak the speech of Rām" means, in a narrow sense, to chant the names of God, and in a broader sense, to devote oneself to God. "The day is dawning," means that it is the time of awakening awareness. "You are a pilgrim of four days" refers to the theory of the four ashrams, or four life stages: student, householder, forest hermit, and renunciant. (This doctrine is elaborated in the texts called the Dharma Shastras.) The line also suggests the brevity of mundane existence. The reference to the caged bird implies that the soul exists in an unnatural, trapped condition in the body. The fundamental points here are that existence is impermanent, death is inevitable, and bhajan is the means not only of salvation, but as indicated in the line about confusion and boredom, even to an aware and purposeful life.

The next one is another concatenation of nirgun conventions but adds a few not seen in the previous songs. It was sung by Kāśī Nāth Gosāī̃ and like some of his other songs seems a bit confused here and there.

90.

Brother, don't be proud of your body; this body is just
  dirt.
Don't depend on these things, they are a trap.
World, money, treasure and wealth will not go with you.
Nor will that which puffs you up with pride help you.
This market lasts but two days; everything will disappear
  and you will regret the way you lived.
Here you purchase merchandise, there you get it.
The buyer of this good always gains and never loses.
Don't be proud of this body; this body is just dirt.
If a person has power in this world he can overcome the
  machinations of death.
In the grip of māyā and greed, you spoiled your entire
  body.
Now concentrate, chant, otherwise you will be
  blindfolded.
They will dress you in a loincloth and at once take you
  out of the house.
If anyone in the world has power, look, brother, he will
  burn you like a pyre.
You came turned around, you go turned around.

This is why knowledge in this turned around world is
turned around.
Oh, the creator, remember him, fix your mind on the
pure saint.
Sing Mohammad, oh my brother, this is the way to
benefit the soul.
Bhairo says: again having mixed these things the market
of knowledge is arranged.
Don't be proud of this body; this body is just dirt.

My helper when this song was recorded, an educated Vārāṇasī man, thought that lines 10-18 were largely improvised padding. We specifically asked about lines 13-15 and 18. Neither the singer nor my helper could make out some of the words. The singer agreed that the lines were obscure but was unable to explain.

"The market lasts but two days" means that this (illusory) life shall soon cease. Therefore one should not take too much stock in material things or in the body (it is just dirt). "Here you purchase merchandise, there you get it," means that one earns salvation in this life and gets it in the next.

Coupled with the importance of devotions to salvation in the following song is the belief that one must attend to the guru, the spiritual master. All of the medieval Hindu cults stressed the importance of the guru.[28] Some even say the guru is more important than the attributeless divine.[29] Unusual, is the coupling in line 5 of Krishna with Rām. This song was sung by the man who learned his songs through participation in the Kabīr Panth Satsaṅg. Sāṛī (the woman's garment) here stands for soul.

91.

Why doesn't the sari come clean, Rām, why doesn't the
sari come clean, fair one?
When will the sari, filthy from birth after birth, go to
the washing place?
Says Kabīr, listen, brother sādhū, when will release be
seen?
Why doesn't the sari come clean, Rām, why doesn't the
sari come clean, fair one?
Take this soap of the name of Rām; make the wash water

of the name of Krishna.
Make the bleach of your guru, wash off the dirt of the body.
Why doesn't the sari come clean, Rāma, why doesn't the sari come clean?

The following three songs are all variations on a common motif, the gaunā or bride-removal custom. Quite commonly a bride remains in her natal home for an extended period after the wedding rites before she goes to his village to live with her husband. Informants said the gaunā ideally takes place one, three, or five years after the wedding. In these songs the gaunā is a metaphor for death.

92.

By force oh Rām, now by force, oh Rām.
My husband is demanding the gaunā, Rām, oh Rām, by force.
Hey the red palanquin has a green cover, hey Rām.
Hey Rām, by force.
Hey thirty-two bearers are engaged.
My husband is forcefully demanding the gaunā, oh Rām.
Hey the red palanquin has a green cover, hey Rām.
By force thirty-two bearers are engaged, oh Rām, by force.
Oh Rām; meet, meet with your girl friends now.
There will be no coming again, Rām, by force.
Hey Rām, there will be no coming again.
Says Kabīr Das, listen brother sādhū, Rām.
There will be no coming into this world again.
By force my husband is demanding the gaunā oh Rām, by force.

93.

Having beautified yourself, dear one, you have to go to Mohan's house alone.
You have to go to Mohan's house, you have to go to Śyām's house.
Having beautified yourself, dear one, you have to go to Mohan's house alone.
Of what is the parrot made, of what the cage?

With what will the merging be?
Having beautified yourself, dear one, you have to go
to Mohan's house alone.
The parrot is of gold, the cage is of dirt.
The merging will be with the earth.
Having beautified yourself, dear one, you have to go
to Mohan's house alone.
I will order a palanquin of green, green bamboo; you will
have to go with the bearers.
Having beautified yourself, dear one, you have to go
to Mohan's house alone.

94.

The heartless husband has come to the door; my pain is
ignored.
Meet and mix with your girl friends,
Father's doorway is being left behind.
I dressed my hair with the comb of love.
I caught the reflection in the looking-glass.
I rubbed on my fingers the lampblack of love.
I applied it around my eyes.
I made a palanquin of green, green bamboo.
I took it to the bank of the Ganges.
Four persons together lifted the palanquin.
They took it to the bank of the Ganges.
The heartless lover has come to the door; my pain is
ignored.

The gaunā, or bride-removal custom, is a very apt metaphor for death in North India. The young bride has no control over her removal to her husband's home, which is generally too far from her natal home to allow frequent visits. As the bride's girl friends gather for a final farewell, so the friends and relatives of the deceased convene before the cremation. As the bearers carry the bride in a palanquin, so the relatives and friends bear the corpse-laden stretcher to the pyre. The bride fears the gaunā as the individual fears death.

In the second song Mohan and Śyām are epithets of Krishna, again showing personalization of the impersonal. The reference to Krishna is unusual in nirgun bhajans of this area. The repetitiousness of this song is typical of women's songs in north India. It was sung my Smti. Sail Kumārī of Kesat, Bihar. The first song was sung by Asir, a Jogī from Khalīsā in Azamgarh District, and the third one by Jagat (mentioned above).[30]

The following song was sung by a Muslim Jogī, Cote Lal, in the railway station in Jakhanīan (southwest of Māu in eastern Uttar Pradesh). He said his home was in a village called Kolhuābān in Āzamgaṛh District; it was fitting that he sing about a "wandering one." The song expresses opposition to religious formalism.

95. Nirgun bhajan

Yes, I the wandering one will sing the qualities of Rām.
I the wandering one will sing the qualities of Rām.
I will go to the pilgrimage place; I will not touch the water.
For love of God will I bathe.
The five pilgrimage places inside this very body I will scrub and scrub.
I the wandering one will sing the qualities of Rām.
Yes, I will go into the forest; I will not touch a leaf, I will not trouble a tree.
All the gods live in every leaf; to them will I bow my head.
I the wandering one wil sing the qualities of Rām.
Neither will I take any bag or mantra, nor will I recite the Vedas.
My guru is the invisible Niranjan; I shall give my love to him.
I the wandering one will sing the qualities of Rām.
Mind the horse, knowledge the quirt, memory the bridle; Kabīr sits on that horse.
Wandering and roaming, I will get that blessed vision.
I the wondering one will sing the qualities of Rām.

The refrain literally reads, "I the wandering one will sing the qualities of the name of Rām (*Rām nām*). Ths usage is reminiscent of the Hindu pall-bearers' chant *Rām nām satya hai*—"the name of God is truth." This identification of God with the word or name pervades South Asian religion. It is the same identification made in the Old Testament: "In the beginning was the word and the word was God." The refrain also brings to mind the Hindi aphorism *Ramtā jogī bahatā pānī*—"the wandering jogī [is ever on the move like] flowing water."

Opposition to religious formalism is a theme expressed by most all of the Hindu saints, including Kabīr. Dadu, a poet-saint who probably followed Kabīr in time as well as sentiment, said: "There is no need of going either to the temple or to the mosque, for the real mosque and the temple are in the heart, where the service and the salutations can be offered to the Lord."[31] Likewise, the yogi in this song avows his pilgrimage places to be within his own body. He will not tear leaves from the trees like the Brahman purohit does for his rituals, nor will he recite the Vedas like they do. His guru is the invisible Niranjan, the eternal spirit which transcends the flawed mundane world. Line 13 expresses the concept of a system of controls within the body: kabīr controls the mind with knowledge and memory. The idea is like that of the Kathā Upanishad in which the body is compared to a chariot driven by a charioteer (the intellect), using the mind as reins to control the senses.

A special category of nirgun bhajan is called *ultabāśī* or *ulatbānī*—"inverted language." These songs, with humorous paradox and absurdity, pique the listener's intellect and, at least in theory, render him or her more receptive.[32] The first one below comes from Jān Mohāmmad.

96.

In the night, wrapped in yards and yards of cloth,
 oh God, I was dying of the cold.
I wear a sari of sixteen yards, and a petticoat of seventeen
 yards,
I swear on the brows of my mother- and sister-in-law,
 half of one leg was naked.
In the night, wrapped in yards and yards of cloth,
 oh God, I was dying of the cold.
I gobbled sixteen rotīs and nine pots of dāl,
I swear on the brows of my mother- and sister-in-law,
 in the night I was hungry.
Nine boys were born in my husband's home, the tenth
 was in the womb,
I swear on the brows of my mother- and sister-in-law,
 I never met with my groom.
In the night, wrapped in yards and yards of cloth,
 oh God, I was dying of the cold.
Says Kabīr, listen, brother sādhū, the person who can
 understand this poem, he is clever and wise.
In the night, wrapped in yards and yards of cloth,
 oh God, I was dying of the cold.

Sometimes the paradoxes encode a secret meaning and are intended to be puzzled out; hence the remark at the end of this song that the person who can understand it is clever. The first six lines of the song above could well be cryptic criticism of formalistic religion, which pretends to provide spiritual comfort and sustenance, but ultimately leaves one cold and hungry. (Rotī is unleavened bread, like a tortilla. Dāl refers to various lentils and, here, lentil soup.) Lines 6 and 7 are more recondite. Sometimes it seems that the funny absurdities are primarily whimsical and have little if any hidden meaning. Rather than burdening the reader with speculations, the third verse and the following song (from Kāśī Nāth Gosāī̃) are left unexplained for the reader to play with.

97.

Now, oh mind, the river is sinking in the boat.
From the mouth of a cap a river is flowing.
Pray, oh mind, a river is flowing.
The boatman is Rām, saints, he is going with Sītā.
I saw another wonder, brother, a monkey is milking a cow.
All the milk was drunk by the monkey.
The butter was delivered to Kāśī.
Now, oh mind, the river is sinking in the middle of the boat.
I saw another wonder, brother, an ant started for his gaunā,
Nine tons of lampblack around his eyes,
An elephant stuck under one arm, a camel hanging at his side.
I saw another wonder, brother.
A well was on fire.
The ice and snow turned into charcoal,
A fish was playing Holi.
I saw another wonder, brother
An ant died on a mountain top, and nine hundred vultures flocked around.
Some of the meal is eaten, some falls to the ground, some gets smeared on the buttocks.
I saw another wonder, brother.
A donkey grew two horns.
Arjun and Bhim pull on the harness to its neck and back.
The inverted speech of Kabīr, the blanket rains and the water gets soaked.
The squash sank, the mortar floated, the water flows from eave to crest.

Line 18 was somewhat garbled, and the translation accordingly inferential. Arjun and Bhim in line 21 were the two most stalwart warriors of the Pandu clan in the epic Mahabharata.

Among those of the Jogīs' songs called only "bhajans" are songs such as the two below that deal with ultimate philosophical and religious questions. The first one proclaims the futility of struggling against fate.

98.

For fate gone bad what can contrivance do?
Dasarath shot the arrow thinking there to be a deer.
Śravaṇ's death has come; what can the arrow do?
If it's in the destiny, what can contrivance do?
If the king is enraged, what can the minister do?
If jail is written, what can the shackles do?
Kabīr resided in Kāśī to practice devotion.
It was written that his death would be in Magah; what
  can Kāśī do?
If it's in the destiny, what can contrivance do?

The sentiments of this song are not the guiding principles of all villagers, by any means, but provide some solace to those who have not or are not what they would wish. The second and third lines refer to Śravaṇ Kumār, a pious man who, as the story goes, was carrying his parents to a pilgrimage place in baskets suspended from a pole on his back. Thirsty, he stopped in the forest, set them down and went to look for water. As he was drinking from a pool, Rājā Dasarath took him to be an animal, and shot and killed him with an arrow. Coming upon Śravaṇ Kumār's parents, he expressed his deep regret, but they cursed him, saying he would be grieved in the same way. (He was, when his son Rām was banished to the forest.) Informants said the story is set forth in the Bhāgavata Purāṇa and the first book of the Rāmcaritamānas and Valmiki's Rāmāyaṇa. It is also circulated in verse form in an inexpensive newsprint booklet published by Ṭhākur Prasād and Sons of Vārāṇasī.

The last two lines refer to legends about the death of Kabīr. Magahar is a place near the city of Gorakhpur in northeastern Uttar Pradesh which has a large population of Muslim weavers. In the past Hindus also associated it with the untouchable Dom caste whose traditional occupation is cremation. According to popular belief, people who die in Kāśī (Vārāṇasī) attain salvation, while those who die in Magahar are reborn as asses. Legend has it that when Kabīr felt that he was near death, he announced to fellow residents of Kāśī that he was going to Magahar to die. The citizens of Kāśī were of course shocked and grieved. (Their disappointment is implied in the final two lines of the song.) Verses attributed to Kabīr in the Bījak and the Granthāwalī express the idea that whether one lives or dies in Magahar or Banāras is of no concern whatsoever; it is the relationship one has with Rām which is all-important.[33] The above song merely states that it was not in Kāśī's fate to be honored by the death of Kabīr. It was sung by Meghū Sāī of Khalīsā.

The next song strings together six ironies to show how inverted and immoral are the times in which we live. Some of these are familiar; others are meaningful only in the North Indian cultural context.

99.

Oh God, when did we go wrong?
Why is the fruit of the mustard tree a seed
 and why that of the vine a pumpkin?
Why is the heron white and why the cuckoo black?
Why does the king rule? Why do the saints become
 beggars?
The saints can't get beans; the pimps eat feast food.
Loyal wives don't get even old rags; the whores go
 tearing around in their saris.
Oh God, when did we go wrong?
Why is the sandalwood tree in the jungle and the castor
 tree at home?
Says Kabīr: don't think it's a lie; it's the fruit of the *kali
 yuga*
Oh God, when did we go wrong?

The cukoo (*koel*) is black, yet it sings night and day and is often a part of erotic natural settings depicted in poetry and song. (See for example, song 108.) The heron (*bakulā*) is white, yet although it stands quietly at the edge of a pond as if in meditation, it is only waiting to spear a fish. The sandalwood tree (*candan*) is fragrant; incense and a cooling paste applied to the forehead in certain Hindu rituals are made from it. Yet it grows only in the forest, while the acrid smelling castor (*rēr*) tree grows at home.

The Viṣṇu Purāṇa, a lengthy compendium of Hindu lore and tradition dating from the first milennium A.D., sets forth the doctrine of the four *yugas*, or ages. The first of the four is a golden, perfect age, but there follows in each age a steady moral and physical deterioriation, culminating in the present kali yuga. This is characterized in a startling passage of the Viṣṇu Purāṇa: "When society reaches a stage, where property confers rank, wealth becomes the only source of virtue, passion the sole bond of union between husband and wife, falsehood the source of success in life, sex the only means of enjoyment, and when outer trappings are confused with inner religion . . . then we are in the Kali Yuga, the world of today."[34] The song was recorded from the above-mentioned Cote Lāl, and a variant from Abul Hassān of Khalīsā.

The final bhajan comes from a man who called himself Kedār Nāth Tewārī, from a village near Māhpur in eastern Uttar Pradesh. He was not a Jogī, but he was a travelling mendicant, and the other songs in his repertoire were those Jogīs would sing. This song denies the interference of the creator in the laws of the universe, an aspect of what some scholars have called deism. "Ocean of Mercy" is here used facetiously, as the author cites various tragic scenes from mythology to disprove the notion of a merciful and omnipotent god.

100.

Refrain: Oh, Ocean of Mercy, your works are inscrutable.
Guru Vaśīṣṭ, the pandit, reckoned the date of the
  wedding.
Then the abduction of Sītā, the death of Dasarath—
  calamity befell house and forest. [refrain]
Why the deceit, why the demon-deer, why was the deer
  grazing?
Rāvan kidnapped Sītā, the golden city of Lankā was
  burned.
Oh, he burned the golden city of Lanka. [refrain]
Hariścandra was sold into low hands; King Bali went
  to the nether world.
Rājā Nṛg donated lacs of cows, but the curse fell
  upon his house regardless.
You destroyed the pride of Durayodhan and the Yādukul
  clan
The pride of Durayodhan and the Yādukul clan were
  destroyed
Oh, you destroyed the Yādukul clan.

Rahū and Ketū collided with the sun and the moon by
chance.
Kabīr says: listen, brother sādhū, whatever is to happen
will surely happen.
Oh whatever is to happen will surely happen. [refrain]

Lines 2-6 refer to the Rāmāyaṇa. Although the date of Rām and Sītā's wedding was astrologically ideal, their life together was marked by catastrophe. Rām's father Dasarath died in grief after Rām was forced to leave Ayodhyā. In their forest exile Sītā was abducted when she was lured out of her dwelling by the sight of a beautiful deer. When Rām battled Rāvaṇa for possession of Sītā the golden city of Lankā was destroyed.

The first part of line 7 refers to a story in the Aitereya Brahmana, the Mahabharata, and the Mārkaṇḍeya Purāṇa. Having offended Viśvamitra, a Brahman sage, Hariścandra offered in recompense anything he might wish—his own son, wife, body, kingdom, even himself. The sage took him at his word and left him nothing but a bark garment and his wife and son. Hariścandra escaped to Vārāṇasī but Viśvamitra found him and demanded the completion of the vow. Hariścandra surrendered his wife and son, then sold himself to a pariah for whom he had to steal the shrouds off corpses. One day a woman came to perform funeral rites for her son, who had died from a cobra bite. They recognized each other and resolved to die on their son's pyre. When Hariścandra sought his master's permission to die, the divine hosts appeared and proclaimed that he had conquered heaven by his humility and good works.[35]

The story of Bali referred to in the second part of line 7 is in the Vāmana Purāṇa and the Bhāgavata Purāṇa. Bali, king of the *asuras* (antigods, demons, or enemies of the gods), had gained dominion over the three worlds. The gods, deprived of their abode and of the fumes of sacrifices, came to Viṣṇu for help. Viṣṇu changed himself into a dwarf and appeared before the virtuous Bali, begging for as much land as he could encompass with three steps. When his wish was granted, he transformed himself. With one step he covered the earthly world, with a second step the heavens, and with a third rested his foot on Bali's head and pushed him down to the nether world. Bali, bound by his promise, had to acknowledge his defeat, but in recognition of his virtues, Viṣṇu left him the dominion of the infernal region.[36] The story of Rājā Nṛg, a royal ascetic who was subject to grave misfortune despite his steadfast piety and enormous sacrifices, is said to appear in the Anuśāsana and Bhisma books of the Mahabharata as well as in the tenth book of the Bhāgavata Purāṇa.

The Religious Outlook of the Songs

The first fourteen of the Jogī's songs, those dealing with death, express a system of belief common to the Jogī repertoire.[37] Fundamental to these songs is the concept of the soul, and its existence independent of the body. This notion is implicit in all of these songs involving the bird/soul metaphor, and explicit in the lines: "When life begins to leave, where does the soul go?" and "Where did the soul come from, where does it go? . . . Oh, the soul came from that-without-form, it went into that-with-form."

Two major concerns of these songs hinge upon the existence of the independent soul: the impermanence of bodily existence, and "salvation," or what is perhaps more accurately called in South Asian religions "spiritual emancipation."[38] Implicitly, of course, all of the songs dealing with death suggest the cessation of bodily existence. The lines, "You are a pilgrim of four days," "This market lasts but two days," and "You have to leave the world, brother," more explicitly express the finitude of corporal being.

The nirgun bhajans hold bhajan to be the primary means to spiritual emancipation, as the following lines from the above songs show: "Concentrate on your chanting, salvation is not achieved without chanting," "Remember God's name always," "Speak the speech of Rām a good while," "Sing, Mohammad, oh my brother, this is the way to benefit the soul," and "Pray! The mind collects māyā." As reflected in the different ways it is translated in these lines and other songs above, bhajan has a broad scope of meanings. In preceding chapters it has been used as a general term for religious song, but it can also mean any sort of audible worship; repetitious utterance of God's name; or even just worship, adoration, or remembrance. More often than not in the nirgun bhajan it seems to refer to repetitious utterance or remembrance of God's name. The repetitious utterance meaning of bhajan gives it something in common with certain yogic traditions. Both repetitious chanting and singing have the effect of turning the mind away from phenomenal experience. The use of the word bhajan, even though it has a different sense than it does in the more popular sagun bhakti, renders the songs more appealing to most villagers, whose religious beliefs and practices are generally more in the sagun vein.

Along with advocating bhajan as a path to salvation, nirgun bhajans promote non-attachment (*nirved*), which goes hand in hand with another concept crucial in these songs—māyā. Māyā is usually translated "illusion" or "web of illusion," but it refers also to the dangerous effects of illusion on the mind. ". . . it means the totality of phenomenal experience and of the relative existence, it denotes the qualified universe as opposed to the absolute, the brahman."[39] The parrot remains in the forest of fruitless trees because it does not realize they are fruitless, that the reality which appears so promising will ultimately deliver nothing—it is false or illusory. But māyā is more than just illusion, it is an illusion in which people get tangled up and bogged down. Attracted by its sweet promises they get stuck in it, as in molasses, or the reward it promises floats away like a flower petal on the wind. This attraction and attachment to the phenomenal world, particularly wealth, and even the body and its sensual pleasures, is futile—"one has to leave the world"—"the treasure and wealth will not go with you, nor will that which puffs you up with pride." Moreover, it distracts one from the divine and the devotions necessary for spiritual emancipation. "I used to count my basil beads (a devotional practice), but in māyā I forgot." In the exegesis of one informant, "The influence of māyā separates the soul from God." (*Māyā ke prabhāv se jīv Iśvar alag ho jātā hai.*)

Two related matters expressed in these songs also deserve comment—the depiction of death and the reactions of the family: "When people are gathered around you on all sides . . . Oh, Mother weeps, oh, my son has died," "Mother grasps the hand and cries; grasping the arm Sister says, oh, my brother," "They will dress you in a loincloth and at once take you out of the house," "The body will burn, everything will burn . . . it will be but a feast for the crows and vultures." This vivid imagery is one aspect of the nirgun bhajans which makes them immediately meaningful to villagers. Concentration on death and the transitory nature of life also leads to serious concern with the soul and its salvation.

A number of scholars have asserted the profound importance in Hindu thought of *karma* (the idea that a person's conduct in one life determines his fate in the next), and rebirth.[40] Yet the word karma was absent in all of the nirgun bhajans collected, and while one song (91) refers to rebirth, there is no emphasis on the idea that what one sows in this life he shall reap in the next, or that the misfortune of this life is the result of some breach of morality in the last one. One reason for this underemphasis of karma is that these songs circulate primarily among the lower castes, to whom the idea of karma is repulsive because it stigmatizes them. This is supported by the research of Pauline Kolenda and Bernard Cohn.[41] Another reason is simply that kārma is more closely tied to the philosophy of the elite, i.e., the philosophy of texts, whereas fate is the more popular explanation of life's ups and downs among the unlettered masses.[42]

The concept of salvation in these songs is undeveloped. The words *mokṣa* or *muktī* appear occasionally, but they are the generic terms for spiritual emancipation and apply to differing concepts of release expressed in different sects and doctrines. Whether the release is to a union with the divine, a state of effulgent bliss, or to an escape from the succession of rebirths is not specified in the songs.

Likewise, the concept of the divine is ambiguous. In only one song is it indentified as the attributeless divine; in others it is personalized. The lack of definition of the divine and salvation, like the reference to bhajan, renders the songs acceptable to people who are not staunch nirgun devotees.

What influence do these songs have in the lives of the people that hear them? Undoubtedly they mean differing things to different groups of people. Many of the songs are addressed to sādhūs—for them they must have validated the ascetic life, defining and unifying the outlook of an ingroup. But the goal of non-attachment coincidentally has meaning for the villagers who are not ascetics—it tells them they can ignore their impoverished condition, their deterioriating bodies, the hunger and starvation which are a part of their lives, the disappointing behavior of their kin, and the affluence of their neighbors. Said one well-educated Hindu: "Nirgun bhajans give solace to the aching heart. Suffering is inevitable—it is in the very order of existence. So the individual comes to know he is not alone in his suffering." Another man cited the proverb: "All are equal in the court of Kabīr." This refers to the levelling concepts of Kabīr's songs, which are shared by many of the nirgun bhajans. They say that ultimately the beautiful, the rich, and the privileged come to the same end as those less fortunate. Not only do they tell villagers that this *saṃsāra*, this fleeting phenomenal world, is of no consequence, but they also say that the only way one can end suffering is through devotion—devotion to a divinity which the songs do not identify. One is simply told to chant.

People also express the idea that even though the songs are inspirational, few people adhere to the discipline they promote. One wise music teacher who was occasionally involved with the translation of these songs pointed out the discrepancy with a smile, saying that people were such that even knowing the right way, they did not follow it.

Jogī Identity

Villagers are ambivalent about Jogīs, as they are about many of the itinerant holy men that happen along. Some believe that there are still yogis who have remarkable mental powers acquired through meditation and concentration, but that most yogis (and Jogīs) are merely beggars who exploit the pious. For the more devout villagers, however, the Jogīs' sacred aspect stands out—they sing songs of God, they give manifestation to the divine. By singing, coincidentally, they establish a mood conducive to donations. Giving alms to the poor is *dharma* (moral duty), and a way of gaining religious merit. Some villagers consider their contribution for service rendered, since even *hearing* the name of god is considered beneficial.

Still other villagers say that the Jogīs are bogus, and some even say they are thieves. One informant said that a few parents attempt to keep their children away from the Jogīs with bogey-man stories about how the Jogīs will kidnap them, hiding them in the numerous cloths in which they keep their donations of grain.

Perhaps because they feared derision or persecution, perhaps because many were Muslims (who constitute a ten percent minority in this largely Hindu area), perhaps because they were afraid of me, the Jogīs were extremely reluctant to reveal anything about themselves. Initially all that could be learned was that many of them were from Āzamgarh District. Many villagers assumed (incorrectly) that they were affiliated with monasteries and that they were in fact the ascetic holy men their title suggests.

Some people said that the Jogīs who came into the village were not true Jogīs, but were only beggars who had made an occupation of their devotional singing, and neither practiced any discipline (*sādhana*), nor received initiation (*dīkṣā*) from a guru. They said the true Jogīs could be found at Gorakhnāth Mandir in Gorakhpur, a monastery founded by the saint, Gorakhnāth, many centuries ago. But at the Gorakhnāth Mandir, some one hundred kilometers north of the village, renunciants said that the only singers of nirgun bhajans they knew of were the beggars who called themselves Jogīs! The initiates of the monastic order are kānphaṭa (split-ear) yogis, which certainly distinguishes them from the Jogīs who came to the village. Although they said that initiates do convene occasionally to sing bhajans, no music was to be heard at Gorakhnāth Mandir save the oleaginous recorded bhajans in film-music style which blared from the temple's loudspeakers.

Subsequently a resident teacher in Indrapur learned of three villages in Āzamgaṛh District said to have sizeable populations of Jogīs: Amīlā Bāzār in Ghosī Tehsil between Mau and Dohrīghāt; Jiānpur Bāzār, north of Āzamgaṛh, and Karahā Bāzār, north of Ciriākot Bāzār. The teacher said that some of these were Hindus and some Muslims.

A visit to Karahā Bāzār leads to the nearby village of Khalīsā, where there are (according to the village headman, a man of the Ṭhākur caste) about fifty families of Jogīs (as well as many families of Hindu castes).

I recorded three Jogīs on that visit and another seven in the same location three weeks later. I did not have the opportunity to observe much other than musical behavior on these two visits but I was told that the adult male Jogīs there do field labor and odd jobs such as repairing metal vessels, in addition to the part-time mendicant singing which some do. The village headman's son said that they are *Sunnī* (as opposed to *Shiā*) Muslims, but that seems unlikely given the preponderance of Shiās among Muslims in the area. The Jogīs said that they generally intermarry with other Muslim Jogīs, sometimes of their own village, and that their rites of passage and other rituals do not differ from those of other lower-caste Muslims in the region.

There was little in their appearance to distinguish the Jogīs from village Hindus. This is probably a consequence of their minority situation, as has been seen elsewhere in Uttar Pradesh. About the Muslim "fakirs" in Karimpur, near Agra, a team of anthropologists observed: "The only money—or—food at the present available for these Muslims is in the hands of Hindu masters. Therefore, they have made themselves as much Hindu and as little Muslim as possible."[43] This is also true in Indrapur, where, with the exception of their Moharram rites, the ten Muslim families went out of their way to remain inconspicuous. I suspect that some of the Muslim Jogīs call themselves by Hindu names for the same reason.

Some intriguing questions remain. What is the place of music in Jogī society today? How are the songs transmitted? (I have seen no printed nirgun bhajans of the type the Jogīs sing.) One Jogī said that they receive no formal instruction in singing or playing the sāraṅgī; they learn when they are young by privately imitating older musicians. It would seem difficult to learn how to tune and play the sāraṅgī without some personal instruction, and there may be an informal guru-celā relationship such as that of the Ahir uncle and nephew in Indrapur. Participant-observation research is needed to answer these questions. It might also shed some light on related historical problems.

It is curious that householders (as opposed to ascetics) of a low Muslim (as opposed to Hindu) caste are called Jogīs (yogis) and have come to be the region's primary transmitters of the nirgun tradition. The common explanation given by villagers is that this Jogī caste descends from clusters of "fallen" yogis—ascetics who took up with women and became householders—but that does not account for their being Muslim. More plausible is the explanation given by the widely respected scholar Hazari Prasad Dvivedi of Vārāṇasī. He suggests that in the middle ages adherents of Nāth jogī cults were forced to become Muslims. He holds that Kabīr, the outstanding nirgun poet, must himself have been brought up among a clan of weavers who were, to translate literally, "Nāth-followers, householder jogīs of a Muslim appearance."[44]

Shashibhusan Dasgupta's work encompassing the yogi castes of Bengal not only supports Dvivedi's idea that the Jogīs descend from adherents of the Nāth yogi cults, but shows that in Bengal as in Uttar Pradesh there is a connection between Jogīs and nirgun bhajans. He states that the yogi castes of Bengal (where they are called *Jugīs*) number about 450,000, residing mostly in northern and eastern Bengal. They are "somehow associated" with the Nāth sect that spread across India between the tenth and twelfth centuries A.D. Members of the castes bear the title Nāth with their names, and are mostly weavers but occasionally cultivators and dealers in betel leaves and lime. They generally bury their dead, though they are now adopting cremation and accepted Hindu funerary rites.[45] Along with the lower Muslim castes of their areas they sing the stories of Gopīcandra and Gorakhnāth as well as "songs of the Nāth-gurus, emphasizing the vanity of life and the pernicious effect of worldly enjoyment and stressing side by side the importance of yoga as the only path for escaping death and decay and for attaining liberation. . . ."[46] In some respects these sound like the nirgun bhajans presented above.

Dasgupta states that these songs of the Nāth-Muslims were the common heritage of both Muslims and non-Muslims of Bengal. The gradual revival of Hinduism in Bengal, with the Caitanya movement as a main thrust, introduced Sanskritic and Puranic elements (by the latter he is no doubt referring to sagun bhakti) which were more attractive to the caste Hindus, leaving the nirgun songs to be preserved only among Muslims and low-caste Hindus.[47]

In Uttar Pradesh nirgun bhajans also circulate primarily among lower castes. I have recorded them among Mussahars, Kohārs and Kahā̃rs, but am reasonably certain they are sung by Camārs, Dhobīs and many other castes. I have also recorded them from Ahirs, a mid-level caste. In a personal interview in 1978, Hazari Prasād Dvivedi gave this differential possession of nirgun bhajans an explanation which complements Dasgutpa's. He said that the Brahmans and upper castes historically had their Vedas, śastras, etc., so they didn't need the nirgun ideology.

In summary, the Jogīs are not Hindu ascetics, but as far as is known, Muslim householders. The songs they sing express ideas probably given definitive form by early medieval Buddhist mystics, and later propagated by the widespread Nāth cults, from whom the ancestors of the Jogīs acquired them. Later generations converted to Islam but retained the ideology, which Kabīr and others then selectively combined with precepts from Sufism, Vedanta, and other ideologies. Apart from the nirgun bhajans they sing, the Jogīs studied appear to have no traditions which qualify them for the name jogī (yogi).

Summary and Conclusion

This chapter has discussed four types of songs sung by unpaid or voluntarily paid musical specialists. In one respect or another all of these genres are more complex or refined than the music discussed in previous chapters. The khaṛī birahā has an intricate melody line, the khisā a long and complex story, the Ālhā an even larger text plus melodic complexity and elaborate drumming, and the Jogīs' bhajans texts of considerable complexity plus an attractive instrumental accompaniment. The increased complexity of these songs, characteristic of specialist, non-participatory music, is prerequisite to their ability to maintain the interest of passive listeners. It also reflects the increased craft and skill of the musical specialist.

The khaṛī birahā texts convey little which is not expressed in other genres, but the form of the message and the situation of its performance give it a unique ability to gain purchase in the listener's mind. The other three genres all convey unique messages: they transmit ideology and attitudes not transmitted in any other medium in the village. Puran Mal stresses the ultimate value of virtue and Ālhā the importance of courage and valor. The nirgun bhajans are particularly important because, to some people at any rate, they convey a world view (non-attachment) and a strategy (the repetitious utterance of God's name and other devotional rituals) which facilitate coping with a difficult environment.

The songs of these genres also constitute diversion for their listeners, and in this respect they have something in common with the professional entertainment genres of the following chapter. But those songs provide, in accord with their expense, more music with the message.

Notes

1 Peter T. Bartis, "An Examination of the Holler in North Carolina White Tradition," *Southern Folklore Quarterly* 39:3 (1975), p. 209.

2 A. H. Fox-Strangways, *The Music of Hindostan* (London: Oxford University Press, 1965), p. 27.

3 The khaṛī birahā on Columbia 9102021, *The Columbia Library of Folk and Primitive Music*, Volume XIII, *Indian Folk Music*, is similar in style to those I recorded but much less robust.

4 W. G. Archer, *The Loves of Krishna in Indian Painting and Poetry* (New York: Grove Press, 1958), p. 53.

5 George A. Grierson, "Some Bihari Folksongs,' *Journal of the Royal Asian Society* 16 (1884), p. 196.

6 Shyam Manohar Pandey, "The Hindi Oral Epic Canaini or Loriki," *Orientalia Lovaniensa Periodica* 2 (1971), pp. 191-210.

7 Prakash Tandon, *Punjabi Century: 1857-1947* (Berkeley: University of California Press, 1961), p. 65.

8 Ved Prakash Vatuk and Sylvia Vatuk, "The Lustful Stepmother in the Folklore of Northwestern India," *The Journal of South Asian Literature* 11: 1&2 (1975), pp. 19-34.

9 D. N. Majumdar, *Races and Cultures of India* (New Delhi: Asia Pulishing House, 1961), opp. p. 374.

10 J. H. Hutton, *Caste in India: Its Nature, Function, and Origins* (London: Oxford University Press, 1969), p. 290.

11 Jack M. Planalp, "Religious Life and Values in a North Indian Vllage," Ph.D. dissertation, Cornell University (Ann Arbor: Universtiy Microfilms, 1956), p. 522; D. N. Majumdar, *Caste and Communication in an Indian Village* (New Delhi: Asia Publishing House, 1958), p. 302; Ved Prakash Vatuk, *Thieves In My House: Four Studies in Indian Folklore of Protest and Change* (Vārāṇasī: Vishavidyalaya Prakashan, 1969), p. 2.

12 Frank E. Keay, *A History of Hindi Literature* (Calcutta: Y.M.C.A. Publishing House, 1960), p. 14.

13 John T. Hitchcock, "The Idea of the Martial Rājput," in Milton Singer, ed., *Traditional India: Structure & Change* (Philadelphia: American Folklore Society, 1958).

14 Shashsibhusan Dasgupta, *Obscure Religious Cults* (Calcutta: Fimra KLM Private Ltd., 1969), p. 369.

15 A variant of this story is in H. A. Rose, *A Glossary of the Tribes & Castes of the Punjab and North-Western Frontier Provinces* (Punjab: Languages Department, 1970), pp. 403-404.

16 George W. Briggs, *Gorakhnath and the Kanhphata Yogis* (Delhi: Motilal Banarsidass, 1973), p. 10.

17 R. C. Pathak, *Bhargava's Standard Illustrated Dictionary of the Hndi Language* (Varanasi: Bhargava Book Depot, 1969), p. 1051.

18 P. C. Bagchi, "Early Medieval Mysticism and Kabīr," *Visvabharati Quarterly* 25 (1959), pp. 160-171. Thanks to Dr. Willard Johnson for pointing this out to me.

19 Thomas J. Hopkins, *The Hindu Religious Tradition* (Encino, California: The Dickenson Publishing Company, 1971), p. 133, and W. T. DeBary, *Sources of Indian Tradition*, volume I (New York: Columbia University Press, 1958), p. 355.

20 Ibid.

21 See, for example, the Mandukya Upanishad III.1.1-3.

22 P. D. Barthwal, *Traditions of Indian Mysticism based upon Nirguna School of Hindi Poetry* (Delhi: Heritage Publishers, 1978), p. 64; B. D. Tripathi, *Sādhūs of India. The Sociological View* (Bombay: Popular Prakashan, 1978), p. 46.

23 Hopkins, *Hindu Religious Tradition*, p. 69.

24 S. M. Pandey and Norman Zide, "Sūrdās and his Krishna Bhakti," in Milton Singer, ed., *Krishna: Myths, Rites, and Attitudes* (Chicago: University of Chicago Press, 1968), p. 194.

25 J. N. Farquhar, *An Outline of the Religious Literature of India* (Delhi: Motilal Banarsidas, 1967), p. 33.

26 Hess, Linda, and Shukdev Sīngh. *The Bijak of Kabir.* San Francisco: North Point Press, 1983.

27 Linda Hess, personal communication, 1979.

28 Ibid.

29 Farquhar, *Outline*, p. 334.
30 Barthwal, *Traditions of Indian Mysticism*, p. 67.
31 See Laxmi G. Tewari, "Folk Music of India: Uttar Pradesh," Ph.D. dissertation, Wesleyan University (Ann Arbor: University Microfilms, 1974), p. 83 for another song in this vein.
32 Barthwal, *Traditions of Indian Mysticism*, p. 258.
33 Ibid, p. 301. Also see Linda Hess, "The Cow is Sucking at the Calf's Teat: Kabīr's Upside-Down Language," *History of Religions* 22 (1983), pp. 313-337.
34 Muhammad Hedayetullah, *Kabīr: The Apostle of Hindu-Muslim Unity* (Delhi: Motilal Banarsidass, 1977), pp. 190-191; Charlotte Vaudevile, *Kabīr* (London: Oxford University Press, 1974), p. 45.
35 Heinrich Zimmer, *Myths and Symbols in Indian Art and Civilization* (New York: Harper & Row, 1962), p. 15.
36 Benjamin Walker, *Hindu World: An Encyclopedic Survey of Hinduism* (London: George Allen & Unwin Ltd., 1968), pp. 429-431.
37 Alain Danielou, *Hindu Polytheism* (New York: Pantheon Books, 1964), pp. 169-170.
38 Cf. S. L. Srivastava, *Folk Culture and Oral Tradition* (New Delhi: Abhinav Publications, 1974), pp. 205-208.
39 The phrase comes from Agehananda Bharati, *The Ochre Robe* (New York: Doubleday & Co., 1970), p. 281.
40 Ibid.
41 See, for example, Farquhar, *Outline*, p. 36.
42 Pauline Kolenda, "Religious Anxiety and Hindu Fate," in Edward B. Harper, ed., *Religion in South Asia* (Seattle: University of Washington Press, 1964); and Bernard Cohn, "Changing Traditions of a Low Caste," in Singer, ed., *Traditional India*.
43 Dr. Willard Johnson, personal communication, 1979.
44 William Wiser and Charlotte Wiser, *Behind Mud Walls 1930-1969* (Berkeley: University of California Press, 1968), p. 33.
45 Hazari Prasad Dvivedi, *Kabīr* (Delhi: Rajkamal Prakashan, 1971), p. 24.
46 Dasgupta, *Obscure Religious Cults*, p. 368.
47 Ibid, p. 370.
48 Ibid, pp. 369-370.

*This song may be heard on the LP disc *Chant the Names of God*.

VIII

Entertainment and Processional Music

Introduction

Villagers often date past events by associating them with weddings—they are the landmarks in family and village histories. Each rite marks the formation of a union of enduring importance between two families, and establishes or renews ties between two villages. It is a time of intense activity, particularly for the bridal family that plays the host role. And it is a time of honor, an occasion for public displays which are of great importance to the families involved and of concern to the entire village. Relative to family incomes, wedding expenditures are quite often extravagant. "It must be admitted that there is a lot more truth in our image as a nation of indigent spendthrifts . . . than of the Scots as wealthy misers. Can anything be more real than the pomp and paupery of our weddings?"[1]

Music is an important part of the pomp. Weddings are the primary occasions for entertainment and processional music. Every wedding includes processional music, and except in the poorest of families, musical entertainment. Wealthier families are expected to spend more for all wedding arrangements, including musical entertainment and processional bands. The family head who doesn't live up to these expectations will be called a *kanjus* (miser) and will lose face. There is accordingly considerable diversity in accommodations, hospitality and music.

Like all the music discussed to this point, entertainment songs transmit much ideology. They share some topics with genres explored in previous chapters—Krishna and Rām, nirgun devotion, and romance.

But their content is also somewhat distinctive. One entertainment genre includes more topical songs, and another transmits unique sentiments of unrequited love. The lyrics and music of most entertainment songs are more developed than most of the genres discussed above. There is more instrumentation, more complexity in the format of songs, and more elaboration in melody and accompaniment.

The Contexts of Wedding Entertainment

The *bārāt* (the groom's party) assembles at a bus or train station near the bride's village. Ideally behind a loud and colorful band and caparisoned elephants hired for the occasion, they parade to the edge of the bride's village for the ritual cordialities with representatives of the bride's family. Poorer families engage smaller, more raggle-taggle bands, but there will always be at least a drum or two. Then with drums banging and horns blaring they make their way in royal style (or what passes for it) to the veranda of the bride's home, where the band's bombast drowns out the voices of the women singing their *dvar pūjā* songs. All the children in the neighborhood, if not the entire village, come running to enjoy the noisy spectacle. Either at the bride's home or at the bārāt's designated encampment the host family then serves refreshments—sweetmeats, potato croquettes (*samosā*) and other delectables, tea, betel leaf and cigarettes. During the wedding and at the gaunā, hosts of the more influential families in the village accommodate the bārāt at some distance from the bride's house, preferably at the edge of the village, and often in the school buildings located there. If the hosts are affluent, they rent a tent (like a small circus tent), to accommodate the musicians and their audience at or near their encampment. Other families borrow as many charpoys as they can, and scatter them about the yards and lanes around their home for bārāt seating, and later, sleeping.

The Informal Performance

More affluent families hire a musical group which performs one of the more artistic genres of music, is probably more skilled, and has a more prominent reputation. Less affluent families have different strategies for obtaining musical entertainment. The musicians who perform for them generally belong to artisan (śudra vārṇa) castes or to untouchable castes or mixtures of the two. Often they are of the same caste as the families for whom they play. The structure of these groups is variable, as is the compensation awarded to them. More ambitious groups rehearse, develop repertoires, and charge employers for their services. Other groups convene more for their own recreation; their loosely structured performances for friends, relatives or patrons are sometimes rewarded with small donations but often represent only the incurrance or fulfillment of an obligation. I call performances of these groups the informal type.

Informal performances contrast markedly with those of the higher paid groups, in both their music and their delivery. The setting of the performance has much to do with the informality. The group performs in a yard, lane or grove, without benefit of a tent for protection from the elements, a dais (raised platform) on which the band can perform, or ground cloths which not only make more comfortable and cleaner seating for the audience, but also localize and define it. Consequently, there is little physical separation of the group from the audience, which at times may be clustered around the group on all sides. This tends to diminish the attention given the music.

These groups usually play only percussion instruments in motley conglomerations which might include any of the following: (a) the *huṛuk*, an hourglass-shaped drum about fifteen inches long with variable tension heads, like the West African talking drums. Of a type found throughout India, the huṛuk is associated with the Goṇḍ and Kahā̃r castes in this area; (b) small and large clay-bowled kettle drums (*nagāṛā*), played with sticks, usually by Camārs; (c) the *daphalā*, a shallow-frame drum approximately two feet in diameter with a buzzing tone produced by holding a small splint of bamboo loosely on the parchment head, played with a stick, generally by Camārs (see Photo 22); (d) the gong, a dished metal disk about eight inches in diameter, suspended from a string held in one hand and struck with a wooden mallet; (e) cymbals (*jārī*),generally larger in diameter by several inches than those used in harikīrtan, and used in fewer groups than the rest of these instruments; (f) the daph, a small tambourine without jangles; and (g) the ḍholak or a double-headed drum of approximately the same size called *mṛdaṅg*. (See Photo 17.) Except for the nagārā drummer, the performers play standing up, and some dance while they play.

In these styles, the alāp, if there is one, is rarely more than a three-or four-second intoning of the tonic. the melodies are simple, with a narrow range. Some of the tunes are similar to those of the men's kajalī, and like kajalī, are antiphonal. In Indrapur the songs were called *kaharavā*, *koharavā*, or *dhobiāv*, indicating their connections with the Kahā̃r, Kohār, and Dhobī castes. Whether these names refer to distinctive musical traits of the genres, or simply to the caste of the singers is a matter needing further investigation. In their repetitious nature, simple solos and imprecise unison singing, these songs are not far removed from the participatory types like harikīrtan and kajalī.

These groups often employ a lauṇḍā (female-impersonating dancer and singer) who may dance opposite a male dancer playing a male role. The role of lauṇḍā is an institutional correlate of purdah, that is, it is a role which fits logically with the seclusion of women from public life. (There are, however, a few women who dance in formal entertainment groups. See below.) The lauṇḍā is a young man who has learned how to look and move like a woman. His coiffured hair has been allowed to grow to a suitable length, or he may wear a hair piece. He wears a padded brassiere and all the garments and jewelry worn by a well-dressed village woman, including ear and nose rings, hair ornaments, necklace or choker, bangels, anklets, toe rings, and the colī, sari, and underskirt. He knows how to beautify his eyes, lips, finger- and toe-nails, and feet. He sings with a peculiar timbre, a falsetto which is intended to represent a woman's voice. The results, given grace, a good face, and careful attention to accoutrements, movement and gesture, can be quite convincing—I sometimes forgot I was watching a male.

The lauṇḍās' performances range from pleasantly sensual to lewd. The lauṇḍā circles and turns with gyrating pelvis, often one hand on his hip and the other behind his head. He might also lean back with his bent legs spread and arms in the air, jerk toward his leering, slightly crouched and pelvis-thrusting partner, who with hand at crotch level motions with his upraised thumb. At low-caste gatherings women sometimes cluster near or around the band and dance with other women, or rarely, male kin, in this style. The following song was appropriate for such dancing, given the thrust of its roughly-joined lyrics.

101.

Brij has become deserted, Brij has become deserted,
  Brij has become deserted.
Without you, Krishna, Brij has become deserted.
Without sustenance the soul is unhappy friend, it's like
  a fish out of water.
Listen, dear, the woman is sad, the woman is sad.
She is wilting day by day.
She sits on the decorated bed, and a sensual feeling
  comes over her.
Her colī snaps.
Wipe off the sweat that has come on me, dear.
The fine orange bedspread on the red bed.
Carefully place your feet on the bed.
The phallus grows erect.

From one side comes the young Rādhā, from the other
Krishna.
In the narrow lanes of Brindāban I got this precious lover.
I bathed in Kartik and the eight months before; I
worshipped Śiva.
What damage you have done, Brahmā, to have written a
young husband into my destiny?

This song, recorded at a Kahār wedding, is a disjointed collation of themes and lines from different genres. First there is the desperate longing of the gopīs for Krishna, which occurs as a refrain throughout the song. This introduces the woman declining in her lonely separation. Unexpectedly her husband is present and the scene erotic, her engorged breasts bursting her colī. They satisfy their desires in the images of Krishna and Rādhā. Line 13 is from a phaguā. Line 14 is from a sohar and Line 15, a non sequitur here, is found in the more recently composed women's recreational songs. Songs such as this one illustrate a common method of the folk composer; one makes a new song by putting together images, phrases and whole lines from extant songs. The next one, whose theme will be familiar, has the same aggregrate character.

102.

I used to play at my father's house until my husband
ordered the gaunā.
This is the way it is, friend, my heart became worried.
This is the way it is.
When the bārāt came to father's house there was a dark
green curtain on the red palanquin.
The band played once; I am worried, friend.
Let us mix together, companions, today I leave my
father's fine house.
What precious babe or who else can I take to play with?
In the house my mother cries, Father at the head of the
palanquin, my brother grabs the palanquin and cries.
This is the way it is, friend.
I left my home; love pained me, friend.
The rain drip-dropped all night; how can I say, friend,
that which is in my heart.
This is the way it is, friend, my eye make-up has dried,
my lungs have withered.

Informants were quick to recognize this song, recorded at a Kohār wedding, as a *nirgun bhajan*. Another with this theme was recorded at a Goṇḍ rite. The last three lines are disjunct transfers from a song of another genre.

The two songs above suggest that the lyrics of informal entertainment songs derive in part from other genres. This is supported by other songs recorded in this context. Krishna songs were perhaps the most popular, but there were also songs about Rām employing episodes from the Rāmāyaṇa, and a sohar which, like the women's nation-devotion song (e.g. Song 1) had been adapted to express topical sentiments. It concerns Hindu-Muslim unity, one of Gandhi's most difficult goals. Its first lines:

103.

Grasp Gandhi's feet!
Worship Nehru and never forget God's name!
Rām and Allah are the same; only the names are
  different.
Hindu and Muslim are brothers; fighting is useless.
Father went to worship at the temple of Śiv.

(The balance of the song is in the mode of a women's devotional song such as 1 and 10.) To grasp someone's feet is to express great reverence. Gandhi, and to a lesser extent, Nehru, were apotheosized by the peasantry.

The Formal Performance: Birahā, Purvī and Qawwālī

More formal performances usually occur at the functions of more affluent families, and symbolize their wealth and prestige. The bands are larger or better known, and better paid. The most expensive one hired during my residence in the village was a well-known group which had recently performed on All India Radio. It was also the largest, most flexible of the formal bands, with two harmoniums, a *bulbultarang* (see below), and several other instruments as well as a dancer. The leader of the group said they were paid eight hundred rupees for three shows; however, he may have been trying to impress me by inflating the amount. Most of the groups (four of five men) working for wealthier families received from one hundred fifty to two hundred fifty rupees for three shows. This is significantly more than the amounts paid to informal groups. One eleven man Goṇḍ-Camār group was paid fifty rupees for one performance, and because it was a large and relatively well-dressed group, it was probably better paid than most groups of the informal type.

The informal groups play on the first evening of the wedding, before and sometimes during the vivāh. They also perform the following morning and often again later in the day. At each performance the listeners collect before them, sitting on ground cloths or carpets as the musicians position themselves, tune their instruments, and fuss with the public address system if there is one. (They are still rarely used in much of the area—public electrical power has yet to reach many villages and is unreliable in all.)

The guests have come to fulfill social obligations, to affirm social bonds, to see favorite relatives and friends, to get away, and to enjoy the ingestables, the conversation, and the entertainment. For most, this time is the high point of the wedding. Often only a core of close relatives and friends observe the vivāh (which would correspond to the church wedding as we know it in the United States). Relatives or servants of the bride's family walk through the collected crowd, which may include several hundred people at its peak, distributing betel leaf and cigarettes. At a few of the weddings I attended a servant circulated in the audience to spray fragrant, cooling rose water on those that so desired, while other menials waved giant palm-frond fans.

The ideal ambience of these occasions is that of the *mahphil*. There are several senses of the word; the one which applies here refers to a private, often somewhat intimate gathering for the enjoyment of a music performance or poetry recitation. The word mahphil is an Urdu word and the institution thrived among elite urban Muslims. The warm spirit of the mahphil can be glimpsed in the film *Bismillah Khan*, when Ustād Khan shares the hukkah with friends while all take turns reciting verses of Urdu poetry.

There is rarely a master of ceremonies, and the musicians are seldom introduced, but each song in the formal performances begins with a musical introduction. This varies in structure, but always includes the *alāp* (the wordless vocal prelude), and often some playing of instruments. The introduction signals the listeners that the performance is beginning, quiets them, and draws them into the main body of the song. It also allows the musicians to warm up—to focus their concentration on performing and limber up their fingers and vocal chords.

Like musicians in many American night clubs, these entertainers must work hard to keep the attention of their audiences. The crowd is silent only when it is intent on what is being sung. If people don't find the performance interesting, they talk with one another and come and go as they please. Children are usually about, making noise. These factors have some bearing on the style of performance—the singers necessarily use the broader, more obvious techniques discussed below at the expense of subtleties which would be lost in the general din. They also influence the entertainer's choice of songs. If the performance is appreciated, members of the audience communicate their pleasure instantly with conventional interjections such as "Wah! Wah!," and by modestly waving rupee notes of impressive denomination in the air, which a band member hastens to collect.

The genres performed in the formal situation are structurally more elaborate and their performance more skilled that those of the informal context. They are discussed below in the order of increasing expense, prestige, and artistry.

Three genres predominate in the music of formal entertaiment: Birahā, purvī and qawwālī. A fourth, called Bhojpurī or lok gīt, is a synthesis of these and other genres. Film songs are increasingly popular but still comprise a small proportion of entertainment music. The program director of All India Radio at Vārāṇasī, Mr. G. S. Sharma, indicated in 1978 that any competent band in Vārāṇasī would perform all of these types. In Indrapur bands which performed birahā performed no other type of music, but bands which primarily played qawwālīs might play purvīs and vice-versa, and either might include a few popular film tunes.

Birahā

Most people associate the birahā with the Ahir caste as they do the kharī birahā. The latter preceded the birahā, but there is little stylistic relationship. In Vārāṇasī, Bihārī Lāl Yādav (1857-1926) is commonly credited with originating the birahā.[2] His last name, Yādav, is the most common family name used by Ahir caste members in this region. Most birahā singers around Indrapur are Ahirs, but men of other castes, such as Nuniās and Bhars, also perform in birahā groups. Recent research in Vārāṇasī showed that ". . . some 30 percent of birahā singers are from other castes" and that "Everyone is proud to state that today there are [birahā] singers from every caste.[3] The Bhojpurī language region is the homeland of the birahā, and the language of birahās is the standard Hindi of the area or a mixture of Hindi and Bhojpurī.

The most common form of birahā begins with an alāp by the leader which ends on the tonic and an open vowel. The support singers raise their voices in unison to the tonic and sustain the tones for a few seconds, adjusting their voices to obtain a unison. The soloist then begins his narrative unaccompanied. At the end of each stanza the chorus joins their voices with his, again sustaining on the tonic. The rhythm section enters at the last line of the verse, and the leader and chorus join together in singing the last line as a repeated refrain over the driving duple rhythms of *kartāl* and ḍholak. The rest of the song alternates between brief unaccompanied rubato solos by the leader and highly rhythmic and repetitious sections by the chorus. This format is similar to and may derive from the religious *qawwālī* (see below). This form can be varied in many ways. For example, in one verse the chorus may repeat each line sung by the leader.

The scale of birahā is fairly close to the Western diatonic scale, and the range is rarely more than an octave and a fourth. The general form and the melodies are said to be a synthesis of Ālhā, qawwālī, phaguā, and other genres. Occasionally, tunes from film songs are used, as was the case for song 105, below.

The distinctive instrument in the musical format of the birahā group is one of the class called *kartāl* (also spelled *khartāl*). This particular kind of kartāl consists of two sets of two iron bars. They are about one foot long, five-eighths of an inch in diameter at the center, and tapered from the center to each end. The player holds two loosely in each hand and strikes one with the other by rapidly curling his fingers, producing a clang of indeterminate pitch (see Photo 18). Of the four to seven members in a group, one or two play kartāl. There is always one ḍholak player, who can produce a wide variety of *tekā*s (rhythmic cycles with specific patterns of accents) and other effects. The harmonium was not used in birahā performances around Indrapur, but seems to be commonly used in Vārāṇasī birahā.

The spirit of the birahā performance is one of intense emotion and authoritative forcefulness. The leader, usually dressed in *khādī*, the handspun cotton which symbolizes Indian nationalism, employs a variety of gestures and facial expressions to convey his deep feelings. At a dramatic point, he may cover his ears with his hands, throw his head back, and sing at the very top of his range with all the force he can muster. (The posture, the force, and the descending melodic contour are reminiscent of the *kharī birahā*.) Birahā groups sometimes sell their services to campaigning politicians, composing special songs to suit the platform of their patron. The style of birahā is well suited to this use.

Birahā texts are usually narrational, like the Ālhā. A few birahās are heard which concern mythological subjects, but most are topical. A birahā singer performs songs composed both by himself and by other birahā singers. Booklets containing the texts of contemporary birahās are sold at bazaars, fairs, and train stations. The following themes from songs I recorded are typical: indictment of the dowry institution using as a basis a story involving multiple murders, suicides, etc.; the wonders of the Apollo 11 space mission; a terrible train wreck in which many were killed; the assasination of Gandhi; and nationalism. Nationalistic birahās were quite popular in 1971 and 1972. The following song, about Alexander the Great (Sikandar) and his invasion of the sub-continent, typifies the verse-chorus format of the birahā, and shows how nationalistic sentiment can transform a traditional theme.*

104.

Sikandar had slept one day in his palace,
awakened and looked at the map of the world.
He made a vow in his heart to raise his flag throughout the world.
I take in hand a full cup of blood; not even in dreams will I know defeat.
[Unintelligible][4]
The world conqueror Sikandar went into India for victory.
He raised his flag on the banks of the Jhelum river.
He had conquered western Asia, Egypt, and Persia.
Wanting India too, he crossed the Sindh river.
At Udammadi he dispersed the forces of the Sindh and Punjabi kingdoms.
There the terrible felon met the Rājā of Taxila.
Between the Jhelum and Cinab rivers there was a man most brave, Rājā Poras.
When he planted the enemy flag on the bank of the Jhelam, the sandy plains cried out for the pride and joy of Poras.
Save the honor of the motherland, brother, protect the dignity of the country with all your might!
Sikandar planted the flag on the bank of the river Jhelam.
The river Jhelam also raised a shout at the billowing sari.
At my border, son, the foe has raised a challenge.
Save your birthland from any stain!
Drive every enemy from our border!
The foe has come and taken his seat; listen to my story.
The bugle blew a signal, the sandy plain raised a shout.
The motherland shed a flow of tears; Sikandar planted his flag.

The forces of Sikandar increased when he met the
stalwart Ambi Naresh of our homeland; the secrets of
the interior were obtained.
Then Poras challenged the Greeks.
Brave one, stop this flowing stream of blood!
[Unintelligible]
Bind the shroud of blood, pick out your biggest soldiers,
go and stop Sikandar.
The strike was on the border; Sikandar planted his flag.
The clouds were rent with incessant torrents of water.
Sons of the motherland, save our dignity; in the
battlefield the flag of the lion began to shimmer.
Save the honor the motherland, brothers, protect the
country with all your might!
Sons of the motherland, save our dignity; in the
battlefield the flag of the lion began to shimmer.
Oh go, young lions, while they are strutting at the
border.
Then take the naked sword in your hands.
The Greek soldiers saw this great man and fled.
There seemed to be darkness in all directions.
Sikandar saw his fleeing troops and called:
"Where are you fleeing, jackals?"
The soldiers clash, sir, look to the border.
The swords fell from both directions.
The elephant troop of Poras bolted.
The huge army scattered.
The support troops of the elephant group fell.
Then they captured Poras.
"I will either give up the kingdom or take the noose;
I'm not afraid of you."
The foreigners cried.
Come, Sikandar, take weapons in hand.
The sari of the motherland was soaked with blood.
[Unintelligible]
"Blessings upon you, son," said the Jhelum river.
Boys, you have saved the honor of our countrymen.
Celebrate the beautiful motherland that you have kept
undaunted!
Guru Bihārī, from Guru Ganeśa [unintelligible] brave
Sikandar.
The poet from Majuī village in Ghāzipur District.
Protect the dignity of the country with all your might!

So says Rām Lakṣman, touching the feet of Sarasvatī.
Protect the dignity of the country with all your might!
Save the honor of the motherland, brother, protect the
dignity of the country with all your might!

The last lines of the song exemplify a conventional ending formula. In addition to mentioning his own home and village, if the singer is the composer, he usually pays homage to his guru and a deity, often Sarasvatī, the goddess of learning and the patroness of the arts and sciences. These lines also serve several mundane functions: to plant the name of the singer and his location in the minds of listeners, which builds his reputation and facilitates other jobs; and to connect the singer with an established, perhaps renowned singer/composer, which further enhances his reputation.

The song is a contemporary interpretation of the defeat of Porus by Alexander the Great (called Sikandar in the song). Its narration of Alexander's movements and battles is consistent in broad outline with history book accounts: Alexander passed the Indus in 327 B.C., and formed an alliance with Taxiles, under whose guidance he reached the river now called the Jhelum. He crossed it after a severe struggle with Porus, a far more powerful opponent than the Persian provincial governors he had previously fought. The story as told in this song may derive in part from a 1950s film by Sohrab Modi called *Sikandar.*[5]

The nationalistic fervor which permeates the song has its basis in the martial ethos discussed in the section on the Alha. The key concepts of *lāj*—honor, and *paniyā*—respect, are the moral values which determine the course of action followed by the heroes of the Ālhā. The same two words are dominant in the song above, but they refer to the honor and respect of the nation rather than the clan. Another metaphor for the patriotic relationship between citizen and country is the primary social relationship, the mother-child bond, expressed in vivid sensory symbols. One word I have translated as "motherland" is *dūdh*, literally, "milk." The other word here translated as "motherland" is *āncal* which means the part of the sari which covers the breasts. Thus the nation is identified with the warmth and succor of the mother's breast.

The invasion of Alexander is interpreted by contemporary audiences as a threat to the motherland, i.e., India, which of course did not exist in its present form at that time. The song shows the extremes to which the nationalistic interpretation is taken in viewing even such peripherally related matters as a two-thousand-year-old invasion.

One birahā used the story of a soldier from the area killed in the 1965 war with Pakistan to extol the glory of dying for the motherland. The song employed some of the same catch-phrases used in the above song, such as "Save the honor of the motherland." One of the soldier's heroic feats was the destruction of Pakastani tanks, which he "lit like a Holī fire." The tanks were called Pattons and their destruction was depicted in the song as a blow to America. Since the 1965 war and particularly during the Bangla Desh confrontation, America has often been regarded as an ally of Pakistan and therefore more an enemy than a friend of India. The next song is also a nationalistic one. Its theme derives from a slogan attributed to former Prime Minister Lal Bahadur Shastri: Hail to the soldier, hail to the farmer! (*Jāya javān, jāya kisān*).

105.

Oh, the marching soldier takes the gun in his hand
  from morning to night at the border.
The farmer puts the plow on his shoulders and takes the
  ox to the field.
The homes of both are in one village.
In childhood they played at the same door.
There, the soldier safeguards the country; here the
  farmer cultivates the fields.
The soldier protects the honor of the country, holding his
  life in his hand.
The farmer mixes his blood and sweat in the soil and
  sustains the country.
There the soldier destroys the tanks and planes; here the
  farmer destroys the alkaline crust of the soil.
There the soldier in his iron hat; here the farmer with
  cow dung and fertilizer.
There the guns fire in salute and the bugle plays the
  signal; here the ankle bracelets jingle as his wife brings
  her husband a snack in the field.
While the soldier marches at the border, the farmer walks
  from home to field with the plow on his shoulders and
  the ox behind.
There the soldier protects the country; here he turns the
  soil into gold.
There the soldier drives out the enemy; here the farmer
  eradicates poverty.
The farmer gives succor to the country; taking his life
  in his hands the soldier protects the nation.
Rām Sevak says both are the pride of India; both are the
  glory of the nation.

These birahās were recorded during the period when India was at war with Pakistan in what was to become Bangla Desh. But the nationalistic sentiment, although it was a common theme in entertainment songs during that period, has been utilized in both entertainment and participatory songs (such as the first song in this monograph) for decades.

The composition of such songs is indirectly encouraged by All India Radio, the govermental network which monopolizes radio and television in India. The local All India Radio stations broadcast regional folk music programs and play local folk music during interludes in the farm news programs. Patriotic songs constituted a substantial proportion of the music broadcast during the first period of this research (1971-1972). Songs stressing the importance of farmers and wage earners to India's development are also heard frequently in the folk music played on All India Radio. The possibility of having one's songs broadcast on the radio is a strong incentive to compose songs in an acceptable mode such as the patriotic one, because the resulting exposure greatly bolsters a reputation.

Music is only one of the means used to promote a sense of national identity. All India Radio and newspapers have also been instrumental in this achievement, and the conflicts with China and Pakistan have provided an abundance of suitable text. State-supported schools are also important in inculcating national awareness. The raising of the flag and national anthem are part of daily opening exercises. The schools also hold special assemblies on Independence and Republic Days, in which the same kind of group cheers found in Holī and mother goddess village ceremonies are used to praise the country and its past and present leaders. The children then march through the village singing national sings and shouting national slogans.

One couldn't ask for a better example of a noted type of change in musical culture. "When a society shifts from a primarily religious to a more secular character, the ceremonial use of music tends to glorify the group and its political leaders."[6] The nationalist sentiments and attitudes reflected in music are now as much a part of village culture as the other topics of village song.

Purvī

Purvī means "eastern." It would seem to refer to the origin of the genre in an area to the east of the Bhojpurī-speaking region, however, one informant said it refers to the Bhojpurī-speaking area itself. The same informant said that purvīs flourished around thirty-five years ago in Chaparā district of western Bihar (which is a Bhojpurī-speaking area), with singer Mahendra Mishra a prime exponent of the genre.

Lyrically and melodically purvīs are among the prettiest of the entertainment songs. They are less strident then birahās or qawwālīs, with interesting but less jagged melodies than the latter. Their melodic contour is one of terraced descent (with a few intermediate rises) from a tonic in the upper register of the singer's range to the tonic one octave lower, with a repeated cadence which begins on the fourth or fifth and works its way down to the tonic. The rhythm is usually the duple meter called *kaharavā*, and the tempos moderately quick (120-130 beats per minute). The scale is generally the Western diatonic major scale with an occasional accidental (sharped or flatted tone). The scale is determined by one of the instruments which accompanies the purvī, the harmonium. This portable organ measures two and a half feet by two feet by one foot and has a piano-type keyboard. Its scale is the equal–tempered chromatic scale of the West, and spans three or, in larger models, three and a half octaves. Squeezing a spring-loaded bellows on the back of the instrument with his left hand, the player depresses keys with the fingers of his right hand.

The use of the harmonium, which was first imported into India from Europe by French missionaries in the nineteenth century, is remarkably widespread. It is used in most formal entertainment genres all across the north, in devotional music, in participatory music like phaguā, in dance and dance dramas, and in Hindustani (North Indian) classical music. Yet musicologists tend to be contemptuous of it, and for good reason. It is worthwhile to consider the pros and cons.

The first and most important argument against the harmonium is that its equal-tempered scale threatens the survival of the diverse and flavorful indigenous scales. A. H. Fox-Strangways, one of the outstanding scholars of Indian music, wrote that the harmonium "has a unique power of making an unharmonized melody sound invincibly commonplace." He suggested that it ruins the musical ear of the Indian performer, and exhorted for its dismissal as the pruning away of an unnatural growth.[7] The equal-tempered scale of the harmonium (so-called because it divides the octave into twelve equal semitones) is that which today is universal in the cultured ("classical") and popular music of the West. It evolved in connection with the increasing use of modulation (key changes) in European cultivated music and gained widespread use in the first half of the nineteenth century. Before the development of the equal-tempered scale a keyboard instrument could be played in only one key without producing disturbingly dissonant intervals. Intervals in the diverse native scales of Indian folk music are seldom if ever uniformly those of the equal-tempered scale. This became clear to me when I tried to play melodies of the participatory songs on my guitar. Not only are the subtle grace notes and ornaments very difficult to render on the guitar or any keyed or fretted instrument, but the pitches of the tones are sometimes subtly, sometimes quite noticeably different from those of corresponding tones in the equal-tempered scale. This is true even in this songs whose scales seem at first listen to be identical to that which we are accustomed to hearing in the West. With its widespread use the scale of the harmonium is supplanting native scales, whose distinctive flavors will be lost forever.

On the other hand, the harmonium does have something to offer the musician: it is durable, does not overpower the vocal, does not require a great deal of technique to play adequately, allows melodic embellishment, albeit more angular than that of vocal music, allows a singer to accompany himself, and stays in tune. Skilled players can also produce intricate melodic interludes on the harmonium, (although in the genres discussed here they tend to be obscured by the percussion instruments), and can fortify an elaborately swirling vocal line with a close unison line. The harmonium also provides an absolute pitch base—when a singer finds the more suitable register for a song he can make a mental note as to where on the harmonium keyboard the tonic or the starting tone of the song lies. The harmonium was a modern instrument not too many years ago, and still connotes urban sophistication. It is so well established in North Indian folk and popular music at this time that it is futile to plea for its dismissal, but it is good to remember the ways in which it is changing Indian music.

The harmonium (and a ḍholak) accompany a purvī singer who is often a launḍā or a female dancer and singer. The style of dance resembles that of the North Indian classical dance called *kathak*. Dancing in the formal context is rarely as suggestive as that of the informal context although the role of the female dancer nonetheless carries a sexual connotation. Female dancers, like the launḍās, have racy reputations. One man assured me that 90 percent of the launḍās are homosexuals and sell their services to men in the audiences they have entertained; I doubt that the proportion is anywhere near that great. Female dancers too have a reputation for prostitution. In Indrapur a female dancer is called *randī*, defined in the dictionary as "prostitute, harlot," which in many instances is misleading. The role of today's female wedding dancer descends from that of courtesan. Today, as in the past, there are several types of courtesans, some of whom do not market sexual favors.[8] Occasionally a female dancer does allude to the courtesan role by making a foray into the crowd during a song, to sing as she sits or dances opposite some man who she thinks will provide a good-humored foil to her coquettish, teasing behaviors (see Photo 18).

Purvīs are predominately songs of the *śṛṅgār ras*—"the erotic or amorous emotion," and they generally employ the virah theme. A few of these songs are explicitly sexual, like the first one below, but one informant said such songs were not of the true śṛṅgār ras, but were *aślīl* (lewd, prurient or indecent). Most purvīs depict a woman separated from her lover or husband, like the second and third songs below. Many, like the third song, use the lovely conventions of natural imagery which appear in early Sanskrit court poetry and no doubt predate it.

106.

I will agree to whatever you say, dear.
Just remove my nose ring and slowly kiss me.
The color of your forearm is so fair.
The tears from your eyes touch the redness of your
  cheeks.
A fire burns throughout my body.
Just remove my nose ring and slowly kiss me.
Phālgun waxes; my heart has gone mad.
The colī strains, the breasts grow full.
Unbutton the buttons, lover, take pleasure.
Just remove my nose ring and slowly kiss me.
I will agree to whatever you say dear.

This song was performed by a female singer and dancer with a small troupe at a large Ṭhākur wedding in the Vārāṇasī District. The image of burgeoning breasts (*jobanawā*) in line 8, often mentioned together with the straining or tearing of the colī, is one of the conventions of *śṛṅgār ras* in folk song.

In the following song, performed by a Camār band for a Camār wedding near Indrapur, a woman complains at the absence of her husband and expresses the anguish and difficulty of her solitude.

107.

You can leave the country, but my eye make-up does not
  leave.
The myrtle stain does not leave my feet.
When I heard you were coming,

I made thousands of preparations.
You have taken my heart and fled, you have deceived me
 and fled.
I swear, friend, he deceived me and left.
If you were just going to deceive me, why did you go
 through with the gaunā?
The night was pleasant; why were you in my dream?
The bed was empty the whole night; I was afraid.
I am unfortunate; he brought me here and left.
Oh God, I got an ill-starred husband.
The era is evil, there are evil men.
Was I suggestive with someone?
Why have people started looking at me suggestively?
They say, "Sweetheart, just come and embrace me!"
The pitcher sometimes bursts and spills.
Hey Sīa Rām, I will not get to be with you.
Oh, if you are going to come, come in my youth.
This empty bed is not at all pleasant.

The song tells that a man brought his bride home, left and did not return when expected. The first line is a pun on *chute,* which means, in different contexts, both "abandon" and "fade away." Indian women not only beautify their eyes on special occasions, they also beautify the soles of their feet and the palms of their hands by painting designs on them with henna or myrtle. The female narrator is metaphorically saying: you come and go as you wish, but I have changed myself irrevocably for you. In lines 14 and 15 she says that the men of the village, knowing her husband is away, try to take advantage of her. In line 16 she signals with a metaphor conventional in this genre that she may suffer a nervous collapse.

The next song focuses on the longing of a woman for her man, which is sharpened by certain phenomena of nature.

108.

At midnight the cuckoo calls.
The pretty woman starts, arises and stands near the bed.
The mango has blossomed, the *mahūā* has flowered.
The sleep of the lady separated from her lover has been
 broken.
The breeze blows over her body.
The door to memories begins to open.

The flowers have blossomed; the bee hovers near,
Why has her husband not come home?
She wrote her sorrows in a letter, posted it, and darkness
began to descend.
Tears flow in her eyes.
Birds began to fly and the sky began to lighten.
The parrot began calling from the cage of her heart.
The hard-hearted one does not remember the love he
gave to me.
God knows when he will remove this sorrow.

A "radio" singer with a rich voice and an agile touch on the harmonium, Rām Candra Harijan, performed this song at a Ṭhākur wedding in Indrapur.* The theme and the conventionalized images used to depict it are found in classical Sanskrit poetry as well as the later Sanskrit poem, the *Gīta Govinda*.[9] The call of the cuckoo, the scents of trees and flowers (the *mahūā* is a tree bearing sweet-scented flowers), the blossoms surrounded by bees, and the motion of the breeze are all thought to increase the desire of separated lovers. The blossoming flowers stand for a woman fully ready to be her consumed by her lover, who is symbolized by the bee hovering near. The theme is again that of virah or virāhāhdukh (the pain of separation in love). It is curious that, as in the West, people enjoy songs which elaborate and augment their own melancholy feelings.

The contemporary songs incorporating these images and themes show that the sentiment of romantic longing has persisted in Indian culture despite institutions which would seem to discourage romance—purdah, arranged marriages, and the absence of courtship. Archer explains this by positing a romantic tendency which can only be expressed in poetry and song.[10] But for some, romantic love, or something akin to it, is not merely a fantasy. There are those fortunate couples who get married and then fall in love, as was the case with a few of my acquaintances in the village. The sentiment of romantic love is thus kept alive by personal experience as well as by song, in which it is an important traditional theme.

Qawwālī

The "popular" qawwālī is another type of entertainment music that often concerns love, but with a complex of feelings very different from that of the purvī. The popular qawwālī derives from Sufi songs which carry the same name.

> Sufism, a major force in Indo-Muslim history and well-established throughout Indian Islam, has developed its own poetry and music as an essential means for devotional expression and the attainment of religious ecstacy. Qawwālī . . . is the musical assembly held by Sufis throughout the year but principally on the anniversary (*urs*) of the numerous Sufi saints at their shrines and wherever their devotees may gather. The term qawwālī actually denotes the Sufi song itself and only by implication the occasion of its performance . . . Its most authentic performers (*qawwāl*) are hereditary professionals tracing their origin and performing tradition to the 13th century Indo-Persian poet and musician Amir Khusrau who was lined with the Chishti order of Sufism. Qawwālī is also performed by many other professionals in a less traditional style and by devotees at various shrines . . . Traditional qawwālī combines group and solo singing and is accompanied by various instruments, principally drum and harmonium and sometimes by handclapping.[11]

In one of the biweekly qawwālī sessions at the shrine of Nizamuddin Aulia in Delhi, the group (see Photo 19) peformed songs of two genres—songs in praise of Mohammed (*na't* or *nat*) and songs in praise of the descendants of Ali (*manqabat* or *śāhīdī*). Nazir Jairazbhoy has stated that a qawwālī performance generally begins with an instrumental called *naghma* (tune) and proceeds through sung genres called *ḥamd* (songs in praise of Allah), the na't and manqabat, and finally ghazal.[12] The ghazal

> is a poetic form employing an indefinite number of couplets, independent in content. Its origin lies in the Persian ghazal and, although Indo-Pakistani ghazals are generally composed in Urdu, they still reflect their origins in style and content. Under court patronage, Urdu ghazal reached its height in the eighteenth and nineteenth centuries with Muslim poets such as Mir, Ghalib and others.[13]

In northern India, the Deccan Plateau, and Pakistan, ghazals are sung independently under that rubric. It is being incorporated as well into the popular qawwālī, whose musical style is quite similar to, and derives from, the qawwālī performed at Sufi shrines. Many of the popular qawwālī lyrics are ghazals which depict unrequited love. The object of the unreciprocated love in some songs, like the first one below, is clearly a woman. Other songs employ an intentional ambiguity: they are simultaneously about the love of man for woman and the love of man for god, love which is spurned in either case. The style of the following song and even the disjuncture of its final six lines are typical of the ghazal-type popular qawwālī.

109.

Yes, I'm troubled by love,
But the trouble will not go away.
I am ruined unless she realizes what she is doing.
Oh, in her eyes are everything but,
In her eyes are everything but,
In her eyes are everything but,
There isn't any passion.
Don't play with my life,
Life isn't that cheap.
A flower has the right to smile,
But why does the sprouting bud smile?
The coquettish look is wrong.
She cries; she doesn't laugh.
He sits on the bank of the river,
He throws the net wide,
How clever are the fish!
Not even one fish is caught!
Oh will the net catch me?
On his hook there is no bait.
[Only the essential repetition has been indicated; most of the lines are repeated two or three times.]

Many qawwālī texts are sung to only a few popular melodies (amply modified, in some cases). This text was set to one such melody by Lālū Prasād (a Camār), who sang it at a casual gathering of musicians and friends in Naria bazaar, just outside the campus of Banāras Hindu University. I later recorded different versions of the text and tune at several weddings. The song employs the simile of a smiling flower to assert that a mature woman has the right to use her beauty to arouse and attract him, but this girl doesn't realize the effect her charms have on him. This simile of the smiling flower is found in one of Mir's ghazals.[14] The disunity of the final six lines is characteristic of the ghazal, in which ". . . every couplet is an independent entity, not necessarily related even in mood to its neighbors."[15]

The language of the more refined qawwālīs is Urdu, which presents two related paradoxes. Among educated people the Urdu ghazal and thus many qawwālī lyrics are highly esteemed, not only because they are ingenious and moving lyrics, but because they connote the elegance and sophistication of the Mughal court and the mahphil. The popularity of qawwālī with Hindu audiences is paradoxical in that Urdu is, for historical reasons, associated with the Muslim population, and historically there has been antagonism between Hindus and Muslims in India. Secondly, Urdu and standard Hindi share a common grammar, but there are many Persian and Arabic words in the Urdu vocabulary. Uneducated and even many educated villagers, who comprise a majority of qawwālī audiences in eastern Uttar Pradesh, do not understand a substantial portion of the pure Urdu songs, but accept the language as an intrinsic part of the qawwālī performance.

Informants said that thirty or forty years ago qawwālīs were sung only by Muslims; today groups performing qawwālīs often include lower caste Hindus. The Hindu-Muslim mixture is also seen in the repertoire of the qawwālī group. At least in the area around Vārāṇasī, this now includes topics from Hindu mythology, as illustrated by the qawwālī below. After a false start it dramatizes an episode from the Rāmcaritmānas.*

110.

In this great expanse, the holy place Brij is best of all.
Nandagā̃o is the best of all places.
In Lanka the name of Rām was made very famous.
Hanumān said, "My Rām is so good."
In Lanka when Angad put his foot down,
He said, "Is there a brave man here who can lift my
  foot?"
When every brave man had lost, then Rāvan came
  forward.
Angad said, "Why did you come to grasp my foot?"
If you would touch it, then go and touch the foot of Rām.
Rām, whoever was touched by your gaze of mercy,
His sin was removed, his spoiled fate corrected.
By your mercy even he who was ruined from the
  beginning was saved.
Ahilyā also received mercy from the feet of Gautam Ṛṣi,
When Rām came forward and put his foot on the stone
  block.
How did Hanumān and the other monkeys meet on the
  sea coast?
Not knowing where Sītā was, he searched here and
  there.
Hanumān crossed the sea and arrived at the mountains.
All the mountains were depressed below the
  underworld.
When Hanumān angrily put his foot down.

This song was performed by the eminent Cānd Pūtalī group of Vārāṇasī at a large Ṭhākur wedding. Aṅgad was the son of Bali, the king of the monkeys who served Rām in the battle with Rāvana. He was sent to Rāvaṇa to obtain the release of Sītā, Rām's wife. After arguing with Rāvaṇa and his aides, Aṅgad wagered (to demonstrate that they would be foolish to do battle with Rām's forces), that no one could budge his foot. All of the aides tried and failed; when Rāvaṇa grasped his foot Aṅgad admonished that he would be wiser to touch the feet of Rām (and thus admit his inferiority and signal his surrender). This episode is not one celebrated in most of the songs lauding Rām.

Ṛṣi Gautam (mentioned in Line 13) turned his beautiful wife Ahilyā into a block of stone as punishment for her sleeping with the god Indra. The Rāmcaritmānas relates how Rām, while in the Dandaka forest, mercifuly touched the stone block with his foot and revived the woman.[16]

The story also refers to the conference of monkeys before Hanumān's departure for Lanka. The last three lines of this song confuse this element of Tulsī Dās' story. According to Growse's translation, Hanumān depressed the mountains on the southern tip of the peninsula when he sprang from them to fly to Lanka. The first two lines of the song also reflect a misunderstanding. Brij is the area around Mathurā, usually associated with Krishna, and is thus out of place in a song about Rām, as is Nandagā̃o, where Krishna was born. Apparently the composer of the song was not well-versed in Hindu mythology.

Like the purvīs, qawwālīs are generally accompanied by ḍholak, harmonium, and in many cases by kartāl. A very few groups use the sāraṅgī. Forward-looking urban groups use an electrified version of an instrument which in India is called *bainjo* or *bulbultarang*. This is unlike any instrument which would be called banjo in the United States. It resembles the Appalachian dulcimer, but the strings are noded by a series of keys much like those on a typewriter. The timbre of the electrified version is one which an electric guitar might produce.

The basic format of the popular qawwālī is like that of the religious qawwālī: solos in free rhythm alternate with heavily rhythmic and repetitious refrains sung by the chorus. (The chorus includes the instrumentalists and, in larger groups, men who only sing and clap.) A song may begin with a harmonium-ḍholak instrumental (*gati*), with a very brief alāp, or with the first solo vocal. The text of each of the solos is a different couplet, and the singing elaborate and somewhat improvisational. The intense, repetitious choral singing of the last line of the leader's couplet over the busy percussion of the ḍholak and the buoyant swells of the harmonium generate much fervor. In one of the later rhythmic choruses of each song the leader or a second singer inserts, in place of the choral singing, a high, wordless "coloratura" passage—a virtuoso passage with much fast melodic movement or sometimes a strategic tone held to great length, that adds to the ecstacy. A qawwālī with only five or six couplets of text may last ten minutes because of the repetition.

Of all the vocal music heard in the village, qawwālī has the most in common with classical musical traditions, in particular with the tradition of *khayāl* singing, which dominates Hindustani classical vocal music today. Qureshi has noted that the religious qawwālī melody freely uses and mixes classical ragas as well as its own type of ragas to form several short tunes within any one song, including many variations of the tunes and melodic improvisations. She also states that the drum patterns of religious qawwālīs are a type of 4/4 meter called *qawwāli tāl*, or, less often, a type of 6/8 meter called *dādra tāl*.[17] These statements would seem to apply as well to popular qawwālī but both matters await detailed musicological analysis.

Like the birahā, the qawwālī is very forceful in its delivery, sometimes to the point of overstatement. The qawwālī employs many passages in a high vocal range, as well as more frequent and more intricate melodic movement and ornamentation. As a result qawwālī often has an even more anguished, strained character than birahā. This is reinforced by the physical appearance of the singer. With his lined brow and bulging neck muscles, he may rise to his knees at dramatic moments, and even throw off his cap and pretend to tear out his hair. In discussing Muslim singers Fox-Strangways stated that the less able singer "is apt to tear a passion to pieces" rather than not challenge the admiration of the audience.

The spontaneous comments men made during and after birahā and qawwālī peformances provide insight into their esthetics. Laudatory remarks about performance often referred to the ability of the singer to generate strong emotional responses in the listener. A typical comment was "this huge wave of force [emotion] hit me." (*Hamke itanī bāṛī jos̒ kā lahar laggayal.*) The term mast (intoxicating) was also used frequently in affirmative comments.

What was surprising was the absence of specific comment on the often dazzling vocal ornamentation and extreme intensity which are characteristic of qawwālī. However, men did comment on "voice" (galā—literally "throat"), and as in our own culture, they were no doubt referring both to vocal timbre and to the skill with which the voice is used. Their comments indicated that sweet as well as strong voices are valued. More investigation is needed to determine what aspects of vocal *skill* are recognized and evaluated.

Another fascinating aspect of performance about which there was very little comment was the drumming, which is usually elaborate without sacrificing a strong drive. One listener did remark that the drummer we were listening to knew only one cyclical pattern of strokes (tekā), which indicates that "good" drumming requires the use of at least several such patterns.

While vocal qualities of some sort are recognized, it appears that the lyrics and story of a song are more important in its success than extreme intensity or refinement in singing. A stentorian vocal didn't stimulate much response unless it was coupled with an arresting lyric. The limited interest people demonstrate in instrumental music, and the incidental role solely instrumental songs play in the repertoire of entertainment groups also suggest that the verbal message is of primary importance.

The challenge to the entertainer at large weddings is to try to please an audience with a variety of interests. In addition to the divisions of qawwālī subjects mentioned above, I heard qawwālīs about such topics as the exploits and glories of Krishna, Rām's journey in the forest, the foibles of a villager in the city, and devotion to the nation. At a wedding which took place shortly after the war in Bangla Desh, following the qawwālī about Rām (above), one of the groom's colleagues shouted that they had heard enough *purānī* (ancient) things; they wanted a song about Bangla Desh. The group obliged with a song lauding Prime Minister Indira Gandhi's strength and determination through the war; the air was full of hands waving rupee notes as the song finished. The variety of topics in songs performed by qavvālī groups has clearly increased in recent years to accommodate the various interests and identities of its expanded and diversified audiences.

Like the English bands discussed below, entertainment bands generally come from outside the village, and in that sense belong to one of the outer of our concentric circles. Moreover, although the themes of their songs are sometimes those of the participatory songs villagers know, the ways they are performed and accompanied are more complex and refined, and in that sense, outside the province of the village culture. Indian writers tend to exclude them from the category folk music, as they would the music of the brass bands.

Processional Music

Throughout India members of untouchable castes are employed to play drums (sometimes with other instruments) at weddings and other festive occasions. The frequent association of drum-dominated music with untouchables is related to a common traditional occupation, the processing of livestock carcasses, which includes the tanning of hides from which they make drum heads. In the surrounding rural areas and even in Vārāṇasī one often sees the noisy Camār rhythm bands called *daphalīs*. These are among the least expensive processional bands that can be hired, and they can double as informal entertainment groups. The groups take their name from the daphalā, the shallow single-headed frame drum. A six- to eight-inch dished brass gong (*kasāvar* or *baṭhalū*) and a pair of kettle drums (nagāṛā) provide complimentary rhythms to the daphalā.*

In and around Vārāṇasī one sees more *śahnāī* bands at the heads of processions than one does in the countryside.* The śahnāī "parties" consist of two or more śahnāīs, of which at least one provides a drone, and a pair of small kettle drums (see Photo 24). One also sees an occasional bagpipe band in Vārāṇasī and other cities in North India (a vestige of the British rule), as well as various motley conglomerations of bagpipes and other Western and Indian instruments.

The loudest, most colorful, and most prestigious of the ensembles that lead processions, however, are the "English bands" (*angrezī baiṇḍs*). They are remarkable syntheses of the diverse elements in Indian culture. Combined with the European costume and instruments are the Islamic identity of the bandsmen, and music deriving from Western, Mughal court, Hindu folk, and modern Indian film traditions. The bands are called "English" because they wear uniforms and play musical instruments associated with, and adopted from, the English military. "A generation ago it was the height of sophistication to have police or 'palace' bands play in public parks—a dignified imitation of the British Governor."[18]

The English band is used primarily to lead processions, and processions are always connected with sacred activities. In the wedding, a band leads women of the groom's family and neighborhood to the village for the final blessing of the groom and dancing by the women. At the bride's village the band leads the bārāt to the home of the bride for the dvar pūjā, after which it entertains the guests briefly. The next day at dawn it customarily plays songs based on Rāga Bhairavī. One of the pleasant surprises of living in the village was to be awakened by the sounds of this contemplative raga).* Later, around noon, the bārāt follows the band to the bride's home for the khicarī ceremonies. It may play again in the afternoon for the entertainment of the wedding guests. The larger bands, consisting of ten to fifteen members, received from one hundred and fifty to two hundred rupees for these services.

Affluent families also hire bands to perform at rites other than the wedding, including the gaunā, janeū (sacred thread) and muṇḍan (first hair-cutting) rites. Bands often play in public ceremonies as well, such as the grand parade of sādhūs in the Śiva Rātra festival in Vārāṇasī. I did not observe bands playing in connection with funerary rites, but informants said that a family might employ a band to play on such an occasion, if the deceased had lived a full and prosperous life and the death was not attended by great remorse.

Brass bands or other processional music are desirable in festive occasions for several stated and unstated reasons. Their brass, bombast and bright uniforms effectively call attention to the event they accompany and assert their sponsor's prestige, signaling even to those somewhat removed from the proceedings that a significant event is underway. (A myth told in the state of Orissa holds that music *originated* in response to a need to signal people in other villages of a wedding or funeral.)[19] Villagers also explained the desirability of the processional bands at festive occasions with the word maṅgal (the same explanation they gave to women's song and other music on public address systems, and the blowing of the conch shell in pūjās). Most villagers appreciate the brass bands' music primarily for its contribution to the exuberant spirit of such occasions. By providing maṅgal, the band contributes to both present and the future good—the more gaudily outfitted the band and louder its music, the happier the proceedings and the greater the chances for the success of the marriage.

Villagers are generally less interested in *bajā*—"instrumental music" than they are in *gānā*—"song." This is seen not only in the lack of close attention paid the brass band performances, but in the incidental role solely instrumental songs play in the repertoires of entertainment groups. Also, villagers visiting my quarters requested me to play my guitar and occasionally complimented my playing. But after listening to it for a short time, inevitably they asked me to sing something, and when I did, asked me to translate. Clearly, the verbal dimension is of prime importance in village music.

Social Composition of the Brass Band

When I asked men of one band why they played, their answer (to what must have seemed a stupid question) was *peṭ-oṭ ke lie*, roughly, "to fill the stomach." They did not mention their ascribed social status, which in several ways channels them toward music. In the area around Indrapur, no caste was thought of as one whose primary traditional occupation was musician (which is not the case in many areas in India). However, the local Muslim musicians, although they belong to castes not thought of as primarily musical in their traditional occupations, in some cases anchor their musical proclivities in the idea that their ancestors were court musicians of Muslim kings and deputy governors. Secondly, most entertainment and English band musicians belong to landless families of low or mid-range Hindu or Muslim castes, in which the education of boys beyond the primary level would deprive the family of essential labor or income. Without education, few of the young men have any alternative to the occupations traditionally associated with their castes. Music is one of these occupations, but for most it is only a secondary source of income, pursued primarily in the wedding season. At the same time, music is for them an immediately accessible occupation. Boys belonging to these castes grow up with music and musicians a part of their environment, such that some music learning takes place informally, and some unconsciously, and to some degree they become musicians without a conscious decision to do so. (See Photo 27, for example.) In some cases they are drafted into bands as soon as they can play adequately. Boys may begin playing drums in the English bands when they are only eight or nine years old.

Around Indrapur the members of English bands were all from lower Muslim castes such as the *Jolāhā* (weaver), *Darzī* (tailor), and *Curīhāra* (bangle seller) castes, as well as from a group who called their caste *Śāh* or *Sāī*, and claimed descent from Muslim *imāms* (religious leaders of Shiā sects). Entertainment musicians are drawn from these castes as well as from lower Hindu castes such as Camār, Mussahar, Bhar, Dhobī, and Nāī, and from mid-range castes including the Ahirs.

Instrumental Composition of the Band

English bands range in size from three members to around fifteen in the countryside and perhaps double that in urban areas. Trumpets, cornets and clarinets usually take the leading melodic roles, and euphoniums, valve trombones, and an occasional saxophone provide support with adumbrate unison or octave lines. The percussion instruments constitute a "rhythm choir"—the lines they play fit together in a complementary way. The *tambur ḍhol*, a snare drum played with two sticks, produces higher-pitched, busier patterns; the *ḍhol*, a larger double headed drum known as the Scottish bass drum in the U.S., played with a short stick and one open hand, produces lower pitched, less dense patterns; the bass drum even less frequent, basic accents. Maracas or cymbals or both add a regular swishing sound on top. (This is assuming a larger band. Small bands may employ only the snare and one of the other drums.)

Instruction

The leader of the band usually plays one of the higher-register instruments (e.g., trumpet or clarinet) and teaches some or all the wind instruments. Instruction is carried out in a traditional guru-celā relationship. The guru plays a phrase and the celā repeats it until he can replicate it satisfactorily.

An older drummer in the band usually teaches the percussion players their parts. In many bands the drummers are young boys, who often play with impressive fierceness and dexterity. They learn by feeling the rhythm—the student holds the sticks in his hands and his teacher holds the student's hands in his own. The teacher then plays the rhythmic cycle on the drum, through the hands of the student, until the child can reproduce it unassisted. There are also *bols* (spoken phrases) which imitate the sounds of a percussive phrase or cycle, to help the student learn and remember it.

Repertoire and Performance

The bands play four classes of music: film songs; marches; folk tunes such as kajalī, phaguā, purvī, and kaharavā; and ragas. The ragas are similar to those played by contemporary, formally trained classical musicians. Raga refers to a performance unit which is based on a certain group of scalar and melodic conventions: "A raga is a group of tones from which a melody is formed . . . [but] the character of a raga . . . [is also determined] by the emphasis placed on certain tones, by certain characteristic turns in the direction of the melody [in descending, especially], by certain deflections from normal pitch, and even by graces or ornamental notes used with certain tones."[20]

As in the orthodox classical tradition, the brass bands play each raga only during a certain period in the day. In fact, of all the musicians I observed, including the classical musicians, the brass bandsmen were the only ones who adhered to the traditional restrictions on the playing of certain ragas at certain times of the day. In the morning the bands play different tunes based on the Bhairavi raga. Classical tunes played in the afternoon are based on the Pīlū raga.* In the evening, they said, the classical tunes played are based on Rāga Śyām Kalyānī. (I did not actually hear any tunes of this raga played.) The other genres in the repertoire can be played at any time of day.

There are interesting similarities and differences between the ragas these bands play and ragas of the same names played in Hindustani classical music. In both systems a raga is the basis of many tunes. Each tune is identified by a distinguishing melodic phrase, often that which leads to the *sam* (the beginning of the rhythmic cycle). In both systems the melody of the tune and improvisational passages also contain brief melodic bits or other characteristics of the subsuming raga. These characteristics are, to a considerable degree, common to the two systems. A formally trained musician would generally recognize a song played by a brass band under the appelation Rāga Bhairavī as such, because it employs the characteristics which he identifies with that raga.

In some cases, however, the song a brass band considers to be based on a certain raga includes melodic phrases which do not manifest the characteristics of the raga by which it is called. For example, one song said by the band leader to be a Rāga Pīlū had an introduction which was identified by a classically trained performer and musicologist as based on Rāga Mālkoś.[21] The subsequent phrase was characeristic of Rāga Pīlū, but the rest of the song did not manifest the characteristics of Pīlū. Such synthesis is no doubt facilitated by the "free" nature of the two ragas (Bhairavī and Pīlū) most commonly played by the brass bands of this area. A "free" raga is one in which there are fewer conventional melodic shapes or other rules which must be observed. There is thus a good deal of latitude in their formulation and elaboration even by classical musicians.

The alāp of the brass band raga is generally a brief rubato section consisting of only a few phrases. The trumpets or other higher register horns play melodic lines over the tonic pedal (sustained tone) of the low register horns, or horns of the two registers play in octave unison. Classical alāps are generally much longer, as are the complete performances of classical ragas. Following the alāp the bands I heard played music in metered cycles of six, eight, or sixteen beats. Cycles of these lengths are common in classical Hindustani ragas. Within these cycles, however, the brass bands use meters (patterns of accents) which are not used in classical performances. This is partially due, no doubt, to the differences in instrumentation. In these passages the higher register instruments—trumpets, cornets and clarinets, generally play the "lead" roles. These consist of playing the melody in unison or heterophony. (In heterophony, each player plays a slightly different version of the melody.) Alternately, during improvisational passages the solo role may be passed from player to player among the better leads. The non-soloing lead horns generally fill in the gaps when the soloist of the moment stops to breathe or rest. This may involve imitating, in brief form, lines he has just played or taking up a melody where he dropped it (often quite surprisingly in the middle of a phrase). Support horns may play the melody in unison or heterophony with the leads, but an octave lower. They also sometimes play a drone, a continuous tone (with brief gaps for breathing) on the tonic. The general organization of the horn parts taken as a whole is similar to that of the śahnāī bands of Vārāṇasī. The śahnāī bands, however, use different percussion accompaniment—a pair of drums similar to the *tablā* and *bāyā̃* drums used in classical music called *ḍuggī* and *khurdak*. (See Photo 27.)

While the sound produced by some bands is little more than loosely coordinated noise, most of the bands play with much snap and verve, and a few of the bands, especially the larger ones, display considerable refinement. Some lead players improvise impressively and have a knack for making a raga out of a simple pop or folk tune. Larger bands also have an effective way of contrasting cooler, moderate passages with hotter, more exciting ones. The effect is achieved through the alternation of sometimes muted solos and restrained percussion with the dramatic resumption of ensemble blowing and more intense percussion. One band leader said that a good band was one that could generate such "climaxes." As occurs with jazz and other instrumental music in the United States, those who are most aware and appreciative of profiency and creativity are the bandsmen themselves. Often their artistry serves mostly to allay their own boredom; most listeners are aware only of the music's gross and spectacular features.

Summary

Weddings are social events of unsurpassed importance to families, and those of more influential families attract the concern of the entire village. The musical entertainment and processional music of weddings signal a family's class standing, as well as providing the gala ambience of the affair and a pleasant and expected diversion for guests.

A family's affluence greatly influences both the style of entertainment music and the surroundings in which it will be performed. Poorer families accommodate guests at their homes, where the often loosely organized bands play simple, heavily percussive music to the listeners with whom they mingle. Many of these performances include the uninhibited dancing of a female impersonator.

It is the music of the more expensive and prestigious formal performances which contrasts most sharply with music examined in previous chapters. Better seating and more space allow the audience a better view of the artists in the formal situation, and there is more worth seeing and hearing—the music involves more instruments and more mastery of instrumental and vocal techniques. The ḍholak provides percussion and drive in all the music of the formal performances, and all of the ensembles except those performing birahās employ the harmonium. (Musicians are unaware of or indifferent to its destruction of native scales.)

The birahā shares with its namesake, the khaṛī birahā, only three general traits: its association with the Ahir caste, its forcefulness, and its descending melodic contour. Topical songs of a wide variety of subjects are composed to the birahā and, to a lesser degree, to the qawwālī forms. Important among these are the nationalistic songs. These develop an awareness of and a feisty pride in the nation, strengthening the nationalistic theme now firmly embedded in village culture.

Purvī, a genre which apparently comes from an area to the east of Vārāṇasī and Ghazipur districts, has gently descending melodies and texts which reflect the same erotic and romantic longing themes found in the men's participatory kajalīs. The other prominent class of music performed in these contexts is the qawwālī, which is derived from music of the same name performed at the shrines of Sufi saints. The highly agile and ornamented melodic line of the qawwālī provides the greatest scope for vocal artistry of the entertainment music. Prominent among its texts are those stemming from a genre of eighteenth century Urdu court poetry called g͟hazal. In Vārāṇasī and other of the region's cities, boundaries between these genres—birahā, purvī and qawwālī—are blurring, and new syntheses like the Bhojpurī and lok gīt are emerging.

Like the formal entertainment bands, the brass bands that lead wedding processions are also important in winning or maintaining the honor of the nuptial families. These ensembles reflect the diversity of Indian culture in their uniforms, instrumentation, and in their repertoire, which may include ragas performed in the Hindustani classical tradition as well as Indian and Western folk and popular music. With their gaudy uniforms and loud, auspicious music, these bands lend much to the festive atmosphere of the wedding.

Notes

1. M. Elias, *Times of India,* April 23, 1978, p. 8.

2 Scott Marcus, "Field Research Report," *Ethnomusicology at UCLA* 2:3 (1984), p. 3.

3 Ibid.

4 Dr. Laxmi Tewari, a native speaker of Hindi, has kindly offered his understanding of this line: *Hilate sikari sejare mahi ke, pairon tale matu tekā jamana* (Every atom of the country and time itself, will touch its forehead to the feet of this fierce warrior.) Review of LP "Chant the Names of God," *Ethnomusicology* 27:2 (1983), p 402.

5 Prithipaul, personal communication, 1983.

6 K. Peter Etzkorn (ed. and add. material), *Music and Society: The Later Writings of Paul Honigsheim* (New York: John Wiley & Sons, 1973).

7 A. H. Fox-Strangways, *The Music of Hindostan* (London: Oxford University Press, 1965), pp. 16-18.

8 See Prakash Tandon, *Punjabi Century: 1857-1947* (Berkeley: University of California Press, 1961), pp. 184-86 for an introduction to the variety of Indian courtesans.

9 See Daniel H. H. Ingalls, *Sanskrit Poetry* (Cambridge: Harvard University Press, 1968), p. 90 and Barbara Stoler Miller, *Love Song of the Dark Lord* (New York: Columbia University Press, 1977), p. 90.

10 William G. Archer, *The Loves of Krishna in Indian Painting and Poetry* (New York: Grove Press, 1958), p. 73.

11 Regula Qureshi, "Indo-Muslim Religious Music, an Overview," *Asian Music* 3 (1972): pp. 15-23.

12 Nazir Jairazbhoy, personal communication, 1979.

13 Ibid.

14 Ralph Russell and Khurshidul Islam, *Three Mughal Poets* (Cambridge: Harvard University Press, 1968), p. 179.

15 Ralph Russell, "The Pursuit of the Urdu Ghazal," *The Journal of Asian Studies* 29 (1969): p. 108.

16 Benjamin Walker, *Hindu World: An Encyclopedic Survey of Hindusim* (London: George Allen & Unwin Ltd., 1968), p. 403.

17 Qureshi, "Indo-Muslim Religious Music," p. 21.

18 B. Chaitanya Deva, *Musical Instruments of India: Their History and Development* (Calcutta: Firma KLM Private Limited, 1978), p. 25.

19 Ibid., p. 71.

20 Howard Boatwright, *Indian Classical Music and the Western Listener* (Bombay: Bharatiya Vidya Bhavan, 1963), p. 4.

21 I am indebted to Professor Nazir Jairazbhoy for his assistance in comparing brass band and classical ragas.

* These items may be heard on the LP disc *Chant the Names of God*.

IX

Field Work: Problems and Prospects

A number of difficulties and dilemmas face the field worker who aims for a thorough knowledge and understanding of folk music and its significance to the peoples of India. A discussion of some of the more important and less obvious problems in field work methods will be of assistance to future field workers in India and elsewhere, and at the same time suggest the limitations of this study.

The Importance of Extended Community Study

Much of the folk music that has been recorded in India and many other parts of the non-Western world has been recorded on the run. The recordist arrives with his recording equipment, arranges for music to be performed, records, and departs with a record of the sonic events in whose creation he unintentionally participated.[1] To what extent is the music collected in this fashion representative of that which is traditional in the society? To be sure, in some cases such music is for all intent and purposes identical with music usually performed in the community. But music obtained in this manner may be an unrepresentative sample, and the music recorded may be substantially altered by the unique situation and the presence of the recordist—and is thus unreliable as social, cultural, and even musical data. Moreover, much of the meaning of the music derives from social and cultural contexts of which the mobile recordist remains oblivious.

Apart from the necessity of gathering relevant economic, social, political and ideological data, there are a number of good reasons why the researcher should live in a suitable community for at least one year after a good command of one of the primary languages spoken in the community has been attained. First and most obvious, many genres are seasonal or are tied to seasonal rituals. To observe them all requires residence through the full annual cycle. If one does not live *in* the community, that is, if one attempts to commute from a nearby city, one misses significant unscheduled musical events, and makes insufficient observations to discern what is unique and what is regular, or what is related to what.

Secondly, the novelty of the ethnomusicologist, with all of his modern gadgets, attracts a great many curious people. With each introduction to a new person or group, be it household, wedding party, or railway coach, the field worker is the target of much attention and a great many questions. On one hand, this disrupts whatever social event may be in process. On the other, he is on continuous display in each new social situation, and this can become quite tiresome. Staying in one community allows people to learn about the researcher, to become accustomed to his strange ways, and to accept his presence with less curiosity. Eventually, this allows him a modicum of privacy, and alleviates many of his hosts' anxieties.

There is another problem alleviated to some degree by extended stay. The field worker may unwittingly change the social and musical phenomena he is there to study. This problem, which social scientists call reactivity, has interesting manifestations in musical situations, as illustrated by the following three examples.[2]

In Indrapur I recorded several women's pre-wedding song sessions characterized by considerable hilarity, not to say hysteria. It was obvious that the women were excited by having a strange male, especially one with something so magical as a tape recorder, sit with them and ask strange questions in a strange language. (Many thought I was speaking in English when I spoke in Hindi.) Playing back the recordings certainly disturbed the normal flow of events and probably caused some self-consciousness. A friend later confirmed my suspicions, saying the women were distracted and agitated when I recorded them, and did not sing well. As could be expected, nervous agitation diminished in subsequent sessions.

When I was recording a group of urban Camārs singing phaguās, a spectator from the community exclaimed that he had heard enough Rāmāyaṇa-related songs, he wanted something juicier (*rasadār*). The singers ignored him. Later I interviewed the singer who had invited me to the session. He said he had told the group not to sing songs containing anything obscene. Perhaps they didn't want a spotted reputation with the sahib, to whom they probably attribute the same attitudes they attribute to their own upper classes. Or perhaps they feared he might play the recording or describe the material to someone who would disapprove, so they sang the loftier Rāmāyaṇa material.

A circumspect, well-educated friend of a friend invited me to attend a wedding at his home, which was in a village I had never visited. En route we talked about my work and I mentioned I had written an article that viewed the institution of galī-singing in a positive way. During the wedding the women sang not a single galī, a unique occurrence in my field experience.

In the first situation my presence negatively affected the quality of the women's singing. I later discovered it was possible in some cases to improve the quality of performance by building rapport with the musicians. (This I did by asking questions about the songs and reacting in an encouraging way to the performance.) In the second, and perhaps the third situation, my presence influenced what was sung rather than how it was sung.

Reactivity tends to diminish with repeated interaction for several reasons. Familiarity reassures and relaxes some people. Others discover that the researcher is not quite the idiot he appeared to be, and they are discouraged from managing false impressions. Obviously, it is not always possible to perceive how one's presence has influenced the usual process, especially when one has little experience for comparison.

The value of repeated interaction in the community is not limited to diminishing reactivity. The more experience the field worker has, the more able he is to discover the factors influencing the course of events in a performance. For example, the quality of specialists' music performance depends in part on the mood of the musicians. This in turn is subject to a variety of factors, including the way they are treated and the amount of their remuneration.

Another problem which can be overcome by a longer stay is the control that a single informant or intermediary can have over a field researcher.[3] For example, I visited one village in which there lived a caste of musicians whose rituals may be closely tied to the music for which they are especially noted. My host in this village was the son of the village headman, who controlled, if not owned outright, most of the surrounding land. The son never left my side while I was in the village, and every question I asked these musicians about their rites of passage he answered himself before they could reply.

An intermediary naturally tends to introduce the field worker to those families with whom he is on reasonably good terms, which automatically delimits the field worker's access to available music, knowledge, and perspectives. In some cases the host may favor a certain kind of folk music and exclude other kinds as not worth recording. A different problem is the host who promises a cornucopia of music but then will not assert himself to make the necessary introductions or arrangements. The field worker who becomes a pseudo-member of the community can make his own arrangements and relate directly to informants with less interference.

Even so, he is still faced with a dilemma. This is the problem that ". . . every firm social relationship (involving an anthropological field researcher) with a particular individual or group carries with it the possibility of closed doors and social rebuffs from competing segments of the community."[4] A field worker concerned with the entire scope of village music must consort with low caste musicians. Yet, unless he is a resident or a relative of one, his presence in the village must be sponsored by an influential person, almost always someone of a higher caste. His association with a high caste sponsor will affect the information lower caste individuals give him, and his association with low caste persons is bound to cause his sponsor some consternation.

A similar problem of mutual exclusivity pertains to the gender of the researcher. No doubt in most field work male researchers have better access to the male sphere of activity and females to the female sphere. Purdah and sexual segregation compound this situation in North Indian society. Women in the neighborhood in which I was a constant visitor honored me by allowing me to attend some ceremonies traditionally limited to women. There were a few rituals, however, to which I was not invited. I also found it difficult to communicate well with uneducated women, who spoke little Hindi. Undoubtedly, there are matters a woman would discuss with another woman that she would not discuss with a man. Clearly, the woman who can speak the vernacular language would have an advantage in researching women's song.

An extended stay also allows the field worker opportunities to cross-check his information. People everywhere are reluctant to say anything which will jeopardize or demean themselves. Band leaders, for example, know that more remuneration suggests a band of greater value. This tends to inflate the payments they report. (Also, most people who ask how much they have been paid for a job are probably considering them for employment. Band members may be accustomed to stating they received more than they actually did for a certain job in order to set a higher starting figure for bargaining.) A bride's father may cite a figure for the daughter's dowry considerably less than what he actually pays if he believes his interlocutor to disapprove the dowry institution and those who practice it, or he is afraid the amount will come to the attention of the authorities. The Dowry Prohibition Act of 1961 has not significantly reduced the practice, but has to some degree driven it under the table.

An unaware field worker can be easily misled. A mendicant singer maintained that he belonged to the Gosāĩ caste, and gave me a vague address. When I went to the suburban area he had described, the people there said that he was on an errand. Hearing that I was interested in music they hauled out some decrepit instruments and made noise for me, then made known their willingness to accept donations. I later discovered that the man I sought did not belong to that group at all, and they had simply been attempting to please me, perhaps to their slight financial advantage. One of my assistants finally located the mendicant's home and discovered that he did not belong to the caste he claimed. Apparently he had maintained a different caste identity because he thought it would lend credence to his qualifications as a singer of nirgun bhajans. I may have invited the deception by asking him, after he told me his name, if he belonged to the caste I was interested in. As often happens, he may simply have told me what he thought I wanted to hear.

Considerations such as these clearly press for an extended period of participant-observation research in a single community. Yet without some research in other communities it is difficult to know what is typical of the area. In like manner, what is unique and what is common in the music and culture of a language region are not apparent until comparative research in adjacent regions is carried out. For example, only from observing weddings outside Indrapur did I learn that the female dancer-singer was not uncommon in the area, although I never saw one in Indrapur. Each community has a somewhat different culture and social structure that result from its size, proximity and access to cities and other villages, and its singular history.[5] Indrapur is not a large village and is somewhat isolated by rivers difficult to cross in the monsoon season. While over fifteen castes live in the village or immediate vicinity, *all* castes found in the area are not found in Indrapur. There are few large landholding families, making for fewer large weddings, hence the absence of female entertainers during my stay. While Indrapur's medium size and isolation may have resulted in a slightly reduced spectrum of music, its isolation may also have led to the retention of music and other culture which is already disappearing from villages closer to the Westernizing and modernizing influences of cities.

There are also matters of chance. In some neighborhoods and perhaps even entire villages, the women's singing is less than musical, while in others good singers are abundant. Some groups elaborate certain rituals which others barely observe. For example, the Brahman *upanayan* or janeū ceremony, the initiation of a boy by his guru and the awarding of the loop of string he will wear which signifies his twice-born status, was observed only once in Indrapur during my stay. The songs associated specifically with that rite were so fragmentary, I did not include them here. There are songs for pilgrimage to and bathing in the Ganges, and no doubt other genres which did not find their way into my tape recorder.

In summary, some comparative study is essential in other villages of a region, but it is best pursued after one becomes thoroughly familiar with the music and culture of one village. This provides a basis for comparison as well as socialization.

Language Problems

The language skills needed to cope with ordinary spoken and written language were listed in the Introduction. Song texts make additional demands. Women's songs are in a variety of languages, including the local Bhojpurī dialect, a dialect spoken in the eastern part of the Bhojpurī region, *khaṛī boli* Hindi, and even a Rajasthani dialect. Bhajans contain words in Āvadhī (a variety of eastern Hindi), and Braj bhāṣā (spoken in the area around Mathurā in western Uttar Pradesh). Birahās use khāṛī boli Hindi and Bhojpurī of one or another variety. Some qawwālīs are in a purer Urdu containing many Persian and Arabic words which even educated Hindus may not know. And Urdu is properly written in a variety of Persian script, rather than the Devanagari script in which Sanskrit, Hindi, and Bhojpurī are written.

English-speaking residents should be employed in the transcription and translation of texts. However, I found it difficult to locate persons fluent in Bhojpurī and English who could take time to assist me, even when I could offer ample recompense. (Most people with enough education to be fluent in English hold full-time positions.) Even a bilingually–fluent assistant cannot solve all transcription and translation problems. Because the language of song texts differs from that of ordinary speech, or because in some cases accompanying music or noise obscures the words of a recorded song, only the singers can make out all of the words. In a few cases the singers themselves do not understand all the words of a song, because they are not in the local vernacular, they are archaic, or they have become garbled in transmission. Thus, accurate transcriptions and translations require consultation with the singers. This is another reason one can't simply go to a site, record, and move on.

I also encountered individuals who tactfully refused to translate obscene material and others who secretly baudlerized it to avoid embarrassment or to protect the dignity of the culture.

Field Assistance

Assistants would seem to be of great help in fieldwork as well as in textual work, but again there are difficulties. Reliable, industrious employees are not always easy to find, and there are some special problems attached to use of field work assistants. Unless the field worker has good control of the language, a native assistant comes to play the role of interpreter. Ethnographers avoid the use of interpreters because unconsciously or otherwise they tend to distort the information they relay to the field worker. Ambrose Bierce put it best when he said an interpreter is "one who enables two persons of different languages to understand each other by repeating to each what it would have been to the interpreter's advantage for the other to have said."

Another problem is reactivity. The educated assistant is often more urbanized and Westernized than the villagers, and few want or are able to downplay their relative sophistication, which may inhibit or otherwise influence the responses of musicians or other informants.

Prospects: Scope for Future Field Studies

Indian village music and its contexts have until now been much neglected by anthropologists and ethnomusicologists. This study demonstrates the abundance of music whose study is worthy in its own right, and the wealth of information it can provide about culture and social structure. The limitations of the study suggest the continuation of certain lines of investigation and the initiation of others.

As a survey even of music of the Bhojpurī-speaking area, the study is incomplete—there are song genres in the region whose study was not possible. In each of the genres mentioned here there are many, many songs yet to be recorded and studied. The transmission of entertainment songs and especially the role played by the inexpensive newsprint song booklets has not been studied, nor has the language of discourse used by these musicians, that is, how they talk about the music.

The perennial unity/diversity problem also suggests numerous investigations. Are the social contexts or uses of song genres in the Bhojpurī-speaking region common to other language regions? For example, do women in all regions in North India sing songs to celebrate the birth of a son? Are the stylistic traits of women's music I have mentioned common in the song of other areas? Are the women's repertoire and song style distinct from the men's throughout India? Is the dichotomy in language families (Indo-Aryan in the north and

Dravidian in the south) reflected in folk music style or social use? Clearly, there are many problems which require further study.

Notes

1 In many cases the field worker will not and in some should not be a male, but for the sake of economy and readability I have used masculine pronouns to refer to the field researcher.

2 Robert B. Edgerton and L. L. Langness, *Methods and Styles in the Study of Culture* (San Francisco: Chandler & Sharp Publishers, Inc., 1974), p. 32.

3. Victor Goldkind, "Anthropologists, Informants and the Achievement of Power in Chan Kom," *Sociologus* 20 (1970), pp. 17-41.

4 Pertti J. Pelto and Gretel H. Pelto, *Anthropological Research: The Structure of Inquiry* (New York: Cambridge University Press, 1978), p. 184.

5 For an introduction to inter-community cultural variation in south India, see Alan R. Beals, *Village Life in South India: Cultural Design and Environmental Variation* (Chicago: Aldine Publishing Company, 1974).

X

Conclusion

While the musical institutions brought to light by this research are interesting in their own right, they also provide new perspectives on social structure and religion.

Classification of the music resulted in the formulation of a dichotomy fundamental to this and, it would seem, many other bodies of folk music: the participatory and the non-participatory. This is a simple matter of form following function. The two types contrast with respect to function (ritual or recreational versus entertainment); form (simple vs. complex); experience (active vs. passive); role of performer (non-specialist vs. specialist); and evaluation (appropriateness to ritual or recreational goal vs. ability to generate emotional response). The dichotomy points out one inadequacy of the term folk music, which includes both types of music. No doubt in some senses the performances of both (in the case of the village musicians) are "folk," but the complexity of the music they perform and the roles that the two different categories of music play in the experience of individuals and the operation of society are quite different.

One of the primary methods of the research was to establish and examine correlations between social categories (or groups) and types or styles of music and surrounding musical cultures. This revealed striking differences between men's and women's participatory music and musical cultures. The contrast is seen in repertoire (women's songs are distinct from those men peform); musical style (women's songs tend to be of irregular meter, men's of foot-stomping rhythm); use or overt function (women's singing is more often a required ritual ingredient, men's singing an end in itself); frequency (women sing more often), spatial location (private courtyard vs. open public area); and song topics (women sing mother goddess songs and songs about family relationships that men don't).

The contrast between men's and women's musical cultures results from the effects of other institutions on musical ones, and from largely unknowable historical factors. Women's and men's lives are, in certain respects, distinct and separate. The place of singing differs because women tend to work and sing in the courtyard, and men outside the house. This arrangement results from the division of labor and from purdah. The uses of their singing differ in that much of women's song is an important ingredient of a larger ritual. Many of their rituals in turn derive from their interest in and responsibility for the welfare of the family, especially the males. This is in turn a result of women's economic dependence on men as a result of patrilocal residence, patrilineal inheritence, and plow agriculture.

Thus, parts of women's musical culture, specifically, the uses of song and the ritual and spatial locations of singing, are seen to result, in an indirect and complicated way, from socio-economic structures and ideology which are themselves interrelated.

Extra-musical institutions also have a limited influence on the contrast in song "style": women and men do not sing together, which aids the maintenance of separate styles. The general absence of driving rhythms from women's music is consonant with the restrained behavior expected of them in their husband's families.

For more explanation of stylistic differences we would have to resort to historical factors, but, as is often the case in the study of folk music, data are lacking. It is possible that the rhythms of men's seasonal songs have been adopted from or influenced by a variety of other music—the semi-tribal music present in the area before the arrival of Rājputs and Brahmans, the ecstatic Vaiṣṇavite devotional music, or the Muslims' religious qawwālī. Perhaps the women's song style diffused from or was influenced by the music of western Asia, where irregular meters are common.

The style of women's song is largely homogeneous up and down the entire caste hierarchy. This is easily explained with reference to ongoing practices involving song transmission: inter-caste singing groups and song trading above the untouchable level, and work-related opportunities for untouchable women to listen to and be heard by upper caste women.

Both men's and women's participatory singing groups consist of people of different and unequally ranked caste. Such intercaste singing groups as well as other rank-free social institutions in village life, contradict notions of rural Indian society as pervasively hierarchical.

It is in the non-participatory music that caste distinctions, their unique histories and discrete musical styles are most apparent. A few of the correlations between castes and particular stylistic features of their music are logical outgrowths of the caste's traditional occupation. The Camārs, who traditionally manufactured drum heads and other leather goods from animal skins, are noted for their drum-based processional and entertainment music. The loudness of the herding castes' *kharī birahā* makes it highly suitable for performance in the wide-open spaces as they tend their animals.

But the other notable stylistic trait of the kharī birahā cannot be explained with reference to caste occupation or other social institution. The tonality which the kharī birahā shares with the Camār shamans' invocations contrasts with the predominating diatonic tonality of village music. Explanation of this difference is limited to the historical knowledge that both groups (Ahirs and Camārs) were indigenous when Rājputs began immigrating.

History also provides a few clues to the association of the *nirgun bhajan* with the Jogī caste. The unusual themes of the Jogīs' songs are attributed to their retention and re-working of medieval Nāth sect ideology and the adoption of the sāraṅgī from the musical accompanists of the court or courtesans in later centuries. History is mute, however, as to why it is members of the Nat caste who perform the Ālhā.

The association of qawwālī, brass and *śahnāī* groups with Muslims is historically more accessible. The popular qawālī derives directly from the devotional music of the same name. The Muslim identity of brass and sahnāī bandsman results from a constellation of factors: the absence of other occupational alternatives, the accessibility of musical occupations through the presence of musicians in the kin group and neighborhood as boys grow up, and possibly for some Muslim castes, a role at some point in the past as accompanists of courtesans or court musicians of Muslim kings and deputy governors.

Music thus alludes not only to the extant divisions in Indian society, but to its long and complicated past as well. A prominent dimension of the past preserved in music is the religious, but before looking at the historical aspect of religion in song, it is useful to review the close relationship of music and religion in the village. This relationship is perhaps the most distinctive feature of rural North Indian musical culture.

Religion is conspicuous and influential in rural Indian culture. Nearly everyone engages daily in some form of religious behavior, and morality is primarily religious. Music is important in religion in India as elsewhere—people in nearly every known society have deemed music an eminently appropriate mode of communication with and about the supernatural. This is exemplified in the village by the shamans' exorcism rites, in which they sing to invoke and manipulate the tutelary goddess, and in mother goddess rites and the *harikīrtan*, in which people sing as a form of worship. It is also seen in the many womens' rites, in which their singing is a highly desirable aid to the accomplishment of ritual goals.

While the importance of music in village religion is not unusual in comparison with other cultures, the fact that the great proportion of all music in rural North Indian culture is one way or another religious—be it in musical belief, lyric, purpose, social setting or attitude of musician—is indeed distinctive. Music is a part of most all rites and festive occasions in the village, and regardless of whether it specifically addresses the supernatural, it has magico-religious significance in these settings because it is believed to be auspicious. Furthermore, in the village and throughout India, many songs not sung in connection with religious ritual refer in their lyrics to the divine, such as the phaguās, kajalīs and wedding entertainment songs whose texts refer to Krishna and Rām. The belief that the uttered name of the deity is the sonic presence of it compounds the religious significance of this music. Thus religion pervades and shapes musical culture in rural North India, providing a quality which renders it distinctly Indian.

To return to the subject of music and India's complex history, the texts of village songs preserve and transmit a thick stratigraphy of religious and other ideology. Those songs of the mother goddess connecting her with the infliction of smallpox could date back to the twelfth century, but probably date from a more recent period of epidemics. Krishna and Rām are the most common topics of songs, in accord with the prominent Vaiṣṇava devotional cults which have persisted since the fifteenth century. Through phaguās, kajalīs, bhajans, khaṛī birahās and even the popular qawwālīs people learn many of the stories told in the Rāmcaritmānas and the principal text of Krishna lore, the Bhāgavata Purāṇa. An important part of the folk compositional process seen in the Vaiṣṇavite songs as in other genres is in the borrowing and synthesis of images, phrases, and whole lines from extant songs. Some poetic conventions can be traced back to ancient Sanskrit court poetry, some have descended from the vernacular poetry of Surdas and other poet-saints, and a few have been borrowed from the Urdu g̣hazal.

Another type of song deriving from the devotional religion which blossomed in the area in the fifteenth and sixteenth centuries is the nirgun bhajan. These songs promote devotion to a formless divine and non-attachment to the mundane world as the paths to spiritual emancipation; they allow villagers to conceptually obliterate upsetting conditions over which they have no control. Their ideological roots go back to early Buddhist mysticism and perhaps even the Vedas.

The many songs depicting Rām's victorious battle (as described in the Rāmcaritmānas), as well as the Ālhā (which dates to the twelfth century) and other epics, reinforce the martial theme in Indian culture. The top stratum in village song, reflecting the most recent ideological movement, combines the martial spirit with patriotic fervor. Along with school rituals, national holidays, and the mass media, it propagates a growing sense of national identity.

Although some women's songs concern Rām and Krishna and other matters treated in the songs men sing, women's songs transmit a social ideology which distinguishes them from men's songs, and is not publicly expressed in another medium. Wedding songs, for example, remind all present that the affinal bonds being forged are double-edged swords, that men as well as women feel acutely the loss of their daughter and sister, and that the bride feels ignominious and betrayed. Mother-goddess songs and sohars teach the importance of sons, and sanction austerities and other rituals thought to insure marriage to a good husband as well as survival of husband and son (who are crucial to a woman's own survival). They also acknowledge problems inherent in a woman's affinal relations. Villagers are aware that, as a by-product, women's song communicates emotional events of the family to the surrounding neighborhood.

Many streams of ideology thus converge in village song, whence they continue to inform village cognition and affect. Remembering also that two-thirds of the population is illiterate, that effective communication relies on redundancy, and that village song is very repetitious, the importance of song to village thought and sentiment is clear.

The final objective of this study was to determine what importance music has in the lives of the people who hear and perform it. The preceding chapters showed the following intentional uses: an important part of religious ritual, a mode of worship, a ritual mnemonic, a means of transcending the phenomenal world, a basis for full and part-time occupations, a source of personal prestige, a medium for creative expression, recreation, a way to express and bolster seasonal moods, and a form of entertainment. We can also speculate on other unintended social and psychological effects: a means of enculturation, particularly of religious ideology, which in turn gives rise to normative behavior; a way to signal the emotional condition of the family to the surrounding neighborhood; a means of cartharsis; a way of establishing and maintaining social bonds; and an enjoyable form of interaction.

The multitude of songs and their many forms, uses and functions indicate that music is indeed important in village life, and its study is therefore requisite to a full understanding of the culture. Futher research of the kind described in this study will probably reveal two things: that the essential social uses of folk music identified here are found throughout northern India, and that the ubiquity of music in the social life of the Bhojpurī-speaking region is matched, if not surpassed, in other regions.

Bibliography

Alexiou, M. *The Ritual Lament in Greek Tradition*. New York: Cambridge University Press, 1974.

Archer, W. G. *The Loves of Krishna in Indian Painting and Poetry*. New York: Grove Press, 1958.

———. *Songs for the Bride: Wedding Rites of Rural India*. Edited by B. S. Miller and M. Archer. New York: Columbia University Press, 1985.

———, and S. Prasad. "Bhojpurī Village Songs," *The Journal of Bihar and Orissa Research Society* (1942);1-48.

Arya, U. *Ritual Songs and Folksongs of the Hindus of Surinam*. Leiden: E. J. Brill, 1968.

Babb, L. A. "Marriage and Malevolence: The Uses of Sexual Opposition in a Hindu Pantheon." *Ethnology* 9 (1970):137-48.

———. *The Divine Hierarchy: Popular Hinduism in Central India*. New York: Columbia University Press, 1975.

Bagchi, P. C. "Early Medieval Mysticism and Kabīr." *Visvabharati Quarterly* 25 (1959):160-71.

Barth, F. *Nomads of South Persia*. Boston: Little, Brown and Company, 1961.

Barthwal, P. D. *Traditions of Indian Mysticism based upon Nirguna School of Hindi Poetry*. Delhi: Heritage Publishers, 1978.

Bartis, P. T. "An Examination of the Holler in North Carolina White Tradition," *Southern Folklore Quarterly* 39 (1975):209-17.

Basham, A. L. *The Wonder That Was India*. Evergreen Books. New York: Grove Press, Inc., 1959.

Beals, R. *Village Life in South India: Cultural Design and Environmental Variation*. Chicago: Aldine Publishing Company, 1974.

Beck, B. *The Three Twins: The Telling of a South Indian Folk Epic*. Bloomington, Indiana: Indiana University Press, 1982.

Bharati, A. *The Ochre Robe*. Anchor Books. Garden City, New York: Doubleday & Co., 1970.

———. *The Tantric Tradition*. Garden City: Doubleday & Co., 1970.

Bhattacharya, D. *Love Songs of Vidyapati*. London: George Allen & Unwin, 1963.

Blacking, J. *How Musical Is Man?* Seattle: University of Washington Press, 1973.

Boatwright, H. *Indian Classical Music and the Western Listener*. Bombay: Bharatiya Vidya Bhavan, 1963.

Brenneis, D. "About Those Scoundrels I'll Let Everyone Know: Challenge Singing in a Fiji Indian Community," *Journal of American Folklore* 88 (1983): 283-91.

———. "The Emerging Soloist: Kavvali in Bhatgaon," *Asian Folklore Studies* 42 (1983):63-76.

Briggs, G. W. *Gorakhnath and the Kanphata Yogis*. Delhi: Motilal Banarsidas, 1973.

Bryce, L. W. *Women's Folk Songs of Rajputana*. New Delhi: Ministry of Information and Broadcasting, Government of India, 1961.

Chatterji, S. K. and S. M. Katre, *India: Languages*. New Delhi: Publications Division, Ministry of Information and Broadcasting, 1970.

Chaturvedi, M., and Dr. B. N. Tiwari. *A Practical Hindi-English Dictionary*. Delhi: National Publishing House, 1975.

Cohn, B. S. "Changing Traditions of a Low Caste," In Singer (ed.) 1958.

———. "Political Systems in Eighteenth Century India: The Banaras Region," *Journal of the American Oriental Society* 82 (1962):313-20.

Danielou, A. *Hindu Polytheism*. New York: Pantheon Books, 1964.

Dasgupta, S. *Obscure Religious Cults*. Calcutta: Firma KLM Private Limited, 1969.

De Bary, W. T. *Sources of Indian Tradition*. Volume I. New York and London: Columbia University Press, 1958.

Deva, B. C. *Musical Instruments of India: Their History and Development*. Calcutta: Firma KLM Private Limited, 1978.

Dimock, E. C. and D. Levertov. *In Praise of Krishna: Songs from the Bengali*. Anchor Books. Garden City: Doubleday & Company, Inc., 1967.

———. "Doctrine and Practice among the Vaiṣṇavas of Bengal," Singer (ed.) 1968.

Dowson, J. *A Classical Dictionary of Hindu Mythology and Religion, Geography, History, and Literature*. London: Routledge & Kegan Paul Ltd., 1972.

Dumont, L. *Homo Hierarchicus*. Chicago: University of Chicago Press, 1970.

Dvivedi, H. *Kabīr*. Delhi: Rajkamal Prakashan, 1971.

Edgerton, R. B. and L. L. Langness. *Methods and Styles in the Study of Culture*. San Francisco: Chandler & Sharp Publishers, Inc., 1974.

Eliade, M. *Yoga: Immortality and Freedom*. Bollingen Series 56. Princeton: Princeton University Press, 1969.

Elias, M. *The Times of India*, April 23, 1978, p. 8.

Etzkorn, K. P. (ed.) *Music and Society: The Later Writings of Paul Honigsheim*. New York: John Wiley & Sons, 1973.

Evans-Pritchard, E. E. *The Position of Women in Primitive Society*. London: Faber and Faber, 1965.

The Far East and Australia 1984-85, 16th Edition. London: Europa Publications.

Farquhar, J. N. *An Outline of the Religious Literature of India*. Delhi: Motilal Banarsidas, 1967.

Fox-Strangways, A. H. *The Music of Hindostan*. London: Oxford University Press, 1965.

Freed, R. S. and A. Freed. "Calendars, Ceremonies and Festivals in a North Indian Village," *Southwestern Journal of Anthropology* 20 (1964):67-90.

———. *Rites of Passage in Shanti Nagar*. New York: The American Museum of Natural History, 1980.

Goldkind, V. "Anthropologists, Informants and the Achievement of Power in Chan Kom," *Sociologus* 20 (1970):17-41.

Greenway, J. *Ethnomusicology*. Minneapolis: Burgess Publishing Company, 1976.

Grierson, G. A. "Some Bihari Folksongs," *Journal of the Royal Asian Society* 16 (1884):196.

———. "Some Bhojpurī Folksongs," *Journal of the Royal Asian Society* 18 (1886):207.

Growse, F. S. *The Rāmāyaṇa of Tulsī Dās* (translated from the Hindi). Allahabad: Rām Narain Lāl Beni Prasād, 1966.

Gupta, G. R. *Marriage, Religion and Society: Pattern of Change in an Indian Village*. New York: John Wiley & Sons, 1974.

Hedayetullah, M. *Kabīr: The Apostle of Hindu-Muslim Unity*. Delhi: Motilal Banarsidass, 1977.

Henry, E. O. "The Meanings of Music in a North Indian Village." Ph.D. dissertation, Michigan State University. Ann Arbor: University Microfilms, 1973.

———. "North Indian Wedding Songs: An Analysis of Functions and Meanings," *The Journal of South Asian Literature* 11 (1975):62-93.

———. "The Variety of Music in a North Indian Village: Reassessing Cantometrics," *Ethnomusicology* 20 (1976):49-66.

———. "A North Indian Healer and the Sources of His Power," *Social Science & Medicine*, 11 (1977):309-17.

———. "Music in the Thinking of North Indian Villagers," *Asian Music* 9 (1977):1-12.

———. Review of R. Schlenker, *Middle Caste Religious Music from India* and *Lower Caste Religious Music from India* (long-playing disc recordings). *Ethnomusicology* 24 (1980):328-30.

———. *Chant the Names of God: Village Music of the Bhojpurī-Speaking Area of India*. 5008 (a long-playing disc recording). Boston: Rounder Records, 1981.

———. "The Mother Goddess Cult and Interaction Between Little and Great Traditions." In Giri Raj Gupta, (ed.), *Religion in Modern India*. Main Currents in Indian Sociology, Volume V. New York: Advent Publications, 1983.

Herndon, M. and N. McLeod. *Music as Culture*. Norwood: Norwood Editions, 1979.

Hess, L. "The Cow Is Sucking at the Calf's Teat: Kabīr's Upside-down Language." *History of Religions* 22 (1983): 313-37.

Hitchcock, J. T. "The Idea of the Martial Rājput." In Singer (ed.), 1958.

Hoebel, E. A. *Anthropology: The Study of Man*. New York: McGraw-Hill Book Company, 1972.
Hopkins, T. J. "The Social Teaching of the Bhāgavata Purāṇa." In Singer (ed.), 1968.
———. *The Hindu Religious Tradition*. Encino, California: The Dickenson Publishing Company, 1971.
Horton, D. "The Dialogue of Courtship in Popular Songs," *American Journal of Sociology* 72 (1957):569-78.
Hutton, J. H. *Caste in India: Its Nature, Function, and Origins*. London: Oxford University Press, 1969.
Ingalls, D. H. H. Foreword. In M. Singer (ed.), *Krishna: Myths, Rites, and Attitudes*. Chicago: University of Chicago Press, 1968.
———. *Sanskrit Poetry*. Cambridge: Harvard University Press, 1968.
Jacobson, D. "Songs of Social Distance," *Journal of South Asian Literature* 9 (1975):45-60.
———. "The Women of North and Central India." In Jacobson and S. Wadley, *Women in India: Two Perspectives*. Columbia, Missouri: South Asia Books, 1977.
Jairazbhoy, N. A. "A Preliminary Survey of the Oboe in India," *Ethnomusicology* 14 (1970):375-88.
———. *The Rags of North Indian Music: Their Structure and Evolution*. Middletown, Connecticut: Wesleyan University Press, 1971.
Junghare, I. "The Position of Women as Reflected in Marathi Folk Songs," *Man in India* 61 (1981): 237-53.
Kaemmer, J. "Between the Event and the Tradition: A New Look at Music in Sociocultural Systems." *Ethnomusicology* 24 (1980): 61-74.
Karve, I. *Kinship Organization in India*. New York: Asia Publishing House, 1968.
Keay, F. E. *A History of Hindi Literature*. Calcutta: Y.M.C.A. Publishing House, 1960.
Keesing, R. M. *Kin Groups and Social Structure*. New York: Holt, Rinehart, and Winston, 1975.
Keil, C. *Urban Blues*. Chicago: University of Chicago Press, 1966.
Keyt, G. *Jayadeva's Gita Govinda: The Loves of Krishna and Rādhā*. Bombay: Kutub-Popular Pvt. Ltd., 1940.
Kolenda, P. "Religious Anxiety and Hindu Fate." In *Religion in South Asia*. Edward B. Harper (ed.) Seattle: University of Washington Press, 1964.
———. *Caste in Contemporary India: Beyond Organic Solidarity*. Menlo Park: The Benjamin/Cummings Publishing Company, 1978.
Lewis, O. *Village Life in Northern India*. New York: Random House, 1958.
Lomax, A. *Indian Folk Music*. Volume XIII of the Columbia World Library of Folk and Primitive Music. 9102021 (a long–playing disc recording). New York: Columbia Records, nd.
———. *Folk Song Style and Culture*. Washington, D.C.: American Association for the Advancement of Science, 1968.
Maity, P. K. *Historical Studies in the Cult of the Goddess Manasa*. Calcutta: Punthi Pustak, 1966.
Majumdar, D. N. *Caste and Communication in an Indian Village*. New Delhi: Asia Publishing House, 1958.

———. *Races and Cultures of India*. New Delhi: Asis Publishing House, 1961.

Maloney, C. *Peoples of South Asia*. New York: Holt, Rinehart & Winston, Inc., 1974.

Mandlebaum, D. G. "Transcendental and Pragmatic Aspects of Religion," *American Anthropologist* 68 (1966):1174-91.

Marcus, S. "Field Research Report." *Ethnomusicology at the University of California at Los Angeles* 2(3):1984.

Marriott, M. "Little Communities in an Indigenous Civilization." In *Village India: Studies in the Little Community*, Marriott, (ed.) Chicago: University of Chicago Press, 1955.

———. "The Feast of Love." In Singer (ed.), 1968.

Mayer, A. C. *Caste & Kinship in Central India: A Village and Its Region*. Berkeley: University of California Press, 1966.

McAllester, D. P. *Enemy Way Music*. Cambridge: Peabody Museum, Harvard University, 1954.

Merriam, A. P. *The Anthropology of Music*. Evanston: Northwestern University Press, 1964.

Miller, B. S. *Love Song of the Dark Lord*. New York: Columbia University Press, 1977.

———. *The Endangered Sex: Neglect of Female Children in North India*. Ithaca: Cornell University Press, 1981.

Monier-Williams, M. *Sanskrit-English Dictionary*. London: Oxford University Press, 1964.

Narayan, K. "Birds on a Branch: Girlfriends & Wedding Songs in Kangra." *Ethos* 14 (1986):47-75.

Nettl, B. *Theory and Method in Ethnomusicology*. New York: The Macmillan Company, The Free Press of Glencoe, 1964.

Nettl, B. *Eight Urban Musical Cultures*. Urbana: University of Illinois Press, 1978.

———. *The Study of Ethnomusicology: Twenty-nine Issues and Concepts*. Urbana: University of Illinois Press, 1983.

Nicholas, R. "Śītalā and the Art of Printing: The Transmission and Propagation of the Myth of the Goddess of Smallpox in Rural West Bengal," In Apte, Mahadev (ed.), *Mass Culture, Language and Arts in India*. Bombay: Popular Prakashan, 1978.

———. "The Goddess Śītalā and Epidemic Smallpox in Bengal," *Journal of Asian Studies* 41 (1981):21-44.

Nketia, J. H. K. "The Juncture of the Social and the Musical: the Methodology of Cultural Analysis," *The World of Music* 23 (1981):22-35.

Norbeck, E. *Religion in Primitive Society*. New York: Harper & Row, 1961.

Opler, M. E. "Introduction: North Indian Themes—Caste and Untouchability." In *The Untouchables in Contemporary India*. J. M. Mahar, (ed.). Tucson: The University of Arizona Press, 1972.

Owens, N. "Mahapatra Wedding Songs: A Preliminary Look at Context and Melodic Structure." Mimeograph, n.d.

Pande, T. "Bhojpuri Folklore and Folk Music." In Biswas, Hemango, (ed.) *Folkmusic and Folklore; An Anthology*. Vol. I. Calcutta: Folkmusic and Folklore Research Institute, 1967.

Pandey, S. M. "The Hindi Oral Epic Canaini or Lorikī." *Orientalia Lovaniensa Periodica* 2 (1971):191-210.

———, and N. Zide. "Surdās and His Krishna-bhakti." In Singer, (ed.) 1968.

Pathak, R. C. *Bhargava's Standard Illustrated Dictionary of the Hindi Language* (Hindi-English Edition). Vārāṇasī: Bhargava Book Depot, 1969.

Pelto, P. J. and G. H. Pelto. *Anthropological Research: The Structure of Inquiry*. New York: Cambridge University Press, 1978.

Planalp, J. M. "Religious Life and Values in a North Indian Village." Ph.D. dissertation, Cornell University. Ann Arbor: University Microfilms, 1956.

Popley, H. A. *The Music of India*. New Delhi: Y.M.C.A. Publishing House, 1966.

Qureshi, R. "Indo-Muslim Religious Music, An Overview," *Asian Music* 3 (1972):15-22.

———"Qawwali: Making the Music Happen in the Sufi Assembly." In B. Wade (ed.), *Performing Arts in India*. Berkeley: Center for South and Southeast Asia Studies, 1983.

Radcliffe-Brown, A. R. *The Andaman Islanders*. New York: The Macmillan Company, The Free Press of Glencoe, 1964.

———. *Structure and Function in Primitive Society*. New York: The Free Press, 1965.

Reck, D. *The Music of the Whole Earth*. New York: Charles Scribner's Sons, 1977.

———"India/South India." In J. T. Titon (ed.), *Worlds of Music*. New York: Schirmer Books, 1984.

Rekesagupta. *Studies in Nayaka-Nayika-Bheda*. Aligarh: Granthayan, 1967.

Richards, A. "The Concept of Culture in Malinowski's Work." In R. Firth, (ed.), *Man and Culture: An Evaluation of the Work of Bronislaw Malinowski*. New York: Harper and Row, 1957.

Rose, H. A. *A Glossary of the Tribes & Castes of the Punjab and Northwestern Frontier Provinces*. Volume II. Punjab: Languages Department, 1970.

Rubin, D. *The World of Premchand*. Bloomington: Indiana University Press, 1969.

Russell, R. "The Pursuit of the Urdu Ghazal." *The Journal of Asian Studies* 29 (1969):107-24.

———, and K. Islam. *Three Mughal Poets*. Cambridge: Harvard University Press, 1968.

Schermerhorn, R. A. *Ethnic Plurality in India*. Tucson: University of Arizona Press, 1978.

Schlenker, R. *Lower Caste Religious Music from India*. LLST 7324 (a long-playing disc recording). New York: Lyrichord Discs, Inc., nd.

Shukla, S. *Bhojpurī Grammar*. Washington, D.C.: Georgetown University Press, 1981.

Singer, M. (ed.) *Traditional India: Structure & Change*. Philadelphia: American Folklore Society, 1958.

———. *Krishna: Myths, Rites, and Attitudes*. Chicago: University of Chicago Press, 1968.

———. "The Rādhā-Krishna Bhajanas of Madras City." In Singer (ed.) 1968.

Singh, C. and Ronald Amend. *Marriage Songs from Bhojpurī Region*. Jaipur: Champa Lāl Ranka & Co., 1979.

Singh, D. *Bhojpurī Lok-gīt mẽ Karuṇ Ras*. Prayag (Allahabad): Hindī Sahitya Sammelan, 1965.

Sinha, A. *Maithili Lok Gīt*. Calcutta: Lok Sahitya Parisad, 1970.

Srivastava, S. L. *Folk Culture and Oral Tradition*. New Delhi: Abhinav Publications, 1974.

Tagor, R. and E. Underhill. *One Hundred Poems of Kabīr*. Calcutta: Macmillan and Co. Ltd., 1970.

Tambiah, S. J. "The Magical Power of Words." *Man* 3 (1968):175-208.

Tandon, P. *Punjabi Century: 1857-1947*. Berkeley: University of California Press, 1961.

Tewari, L. G. "Folk Music of India: Uttar Pradesh." Ph.D. dissertation, Wesleyan University. Ann Arbor: University Microfilms, 1974.

———. *Folk Music of India (Uttar Pradesh)*. LLST 7271 (a long-playing disc recording). New York: Lyrichord Discs, Inc., 1976.

———. "Ceremonial Songs of the Kanyakubja Brahmans." *Essays in Arts and Sciences* 6 (1977):30-52.

———. Review of E. O. Henry, *Chant the Names of God*, in *Ethnomusicology* 27 (1983): 402-404.

Titon, J. T. *Worlds of Music: An Introduction to the Music of the World's Peoples*. New York: Schirmer, 1984.

Tiwari, U. N. *The Origin and Development of Bhojpuri*. Calcutta: The Asiatic Society, 1960.

Tripathi, B. D. *Sādhūs of India: The Sociological View*. Bombay: Popular Prakashan, 1978.

Turner, V. *The Forest of Symbols*. Ithica: Cornell University Press, 1967.

———. *The Ritual Process: Structure and Anti-Structure*. Chicago: Aldine Publishing Company, 1969.

———. "Symbols in African Ritual," *Science* 179 (1973):1100-05.

Upadhyaya, H. S. "The Joint Family Structure and Familial Relationship Patterns in the Bhojpurī Folksongs." Ph.D. dissertation, Indiana University. Ann Arbor: University Microfilms, 1967.

Upadhyaya, K. D. *Bhojpurī Lok-gīt* (part 1). Allahabad: Hindi Sahitya Sammelan, 1954.

———. "An Introduction to Bhojpurī Folksongs and Ballads," *Midwest Folklore* 7 (1957):85-94.

———. *Bhojpurī Lok-gīt* (part 2). Allahabad: Hindi Sahitya Sammelan, 1966.

Vatuk, S. "Trends in North Indian Urban Kinship: The Matrilineal Aysmmetry Hypothesis." *Southwestern Journal of Anthropology* 27 (1971):287-307.

Vatuk, V. *Thieves in My House: Four Studies in Indian Folklore of Protest and Change*. Vārāṇasī: Vishwavidyalaya Prakashan, 1969.

———, and S. Vatuk. "The Lustful Stepmother in the Folklore of Northwestern India," *The Journal of South Asian Literature* 11 (1975):19-44.

Vaudeville, C. *Kabīr*. London: Oxford University Press, 1974.

Venkateswaran, T. K. "Rādhā-Krishna Bhajanas of South India: A Phenomenological, Theological, and Philosophical Study." In Singer (ed.) 1968.

Wade, B. "Songs of Traditional Wedding Ceremonies in North India." In *1972 Yearbook of the International Folk Music Council*. Urbana: University of Illinois Press, 1972.

———. "India: Folk Music." In *The New Grove Dictionary of Music and Musicians*. Washington, D.C.: Grove's Dictionaries of Music, Inc., 1980.

Wadley, S. S. "Dhola: A North Indian Folk Genre." *Asian Folklore Studies* 42 (1983):3-26.

———. "Folk Literature in Karimpur," *Journal of South Asian Literature* 9 (1975):7-18.

———. "Popular Hinduism and Mass Literature in North India: A Preliminary Analysis." In *Religion in Modern India*. Vol. V of G. R. Gupta (ed.), *Main Currents in Indian Sociology*. New Delhi: Vikas Publishing House Pvt. Ltd., 1983.

Walker, B. *Hindu World: An Encyclopedic Survey of Hinduism*. London: George Allen & Unwin Ltd., 1968.

Wallace, A. F. C. *Religion: An Anthropological View*. New York: Random House, 1966.

Wiser, W. and C. Wiser. *Behind Mud Walls, 1930-1960*. Berkeley: University of California Press, 1968.

Zimmer, H. *Myths and Symbols in Indian Art and Civilization*. New York: Harper & Row, 1962.

Appendix A.

TRANSLITERATED SONG TEXTS

1. Tilak

1. ūṭho bhārat bāsī, uṭho bhārat bāsī
   gā̃dījī ka caran dharo re dharo
2. kab ke tum soyo, kab ke soyo
   abahī se khyāl karo re karo
3. kā to carake kā sūtā, kā to carake kā sūtā
   kaddar par dhyān dharo re dharo
4. choṛo vidhyā ãgrezī, choṛo vidhyā ãgrezī
   hīdī par khyāl dharo re dharo
5. śiv śãkar dānī, śiv śãkar dānī
   kar mẽ tirasul birājī rahī
6. hāth sobhailā ḍamarū, hāth sobhailā ḍamarū
   lilarā par cãdan bīrājī rahī
7. khālãi bhā̃g ka golā, khālãi bhā̃g ka golā
   baiṭhe bäilava ke piṭh mẽ
8. gale mũd ka mālā, gale mũd ka mālā
   hāth tirasul birājī rahī

2. Tilak

1. beriyā ki beriyā ham barajī ho rāmdhārah sīh
2. jhinavā mat e besā ho lāl mãi to barajī rahū̃
3. jhinavā pahirelī̃ chinarȯ e murat ka bahina
4. jhalkai unke medanī ka bār

3. Tilak

1. nadī kināre ninuā boī hariar rāg rāgayo jī
2. sacatā kī bahan gāvane jāke koī nā mile cahũpāve ke
3. hamare kapil mun äise rasiyā āī gäile cahũpave ke
4. kaṛe phalāg par cumā mā̃ge aur ḳhare ḳhare hirakāne
   ko

4. Sagun

1. rājā kãgaresiyā bhäilãi jiabai ta häiye na
2. jīab ta häiye nāhī̃, jevanā ta jei hãi nāhī̃
3. binu re surajavā lehalẽ duare ta āī hãi na
4. jīab ta häiye nāhī̃, gaṛuā ta pī hãi nāhī̃
5. binu re surajavā lehalẽ, āgane ta āī hãi nāhī̃

6. binu re surajavā lehalẽ, bīravā ta khāī hāĩ na
7. binu re surajavā lehalẽ, sejiyā par soī hāĩ na

5. Sagun

1. kiyā khatā mujh kīnā balam itanī dukh dinā
2. kiyā mãĩ rājā re jevanā bigaṛalõ kiyā namak kam kīnā
3. kiyā mãĩ rājā re jevanā bigaṛalõ kiyā taj kam kīnā
4. kiyā atar kam kīnā balam itanī dukh dinā
5. kiyā tor rājā re biṛavā bigaṛalõ
6. kiyā tor rājā re khair bigaṛalõ
7. kiyā tor rājā re sej bigaṛalõ
8. kiyā sulan kam kiyā

6. Sagun

1. hamẽ dhānī rāg sāṛī māgādā piā
   binā pahane na māne morā jiarā
2. koṭhā uṭhāī dā atārī uṭhāīdā
   ek ṭhe choṭā sā jāgalā katāī dā piā
3. binā jhā̃ke na māne hamār jiarā
4. binā tāke na māne hamār jiarā
5. hamẽ dhānī rāg sāṛī māgādā piā
   binā pahane na māne morā jiarā
6. bāgo lagāīda bagäicā lagāīdā
7. ek ṭhe choṭā sā nībū lā lagāīdā
8. bin toṛe na māne hamār jiarā

7. Sagun

1. koi aisā gajab se āī ā re larikā amirõ kā
2. maurū jetero lākh kā jhālar hajārõ kā
3. joṛā jetero lākh kā jāmā hajārõ kā
4. jūtā jetero lākh kā, mojā hajārõ kā
5. dulahin jetero lākh kā, paradā hajārõ kā

8. Sagun

1. kṛṣṇa kī āī sagāī sakhīnā sab a nācan koi āī
2. kakaṛī becārī kā kambhā gaṛā hai (2x)
3. pānan a māro cavāī sakhīnā sab a nācan koi āī
4. kelā becārā ka dulahā banā hai (2x)
5. nāvarangī kī dulahin banāyī sakhīnā sab a nācan koi āī

6. koharā becārā ka tablā banā hai (2x)
7. ninuā ki banī śahnāī sakhīnā sab a nācan koi āī
8. ālū becārā cale hai bārātī (2x)
9. murāī ka cāvar dolāī sakhīnā sab a nācan koi āī
10. palakī becārī kā sejā lagā hai (2x)
11. laukī ki takiā lagāī sakhīnā sab a nācan koi āī

9. Sagun

1. madha jamunā jī ke tir lāl mor abharan lūtā̃ī
2. brij kī banita cale ho jalbharane jamunā tat kī orī
3. yahī bīc mohan āī pare ho ham se karai balajorī mor śyām abharan luṭā̃ī
4. dahī mor khāilā̃ī maṭuk ki sir phoralā̃ī geṛūrī jamunā bahāī
5. leke cir kadam chaṛhī baithā̃ī lekar cir kadam chaṛhī baithā̃ī
6. ham jalamājh ughārī, lāl mor abharan lutā̃ī
7. cir ka badala pitāmbar debai ho jāibū jalavā se nyārī
8. tu to lāl hav, nāda bābā kay maī bṛṣbhan dulārī
9. kabahū̃ke lāl bhetāibā mil galiyan mē lebai dūno galavā nimorī
10. purāin pat pahirī rādhe niklā̃ī (2x)
11. kṛṣṇa bajāvat tālī, lāl mor abharan luṭā̃ī
12. barajā jasodā māiyā āpan kanhaiyā
13. ham se karat balajorī, lāl mor abharan luṭā̃ī
14. abahī ta lāl khelat galiyan mē
15. kab tūse ki e balajorī, tu ta jasodā māiyā lāl na khūjhe
16. bolat kūj kī orī, lāl mor abharan luṭā̃ī

10. Sagun

1. ādat par gaī hai pītā jī, ādat par gaī hai (this is refrain)
2. rām nām japane ko pītā jī (refrain)
3. sone kī ṭhālī mē jevanā banāī, jevanā na jebā̃ī prahalād pītā jī (refrain)
4. āgī mē jalā do cāhē pānī mē dūbā do, cāhē kambhā mē bā̃dh pītā jī (refrain)
5. jhajhar jhārī himalaya ka pānī paniyā na pīe prahalād pītā jī (refrain)
6. lavāg khilī khilī birā jorāiyo biravā na kūcai prahalād pītā jī (refrain)
7. phulā hajārī ka sej lagāyō sejiyā na soe prahalād (refrain)

11. Haldi

1. jinare deī ko khel to na dekho se māī re dekhalõ cäuk caṛhī
2. cäuka dekhailõ baṛā sūdar cäuka dekhailõ baṛā sūdar (2x)
3. are mäi nahī̃ jāno näunī ke potalai nahī̃ jāno ________

4. kalaś dekhailõ baṛā sūdar kalaś dekhailõ baṛā sūdar
5. are mäi nahī̃ jāno koharā ke gaṛhalā̃i nahi jāno ______

6. hariśi dekhailõ baṛī sūdar hariśi dekhailõ baṛī sūdar
7. are mäi nahī̃ jāno lohār ke gaṛhalā̃i nahī̃ jāno kaṭale
8. dulahin dekhailõ baṛī sūdar dulahin dekhailõ baṛī sūdar
9. are mäi nahī̃ janõ daivā ke gaṛhalā̃i nahī̃ re janamole

12. Haldi

1. koirin koirin tū̃ baṛī rānī re
   kahāvā̃ ke haradī upar käilū āj are
2. hamarī radhikā deī asa sukuvār re sahahi na jānelī haradiyā ka jhā̃kare
3. telin telin tū̃ baṛī rānī re
   kahāvā̃ ka telavā upar käilu āj are
4. hamarī radhikā deī as sukuvār re sahahi na janelī kaṛūvā ka jhā̃kare

13. Haldi

1. jäisan hamahū̃ rasīlī väisan sājan nā mile
2. jäisan bāravā hamār väisan bāravā nā mile
3. jäisan līlarā hamār väisan tikā nā mile
4. jäisan rāgavā hamār väisan rāg nā mile

14. Dvar Puja

1. kehī dal utar are amā imilī tar jinare kadam juṛ chā̃h
2. tohar balihariyā bābā ho markāde rām jehare khojailā
3. bar ke māthe sir chat birajailā avela rājā dvarare bālī

15. Dvar Puja

1. lo le lo le sasurarī mẽ ailā̃i
2. sughare bar sasurarī mẽ ailā̃i

16. Dvar Puja

1. pakalī mochiyā muräighalā e bar
2. lāvā bhāgareyā ka rāg
3. mardāpur ka log are karahū ajorare äilāī dudhaurā ka cor
4. mäi ka cor bahiniyā ka corare äilāī dudhaurā ka cor

17. Dvar Puja

1. hāthī hāthī śor käilā hāthī nā liäilā ho
2. torī bahan ka gapadā māro hāthī nā liäilā ho
3. mor gäurā luṭāī äil ho
4. bājā bājā śor käilā bājā na liäilā ho

18. Dvar Puja

1. jab baratiyā duare bhiṛī lagäile
2. hani hani maraila niśānī jī

19. Vivah

1. māganī ka gahana liāke maṛavā mor jhamakavalā ho
2. toharī bahin ke bhasur māro mor bigaṛāl ho

20. Vivah

1. ḍāl maunī leke bar maṛave āe
2. äire bar āī senur sinhorā leke bar maṛave āe
3. äire bar āī sonahulā rupahulā leke bar maṛave āe
4. äire bar āī dhumadharakkā leke bar maṛave āe

21. Vivah

1. ehire bhasuravā ka cilam äisan nakare
2. yahī māṛo tākayalā gäura hamārire
3. bhasuravā ka lābī lābī ṭāgare
4. vahī ṭāgi nāpayalāya maṛavā hamārire
5. vahī bhasuravā ka lābā lābā dānte cīrelā cäilā hamarare

22. Vivah

1. mäi tose puchailū supher dularū maṛanā kāhē gūnā
2. mäi tohār sutelī̃ khajūr tare maṛanā vahī̃ gūnā
3. mäi tohār sutelī̃ kukur tare kariyā vahī̃ gūnā

4. mäi tose puchailū supher dularū bhā̃knā kahē gūnā
5. mäi tohār sutelī̃ hū̃ṛār tare bhā̃knā vahī̃ gūnā

23. Vivah

1. koṭhā ūpara dulā mäuru asavaraya (4x)
   (savarayalaya is the spoken pronunciation)
2. jahā̃ dulā ka mäiya surujū manāvelī surujū manavelī
3. ājū dulahā bara ke najaro na lāve koi (4x)
4. koṭhā ūpara dulā sonavā savaraya (4x)
5. jahā̃ dulā ka phuā surujū manāvelī surujū manāvelī
6. ājū dulahā barake najaro na lāve koi (4x)
7. koṭhā ūpara dulāra jamā asavaraya (4x)
8. jahā̃ dulā ka bahnī surujū manāvelī surujū manāvelī
9. ājū dulahā barake najara na lāve koi (4x)
10. koṭhā ūpara dulā dhotiyā savaraya (4x)
11. jahā̃ dulā ka kākī surujū manāveli surujū manāvelī
12. ājū dulahā barake najara na lāve koi (4x)

24. Vivah

1. mäuru dekh jin bhulī hā e bābā mäurū hav mā̃gan kā
2. dulahā hav chinār kā, dulahin hav phacibaratā
3. kāganā dekh jin bhulī hā e bābā kāganā hav māganī kā

25. Vivah

1. caranā pahiro uparanā julahā bape ka binal hav
2. pahirā chinārī pūtā ī dhotiā ranivāse ka kātalī hav
3. pahirā hajarī pūtā ī dhotiyā ranivās ka kātalī hav

26. Vivah

1. bidhī bidhī rāma milāī
2. näuā khojala bar bamanā socailā din
3. are bābā bahut dur mor chalavā bichāire māī
4. bidhī bidhī rāma milāī
5. näuā ka daṛhī jaro bamanā ka phothī jaro
6. are bābā ke kavana sarāp re māī

27. Vivah

1. kavan garahanavā lāge sā̃jhe se bihanavā
2. kavan garahanavā lāge ādhī rāt
3. kavan garahanavā lāge mājhe maṛavā

4. kab jāī ugrah hoi
5. kavan garahanavā lāge bhinusār
6. are suruj garahanavā lāge sā̃jhe se bihanavā
7. dhīā cādra garahanavā ādhī rāt lāge mājhe maṛavā
8. bhore mē ugrah hoi

28. Vivah

1. are bhäiyā dasarat rām dhariyā na ṭuṭe ho
2. dhariyā ta ṭuṭī jāī hā̃ī bahiniyā se rusit jäibā ho
3. bhäiyā dasarat rām tir dhanūhī̃ bānhī ghalā ho
4. are bhäiyā āvat ta hoi hā̃ī bahanoiā ta kurakhet laṛ jāī na ho
5. din bhar mere bhaiyā laṛelay ta sā̃jhī ber hārī gäilā̃ī ho
6. are haralā̃ī tīlā deī bahiniyā ta supher dularu jīt gäilā̃ī ho
7. are bhäiya dasarat rām kavane matī bhulī gäilā ho
8. bhäiyā gäiyā bhā̃isī nahī̃ haralā bahinī harī gäila nā ho
9. are are bahini tīla deī bhale mati bhūlī gäilī ho
10. bhäiya gäiyā bhā̃is hamarī lakṣmī bahini parāye bas ho

29. Vivah

1. baratihavan kaya pā̃ḍit paniyā bahāne āpan bahini bolāve
2. hane bajaṛ kevāṛī ho bābā ke lajiyā maī marō̃
3. mor bhäiyā amala dhārī ho
4. kul baratihavā āpan bahini bolāvan

30. Vivah

1. jaise ghurvā par cäurāī vaisan bābhanā ka mäi
2. suno bābhan bābhan hālī hālī ā hutī de hu dhiyā morī
3. bārī cal ta sukuvārī ta dhuāvā biyaya gäilā̃ī ho
4. jaise pokharī ka cakkā vaisan bābhanā ucakkā
5. suno bābhan bābhan hālī hālī ā hutī de hu dhiyā morī
6. jaisan baniyā ki daṛī vaisan babhana ka aṛhī
7. jaisan bā̃s kaya kainiyā vaisan pā̃ḍit ka bahiniyā

31. Vivah

1. mor lāvā tor lāvā ekaya mē milāī dā
2. mor bābū tor māī ekaya mē sutāī dā
3. mor cācā tor cācī sutāī dā

32. Vivah

1. mãi bābāke lajiyā mãi marū̃ mor bābā jaṭādhārī ho
2. mãi cācā ke lajiyā mãi marū̃ mor cācā jaṭādhārī ho
3. mãi bhäiyā ke lajiyā mãi marū̃ mor bhäiyā jaṭādhārī ho

33. Vivah

1. are bābā hi bābā pukārelō bābā na bolãi
2. are bābā ki bariäiyā senur bar ḍālelaho
3. are cācā ki bariäiyā senur bar ḍālelaho
4. bhäiyā bhäiyā ki bariäiya senur bar ḍālelaho

34. Vivah

1. saṭhī̃ ka cäur hālarī dūbīre cumahin calãilī̃ chotū a rām dhīarī re
2. mathavā cumi cumi dihalī̃ asīsarī
3. jiyasū mor dulahin dulaha lākh barīsare
4. jasare jiyasu jas dharatī hi dhānare vasare
5. bhugut vas rainī ka cānare

35. Vivah

1. kā̃cī pitariyā ka i hai navā kohabar
2. halabal halabal bar cale haravāhe ka janamal ho
3. dhire dhire morī dhīā cala patiśāh ka janamale ho

36. Vivah

1. päiṭhī jagāvelī̃ mäire kavanī deī bahini ho tīlā deī
2. uṭhu pūtā bhäilãi bhinusārarare
3. äisan mäi turuk hāthe beco, pathān hathe becatū̃ mōgal hāthe beco
4. ādhi rātī bole bihānare

37. Khicari

1. bhāī paṭnā śahar gulajārare bhāī paṭnā śahar gulajār
2. bacapan ke bigaṛe bhaṛūe henarī rām rāmsāgar miśra
3. unki bahina bigaṛ gaī mahtar rām se cādā chip gaī
4. unkar bahina bigaṛ gaī rām nāth se
5. apane bahin ke sagāī khālãi ā̃ko mē ave rulāire

6. apane bahin ke henarī rāmsāgar sagāī khālā̃ī
7. apane marāve gaṛī re bhāī paṭnā śahar gulajār

38. Khicari

1. ū̃cā talāb ka nīcā ghāṭ bāgalā man bhāvelā
2. vahī mē̃ henarī ka bahin racai nahān
3. dayā śākar ka bahin racai nahān
4. tahā̃ kesauram mār gāilā sān bāgalā man bhāvelā
5. tahā̃ laukāī rām mār gāilā sān bāgalā man bhāvelā
6. kholā gughat dekhab gāl
7. gāl ta hāue jāise īgur ka dhār
8. kholā colī dekho māl
9. māl hāue jāise nībū anār
10. kholā pupati dekhab cā̃d
11. kholā lahāga dekhab cā̃d
12. ihāi ta hāi jāise bijalī ka cā̃d

39. Khicari

1. barasan lāgal megh badariyā galiyā ki galiyā nirarmal
2. nisaran lāgal sone ka kharauavā bice āgan ṭhaharāi jī
3. mā̃ī tose puchailõ bābū ho henari rām bahinā tohār nisaral jāī jī.
4. mā̃ī tose puchailõ bābū ho rām sāgar rām bahinā udaral jālī jī
5. i hai niahayā re katahū na ṭūṭele ṭūṭe indra jīt rām dvāre jī
6. das pā̃c babhanā khiāvā ho henarī rām
7. das pā̃c babhanā khiāvā ho rām sāgar rām
8. pāp katit hoi jāī jī
9. kāśī viśasar gāj nahvāva ho henarī rām
10. ham to rakhī apane bāp ka biṭiyavā apanī ājā natiniyā
11. ekar kaun niaiyā jī

40. Khicari

1. bhāge bhaṛuā bhage jāe āge āge dili jāe
2. dilī pare ret mē̃ henarī ka bahin marāve khet mē̃
3. hinuvānā turkānā vah jirā vah dhaniā vah āg vah pac cõdā̃ī
4. tohare bāp ke muh mē̃ lār tohare bāp ke muh mē̃ pānī
5. māre gariyā ka dām deī dā ho henarī rām deī nātavā
6. tohare bahinin ke mor kamalā leī ho bahin cõd, deī nātavā

41. Sohar

1. kahavā̃ se āvelī̃ kālī mäiyā kahavā̃ se bhavānī mäiyā ho
2. kahavā̃ se āve śiv śākar kahā̃ se satya narāyan bābā ho
3. purval le āve kālī mäiyā pachim bhavānī mäiyā
4. are dakhinā le āve satya narāyan utar śiv śākar
5. kahā̃ baisāve kālī mäiyā kahavā̃ bhavānī mäiyā
6. kahā̃ baisāve śiv śākar kahā̃ re satya narāyan
7. bagiyā bäithāve kālī mäi äuru bhavānī mäi
8. āraghī bäiṭhāī śiv śākar caukiyā satya narāyan
9. kāre caṛhäilā kālī mäiyā kāre bhavānī mäiyā
10. ab kāre caṛhāve śiv śākar kāre satya narāyan
11. dhariyā caṛhäile kālī mäiyā phulavā bhavānī mäiyā
12. akṣat caṛhāe śiv śākar mevatiyā satya narāyan
13. kā mohī̃ de halī̃ kālī māīyā kāre bhavānī mäiyā
14. kā mohī̃ dehalī̃ śiv śākar kāre satya narāyan
15. sātat dehalī̃ kālī mäiyā äuru bhavāni mäiyā
16. sāpat dihalā̃i śiv śākar mukut satya narāyan
17. je yahi māgal gavelā gāy ke sunāvelā
18. se bäikute ha jāī sadā phal khāī

42. Sohar

1. canan he kerī cäukiyā ta ām nahalā̃i ni ho
2. sakhiyā sīta se puchē sab sakhiyā kāvan tapa käilu ta rām bar pāvelu sakhiyā sīta se puchē sab sakhiȳ kāvan tapa käilu ta rām bar pāvelu
3. jeta rahila ekādasiyā äuru duadasiyā ho
4. sakhiyā bidhī ka rahila atavār mā̃i rām bar päilā sakhiyā bidhī ka rahila atavār mā̃i rām bar päilā
5. māgarhi māsawāna nahäilī̃ agini nāhī tāpela ho
6. sakhiyā niti uṭhi pujīlā śiv śākar mā̃i rām bar päile sakhiyā niti uṭhi pujīlā śiv śākar mā̃i rām bar päile
7. nevatī ke bamhānā javäilā mā̃i juṭhavā uṭhāvalo ho
8. sakhiyā sīr rakhi dahiyā parosalō mā̃i rām bar päile

43. Sohar

1. āgan bedī paṭila o paṭaṭhārilā
2. bahini bah par bäila satya narāyan oṛhale pitābar
3. jäumā̃i janitō satya narāyan oṛhale pitābar
4. bahini nihuri nihur goravā lagatu caran dhoike pīatu

5. māgan ki cumā̃git sasuru mē mā̃gu rājā dasarath sāsū kausiliyā rānī
6. bahini potiyā bā̃cat mā̃go bhasur
7. nanadā akelī mā̃gu rām isan mā̃gu puruś
8. lakṣman äisan devar bahin dhiāvā mā̃golo lavāg yas pūtavā keval yas
9. sasuru mā̃ī pavalu rājā dasarat sāsū kausiliyā äisan
10. nanad akelī pav rām äisan pavalo purus lakṣman äisan devar
11. bahin dhiāvā pavalo lavāg yas putav keval yas
12. hamarī burukī suphal hoi gäilī̃ avadapur ke basale

44. Sohar

1. sabavahī̃ bäisalā rajavā ta raniyā̃re araj karē ho
2. rājā ekare bāsare kulavā hānī hamahū̃ hobai jogin
3. jab rānī hobū joginiyā ta ham hobe jogī (2x)
4. rājā dono jānī bhabhūtire ramäibai jāgal bhikṣā mā̃gabai
5. barah baris biti gäilā ta baramhā ke ban me na ho
6. baramhā sabke ta balakā re urehalā ulaṭī nāhī̃ citavelā
7. jāho tu bajhinīre apane gharavā tohākere hukum nāhī̃ ho
8. bājhin baramhā ke hāthe masi haniyā ta kikhalē re narāyan

45. Sohar

1. milahu na sakhīyā sahelarī hamarī gotīn ho
2. sakhīyā gangājī ka nirmal pānī ghaṛīlawā borīlīāī ho
3. koi sakhī pānī bher koi sakhī bālū bhare ho
4. bahinī koi sakhī ṭhāṛhī ho tawalīn ghaṛīlawā nahī̃ boraū ho
5. bharo na e bahinī ghaṛīlā lawaṭī gharawā calahū ho
7. kīya tore sāsu jo maralīn nanad garīaulīn ho
8. bahinī kīya tore kantā madhuban jāle
9. ṭhāṛhī ho tawālīn ho ghaṛīlawā nāhī̃ bharalū ho
10. nāhī more sāsu jo maralīn nanada garīaulīn ho
11. sakhīyā nāhī̃ more kantā madhuban jālen
12. ṭhāṛhī tawalīn ghaṛīlawā nāhī̃ bharalu ho
13. bahinī kokhīyā ka marala ho mehanawā sahal nahī̃ jālā īa ho
14. bharo na bahinī gharilavā lawaṭī gharawā calahū ho
15. bahinī duī ṭhelī hamare gherilawā ek ṭhe leī līha

16. apan kaike rakhatū meṭawāyī ho
17. nūnawa ta milalā udharawā ta tel beūharawāī ho
18. bahinī kokhīyā ka kauan ho udharawā
19. kharīdale na mila besahale na milaī ho

46. Sohar

1. rājā apane mäiyā re bulāī leī avatā ho
   daradiyā hole bhārī ho daradiyā hole bhārī (refrain)
2. choṭan hoi rājā jāīhā ta baṛāhoi manāīhā ta baṛāhoi manāīhā tū ho
3. gotan dhäilī hā̃ī patarī ḍagariyā ṭhumukat gharavā āī hā̃ī
4. buṛha dhäilī hai patari dagariya ṭhumukat gharava āī haī
5. jabatū e buṛhā cäukaṭhavā̃ caṛhī baiṭhalū cäukathavā̃ caṛhī baiṭhalū
6. tu buṛha läikan ka kalevā jab khäibyū ta jhoṭā jhoṭiyäibā ho
7. rājā apani bhaujī bulavtā daradiyā bhārī hole (2x)
8. choṭan hoi rājā jāīhā ta baṛāhoi manāīha ta baṛahoi manāīhā tū ho
9. buṛha dhäilī hā̃ī pātarī ḍagariyā ṭhumukat gharavā āī hā̃ī
10. äilū ta ho gotin dhäilū palāgiyā caṛhī baiṭhahū ho
11. e gotin pātar piyavā mor bhoräibyu ta jhoṭā jhoṭiyäib ho
12. rājā apane bahini re bulāī le avatā ho daradiyā hole bhārī ho daradiyā hole bhārī
13. baṛan hoi rājā jāī ha ta choṭ hoi manāīhā hū̃
14. rājā dhäilī hā̃ī pātari ḍagariyā ṭhumukat gharavā āī hā̃ī
15. ab ta äilū e nanado palāgiyā caṛhī baithalū palāgiyā caṛhī baithalū
16. ho nanado khudiyā ka kuṛavā jab tu kholabū ta jhota jhoṭiyäib ho

47. Sohar

1. ab bāje lāgal anadh bajäiyā gotīn sohar gāv ho nā
2. ab bāje lāgal anadh bajäiyā gotīn sohar gāv ho nā
3. beṭawā maiyā ke godīyā me halar
4. bābū godīyā halaral ho nā
5. ham na nanadīyā boläib balam morā
6. Ham na jhaläiyā boläib balam morā

7. nanadā boläib mā̃i neg cār māngäiha
8. unke ham neg kahā̃ päib balam mora
9. sāsu boläib mā̃i dewata manäiha
10. unke mā̃i piarī kahā̃ päib balam mora
11. okhari mangäib mā̃i sonth kuṭawäib
12. säiyā̃ morī kuṭī ham cālab balam mora
13. sīlā mangäib mā̃i sonṭh pisawäib säiyā̃ pakäiha ham khäib balam mora
14. nanadā ke badale ham bahin bolawäib onahī ke neg cār deb balam mora
15. ham na nanadīyā boläib balam mora ham na jhaläiyā boläib balam mora
16. ham na akel pīya sab na luṭāy diyā
17. sāsu morī aïha jo devatā manäiha paisā corāy liho kauṛī dikhāy diho
18. nanadīyā mor aïha jo saurī potan ko baṭuā corāy liho haṛiyā dikhāy diho
19. gotīn morī aïha jo sohar gavan ko panawā corāy liho surtī dikhāy diho
20. paṛosīn mor aïha dularuā dekhan ko mūhavā corāy liho goṛawā dikāy diho
21. ranīya mor äiha jo jewanā banāwan caukā corāy liho belanā dikāy diho
22. e bhaujī jab se sunal torā saguna e bhauji leb jaṛavdār kanganā
23. macīan baiṭh mor bābā baṛhäitā
24. e bābā leb jaṛāvdār jhabīya
25. macīan baiṭh mor bhayā baṛhäita e bhäiyā leb jaṛavdār bindiya
26. macīan baiṭh mor mäiyā baṛhäitin e mäiyā leb kusum rang cundarī
27. e bhaujī jab se sunal torā saguna e bhaujī leb jaṛavdār kanganā

48. Sohar

1. panawā yesan pātar kusum rang sundar ho
2. morī raniyā sutalīn harī ke sejariyā ho
3. sutalīn sukh nīnīyā ho sutalīn sukh nīnīyāī ho
4. hot ho bhor bhayal bhīn saharā
5. rājā choṛī dehu hamar ancarawā
6. hot ho bhor bhayal bhīn saharā
7. morī raniyā kīyā tore sāsu ghorāwāū nanad hānk ḍäläu ho

8. morī raniyā kīyā tore godī mẽ balakawā
9. ta roī rahī jagāw ta roī rahī jagāwl ho
10. nāhī more sāsu ghorāw ho nanad hānk ḍāl ho
11. more rājā nāhī more godī mẽ balakawā ho
12. mehanawā matī mār ho mehanawā matī mārāī ho
13. bhor bhayal bhinusaharā ho äuro bhinusaharāī ho
14. more rājā choṛī dehu hamar ancarawā ho
15. bhayal bhinusaharā ho bhayal bhinusaharāī ho
16. yetanī bacan rānī sunalīn ho rānī sunahī nahī päulī ho
17. morī raniyā choṛ dehalīn laharā paṭorawā ho
    lugariyā pahirī lehalīn ho
18. morī raniyā choṛ dehalīn laharā paṭorawā ho
    lugariyā pahirī lehalīn ho
19. morī raniyā pahiralī phaṭahī lugariyā ho
20. rūsal näihar jālī ho rūsal näihar jālīn ho
21. ek ban gäilī dusar mẽ awaro tīsar ban ho
22. morī raniyā tīsare mẽ bābā ka mahaliyā ho
23. mahaliyā bicawā jālī ho mahaliyā bicawā jalīn ho
24. ek lāt näili duarawā ho dūsar lāt ḍewaṛhiyā ho dusar
    lāt ḍewaṛhiyāī ho
25. morī lalanā tīsare lāt osariyā ho
26. morī raniyā tīsare mẽ bābā ka owariyā ho
27. ta babuā janamal ta horīlā janamal ī ho
28. dhābo na gãuā ka näuā ho begam calī āwäi ho
29. more näuā yehī ho locanawā leī jāy ho
30. ta rām jīn janāy ho ta rām jīn janāyi ho
31. pahil locanawā hamare sā̃su dūsar locanawā sā̃sarū
32. more näuā ho tīsar ho locanawā lachiman dewar ho
33. ek ban gäil dūsar ban awaro tīsar ban ho
34. more lalanā tīsare mẽ sā̃sarū sagarawā
35. ta rām datuan karäi ho ta rām datuan karäi ho
36. more näuā käun ho sagunawā leī äīl ho
37. ta māthe tohare bhathakal ta māthe bhathakal ho
38. pahil locanawā hamare sā̃su dūsar locanawā sā̃sarū
39. more näuā ho tīsar ho locanawā lachiman dewar ho
40. itanī bacan rājā sunalan sunahī nāhī päulan ho
41. phekī dehalan pāncis ta rupäiyā ta rupäiyā
    ta hāth ka munariyā ta hāth ka munariyā i ho
42. more näuā ho locanawā leī lihā
43. ta rānī̃ jīn janāya ho ta rāni jīn janāyaī ho
44. uhawā̃ ka uṭhal more näuā ho sabere calī gäil ho
    savere calī gäil ho savere calī gäilī ho
45. more näuā pahil ho locanawā onake sā̃saru ho
46. dūsar locanā sā̃su ho dūsar locanā sā̃su ho

47. more näuā tīsar ho locanawā lachiman dewar
48. ta rām jīn janāy ho ta rām jīn janāy ho
49. sā̃su jo uṭhalin gāwat ta nanadā bajāwat ho
50. more lalan lachiman ho dewarawā mohar bajāwat ta päisā luṭāwat ho.

49. Sohar

1. ab bāj lāgal anadhā badhäiyā sotī ka näuā jāgal bhäiyā nā
2. lālan bāj lāgal anadhā badhäiyā gotin gāw sohar ho nā
3. ab mor rājā pichawarawā sundar maliyā begar calī äib ho nā
4. maliyā kāhẽ ka häuā to kudariyā kāhẽ ka ḍalariyā ho nā
5. maliyā kāhẽ ka lalī tor kudariyā kāhẽ ki ḍaläiyā ho nā
6. raniyā sonawan ka häuan mor kudariyā rūp ka ḍaläiyā ho nā
7. maliyā jäib tu kedarī ka banawā liäib kandamulawā ho nā
8. bahanī kanhawā par lehalan kudariyā sir par ḍalariyā ho nā
9. maliyā ek banawā gäil duī ban tīsar banawā gäil ho nā
10. maliya jāī pahunc kedarī ke banawā jahā̃ ka kandamulawā ho nā
11. lalanā pahalī kudariyā calāve ban sattī manāwe ho nā
12. raniyā dusarī kudariyā calāv mātā pitā sumira ho nā
13. lalanā tīsarī kudariya mor calāv nikal kandamulawā ho na
14. lalanā khodī khād bharal ḍalariyā rānī jī ka okhad ho nā
15. ab more kanhavā par lehalan kudariyā sir par ḍalariyā ho nā
16. maliyā ek banawā äil duī ban tīsar banawā äil ho nā
17. maliyā āī gäil gā̃w ke goiṛawā ajodhiyā ke tajike ho nā
18. ab mor khabar pawalī jo kosilyā rānī mālī hamarī āw ho nā
19. raniyā kahawā̃ ka silīhā silawṭī kahawā̃ ambar lorhā ho nā
20. raniyā kahawā̃ ka nanadäi boläib ragaṛ pisawäib ho nā
21. raniyā purab pachiawā ka silihā awadh ka lorhā ho nā
22. raniyā dur ka nanadäi bolawäib ragaṛ pisawäib ho nā

23. ab mor bharī khorā pialī käusīla dūsar sumitara ho nā
24. raniyā sil dho ke pia rānī kekahī janamawā ka bājhin ho nā
25. raniyā ohī re okhadawā ke piate tīnõ raniyā bedan ho nā
26. raniyā agab janäil käusilā äuro sumitarā ho nā
27. raniyā aüro janäil rānī kekahī janamawā ka bājhin ho nā
28. lalanā janame käusilā ke rām jī sumitarā ke lachiman ho nā
29. rānī kekehī ke bhārat caturgun tinõ gharawā mangal ho nā
30. raniyā sur gäiyā gobar mangāv anganā lipawäi ho nā
31. raniyā gājī motī cauka purawalan paṇḍit bolawal ho nā
32. ab mor āī jäib kāśī jo paṇḍit jī angan more bäithäu ho nā
33. paṇḍit kholī deb pothiyā puranakī bānc ke sunäibā ho nā
34. raniyā kawan lagan beṭā janamal kawan sukh säit ho nā
35. ab morī bhalī ghariyā janame rājā rāmacandr śubh ghariyā lachiman ho nā
36. ab mor tīsar ghariyā bhārat caturgun ajodhiyā ka mālik ho nā
37. ab mor janamele kawasīle ke rām jī sumitar ka lachiman ho nā
38. rām bārah barisawā ka hoihan ajodhiyā ke taj deih ho nā
39. ab morī caṛhī ke lankā par jāiha rāvaṇa mat māral ho nā
40. rājā rāvaṇa ke mār ke giräiha sītā harī leihā ho nā
41. sīta ranī jī ka ḍoliyā phanawal ajodhiyā basāwäi ho nā
42. sītā caumukh dianā jalāī ke
43. girijā pūjan jalīn ho nā
44. bahinī girajā pūjan sītā käilīn māngan pānc māngāī re nā
45. ab mor pahilī manganawā sītā māng jäure vidh pujäu ho nā
46. sītā māng ajodhiyā ka rājā sarajū ka darśan ho nā
47. lalanā dūsrī manganawā sītā māng jäure vidhī pujäu ho nā
48. sītā māng kausilyā äisan sās sāsur rājā dasarath ho nā

49. lalanā tīsarī manganawā sītā māng jäure vidhī pujäu ho nā
50. sītā māng lachiman äisan dewar patī rāmcandr ho nā
51. ab morī cäuthī manganawā sītā māng jäure vidhī pujäu ho nā
52. sītā māngalīn phūlawan ka sejiyā godiyā horil māng na
53. lalanā pancäī manganawā sītā māng jäure vidhī pujawäi ho nā
54. ab mor phulawan ka sejiyā sītā mangalīn godiyā horīl mang nā
55. lālan bāj lāgal anadha badhaïyā gotīn gavāī sohar ho nā
56. ab bāj lāgal anadhäī badhäiyā sukkhū ka näua jāgal bhäiyā nā
57. lālan bāj lāgal anadhan bajäiyā gotīn gāvai sohar ho nā

50. Sohar

1. maciyā je bäiṭh a kauśilyā devī sinhāsan rājā dasarath ho
2. rājā rām ka paral ho tilakawā nevatava ghumāyī ho
3. arīgan newatäu ye rājā parīgan newatäu ho rām nanī äur ho
4. rājā ek jīn newatäu ho kakahiyā kakahiyā hamare bairan ho
5. arīgan awalen ye rājā parīgan āwale an rām nanī aür ho
6. rājā ek nahī̃ äilī ho kakahiyā anganawā sunn lāgal ho
7. yetani bacan rājā sunalan sunahī nahī̃ pawalan ho
8. rājā caṛhī bhäilan sone keho kharäuā ta kekäī ho manāve ho
9. sutalīn ranīyā jagäulan palathī bäiṭhäulan ho
10. raniyā choṛ deū man ka ho birodhawā calahu hamare angan ho
11. nahī̃ choṛab man ka birodhawā nahī̃ re calab angan ho
12. rājā rām ke likhā banabās bhārat rājā likhā
13. tabahī ho calab angan ho
14. äisan boliyā tu bolalu bolahī nahī̃ janalu ho
15. ranīyā däulu karejawa mẽ hātha karejā kaṛhī lehalu aho

51. Mātā Māī

1. Mäiyā morī khelelī re jhumariyā e maliyā torī re bagiyā nā
2. sāto samē khelelī re jhumariyā e maliyā torī re bagiyā nā
3. candan caukī jaṛāv kī re sāto bahinā ke āsan lagäure maliyā torī re bagiyā nā
4. sāto bahinā khelelī re jhumariyā e maliyā torī re bagiyā nā
5. jhanjhar gaṛuvā gangā jal pānī
6. sāto bahinā ke päuvā paravārū re
7. maliyā torī re bagiyā nā
8. sone ke chippi mē garī chohārā sāto bahinā ke bhog lagäu re maliyā torī re bagiyā nā
9. gāī ke ghīv kapūr ke bātī sāto bahinā ke āratī utāru re maliyā torī re bagiyā nā

52. Mātā Māī

1. nibiyā kī ḍariyā mäiyā nāwalīn jhaluawā ho ki jhulī jhulī nā
2. mäiyā gãvalīn gītiyā ho ki jhulī jhulī nā
3. jhulāī je bäiṭhalī sātāu bahiniyā ho ki peng mār nā
4. lālcand rām dularuā ho ki peng mār nā
5. agivan sing dularuā ho ki peng mār nā
6. ḍīh bābā dularuā ho ki peng mār nā
7. dhīre dhīre peng mār lālcand dularuā ho lahasī jäi hāī nā
8. ālar nibiyā ki ḍariyā ho lahasī jäi hāī na
9. jhulat jhulat mäiyā lāgalīn piasiyā ho ki calī bhäilī nā
10. ohī mālīnī ḍagarīyā ho ki calī bhäilī nā
11. bhītarā i bāṛu ki bahare malaniyā ho ki būn ek nā
12. hamke paniā piawā būn ek nā
13. käise ka paniā piāw sitalā māī ho ki godiyā hamare na
14. bāyan sevak tohār ho ki gōdiyā hamare nā
15. bāyan ganapat balakawā mäiyā godiyā hamare nā
16. ganapat sutāwahu mālīn sone ka khaṭolawā ho ki būn ek nā
17. detu pāniya piāī mālīn būn ek nā
18. käis ka paniyā piāwäu sātō bahīnī ho ki godiyā hamare nā
19. bāyan sewak tohār ho ki godiyā hamare nā

20. sevak sutāwahū mālīn sone ke khaṭolawā ki būn ek nā
21. detu paniyā piawāy mālīn būn ek nā
22. sone ka khaṭolawā mäiyā tutī-phutī jäi hā̃i ho ki bhuiyā loṭ nā
23. maïyā sevak tohār ho ki bhuiyā loṭ nā
24. jā̃u mor sevak mālīn bhuiyā loṭ lag hi ho uthāī ho leb nā
25. apne sone ke ancarawā ho uṭhāī ho leb nā
26. dahīne ke hathawā lihalīn jhajhuṛhā gaṛhulawā ho bāye re hathawā
27. ohi reśamawā ka ḍoriyā ho bāye re hathawā
28. calal calal mālīn gäilīn sākar kũawā ho ki ḍhīl lag nā
29. tāl gäil kūā patāl bhäil panīyā ho ki käise ka nā
30. mäiyā ke paniyā piāwäu ho ki käise ka nā
31. jā̃u tūī hotī mālīn gunawā ka āgar ho ancarawā jorī ke nā
32. hamke paniyā piāyā ho ancarawā jorī ke nā
33. ek loṭā kaṛhilin mālīn hāth goṛ dhoalīn dusare loṭawā
34. mäiyā ke paniyā ho piāw ho dusare loṭawā
35. sab devī ke paniyā piāw ho dusare loṭawā
36. bhūl cūkal ke paniyā piāw ho dusare loṭawā
37. jais tu mālīn ho ham juṛawaul ho ki väis-väis nā
toharī ṛheriyā juṛāy mālīn väis-väis nā
38. toharī patohiyā juṛāy mālīn väis väis nā
39. toharī nagariyā bakasal jāy väis väis nā

53. Mātā Māī

1. kathin ke morī mäiyā ke mandilawā kathī lāgal kẽwāṛ
kathī lāgal kẽwaṛiyā mäiyā
2. ancare mandil raure jharabō̃ sir senur lāgī mäiyā
3. sonn de morī mäiyā ke mandilawā rupe lāgal kẽwāṛ
4. candan lāgal kẽwaṛiyā mäiyā
5. ancare mandil räure jharabō̃ sir senur lāgī mäiyā
6. kathin ke mäiyā käne kanaphulawā kathiye gare hār
kathiye gare harawā mäiyā
7. palakan ḍagar baharabo sir senur lāgī mäiyā
8. sonn ke mäiyā kāne kanaphulawā motiye gare hār
dawanā gare harawā
9. mäiyā āsuan caran parawarabo sir senur lāgī mäiyā
mandil räure jharabō̃
10. gode bālak lāgī mäiyā rase rase beniyā̃ ḍolāibo

54. Mātā Māī

1. phulavā māĩ loṛhī loṛhī haravā gachavalū
2. le gāilā śitala darabar māiyā morī
3. le gāili kālī darabar māiya morī
4. sutalī bāṛū ki jāgalī kaliyā māiyā
5. duare maliyavā bāṛe ṭhāṛh māiya morī
6. mãgo mãgo malini je kichū mãg dehulā je tohare hirde samāī, malini
7. bhītar bāṛū ki bahare sātõ bahini
8. kab ka duare maliniyā bāṛe ṭhāṛh māiya morī
9. mãgo mãgo malini je kichū mãg dehulā je tohare hirde samāi, mālini
10. dhan se putra māiya tohare dihal bāṛe
11. maliyā amar kai dehũ māiya morī
12. puruv ka cān pachim cali jāi hãī tabo maliyā amar nahĩ hoi mālini

55. Mātā Māī

1. sīghā caṛhalĩ śītalā garajatī ave ho gavaiyā logavā
2. māi ke cinhabo na karãī ho gavaiyā logavānā (this is the refrain)
3. cinhī hai ta cinhī hai śītala mālī ka chokaṛavā haravā
4. devī ke ṭhaṛhi darajavā haravā lehalenā (repeated many times)
5. sīghā caṛhalĩ kālī garajatī ave ho gavaiyā logavā (refrain)
6. cinhī hai ta cinhī kālī sevā ke chokaṛavā ahūtiyā lekenā
7. devī ke ṭhaṛhī darajavā ahutiyā lehalenā (repeated)
8. sīgha caṛhalĩ duṛgā garajatī ave ho gavaiyā logavā
9. cinhī hai ta cinhī hai duṛgā gaṛeriā ka putavā kasiyāvā lehalenā
10. devī ke ṭhaṛhī darajavā kasiyā lehalenā (repeated)
11. sīgha caṛhalĩ amaliyā garajatī ave ho avaiya logavā (refrain)
12. cinhī hai ta cinhī hai amaliyā koharā ka chokaṛavā ho kalaśavā lehalenā
13. māiyā ke ṭhaṛhi darajavā kalaśavā lehalenā (repeated)

56. Mātā Māī

1. māiyā morī pātarī pātarī kamaṛuā deśavā ārujhe ho
2. kekarā ke dehale śītalā (repeated)

3. kekarā ke dehale kālī
4. das pā̃c putavā ho (repeated)
5. kekarā ke käinū nirasātaniyā ho
6. dharamī ke dehalu sev kā
7. das pā̃c putavā ho
8. garabhī ke käila nirasātaniyā
9. kekarā ke dehale mäiyā
10. mäiyā morī pātarī pātarī kamaṛuā deśavā ārujhe ho
11. das pā̃c gotiyā
12. kekarā ke pīṭhiyā āgaravā ḍaro ho nā
13. dharamī ka dehalo sev kā, das pā̃c gotiyā
14. garabhī ka piṭhiyā daro āgaravā ho
15. mäiyā morī pātarī pātarī kamaṛuā deśavā ārujhe ho

57. Mātā Mäī

1. ālhar näihar tor bahut garīb ye mäiyā
2. akhare i jäuā ka roṭī ye mäiyā
3. mäiyā uparā cakawaṛhe ka sāg ye mäiyā
4. sītalā mäī näihar tohar bahut garīb ye mäiyā
6. akhare ye jäuā ka roṭī ye mäiyā
7. mäiyā uparā cakavaṛhe ka sāg ye mäiyā
   (from this point the paradigm is repeated again and again, inserting the gods' names as indicated in the translation)
29. sab devī devtā näihar tohara bahut garīb ye mäiyā
30. bhūlal cukal näihar tohar bahut garīb ye mäiyā
31. akhare ye jäuā ka roṭī ye mäiyā
32. mäiyā uparā cakavaṛhe ka sāg ye mäiyā

58. Mātā Mäī

1. choṭī choṭī bīṭiyā bā̃se ka dalavā ho phulavā loṛhai e devī
2. maliyā phulavariyā ho apani mādil hoi ke
3. maliyā pukare ho kekare bīṭiyā e logõ
4. dhāgäilai phulavariyā ho kekar bīṭiyā logõ
5. nahī̃ ham biṭiyā nahī̃ ham patohiyā
6. ham ta hai e mālin śītalā ka satavā̃ bahiniyā
7. vīdhyācal bhagavatī ho ham ta kālī ka bhavānī ho

59. Ropanī

1. mãĩ tose pūchailõ maina morī nanadiyāre
2. kaise torā gāl piyarailãĩ mor nanadiyāre dilavā rasiyāre

3. bābā kī bagiyā pīsā̃i gäilī̃ haradiyā haradī citikiyā muhavā̃ piyar dilavā rasiyāre
4. käisan toharā petavā phulal āve mor nanadiyāre
5. bābā kī bagiyā pīsā̃i gäilī̃ satuvavāre are khäilī̃ satuvavā petavā phulal dilavā rasiyāre
6. käisan tohari chatiyā savaräilī dilavā rasiyāre
7. bābā kī bagiyā bhavjī mājai gäilī̃ baṭuliyāre baṭulī karikhiyā chatiyā sāvarī̃ dilavā rasiyāre
8. maciyā hi baiṭhalā̃i sasuru baṛhäitāre maina ka uvadavā dhäi dā ho dilavā rasiyāre
9. abahī ta maina mor laṛikā gadelavāre kheltī hoi hā̃i suyali mauniyā dilavā rasiyāre
10. devarā ki coriyā̃ bhavjī bhejäilī citṭhiyavāre maina ka baduā lei jā dilavā rasiyāre
11. jabare baratiyā goiṛavā dhäi äilī̃ maina ka bathe kapār dilavā rasiyāre
12. jabare baratiyā āganavā mẽ äilī̃ maina ke janamai nāda lāl dilavā rasiyāre
13. bacce ke rone ki āvāj sunī bhäiyā dhunailā kapaṭiyā biyahal bajāi ki sudevas dilavā rasiyāre
14. bati mori mānā bhäiyā jin dhunā kapaṭiyāre duno rāg lakaṛī bajäihā dilavā rasiyāre

60. Milling (*Jatsār*)

1. sonavā ke kūchiyā e rāmā āganā bahārī le
2. āgana bahārata e rāmā chutele ho ācarav
3. maciyā baithalī e rāmā sasur tuhū̃ baṛhäitin (2x)
4. bhäiyā khāū̃ bhāvjī ho khāū̃ äurū ho batijav
5. sāsur tohare ihalī ho rāmā sone ke ho garīlava
6. hathavā ke lihalī ho rama resam ke ḍoriyā
7. garīlā ke bharī ho bharī däili ho araravā
8. apane dubelī e rāmā jāī jamunā bica (2x)

61. Phaguā

1. are suno janaka kī batiā sakhiā, suno janaka kī batiyā
2. rājā janaka jī paran ek ṭhāna
3. duare par dhäile pinakiā
4. deś deś ke bhupatī āe
5. tāre na tāre pinakiā sakhiā, suno janaka kī batiyā
6. bārā sur rāvan calī āī
7. uho bhāgäi ādhi ratiyā sakhiā suno janaka kī batiyā

8. munī ke sāg duī bālak āe
9. u dhāi torā pinakiā sakhiā, suno janaka ki batiyā

62. Phaguā

1. le lo dahī nāda lāl, lāl dahiyā morī le lo (refrain)
2. kahawā kā tū gop gwālī
3. kā tumāro nām lāl dahiyā morī le lā
4. mathurā ki ham gop gawāle
5. rādhā hamāra nām lāl dahiyā morī le lā
6. ī dahiyā morī sāsu jamolī
7. becan calī ham āj lāl dahiyā morī le lā
8. kab kar dūhal, kab kar jamāval
9. kab kar jaranav dāl lāl dahiyā morī le lā
10. bhoravā ka dūhal, sājh hi ka jumaval
11. sājhavā joran dia dāl lāl dahiyā morī le lā
12. i ha cahakavā kalp nāth pāḍe gāve
13. henarī bāithale āj lāl dahiyā morī le lā
14. āj ka dinavā hāue mehamanavā
15. holī ka hāue tyohār lāl dahiyā morī le lā

63. Phaguā

1. vrij mē harī horī macāī, lalā (this is the refrain)
2. rādhā ji cāynā diyā sakhiyan ke
3. jhūda jhūda sab āī lale (refrain)
4. kisne lie mohan mālā muraliyā
5. ham nakabesar pahirāī (refrain)
6. kahā gāiyā tār nāda bābā jī
7. kahavā dasomat māī (refrain)
8. kṛṣṇa kahai mukh morī ke
9. kahā gaī caturāī

64. Phaguā

1. sakhī kā ho takasir hamarī tajeho banavārī
2. jet mās tan tapai āg bhāve nā sāṛī
3. bāṛhe birahā asāṛh nakhat ādra lalakārī
4. sāvan mās sohāvan lāgat
5. jhulai gāilī amavā kī ḍāri ho āvadh bihārī
6. bhādō gagan gamhir pīr ati hiraḍe majhārī
7. karigai kvār karār savatasāg pasai murārī
8. kartik rās racat man mohan
9. koel bole lagalī amavā kī ḍarī ho āvadh bihārī

65. Phaguā

1. mārī dil jānī nayan bhālā
2. tab se cāynā parat na dil mẽ
3. vah tāmas lagai uṭhe joālā
4. mārī dil jānī nayan bhālā
5. khān pān kuch dil nahī̃ na bhāve
6. bhītar me ho gae ho joālā
7. mārī dil jānī nayan bhālā
8. śiv parśād bolāe na bolai
9. mānā ho mārī gae kālā
10. mārī dil jānī nayan bhālā

66. Phaguā

1. bābū darogā jī kavane gūnahiyā̃ banhalā piyavā mor bābū darogā jī
2. nā piavā mor atar patar nā piavā mor choṭ
3. bhāgiyā ka mātal mor matavalavā gāila sarakiyā par soe
4. pā̃ch rupayā sipāyā ke debai das debai kotvāl
5. bālā jobanavā phirāgiyā ke debai das debai kotvāl
6. sāīyā ke lebai choṛāya

67. Phaguā

1. nayā phaiśan mẽ sabahī lubhāe, bhāiyā, sab cal purānī bhulāe, bhāiyā
2. are gore mẽ jutā būṭadār cāhī
3. rāge birāgā kā lūgī lag gaī
4. motiyā dhotī mane nahī̃ bhāī
5. bāro mẽ bagalā kaṭae bhāiyā
6. laṛaka biṛī piyẽ harkhāī
7. tel aur sābun sugādh lagāī
8. kāmõ par jāte khūb pāno ghulāī
9. dhur māṭī kiye bisarāe bhāiyā, sab cal purānī bhulāe, bhāiyā
10. ek to ā gaī mahāgāī
11. ghare kā ghī sapnā hoi jāī
12. catanī caukhā se peṭ bharāī
13. iśkabanī mẽ̃ man khūb lagāe, bhāiya, sab cal purānī bhulāe, bhāiyā
14. pahale ka javān sir kā nām baṛhāī
15. bacau śer ke mārī girāī

16. madhu kuśtī mẽ nām kar jāī
17. kahe nāgau samijhāe, bhäiya, sab cal purānī bhulāe, bhäiyā

68. Jogirā

1. bājā bāje bāg mẽ bajāvanvālā kaun
2. dharatī mäiyā so gaī jagāvanvālā kaun
3. yahā̃ par mil ke nāco
4. calī calījā bāg mẽ mevā khilāū̃gā
5. mevā kī ḍār ṭuṭ gaī cadar bichāū̃gā
6. cadar kā konā phaṭ gayā darjī bulāū̃gā
7. darjī kā suiyā ṭuṭ gaī ghauṛā daurāū̃gā
8. ghauṛa kā ṭā̃g ṭuṭ gaī hardī lagāū̃gā
9. hardī nā choṛhe jardī, jardī nā choṛ rāg
10. buṛhavā nā choṛhe buṛhiyā, buṛho kā marī gaṛh

69. Kabīr

1. sunīlā morī kabīr henarī, kahat jā
2. henarī ke bahin ka buriyā baṛhäile jaise ujainī ka tāl
3. ādhe mẽ henarī satuā sanāĩ ki ādhe āskar nahāĩ
4. dono dā̃ti darerat jāī laṛhavā
5. bhūsaraibū ta tīgā kātī leb burī rūnaho magoicā ke kā̃te se
6. burī kū̃co kudāri ke pāse se
7. hāī hāī horiyā lauṛhe par caṛhai tohār buriyā

70. Kajalī

1. kharī ho ke araja karāĩ ho brajanārī
2. dedā kā̃dhā cira hamārī nā
3. leke cira kadam caṛhi baiṭhāĩ
4. ham jāl mājh ughārī nā
5. sawaliyā̃ mājh ughārī nā
6. tohāre cir jabai ham debe
7. hoi jäibū jalavā se nārī nā
8. sab sakhiyā̃ mil araj karat hāĩ
9. rakhā lāj hamārī nā
10. sawaliyā̃ lāj hamārī nā
11. pūräin pāt pahir rādhā nikalāĩ
12. kṛṣṇa bajāve tālī nā
13. sawaliyā bajāve tālī nā

71. Kajalī

1. gujariā dhīraj dharā bāraho mahīnavā (this is the refrain)
2. asarh yārī chorā hamārī dhiraj dharā manavā
   dhiraj dharā manavā ho pyārī dhiraj dharā manavā
3. sāvan mē dhulamil ke gāvā sakhiyan sāg mē ganavā
4. bhādō bhar tu rahā bhavan mē mat jāi hā̃i nāiharavā
5. kal kuār kare nā pāi hā̃i mat karā rudhanavā̃ (refrain)
6. kārtik mē ek patī bhejab ciṭṭhī bairanavā
7. agahan mē sab sāg kae sakhiyā calelī gavanavā (refrain)
8. pus mē tohāke khelai bade bhejab ek suganavā
9. māgh mē makar nahāyā jāke prayāgarāj sthānavā
10. phāgun phāg ṭarai nā pāī hā̃i cunarīn par rāginavā
11. cait mē cītā karake pyārī bhejab ek dhavanavā (refrain)
12. bāiśāk mē as pujāibe toharī jab āibe bhavanavā
13. jaith mē bhēṭ karab ham tohāse hoi jāi hā̃i milanavā (refrain)

72. Kajalī

1. kahanā mānā mati jā be jānalā ḍagariā ho balamū
2. arabar deś śahar bāgālā
3. jātai hoi hā̃i suratiyā kālā
4. paniā lagā̃i karejavā paṛī jāi hā̃i jhajhariā ho balamū
   ab jhajhariā ho balamū
5. nariyar kelā kay adhikārī
6. jekare khāile hoke bīmārī
7. okare khāile baṛhe bīmārī
8. sastā bikai barābar carī aur bajariyā ho balamū
9. sastā bikai barābar caṛī aur śahariyā ho balamū
10. ek ṭhe narī catur bāgālī
11. ek ṭhe narī catur bāgālī
12. o sab jyādū karanevālī
13. lābī kes suhavan patarī kamariyā ho balamū
14. batiyā samajh na pāiba teṛhā
15. jyadūā mār banai hā̃i bheṛā
16. bas mē kāike rakhī hā̃i apanī sejariyā ho balamū

73. Kajalī

1. pātī ī lehale jāi hā bābhanavā

2. bital jālā savanavā na (2x)
3. pātī hamār lihale jäi hā pir gagan dhan garajanā
4. sāvan phūle gavanavā na, savaliyā phūle gavanavā
5. bhādō räin pāth nahī̃ sujhe
6. ṭapaṭap cue āganavān
7. kuār mās nit sarag cā̃danī
8. kārtik jare diyanavān, savaliyā jare diyanavān
9. agahan nīk tanik nahī̃ laga
10. sakhī sab calelī gavanavān
11. pus mās muhi sit satave
12. maghavā ṭhaṛhī āganavān savaliyā ṭhaṛhī āganavān
13. phāgun phāg kekarī sāg khelab
14. harī mur madhubanavān gaelā̃ia harī madhubanavān gaelā̃ia
15. cait mās banatesur banapūle bahi pavanavān, savaliyā bahe pavanavān
16. jaitavā mē śyam sūdar nahī̃ äilaia
17. bitī gäelā̃ia baraho mahinavān

74. Kajalī

1. gurahin pānī bharajā bābū log khariyān
2. gorikā kajarā hai kaṭīlā
3. ūke dūno nayan mē khirā
4. nīlā lahāgā pahine patarī kamariāna
5. gorika coliā hav mulatānī
6. bā̃h mē curiā dhānī
7. dhakavā chāp cunariā odaile gujariā na ho
8. gori ke kābar mē karadhaniā
9. pair mē karā charā paijaniā
10. goriā calat ka rahiyā pheraile najariyā na
11. gatē caubejī ostād
12. kajarī nayā nayā taiyār
13. jīlā gāzipur indrapur makanavā ho balamū
14. gurahin pānī bharajā bābū log khariyān

75. Khaṛī Birahā

1. kahai e bhā sugavā hi jān hamē dudhavā piyavalū sugavā mudäiā baṛe
2. are jab bhā janatō sugavā hoi hā̃i mudäiyā are nanhave ḍayanavā baṛe re pajiyā
3. are nanhavā ḍayanavā are hiravä tor

76. Khaṛī Birahā

1. are kahā̃i rām bhäiyā rām bhäilā̃i jogiyā lakhan bairagiyā
2. lekin dūno bhäiyā ho gäilā̃i phakir
3. are i hai garavā mē nāvat häue tulasī ka malavā lekin
4. ghumke mā̃gat bāṛe nagariyā mē bhīkh

77. Khaṛī Birahā

1. are kahā̃i sakatiā banavā ta ho gailai rahal Lakhanjī ke bhāī lekina
2. a Rāmjī ta rowat rahe leke jhangiā par bilakhai (ha)
3. are hot hī āī hā̃i bhoravā Lakhan Mār jāī hā̃i lekin
4. ho are keke leke Awadhabapurī re
5. are keke leke Awadhabapurī mē jā wā (ha)

78. Khaṛī Birahā

1. bīdarā banavā mē rahai pakalī bäiriyā lekin
2. radhikā onhavale rahai dar ta ekahu bairiya radhe torahi na pavali
3. ta kanhaiā dahalire basiyā bajāe kānhā

79. Khaṛī Birahā

1. jhākay nārī gokulavā ka dhani re kubariyā torī bāṛī bhāg
2. sab ke ta mil gäilē lāgar a lūjavā
3. a kubarī ke kesun murarī

80. Khaṛī Birahā

1. kahā̃i kavanī samäiyā mē dharatī ta hilal rahalī̃ ki
2. kavanī samäiyā mē doli gayal rahal asamān
3. kavanī samäiyā mē sītajī hari gäil rahā̃i
4. kahavā̃ gayal rahala bhagavān

81. Khaṛī Birahā

1. are kahā̃i kaläu samäiyā mē ta dharatī ḍolal rahalī bhāe
2. lekin satajug samäiyā mē ḍol gayal rahal asamān
3. treta jugavā mē māī jānakī har gäilī̃
4. jahā̃ miragā mārā̃i mere logavā
5. are miragā mārā̃i gayal rahā̃i bhagavān

82. Nirgun bhajan

1. Prān panchī ban jāī ha͠i rām, jāhi dinawā̃
2. are tan ta jarat sabhī jal jāī ha͠i
3. are ḍār pāt sab jhar jāī ha͠i
4. ye dehiyā ke gumān mat karā bhāī
5. nahī̃ ta kāg ya gidh mila khāī ha͠i
6. jo vyāhī mukh pān khilāī ha͠i ara uhao dekhike ghināī ha͠i
7. are jaldī nikālā ghar se bāhar nāhī̃ ta bhūt bani ghar khāī ha͠i
8. jab rāj karat rājā calī jāī ha͠i are rup nirekhat rānī are bed paṛhat sab hī calī jāī ha͠i
9. are logawā jāī ha͠i abhimānī
10. are cānd je chuṭī ha͠i are suruj chuṭī ha͠i are jinkar jot ujiyārī
11. are kahat kabīr dharam nāhī̃ jāī ha͠i
12. are rahi jāī ha͠i nam wa niśānī
13. jāhi dinawā̃ prān panchī ban jāī ha͠i rām jāhi dinawā̃

83. Nirgun Bhajan

1. ek din hogā śarīr mẽ corī
2. are he man caukas hokar rahnā
3. are ek śarīr mẽ das darawāja
4. jab log ghere cārī or
5. jab prān dās jab chuṭan lage
6. are hans jālī kaünī orī
7. are mātā e rowa͠i are lalan mar gaye
8. are bahan rowa͠i merā bhāī
9. jab cor dinan ki vyāhī jab rovaī
10. are cetat prān e āśā
11. are kahat kabīr suno ho bhāī sādhū
12. kaṭilā narakhar bānhīlā ṭaṭī
13. nahī̃ jāne rām ho kahā̃ lāgī māṭī

84. Nirgun Bhajan

1. he lakaṛī tū ban lakaṛī ab dekh tamāsā lakaṛī kā
2. garbh wās se bāhar āye jo jhūle pālanā lakaṛī kā
3. jab pānc varṣ kī umr bhāī jab hāth khelawanā lakaṛī kā
4. he lakaṛī tū ban lakaṛi ab dekh tamāsā lakaṛī kā
5. bīs varṣ kī umr bhāī jab jab phikr lagī vyāh karne kī
6. jab palkī sajī tulasī lakaṛī kī

7. cālīs varṣ jab umir bhāī jab phikr lagī ab buṛhāyā kī
8. sāṭh varṣ kī umar bhāī jab hāth sahārā lakaṛī kā
9. jab asi varṣ kī umar bhāī jab phikr lāgī ab calne kī
10. jab cār jane mili khāṭ uṭhāvā̃i vimān banāyā lakaṛī kā
11. jamunā taṭ par le jākar ke snān karāyā gangā kā
12. nice lakaṛī ūpar lakaṛī citā sajāyā lakaṛī kā
13. jas phūnk diyā thā phāgun ki holī bhāī ṭhokar mārī lakaṛī kā
14. kahat kabīr suno bhāī sādhū sab khel tamāsā lakaṛī kā
15. he lakaṛī tū ban lakaṛī ab dekh tamāsā lakaṛī kā

85. Nirgun Bhajan

1. taruar as maydān biyārī nahī̃ jelat ho rām
2. hā̃ ta ihā jag koi nahī̃ āpan ta kehū̃ se na bolal ho rām
3. hā̃re hans kahelā sun sarwar ham ta uṛī jāīb ho rām
4. torā morā ihā mulukāt bahurī le na āīb ho rām
5. hā̃re kahūwā se jīv āīl ta kahawā̃ samāil ho rām
6. kahawā̃ tu käil mokām kahawā̃ ta lapaṭāil ho rām
7. are nirgun se jiv āil, ta sargun samāil ho rām
8. kāyā gaṛhāy kaile mokām māyā me lapaṭāil ho rām
9. Hā̃ re kahawā̃ se sowal ek ṭhag ta sab log ṭhagāil ho rām
10. hā̃ re kabīr ṭhag cinhī ke acal umar ghar pāwal ho rām

86. Nirgun Bhajan

1. e ab koi hīrā ratan gāvā ke jagat se jāne ho bhāī
2. hīrā ratan jatan se rākho tālā kunj lagāī
3. āj āī hā̃i koi sant gahakiyā hīrā mahang bikāī
4. jagat se jālan ho bhāī
5. gīlā guṛ par makkhī baithe pā̃v agayī lapaṭāī
6. jab uṛane ki śaktī nahī̃ hai bharamī mari jāī
7. jagat se jalanā̃i ho bhāī
8. semar kāṭh kā jangalā rah phulawā suganā dekh lo bhāī
9. jab uṛane kī śaktī nahī̃ hai bharamī mari jāī
10. jagat se jalā̃i ho bhāī
11. e kahai kabīr suno bhāī sadho bhajan karat cit lāī bina bhajan ka mukti na bani hā̃i
12. virathā janam gāvāī
13. jagat se jalā̃i e bhāī

87. Nirgun Bhajan (Khari biraha)

1. kahā̃ ki jāe ke rahalī badrī nārāyan ki baramhā ji lehalā̃ belhamāi
2. pherāi ke rahalõ tulasī ka malavā gāilī̃ māyāvā mẽ bhūlāi
3. are māyāvā mẽ apane gāile bhūlāi

88. Nirgun Bhajan

1. bhāī abai manai māyā māyā ho abai manai māyā ho māyā
2. bhāī ab man māyā joṛe bhajan ab man māyā joṛayo
3. hāthī joṛe ghoṛā joṛe bailā lākh karoṛayo
4. kund phān ke sampat joṛe jabahu kahe dhan thoṛe
5. bhajan man bhāī ab man māyā joṛayo
6. pānc pacīs mili āye barāti caṛhe kaṭh ke ghoṛe
7. āpan cale prabhu mukh na bolyo sir se cādar oṛhe
8. ab man māyā joṛe bhajan man ab man maya joṛayo
9. ham jānī koi sang calega gāī bhā̃isiyā dhan ghoṛayo
10. gā̃ṛ langoṭī khole cale hai are lag gāil prabhu ji ke ḍorayo
11. ab man māyā ho māyā ab man joṛayo ho are man joṛayo
12. hāth pakaṛi ke mātā rowat bā̃h pakaṛ bīri mere
13. bhajan man bā̃h pakaṛ bīr mere
14. kahe kabīr mātā ab kyõ rotī tin joṛayo un toṛayo
15. are man māyā ho māyā bhāī abai man joṛayo

89. Nirgun Bhajan

1. are mainā rām kī bolī bol
2. bol re mainā tū rām kī bolī bol
3. kyõ gaphalat mẽ sote maina howan lāge bhor
4. cār dinā ke ab tū hī musāphir
5. jānā hai jag choṛ mainā rām kī bolī bol
6. kuch gharī rām kī bolī bol
7. kin pijaṛan mẽ rahat mainā (incomprehensible) lagāye ho
8. nikal jāyegā sā̃s ka panchī bas nā calī hai tor
9. are bol re maina kuch gharī rām kī bolī bol
10. cār pahar dhandhā mẽ bite kyā baiṭhe mukh mor
11. kahat kabīr suno bhāī sādhū bhajan karo sagaro
12. mainā rām kī bolī bol kuch gharī rām kī bolī bol

90. Nirgun Bhajan

1. bhāī tan kā āpan gumān mat kar ī tan bilkul matti hai
2. inkā bharosā kabhī na karna ī dhokē ki ṭaṭṭī hai
3. duniyā daulat māl khajāna tere sang jā jāyegā
4. jisko dam par phūl rahe bābū wah bhī kām nā āyegā
5. do din khātin lagā hāṭ sab uṭh jāye pachatāyegā
6. yahū̃ tahā̃ se kar ik sādā rehū̃ tahā̃ se pāyegā
7. e sauda ke kharīdār ko naphā choṛ na ghaṭṭī hai
8. tan kāyā par gumān mat kar ī tan bilkul maṭṭī hai
9. kisi kā jag mē khuśī lahī to jītī jam ke sabhī jatan
10. bhai māyā lobh mē phãs kar ke barabād kiyo sab apan tan
11. abhī ta cetau bhajan karo nahī̃ badhõ ānkh mē paṭṭī hai
12. ek langoṭī pahanā kar ke ghar se nikālēge phauran
13. kisī kā jag mē khuśī lahī to dekho bhāī jalai diyā thā jaise citai ki bhaṭthī hai
14. are ulaṭā āe ulaṭā jāe ulaṭā sabhī samān huā
15. ulaṭe na duniyā ke andar isī se ulaṭā gyān huā
16. bidhanā re unhī kahale khare san par dhyān huā
17. gole muhammad tat hamāre i prānī kalyān huā
18. kahe ta bhairo milajil ke phir gyān kī maṭṭī hai
19. tan kāyā par gumān mat kar ī tan bilkul maṭṭī hai

91. Nirgun Bhajan

1. ancarā kāhē nā dhulāī rāmā ancarā kahē nā dhulāī goriyā
2. janam janam kī mailī cunariyā jab panighaṭ pe jāī
3. kāhē kabīr suno bhāī sādho kab muktiyā se dekhāī
4. ancarā kāhē na dhulāī e rāmā ancarā kāhē nā dhulāī
5. rām nām kā sābun karle kṛṣṇanām dariyāī
6. apane gurū kā banā le rīṭhā tan ka mail choṛāī
7. ancarā kāhē nā dhulāī rāmā ancarā kāhē nā dhulāī

92. Nirgun Bhajan

1. baljorī se ho rām ki ab bal jorī se ho rām
2. saiyā̃ ye māngelā gawanawā rām ki hāy rām baljorī se
3. e lālī lālī ḍoliyā kā sabujā oharawā he rām
4. ki hai rām baljorī se
5. hai lāge batīso kaharawā̃ lāge ki he rām baljorī se
6. saiyā̃ baljorī se rām mangelā gawanawā

7. e lālī lālī ḍoliyā ka sabujā oharawā he rām
8. ki baljorī se he lāge batiso kaharawā̃ ho rām ki baljorī se
9. he rām mil lehū mil lehū sakhiyā salehar rāmā ab hai
10. ab phir na hoi hãī awanawā rām ki baljorī se
11. he rām hoi hãī nā awanawā rām bal jorī se
12. e kahat kabīr dās sun bhāī sādho rām
13. e jag phir na hoi hãī jag awanawā rām
14. baljorī se he saiyā̃ ye mangelā gawanawā rām ki hãy rām baljorī se

93. Nirgun Bhajan

1. karke singār alabelī akelī mohan ke ghar jān hogā
2. mohan ke ghar jāna hogā re śyāmo gharawā jānā hogā
3. karke singār alabelī akelī mohan ke ghar jān hogā
4. kathī ke suganā kathī ke pinjaṛā
5. kathī mẽ mil jānā hogā
6. karke singār alabelī akelī mohan ke ghar jān hogā
7. sone ke suganā maṭī ke pinjaṛā
8. maṭī mẽ mil jānā hogā
9. karke singār alabelī akelī mohan ke ghar jān hogā
10. kānce kānce bāsawā ke doliyā mangaibo kahāran ke sang jānā hogā
11. karke singār alabelī akelī mohan ke ghar jān hogā

94. Nirgun Bhajan

1. äile duarawā sajan niramohiyā nā māne darad hamār ho
2. mili lehu juli lehu sakhiyā salehari chuttā re bābā ke duar ho
3. prem ke kangahī se mathawā sãwaralī
4. aina mẽ lehalī utār ho
5. prem ke kājar anguriyā mẽ boralī
6. ankhiyā mẽ lihalī utār ho
7. kānce kānce basawā ke ḍoliyā banawalī
8. le gäilī gangā ke kinār ho
9. cār janā mili doliyā uṭhawale
10. le gäile gangā ke kinār ho
11. äile duarawā sajan niramohiyā nā māne darad hamār ho

95. Nirgun Bhajan

1. hā̃ ramatā mãi rām nām gun gäiho
2. ramatā mãi rām nām gun gäiho
3. tirath jäiho jal na chuihõ
4. nām ratī nahawäihõ
5. pā̃cõ dham yahi ghaṭ bhītar inhī̃ ke mal mal dhoihõ mãi ramata
6. hā̃ ramatā mãi rām nām gun gäiho
7. hā̃ ban mẽ jäiho pat na chuiho na virichā sanatäihõ
8. pāt pāt sab dev vasat hãi unhī̃ se sir jhukäiho mãi ramata
9. hā̃ ramatā mãi rām nām gun gäiho
10. hā̃ nā lihõ mãi jholī mantrā nā mãi bed kahäihõ
11. mere gurū wohi alakh niranjan unhī̃ se nehiyā̃ lagäihõ
12. hā̃ ramatā mãi rām nām gun gäiho
13. hā̃ man kā ghoṛā gyān ka ankuś surat lagām lagaihõ opar baiṭhe prabhū dās kabīr
14. ghūm phiri darśan päihõ
15. hā̃ ramatā mãi rām nām gun gaiho

96. Nirgun Bhajan

1. ratiyā jhin jhin oṛhe ke rāmā jāṛan maralī̃ rām
2. solah gaj ki sāṛī pahinū̃ are satarah gaj kā lahangā
3. sāsu nanad ke māthan kiriyā ādha ṭāng ughārī
4. ratiyā jhin jhin oṛhe ke ratiyā jāṛan maralī̃ rām
5. solah roṭī mõ sarapoṭī are nau baṭule kī dāl
6. sāsu nanad kī māthe kiriyā ratiyā käilin upawās
7. nau laṛikā näihar bīc janamẽ dasawo rah gayē peṭ
8. sāsu nanad ke māthan kiriyā nā säiyā̃ se bhenṭ
9. ratiyā jhin jhin oṛhe ke rāmā jāṛan maralī̃ rām
10. kahat kabīr suno bhāī sādhū ī pad ke je samujhe bujhe uha catur gyānī
11. ratiyā jhin jhin oṛhe ke rāmā jāṛan maralī rām

97. Nirgun Bhajan

1. abai man nāw mẽ nadiā ḍubal na jāī
2. ek ṭopī ke mūh se yāro nadī nal bahi jāī
3. bhajal man nadī nal bahi jāī
4. khenewālā kewaṭ rām sant siyā sang jāī
5. ek acaraj auro dekhe bhāī bandar duhai la gāī
6. dudh dudh sab bandar pī gaye

7. makhan kāśī jī pahuncāī
8. abai man nāw bice nadiyā ḍubal na jāī
9. ek acaraj mā̃ī auro dekhe bhāī ek ciunṭī jī calī gawanawā̃
10. nau man kājar lagāī
11. hāthī mār bagaltar dābai unṭai let laṭakāī
12. ek acaraj mā̃ī auro dekhe bhāī
13. ek kū̃iyā par lāgī āg
14. pālo kālo jarike koilā hoi gāī
15. macharī khelat ab phāgai
16. ek acaraj mā̃ī auro dekhe bhāī
17. ek ciunṭī jī mari pahār par nau sā gidd meṛarāī
18. kuch khāw karai kuch bhuiyā girāwat kuch garilatar jawāī
19. ek acaraj mā̃ī auro dekhe bhāī
20. ek gadahā jāmī do singh
21. pīṭhī galī par rassī lagaī ghīncai arjun bhīm
22. kabīr dās kī ulṭā bānī barasai kammal bhījai pānī
23. laukī buṛe sīl utarāī oriyan panī baṛerī caṛhī jāī

98. Bhajan

1. takdīr bigaṛ jāne se tadbīr kyā kare
2. dasarath ne mārā bān to mirigā ke jānā ke
3. saravan ke kajā ā gaī to tīr kyā kare
4. takdīr mẽ yahi hai to tadbīr kyā kare
5. khaphā hai jo bādśāh to wazīr kyā kare
6. likhā hai agar jel to janjīr kyā kare
7. baiṭhe kabīr kāsī bhagatī ke vāste
8. likhā marnā hai magah mẽ kāsī kyā kare
9. takdīr mẽ yahi hai to tadbīr kyā kare

99. Bhajan

1. hā̃ kab kar cuk hamārī prabhū
2. kāhẽ tarivar par phar sarsõh kāhẽ kõhaṛ phar bhārī
3. kāhẽ bakula ujar barnu hai kāhẽ koyal bhai kālī
4. kāhẽ rājā rāj karte hā̃ī kāhẽ sant bhaye bhikhārī
5. sādhū e hokar cannā na pāve bhaṛuā khāt sohārī
6. satvartā hokar lugārī na pāyẽ beśyā phārat sāṛī
7. sādhū e hokar cannā na pāve bhaṛuā khāt sohārī
8. kāhẽ jangal pharā̃ī cannan peṛawā reṛ kāhẽ ghar bārī
9. kahai kabīr jhuṭh mat samjho kal jug kī balihārī
10. sādhū e hokar cannā na pāve bhaṛuā khāt sohārī

100. Bhajan

1. are gati terī lakhi na parī re dayānidhi (2x)
   (This is the refrain)
2. gurū vaśiṣṭh pāḍit as jānī sodhi ke lagan dharī (2x)
3. sīta haran maran dasarath ko ghar ban vipat paṛī e dayānidhi
   (refrain)
4. kāhāvah phād kahā̃ mrig māric kāhava mrig cari (2x)
5. sīta ko hari le gaye ravaṇ suvarṇ lāk jarī e dayānidhi
   (refrain)
6. are suvarṇ lāk jarī e dayānidhi (refrain)
7. nīc hāth haricād bikāne hali pātāl dharī
8. koṭi gāu rājā nrig dinhe to ghar kop parī e dayānidhi
   (refrain)
9. pādav dal ke āp sārathī tin par vipat paṛī
10. duryodhan ke garab mitāyo yadukul nāś karī e dayānidhi (refrain)
11. are yadukul nāś karī e dayānidhi (refrain)
12. rahu ketu aru bhānu cādramā bidhi sanyog paṛī (2x)
13. kahat kabir sunā bhāi sadho honī hoke rahī e dayānidhi (refrain)
14. are honī hoke rahī e dayānidhi (refrain)

101. Kahā̃ravā

1. birij bhāilā̃i sūnā birij bhāilā̃i sūnā birij bhāilā̃i sūnā
2. tohā̃i binu śyām ho birij bhāilai sūnā
3. an binā prān dukhi ta bhāilā̃i sajanī jalabin tarapat mīnā
4. sun balam nārī dukhi ta hai nārī dukhi ta hai
5. din din hole malīnā tohai binu śyām ho birajī bhāilā̃i sūnā
6. kari ke sī̃gar palāg caṛhī baiṭhā̃i romarom ras bhīna bhīna
7. cole ka bād dharā dhar ṭuṭe
8. pōchā balam hamare cūelā pasena tohā̃i binu śyām birij bhāilā̃i sūng
9. lāl palāg par jarad bīchauna tāpar kāpar jhīna
10. dhire se pāv dharo palāge par
11. līga līga lāve caṛhīnā
12. idhar se avelī naval rādhīkā udhar se kuvār kanhai
13. śrī bṛndabanabā ke kūjagalin mē mil gailā̃i pīavā nagīnā
14. āṭh mās nav kātik nahāilī̃ śiv bar pūjan kinā
15. he vidhanā tohare kāre bigāṛalī choṭ balam likh dīnā

102. Koharavā Nirgun

1. khelat rahalõ mãi bābā ke bhavanavā tab le piyā ho mor bheje paravanavā
2. ki a ho saganī pari gāilāi gavane kā din jīā ghabaṛāī gāilā ho na kiyā ho sajanī
3. jab āilī ho baratiyā ho baba ka bhavanavā lālī lālī ḍoliyā par sabaj oharuvā
4. bajale ek bar ho baganavā ke dil ghabaṛāī gāilē ho sajanī
5. milī le hū̃ milī le hū̃ sakhiyā saheliyā āj chuṭaile more bāba kā habailiyā
6. choṭe jale gõdi ka naginavā ki keke leke la khelāīb
7. ghar mē morī mātā rove bābā sirhanavā ḍoliyā pakaṛke rovē bhāiyā mor biranavā
8. nāiharavā choṛavalāi ta mohiyā satāvelī honā sajanā
9. rim jhim buniyā paraile sārī ratiyā kaise kahõ re sakhī dilavā ka batiyā
10. ki a ho sajanī kājar gailai jhurāī kaval kumhī lāī gailī hona

103. Dhobiav

1. e jī gā̃dhī jī ke caraṇ gahā
2. javāhar ke sir nām bhajan karū̃ parameśvar ka kabhī na bhūle nām
3. rām khudā ekahī hāi sab alag alag hāi nām
4. hīdū musalim bhāī hāi laṛate ho bekār
5. bābā to pūjan gāilī̃ śiv ki mādiravā

104. Birahā

1. soyā thā ek din mahal mē sikādar uṭhāke dekhā duniā ka khākā
2. dil mē tamannā sākalp sādhā sāre jamīn mē uṛā dū̃ patākā
3. kar mē lekar khunõ ke pyāle labābab sapanõ̃ mē nasīkhā jhāda jhukānā
4. hilte sikarī se jarre mahī ka pair utale matu ka kā jamānā
5. visva vijeta bir sikādar vijāi calā hīd ke ādar
6. jhāda gāṛ diā jhelam nadī kinār
7. kabje mē paschamī esiā kiā misar irān śahar
8. kādahīd kā basā najar gayā sīd nadi ko gaya utar
9. udamādi mē sīd aur pājāb rāj ko titar bitar

10. ghor patakī takacasilā kā rājā ābī milā udhar
11. jhelam aur cināb ke bic thā ek rājā poras vahā̃ ka bali bahādur ek
12. jhāda dusamān ka gaṛā jhelam nadi kinār poras ke puruṣārth ko reti uṭhī pukār
13. dūdh ka lāj bacäi hā bhäiyā bhar javaniyā vatan ka rakhihā jīda pāniyā
14. nadī jhelam kinār jhāda sikādar ne gāṛā
15. nadī jhelam jhilmil ā̃cal bhī phukār uṭhā
16. merī sīma par beṭā bairī to lalakār uṭhā
17. lage na dāg janābhumī bacāū koi
18. hamāre sime se dusaman haṭāo koi
19. ākarake bairī birājā ho suno batiyā hamār
20. bājā bigul hai bajāyā uṭhī retī phūkār
21. rotī hai mātā mahīkī bahe asiā ki dhār jhāda sikādar ne gāṛ
22. bali ābī nareś hāī hamare ghar ke milā baṛhā jātā sikādar bhed thā ādar kā milā
23. tabhī poras ne lalakāra yunānvālō̃ ko
24. bahādur rok lo bahate lahuke nāle ko
25. mātā ka poras dulārā ho gale gajarā ke ḍāl
26. bā̃dhe lahukī kaphaniyā lie senā biśāl nikāl jākar sikādar ko rokā
27. hui sīmā par mār jhāda sikādar ne gāṛ
28. cācal calā gagan se pānī meghaiyā ko phār
29. vatan ka beṭā rakhihā pāniyā ran mē̃ lagī jhumane nāhar ka nisaniyā
30. dūdh lāj baceyā bhäiyā bhar javaniyā
31. vatan ka beṭā rakhihā pāniyā ran mē̃ lagī jhumane nāhar ka nisaniyā
32. are calalbā baghelavā jab jhumat ho simavā par
33. hathavā mē̃ jab lehale nāgī ho talavār
34. bhāgelā sipāhī ho yūnānī dekhi ke biravā
35. ākiya se bābū caumukh lāge ādhiyār
36. dekh ke sipahī bhāgi bolelā sikādar
37. kahā̃vā̃ bhāgi jālā ban ke gīdar ho sīyar
38. javanavā bābū dekhā simavā par
39. donō̃ oriyā se cale lagal talavār
40. bharakā hai gajadal rājā poras ka
41. bhārī senā gaī ho chitarāī
42. bhuiyā javanavā giral ba gajadal ke
43. bādh līā unko us bar
44. cahe de dā rāj cahe le la phāsiyā tohase ḍarabai na
45. videśiyā bahäibe asiyā

46. ājā ho sikādar hāthe lelā hathiyaravā
47. khunavā se bhīg gāilā mātā ka acaravā
48. kahalā sobariyā banāvelā siyār tohase ḍarabe na
49. jīo jīo beṭā bolal jhelamvālā paniyā
50. laṛake bacavalā hamare hīdvāle saniyā
51. bāje la acaravā sohāle basiyā tohse ḍarabe na
52. guru bihārī guru ganeś (unintelligible) bir sikādar
53. grām majuī bhāil kavī gājipur ke ādar
54. kahate rām lakhan dhar sārad ka caraniyā
56. vatan ka beṭā rakhiha jīda paniyā
57. dudh ka lāj bacāi hā bhāiyā bhār javaniyā vatan ka rakhihā jīdā pāniyā

105. Birahā

1. are ta hathavā mẽ gan lehale ho sajhavā bihanavā simavā par jhume javan ho
2. kāhavā par halavā bayalavā ke dharale khetavā mẽ jālā kisān ho
3. bāre ek gaua̐ mẽ dūnõ ka gharavā
4. khelale laṛakapan mẽ eke duaravā
5. oharo javān deś ke rakhavaravā eharo kisanavā banal kheti haravā
6. deśavā ka lajiā javanavā bacavaīla rakh ke hathelī par jān ho
7. maṭiā mẽ khunavā pasīnavā milāke deśava bacāve kisān ho
8. ohar javān toraī ṭaīk ho jahājiā, iharo kisān tore usar paratiyā
9. oharo javān sir lahava ka ṭopiyā, iharo kisān ke gobarā aur khādiyā
10. vaha̐ ta da̐gele ṭopiyā salāmī bajelā bigul niśān ho, iharo ta ṭhumuk ṭhumuk nāce payaliā goriyā li āve jalpān ho
11. gharavā mẽ taharaile sājhavā bihanavā sīmavā par jhumẽ javān ho kāhava par halavā bayalvā ke dharale khetavā mẽ jālā kisān ho
12. oharo javanavā deśava bacāve, iharo ta matiyā ke sonavā banāve
13. oharo javanavā dusaman bhāgāve, iharo kisanavā garībī miṭāve
14. deśavā ka pālan kisanavā karailā, rakhi ke hatelī par jān ho rakṣa karaila javān ho
15. rām sevak donõ bhārat kay gaurav donõ hai̐ deśavā ka śān ho

106. Purvī

1. jawan jawan kahī piyā mānab sab bacaniyā
2. dhire se cummā leil tanī ṭārī ke jhulaniyā
3. gorā-gorā rang bāṭ gorī bā kalāiyā
4. ankhiyā se ras cuwe gāl se laliyā
5. āg mor lāgal bā are sagarō badaniyā
6. dhire se cummā leil tanī ṭārī ke jhulaniyā
7. caṛhat phagunawā jīyā baurāy gāil
8. ṭas-mas colī karai baṛhalā jobanawā
9. kholī ke baṭaniyā piyā maujawā uṛāw
10. dhire se cummal leil ab tari ke jhulaniya
11. jawan jawan kahī piyā mānab sab bacaniyā

107. Purvī

1. deś chūṭe kajarā na chūṭe
2. mẽhadi na chūṭe mere pāvan kī
3. koṭin koṭin upay karī
4. haliyā̃ jo sunī āvan ki
5. dil leke bhāgā dagā deke bhāgā
6. kasam goiyā̃ säiyā̃ dagā deke bhāgā
7. dagā denā hi thā to lāye gavanavā kāhẽ
8. sohanī rāt mẽ tu bhäilā sapanavā kāhẽ
9. sejariyā sunī sārī rāt bhayāvan lāge
10. mohī abhāgin piyā lake gavanavā gäilā
11. are he ho gosäiyā̃ säiyā̃ are milā mor abhāgā
12. jamānā burā hair isasān bure hote hãi
13. javānī joś mẽ imān bure hote hãi
14. karār kese käilū log lagāve jhakiyā
15. kahãi dil jānī jarā āke lagā lo chatiyā
16. phūṭ jaegī kabhī chalak jāe gagariyā
17. e siā rām tere sāth nahī̃ paũgī
18. are ānā ho to javānī mẽ ājā
19. morī sunī sejariyā säiyā are nīkõ nā lagā

108. Purvī

1. adhī adhī ratiyā ke bole koilariyā
2. cihũkī uṭhī goriyā sejariyā se ṭhāṛh
3. amavā mojarī gäilāya mahuvā kocāī gäilāya
4. mor birahiniyā̃ ke niniyā bhorāī gäilāya
5. rahi rahi dehiyā̃ se bahailī bayariyā
6. khulan lāge sudhiyā ke dehalo kevāṛ

7. phulavā phulāī gäilā̃ī bhāvarā lobhāī gäilā̃ī
8. kavane kasuravā s̱e piyā ghar nāhī̃ äilā̃ī
9. likh likh patiyā paṭhavalī vipatiyā bahan lāge ratiyā
10. nayan jaladhār
11. pāchi uṛan lāge gagan magan lāge
12. manavā ke pijaṛā se suganā bolan lāge
13. hamaro sanehiyā na gune niramohiyā
14. däiv ho jāne kahiyā le kaṭihani gāṛh
15. adhī adhī ratiyā ke bole koilariyā

109. Qawwālī

1. hā̃ pareśān hū̃ mohabbat se
2. magar paresānī nahī̃ jātī
3. ki mā̃ī barabād hū̃ ki unkī nādānī nahī̃ jāyā
4. are uskī ā̃kho mē̃ sab u kuch hai lekin (repeated three times)
5. dāvatē̃ kaiph mastī nahī̃ hai
6. mere jīdagī se na khele
7. jidagī itanī sastī nahī̃ hai
8. phūl ko mussa ārane ka hak hai
9. phir kalī kislae musakarāī
10. bā̃kī bā̃ka najariyā galat hai
11. vo rotī hai hāstī nahī̃ hai
12. vo to baiṭhā hai dariyā kināre
13. jāl ḍāle hue khūb macherā
14. machaliyā̃ hā̃ī ye kitanī sayānī
15. ek bhī machalī pāsti nahī̃ hai
16. are kyā pāsāegā jālī vo mujhko
17. uske kaṭihe mē̃ cārā nahī̃ hai
18. uskī ā̃kho mē̃ sab kuch hai lekin
19. dāvatē̃ kaiph mastī nahī̃ ha

110. Qawwālī

1. is caurāsī mē̃ vṛjdhām bahut acchā hai
2. sarī isthānō̃ se nādagā̃v bahut acchā hai
3. rām ke nām ka lāka mē̃ bajāya ḍākā
4. bole hanumān merā rām bahut acchā hai
5. lāka mē̃ jab se rakh dīā āgad uṭhāke pā̃v
6. bole jo bir hone haṭā de āke pā̃v
7. jab sab bir hāre tab calā rāvan baṛhāke pā̃v
8. āgad jī bole dhartā hai kyū̃ merā ā̃ke pā̃v
9. agar chūnā hai to chū bhagvān ka jāke pā̃v

10. bhagvān jidhar tumhāri dayā ki najar gaī
11. pāp inkā pāp kaṭ gaī bigaṛī sāvar gaī
12. tumhārī kṛpā se dubtī nayā ubhar gaī
13. gautam ṛṣī ke pā̃ve ahalyā bhī tar gaī
14. jis dam śilā par rakh diā raghubar baṛhāke pā̃v
15. kaise kay sīd kapi kapiõ se milkar
16. sīta kī sudhī nā pāī ke ḍũṛhā idhar udhar
17. hanumat samudra lā̃gh ke pahũcā pahāṛ par
18. sārā pahāṛ dhās gayā pātāl ke ādar
19. are rakhā pavanakumār jo gusse mẽ ake pā̃v

Appendix B

Musical Notations: Transcriptions of Representative Songs

General information on the transcriptions:

1. The songs have been transposed to facilitate transcription. The note in parentheses at the beginning of each song represents the singer's actual starting pitch.

2. An arrow pointing up or down over a note means that it is approximately one quarter tone higher or lower than written.

3. Where letters are used to indicate the order in which the strains of the song are sung, a letter followed by an asterisk indicates singing by the second half of the group.

4. The structure of the women's songs is discussed on pp. 105–108. Structures of the other types are discussed in their respective chapters.

5. Songs with asterisks at the ends of the titles can be heard on the LP record Chant the Names of God (Henry 1981).

1. Sagun (Text 8)

Sequence: AA* B CC* CC*

Scale/Melody: It is not clear which tone is the tonic. I hear it as e, a fifth below the starting and ending pitch. The melody is typical in that it is divided into two parts, and the range of the second, or B part, is higher than the range of the A part. In this case the scale of the B part also differs from that of the A part in that the sixth tone is a half step higher. This slight difference between the scales of the A and B parts is also common among women's songs.

Rhythm: The meter is regular, that is, there is a regularly recurring pattern of pulses. This particular pattern, 7/8 time, is not uncommon in women's songs, but I recorded it in no men's group songs.

1. Sagun (Text 8)

2. Sagun (Text 23)

Scale/melody: This song also has the two-strain melody, the second strain raised slightly by a bit of major third.

Rhythm: The rhythm is also of a type common among women's songs. The strains have unequal numbers of beats, and seem neither to comprise a pattern of accents nor to contain a repeated pattern of accents.

3. Haldī (Text 12)

Scale/melody: This song was pitched relatively low, probably because it was sung by old women. The tonality is clear and the melody lovely.

Rhythm: The meter that emerges from the notation is 5/4, but whether that is an artifact of the transcription, whether it is intentional or accidental, whether the singers are aware of the song's meter and its distinctiveness, is not known. Women who have not formally studied music generally lack technical vocabulary for discussing music. Women usually do not clap or gesture to express the rhythm. (The problem of determining how native musicians hear and understand their music is a common one. See Nettl's *The Study of Ethnomusicology.*)

Although a 5/4 meter is absent *per se* from Indian classical music, there is a *ten*-beat meter (*jhaptāl*), to which this is at least numerically (if not genetically) related. Song 7 below also has a meter which could be interpreted as one of ten beats.

4. Vivāh (Text 26)

Sequence: AA BB CC

Scale/melody: The melodic structure is flexible and seems dependent on the text, as seen in comparing stanzas A and B.

Rhythm: The metric structure is irregular.

5. Sohar (Text 42)*

Sequence: A BB*

Scale/melody: The impressive melodic elaboration here typefies vocal virtuosity in Indian folk and classical music. The other women sang in unison with the lead singer, Launjārī Devī Paṇḍey, as best they could.

Rhythm: No regular beat could be discerned.

5. Sohar (Text 42)*

= 124
A
je- ta ra- hi- la- a e- kā- a
da- si- yā äu- ru du- a-
da- si- yā ho
B
a sa- khi- ā bi- dhī
ka ra- hi- la a-
ta- vā- ra mai̐
Ra- ma a- bar- a pa-
i- -la

6. Mata Mäī (Text 54)

Sequence: AA BB* BB*

Scale/melody: The opening melodic formula is the same as that of the sohar and haldī above: beginning on the tonic, the melody moves to the second and then to the fourth. This is a common pattern, but not a prevalent one. The B part is made to contrast with the A by means of the major third near the beginning of the stanza instead of the fourth as in the A part, and by the resulting narrower range. The song employs only four tones, which is not unusual.

Rhythm: the meter is again irregular.

♩= 117
A
su- ta- lī bā- ṛū ki jā- ga- lī Ka- li-
B
yā Mä- i- yā du- a- re Ma- li- a-
vā a bā- ṛe ṭhārh e Mä- i- a
mo- rī

7. Milling Song (Jatsār, Text 60)

Scale/melody: Here the "strains" are so brief they seem only parts of one long phrase, but the second part does go higher than the first.

Rhythm: Not counting the eighth-note rest there are ten beats in each strain. This presents the same problem as seen in Song 3 ("How do *they* hear it?"), with a meter that may be the same as or closely related to that of Song 3.

Singers: Shīlā Rānī, Pāṇḍe and Ushā Rānī Pāṇḍe of Nārhī, District Balliā.

= 120
a- ṅga- na ba- hā- ra- ta e
Rā- mā chu- te le ho an-
ca- rav

8. Phaguā (Text 61)*

Sequence: AA* BB* CC* DD* DD* EE*

Scale/melody: The scale is major and diatonic, with a range of a sixth, and similar to that of the local harikīrtan. Surprising is the complexity of the form, with five different parts (A-E).

Rhythm: Performance of songs in this very rhythmic genre usually includes a drum and other percussion instruments such as small cymbals or shaken metallophones (*jhānjh*). The tempo increases in this as in most phaguas, a practice also typical of the harikīrtan.

8. Phaguā (Text 61)*

Ja- na- ka jī pa- ra- na e- ka ṭhā- na
E
3
a- re du- a- re par dhäi- le pi- na- ki- ā
a- re du- a- re par dhä- i- le pi- na- ki
ā sa- khi- ā su- no Ja- na- ka kī ba- ti- ā

9. Phaguā (Text 62)

Sequence: AA* AA* BB* CC* CC* DD* EE* FF* FF* CC* CC* AA* EE*

Scale/melody: The only difference from the previous song is the expanded range (one octave). Again there are many small parts (A-F).

Rhythm: This song has the same driving rhythm of the previous one.

9. Phaguā (Text 62)

10. Kajalī (Text 70)

Sequence: AA* B*

Scale/melody: The A part of the song is minor and the B part major. The range is only a fourth.

Rhythm: The men snapped their fingers as they danced to this tune which they, themselves sang.

♩= 96
A
Kha- rī ho ke a- ra- ja ka- rāi ho braj- a-
nā- rī de- dā kān- dha ci- ra ha- mā- rī
B
nā le- ke ci- ra ka- dam- a ca- ṛhi
ba- i- thāi ham- a jā- la mā- jha u- ghā- rī
na sa- wa- li- ā̃ mā- jha u- ghā- rī
nā

11. Kajalī (Text 72)*

Sequence: AA* BB* CC* DD* E DD* BB* CC*

Scale/melody: This song is minor until the end, when the third is elevated.

Rhythm: Same as previous song, but the tempo increases.

11. Kajalī (Text 72)*

jha- ri- ā ho ba- a- la- mū ab- a jha-
jha- ri- ā ho ba- la- mū

12. Kharī Birahā (Text 77)*

Scale/melody: The kharī birahā's array of tonal features render it unique in the region's music. Each of its first three lines consists of a monotonic chant that is embellished with initial ascending and terminal descending grace notes, the descending motion ending with a portamento into a spoken syllable (represented as (x)). The singer frequently, but not always, applies a startlingly wide vibrato to tones a quarter note or longer throughout the song, especially at the end of each phrase. In the fourth stanza the vocal line makes a dramatic jump to the sixth degree of the scale (in this song, the seventh in others of this genre that I recorded), descends gradually with some intervals of less than a semi-tone and considerable gracing, terminates in a tour-de-force vibrato held at conspicuous length, then optionally steadies, then rasps, drops down a third momentarily (still rasping) and finally concludes with the portamento into a spoken, nasal syllable. The fifth line has roughly the same contour.

Rhythm: The rhythm is free (rubato); the time values indicated here only suggest gross relative durations of tones.

12. Khaṛī Birahā (Text 77)*

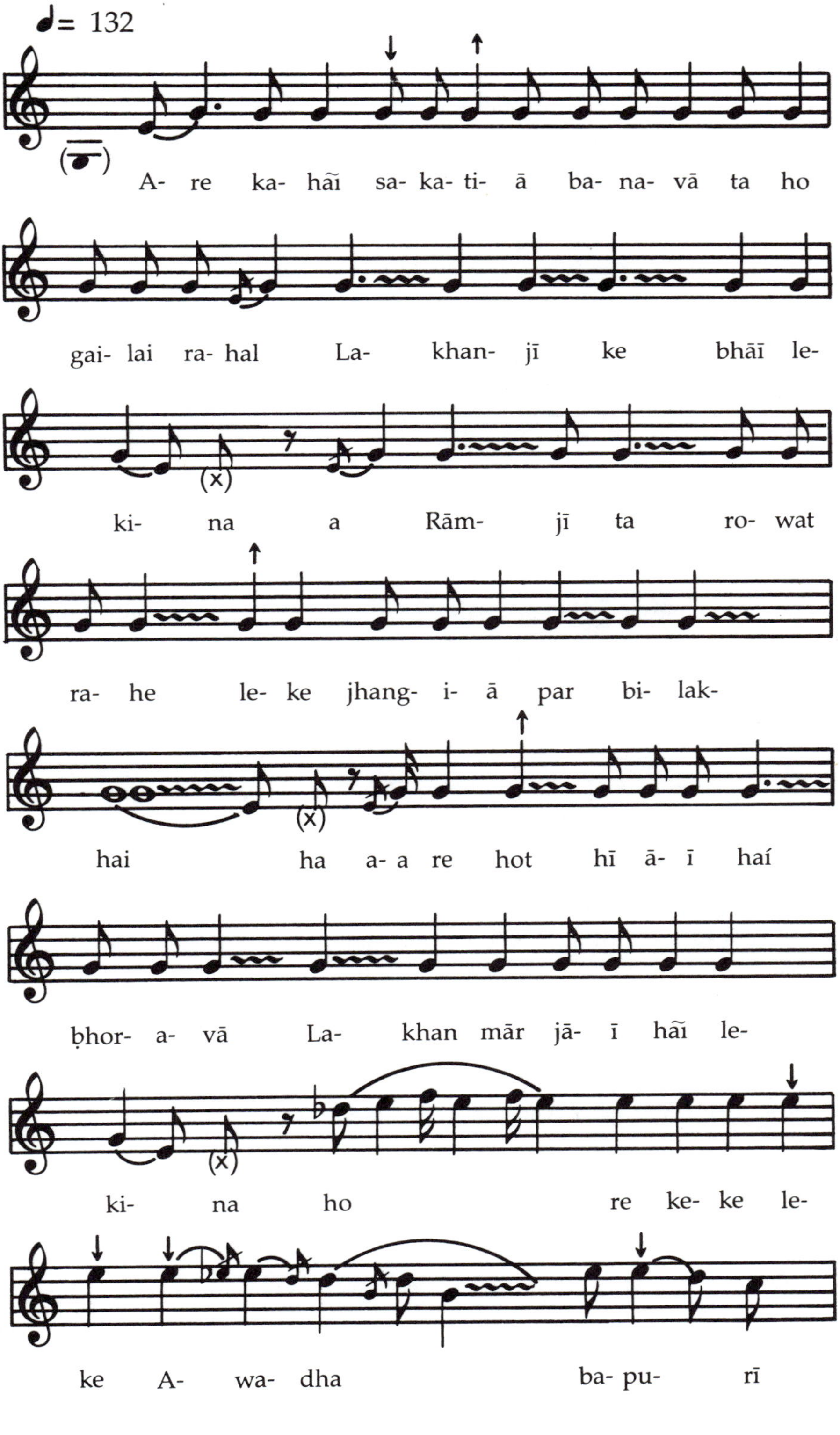

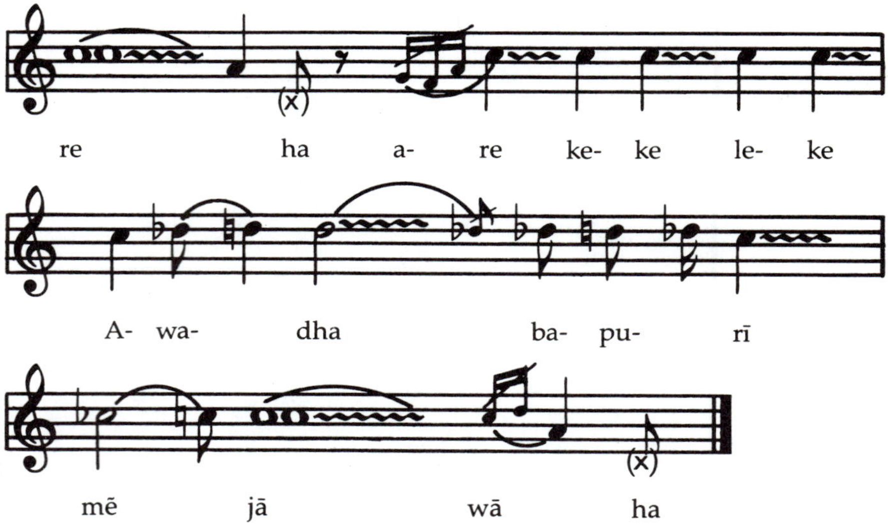

13. Nirgun Bhajan (Text 82)

Jogī Jān Mohāmmad sang this song and accompanied himself on sāraṅgī. The actual pitches were an octave higher than indicated. The sāraṅgī is in rough unison with the vocal throughout the song, which is not shown in the transcription. Notes with no text beneath them indicate the sāraṅgī solos, which always included the drone on e indicated by a whole note on the first line of the staff. An S on the text line indicates a sāraṅgī interjection. The quarter notes on the line below the staff indicate the sound of the jingle bells tied on the end of the sāraṅgī bow.

13. Nirgun Bhajan (Text 82)

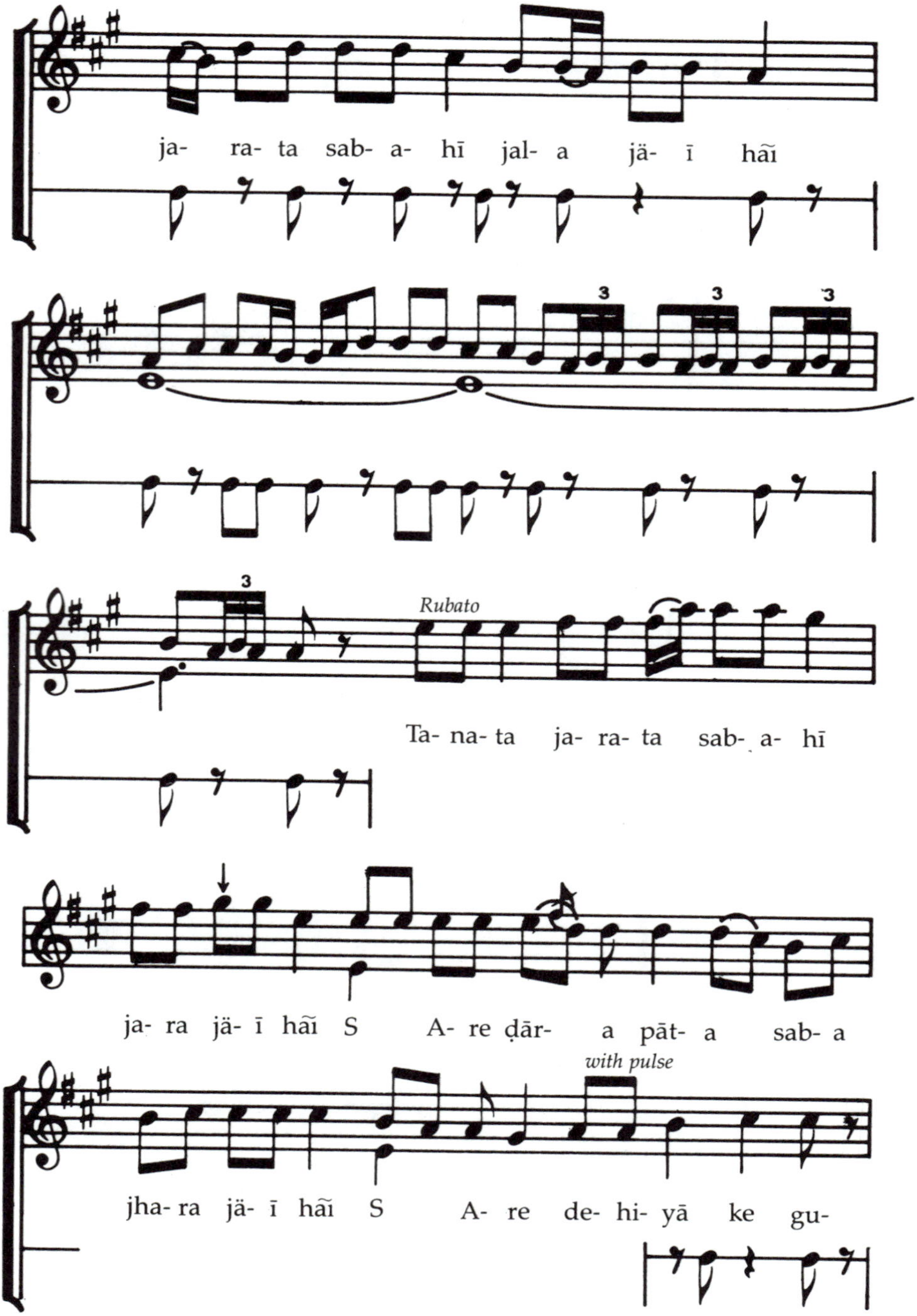
ja- ra- ta sab- a- hī jal- a jä- ī hāĩ
Rubato
Ta- na- ta ja- ra- ta sab- a- hī
ja- ra jä- ī hāĩ S A- re ḍār- a pāt- a sab- a
with pulse
jha- ra jä- ī hāĩ S A- re de- hi- yā ke gu-

mān- a mat- a kar- ā bhā- ī
3
5
Rubato
Ye de- hi-
yā ke gu-mān- a mat- a kar- ā bhā- ī na- hĩ
ta kā-ga- ya gi- dha mi- la khā- ī hãi
with pulse
a- ra- jo vyā- hī mu-kha pān-a khi- lā- ī hãi

Jo vyā- hī mu-kha pān khi- lä- ī

hãi Ar- a u-ha- o de-khi ke ghin- ä- ̣

ī hãĩ Ar- a u-ha- o de- kha ghin- ä- ī

hãĩ Ar- a jal- dī ni- kal- ä gha- ra se ya bā-

har- a

Index